PIONEER FAMILIES

OF

SUMTER COUNTY, ALABAMA

By

NELLE MORRIS JENKINS

Southern Historical Press, Inc.
Greenville, South Carolina

This volume was reproduced from
An 1961 edition located in the
Publisher's private library,
Greenville, South Carolina

All rights reserved. No part of this publication may be reproduced,
stored in a retrieval system, transmitted in any form, posted
on to the web in any form or by any means without the
prior written permission of the publisher.

Please direct all correspondence and orders to:

www.southernhistoricalpress.com
or
SOUTHERN HISTORICAL PRESS, Inc.
PO BOX 1267
375 West Broad Street
Greenville, SC   29601
southernhistoricalpress@gmail.com

Originally published: Tuscaloosa, AL. 1961
Reprinted by:
Southern Historical Press, Inc.
Greenville, SC
ISBN #0-89308-944-3
All rights Reserved.
Printed in the United States of America

CONTENTS

CHAPTER I
   Sumter County, Alabama........... 7

CHAPTER II
   Sumterville..................... 15

CHAPTER III
   Payneville...................... 85

CHAPTER IV
   Emelle..........................126

CHAPTER V
   Family Cemeteries...............160

CHAPTER VI
   Death Notices from Early Newspapers........................183

CHAPTER VII
   Tract Book Records..............222

ERRATA..............................250

INDEX...............................251

ACKNOWLEDGMENT

My interest in local history began after World War I, when Mrs. Rosa Little Meek of Panola told me so much about the pioneer families of Warsaw. Later on Hon. John A. Rogers, late of Gainesville, gave me in his own handwritting the history of his town. Mr. John T. Simms; my father-in-law Mr. T. L. Jenkins; Mr. Phillip Willingham, Sr.; my husband, the late Bertram Andrews Jenkins, and Dr. Robert Spratt of Livingston, all fed my growing interest in the early settlers of our county. My good friend, Mrs. Julia Praytor Killingsworth, and our Probate Judge, Wilbur Dearman abetted me in my efforts in collecting data for this volume. To the families of those who have passed on, and to those of you who are still living, I wish to express my feeling of gratitude for stirring within me the desire to set down, for posterity, what I have gleaned from them and from you.

Nelle Morris Jenkins

CHAPTER I

SUMTER COUNTY, ALABAMA

HISTORY OF SUMTER COUNTY

Sumter County was not one of the original counties organized when Alabama was admitted to the Union in 1819. At that time the land which is now Sumter County belonged to the Choctaw Indian Nation. Negotiations, which were begun between the Choctaw Indian Chiefs and the United States Government in 1804, were not consummated until 1830 and it was not till 18 December 1832 that this land was made into a county. Sumter County was named for General Sumter of Revolutionary fame from South Carolina.

It was in 1824 that the mighty Choctaw Indian Chief, Pushmataha, visited Washington with the avowed purpose of bringing into closer relationship the Choctaw Nation and the United States Government. He became the toast of the town. He was tall and very erect, and quite proud. Whenever he entered a room he would announce in an eloquent and a grand manner, "I am Pushmataha." He took quinsy while in the capital city and when death seemed eminent he asked that the big guns be fired over his grave. He was buried at Arlington Cemetery and the great of the country followed his body to its last resting place. He was accorded a full military funeral with the firing of the guns and the sound of taps.

On the 27 September 1830 representatives of the United States Government and of the Choctaw Nation met on the banks of Dancing Rabbit Creek near Macon, Mississippi and signed a treaty giving to the United States the Choctaw lands west of the Tombigbee River. The Indians were to be transported to Oklahoma. This treaty is known as "The Treaty of Dancing Rabbit Creek."

The Indians went into a period of mourning before the long and tragic trek west. It had been handed down from father to son of another transplant of their nation when their Chiefs bet their hunting ground on the outcome of a ball game and lost to another Indian Nation. The Choctaws boasted of the fact that they had never shed white man's blood in battle.

As the French, the Spanish and the British had maintained a fort (called Tombecbee and later Fort Confederation) at different times on Sumter soil at the bluffs on the Tombigbee River at what is now known as Epes, and that these people had always maintained a friendly relationship with the Choctaws one can readily see why there should have been a peaceful co-existence.

Many of the French, Spanish and English took Indian wives. Some American men who wandered into the Indian Territory prior to 1830 married Indian maids, also. These men were known as squaw-men. Coleman at Gainesville, Brashier at Jones' Bluff, a freeman (Negro) by the name of Tom and many more were squaw-men. By virtue of this they were awarded so much land under a provision of an article in the Treaty of Dancing Rabbit Creek.

A commission was appointed by Governor Gayle to select a County Seat and to organize the county. Those appointed were: Judge William G. Anderson, Edward B. Colgin, Warham Easley, Dr. Charles J. Puckett, Andrew Ramsay, John C. Whitsett and William O. Winston. Judge Dillard stated in his unpublished history of Sumter County which may be seen at Court House in the Probate Judge's office, that little was known about the background of William G. Anderson except he had a meagre education, but had an abundance of common sense, native shrewdness and decision of character. He was arbitrary in disposition and quick in temper. He also stated when the commission met to select the location for the county seat that William O. Winston had illness in his home so did not attend the first session. It looked as if Hickory Hill, just out of what is now Sumterville, would be selected as the County Seat, and it struck the irascible chairman (Judge Anderson) as being so preposterous and so excited his fears that it would be selected that he denounced the entire proceedings as tomfoolery and vented his abjurations on the commission in the tersest Saxon, enlivened by an occasional ejaculatory oath that pooped out with a bang. He clutched his hat and swore he would not preside over such a set of fellows. Judge Dillard went on to say that this pleased Major Whitsett and Dr. Puckett so they tore up the minutes.

The next day William O. Winston made his appearance and saved the day by casting his vote for the present site of Livingston for a County Seat. Andrew Ramsay had nominated Hickory Hill; Dr. Puckett had nominated present site of Livingston, Warham Easley nominated Chiles' Place or Mill across and down Sucarnoochee River from Livingston several miles.

The commission selected the name of Livingston as a name for the new county seat. It was named for Edward Livingston who at that time was Secretary of State in President Jackson's Cabinet.

Judge Anderson's father was William Anderson and his mother was Elizabeth Easley. Her great grandfather was Warham Easley who married Sara Barnes. Warham's father was Robert Easley the immigrant forebear. Judge Anderson's great grandfather was James Anderson, born in Scotland and who went to Ireland from where he emigrated. He landed in Philadelphia and went to Augusta County, Virginia. His wife's name was Jean. Their son John went to Madison County, Kentucky. His wife's name was Ann

Erwin. Their son William married Elizabeth or Betsy Easley in Greenville County, South Carolina and removed to Kentucky and then to Clark County, Alabama where we find him in the 1816 Census - a special Census taken of Alabama inhabitants in the Mississippi Territory of which Alabama was a part before it became a state. (See Alabama Genealogical Register, page 183 Volume 1 number 4). There were some Easleys in this census also, among them was Warham Easley who was later a member of the Sumter County Commission. (See the various members of the Anderson family elsewhere in this book.)

Edward B. Colgin, a wealthy planter, was from Gainesville, Alabama. His history will be given in Volume 3, Pioneer Families of Sumter County.

Andrew Ramsay was from near Sumterville. He was a brother of Alexander Ramsay who was born 1799 in Pendleton District, South Carolina. Andrew and Alexander Ramsay were the sons of Alexander Ramsay born 1747 in Scotland and his wife Mary Egger was born 1755, also in Scotland. It is said that Andrew H. Ramsay, who patented land near Sumterville, was a son of Andrew Ramsay. We know that Andrew Ramsay, the member of the Commission to form Sumter County returned to Tennessee after a short time in Sumter County, and from there he went back to South Carolina. Andrew H. Ramsay was here much longer. His daughter, Margaret married Furney Richardson in 1845. G. W. Ramsay of Sumter County married his first cousin, Willie Ramsay both of whom were grandchildren of Alexander Ramsay, who married Sara Hartgrove Ried in Pickens County, South Carolina.

Warham Easley was in Clark County in 1816 (see Alabama Genealogical Register page 184 Volume 1 number 4.) Roderick Easley was also named in this census of 1816 along with Warham Easley. We next find them in Marengo County, Alabama when Roderick's estate was settled (Will Book A page 189.) It seems that the Easleys, the Andersons, the Moores, the Mitchersons, the Hollands, the Cherrys, the Davises, the Lacys, the Darnells, the Jenkins, and the Brownings came from Kentucky. We believe that the William Andersons, the Lacys, the Easleys came first and were later joined by other members of the families. We found them living together in Kentucky and later in Marengo County and still later in Sumter County, Alabama.

Charles J. Puckett patented quite a lot of land in Township 19N Ranges 3 and 4 West and he was one of the founding fathers of Payneville. He was also a practicing physician, and became Paynesville's first postmaster in 1837.

Major John C. Whitsett was born in North Carolina, came to Sumter County before it was organized. He was trustee or a Factor for the many Indians who received land in Sumter County by virtue of a clause in the Treaty of Dancing Rabbit Creek. They could not sell the land without permission, that is to see that they were not taken advantage of by unscrupulous settlers. More will be given about Major Whitsett in volume 2.

William O. Winston was a large landholder in Township 21N Range 3 W. He married Amanda Morrison (2nd wife) and they were parents of six children. Mr. Winston was a member of a large and prominent family in Sumter County and as they lived in and around Gainesville their history will be given in Volume 2 "Pioneer Families of Sumter County."

On the 22 December 1814 the Governor of Mississippi Territory, which did not belong to the Indians of which Alabama was then a part, had a bill passed providing for militia duty in case of emergency. (See page 586 Digest of Alabama Laws, Published 1823.) On 31 December 1822 a bill was passed in the Alabama Legislature which amended the preceding act. It stated that all free white men between the ages of 18 and 45 be compelled to register with the Military Authorities within 30 days after immigrating into a county. Everyone had to serve when called upon except all public officials, Ministers of the Gospel, public ferrymen, Justices of the Peace, Postmasters, postriders and millers except in invasion or insurrection. Every county had its Battalion or Regiment, and each beat had its company with officers. The companies had to be mustered out once each year upon a 30 day notice.

Much of the social life of Sumter County centered around the military Companies in each beat. Once a year a Military Ball was held either in Livingston or Gainesville.

Another bill passed 7 December 1811 (same book page 623) related to Mills and Millers. One section provided for the erection of mills so as to not overflow any other mill or create a nuisance to the neighborhood. In 1821 the act was amended to provide that each take his turn in grinding and that the miller could legally take only 1/8 part of grain ground for toll. As Sumter County was and is well blessed with waterways, several people applied the first year of the organization of the county for permits to erect mills.

Another interesting bill enacted in 1807 was the one requiring persons who wished to sell liquor to present a petition with names of freeholders saying that the person was of good character before he could obtain a license.

In 1815 a levy of 20¢ on each $100.00 value to be paid on all land.

In the early years after Alabama became a state all divorces were granted by the Legislature. Before the County Courts were established couples were known to announce in what was called "bans", their intention of marrying. Later, when a minister came into the community, they had him do a better job of it. Funerals were held months after death because no minister was at hand when death occurred. The colored people continued this custom for a century after it was discontinued by the whites.

In an article "Alabama Black Belt" by the Reverend Renwick C. Kennedy, in the Alabama Historical Quarterly Number 3, Volume 2, 1940, page 282, gives the following: "The Alabama 'Black Belt' is a fair-spoken term and corresponds not merely to the 'right side of the tracks' but to the old, exclusive, best-family streets; being from the 'Black Belt' is like being from the Low Country in South Carolina, or the Blue Grass in Kentucky or Tidewater in Virginia.

"The Virginians and South Carolinians are still proud of the states that gave them birth. Virginia and South Carolina are the two states in which pre-Confederate, Southern aristocracy reached its zenith. In Alabama the Black Belt counties achieved the most exalted aristocracy of any other section in the state.

"The type is nearly extinct, but not entirely. In the Carolina Low Country, the Mississippi Delta, a few parishes in Louisiana, a few counties in Georgia and in the Alabama Black Belt the strain still survives, somewhat tainted by the Twentieth Century, but preserved well enough to be recognized. Nowhere is it more authentically intact than in the Alabama Black Belt. Nowhere is it preserved in a larger area than here. Yet of all the museum pieces of the Old South that remain, none has received less publicity and none is less widely known. So, unsung and unknown and relatively unexploited, it has gone its quite, calm way, restoring much of its former grandure."

THE EARLIEST SCHOOLS (1830s - 1840s)

IN SUMTER COUNTY, ALABAMA

The 16th section in every Township was set aside by the State Legislature to be used for schools. The land was rented or gradually sold off and the funds were used to build schools, to help pay salaries of teachers whenever parents were not able to pay tuition, and for other school purposes. At the organiztion of the county the governor

other school purposes. At the organization of the county the governor of the state appointed commissioners to look after these sections, as well as the schools within the various twonships.

Township 16, Range 2 West was the Gaston District. George Kennard, Pleasant White and Solomon Williams were the commissioners in 1841. 13 November 1841 the citizens voted on whether to consolidate their schools. There were two factions in this township so finally two academies were organized. As this was an important section of the county I will give names of those voting in this election, as follows: John Dill, Thomas Young, J. H. Simmons, J. J. Shields, J. H. Kennard, Thomas Nelson, G. J. Wilson, R. L. Hunter, John C. Ward, Bird Wheat, Jacob Kuhn, John Kuhn, N. A. Davis, W. Ward, James Auld, John Gilmer, John Wayne, Geo. W. Kennard, Solomon Williams, Samuel Halsell, Hiram

Brown, Nathan Halsell, Benj. Lewis, James Anderson, Mathias Ethridge, James Grimes, John C. McCormick, Simon C. McLendon, Dempsey S. Haize, Bryant McClendon, James Ingram, Charles Page, R. T. McCormack, John J. Stephens, Jesse Ward, Burwell McClendon, Henry Cahoon, E. Peters, C. A. Spear, W. W. Hall, J. C. Talmage, Nathan Fuller, N. M. Foster, A. Haley, M. Callums, J. M. Rogers, William Wheat.

Prof. T. A. Lilly and his wife, Mrs. Lilly were co-principals of Gaston Institute; there was a Gaston Male and Female Academy at the same time as the Gaston Institute; Sumterville Male Academy under direction of Rev. S. S. Cross; West Alabama Military Academy at Sumterville with C. A. Derby and P. B. Burwell teachers; and the Classical and Mathematical School was near Sumterville with Benj. P. Burwell, Principal; Mt. Moriah Academy at McCainville; Gainesville Female Academy Wm. R. Poindexter, Principal and with Prof Lockett and Prof. Jordan, "late of Kemper Springs Academy teachers"; Livingston Female Academy with C. E. Brame and wife, James Harran, C. S. Danneburg teachers in 1852; Sumterville Female Academy with Prof. and Mrs. M. F. Davidson and Miss Elizabeth Eason teachers. There was a Pleasant Hill Academy in Township 20 R 2 West, and Central Academy in Township 23 Range 3 West - Benj. Turner, James M. Stanton and John W. Geiger were School Commissioners of the latter Township in 1842, (No one knows anything about either academy today) - page 292 of 16th Section Book; Blake Little and Samuel Taylor were commissioners in Township #23 R 3 W in 1837; Township 20 Range 2 West had teachers A. E. McEnnis, Elizabeth Muldrew, George J. Colgin, George Barrows, Mrs. Joanna Roberts, John P. Hampton, E. Root, Thomas M. Tobin, and N. O. Smith. In 1845 teachers in Township 21 Range 2 West were: L. D. Myers, Miss Mary Brown, James Ellison, O. M. McDaniel, Woodson Hubbard, George Belton, Aaron A. Kemble, Susan Craven, Willis V. Hare, Thomas J. Davidson.

Township 22 Range 3 West Elisha Meredith, C. A. Hatch, and Charles Beasley were Commissioners in 1844, James B. Tartt was Justice of Peace.

Township 18 Range 4 West the following were appointed Commissioners in 1842: Benj. Stone, R. R. Shelton, G. W. Grant, F. M. Grant, Jabal Faulkner. In Township 18, Range 3 West Richard Yarbrough was J. P. and Stephen and C. P. Yarbrough figured in the school business in 1838 with Stephen Webb, Thomas Porter, R. D. Twomby (?) and P. M. Fullingham were teachers. In Township 19 Range 3 West David Boyd, Amos Travis, Micajah Frazer were Commissioners in 1840; in Township 21 Range 2 West Ferney Richardson, A. H. Ramsay, William R. Colgin and Mitchell Malone were Commissioners in 1835 with John McNiece and John Griswold teachers. In 1848 Elias N. Wrenn, Thomas Lacy, and Warren Woodson were teachers.

There was Black Jack Academy at Bluff Port, Prof. Nuffer was the first master of this academy; then Prof. T. A. Hunter, a Harvard graduate was master; other teachers were Prof. Johathan May, Mr. Hoit, Miss Dutch Cook and Miss Mary James.

Old Payneville had a famous academy headed by the Rev. Hadden, a Presbyterian minister. Mr. Farrah was an early teacher. There were other academies and schools in the county, which will be mentioned as we give the histories of different towns and villages.

According to Mr. Joel Campbell DuBose in his "History of Alabama" the young people in these early academies studied Quackenbos' Rhetoric, Caesar's Gallic War, Virgil's Aeneid and all the Bucolics and Georgics, Orations of Cicero, Horace entire, Juvenal's Satires. The course in Greek embraced the four books of Xenophon's Anabasis, Homer's Iliad, Herodotus, Cyropaedia, De Corona and others.

In the field of mathematics they were proficient in University Algebra, Davies' Legendre, and Surveying and Navigation. Grammar and rhetoric were studied year in and year out. Every Friday afternoon was devoted to reading of compositions and to "speaking". The close of the session was about July 1st with public examinations, which swept the whole range of poetry, music, philosophy, science and nature. A great public dinner was a climax to the school closing; perhaps this custom was the beginning of our barbecues for which Sumter County is so famous.

SOME " FIRSTS " IN SUMTER COUNTY

First Probate Judge in Sumter County was William G. Anderson.

First Tax Collector in Sumter County was Albert G. Anderson.

First Sheriff in Sumter County was George W. Harper.

First County Clerk in Sumter County was James Savage.

First County Treasurer in Sumter County was James Parker.

First Surveyor in Sumter County was Alfred Moore.

First Auctioneer in Sumter County was John B. Cooper.

First elected Commission of Roads and Revenue in Sumter County: William Godfrey, Wilson G. Myers, Lewis Brock and M. McGee, August 1836.

First entry in Deed Book A page 1 was the recording of the sale of a slave from Winchester J. Harman to Jesse Brashiers, a Choctaw Indian Chief, who was part French. The sale took place 27 July 1825 but was not recorded until 19 August 1833.

The first Post Master at Gainesville was John E. Whitsett, 1835.

The first Post Master at Livingston was William B. Ogletree (1835), followed by Handcock and then Houston.

First Postmaster at Sumterville was Charles Hinsdale, 1835.

First Post Master at Payneville was Dr. C. J. Puckett, 1836.

First Post Master at Jamestown (Warsaw) was

The first court house in Sumter County was a log cabin which stood at the site of the present court house.

Sumter County's first Circuit Court was organized by Judge Sion L. Perry of Tuscaloosa.

First Ministers of the Gospel: Eli Davis, Mr. Campbell, Payneville, Wiley Stanton,

First Doctors in Sumter County: J. L. McCants, J. A. Smith, C. J. Puckett, Robert F. Dalton, M. B. Posey to name a few.

First Lawyers in Sumter County: William H. Green, Murray F. Smith, Samuel B. Boyd, R. K. Chamberlayne, James Hair and many more.

First merchants in Sumter County: D. L. Ayers and Company, Drapers and Taylors; William Moore & Co., Williams and Dillard; W. H. Norvill & William Land, Watch Makers; Anthony Arrington and S. F. Miller; Moffett and Watson's Ware House, Gainesville; M. C. Ward, Taylor; Rix, Rich and Rix, Sumterville; others will be mentioned in later volumes.

CHAPTER II

SUMTERVILLE

HISTORY OF SUMTERVILLE

In pioneer days most communities grew up around churches which contributed to the social as well as to the religious life of the people for miles around, but Sumterville was different from the average pioneer village. The people, as a whole, were well educated and many of them were men of means; so their first thoughts were, not only of churches, but schools as well. From the earliest days Sumterville boasted of three churches; the Presbyterian which was really three miles west of Sumterville; Old Side Baptist Church and an Episcopal Church; and at the same time a boys' Military Academy and a Female Academy were organized. Around 1844 another school was organized near the Presbyterian Church which was near the present Bethel Memorial Chapel. This school had as its head master, Professor Benjamin P. Burwell who saw to it that his pupils were quite proficient in Greek and Latin. This school was more centrally located so served not only Sumterville but the Old Ramsey community, as well. Professor W. Fayette Davidson was Head Master of the Boys' Academy for many years.

The northern part of Sumter County, the part of the county in which Sumterville is located, is in what is known as the "Black Belt". The black, waxy soil was too heavy for the average farmer of that day to till with the equipment he brought with him from sandy areas, so he sold out to his neighbor who had slaves to work the soil. In that way the whole area finally fell into the hands of a few land lords. Many tales have been told about Sumter County mud but the poem written in 1852 by Professor W. Fayette Davidson and published in "Sumter Democrat" aptly tells the tale as follows:

SUMTER COUNTY MUD

I've wandered in distant climes
And seen a host of sights
By day light and by moon light
In fact all sorts of lights;
But ne'er yet where e'er I'd stray
In regions ill or good

Did I ever find one thing to match
This Sumter County Mud.

The whole area was covered with tall cane when the first settlers moved in; the trees were oak, cotton wood and hickory, but the cedar trees which now grow everywhere were imported from another county. The dogwood and red bud trees were abundant. This limerock, hilly land was noted for its beautiful and brilliantly colored flowers which covered the country side in the spring.

A few white people began to trickle into the Indian Territory before the Choctaw Indians left for Oklahoma after the Treaty of Dancing Rabbit Creek. Clark Crocker and Anthony Phariss were among those who came to Sumterville area while the Indians were yet there. They told how the Choctaws met on a hill just east of what is not Sumterville and went into a period of mourning because they were being transplanted to another soil. A free Negro by the name of "Tom" had wandered into the Indian territory and married an Indian woman. By virtue of this marriage he acquired quite a bit of land under the Treaty of Dancing Rabbit Creek, this land lay just north of Sumterville; and a creek called Tom's creek bears his name, even today.

The first settlers of Sumterville and environment were William Patton, Randle Jackson, Seaborn Jackson, Jacinth Jackson, the Webbs, John E. Brown, Jeremiah Brown, Terrance Foy, Bryant Richardson, Evan Bryant, William Gilbert, John Holland, William and John Kerr, Tom Ormand and many others. They built their homes on the hill tops and tilled the lower ground. At first there were many springs flowing from the lime rock hills, but after the land was cleared and worked the springs stopped flowing. The Foys, Bryants and Ormonds suffered the first years from lack of water. Every two weeks they took their clothes to the Parker place on the Sucarnoochee River, five or six miles from Sumterville, to wash. Later on they dug wells in the bottom land and hauled water to their homes, this was before they learned that wells dug on the hills would produce water.

The old road built by the French from Fort Tombecbee to the outpost, which was located at the present cite of Old Payneville, ran through Sumterville. In places, yet, our modern roads follow the old roads or trails as set forth by the French, Spanish and English in those days before the "Treaty of Dancing Rabbit Creek".

Sumterville was first called Patton's Hill for Mr. William Patton whose home was just behind that of the one we know as the Dr. Wrenn home. Mr. Patton's grave has not been located, perhaps it is unmarked or the stone has crumbled. But we know from his will and settlement of his estate that he died 7 April 1838. He had a son, William S. Patton who studied medicine in Philadelphia, Pennsylvania, and later became a practicing physician; his daughter was Cynthia M. Myers, and he left a widow, Eliza

Patton. The town was still called Patton's Hill until after 1841, for on that date the Poll List was headed "Patton's Hill". It is said that John E. Brown was instrumental in getting the name changed to Sumterville when in 1844 the town was incorporated.

In the early 1840's Sumterville boasted of eight business houses, Masonic Lodge, three Churches, two schools, and an Inn for the convenience and comfort of stage coach travellers. The stage road ran between Gainesville and Sumterville and on west toward Jackson, Mississippi through DeKalb. Mr. Webb was proprietor of the Inn. Charles Hinsdale was Post Master in 1837.

The Old Side Primitive Baptist Church was the first one organized in the north western part of the county; the building was erected 6 July 1833. The Methodist Church was built in 1841. The Presbyterian Church was three miles west of Sumterville where Reverend Carothers preached a year or two prior to the erection of the building in 1835. In 1897 this Presbyterian Church building was moved to Sumterville.

The organizing and charter members of the Primitive Baptist Church were: Asa Wright, Clark Crocker, Thomas Hogger, Randle Jackson, John Arnold, Elisha Thomas, P. McDaniel, Armaton Smith, James Williams, Sara Irwin, Henry Smith, E. N. Bryant, Wright Jones, Lermel Mathress, Ben. J. Richardson, Coin Richardson and Washington Richardson. (From the original Minute Book of Old Side Baptist Church.)

The organizing and charter members of Bethel Presbyterian Church were: P. R. Fleming, Mary B. Fleming, Jennett (Spence) Dial, Mary Dial, Sara Kerr, Margaret Kerr, Robert S. Lavender, Jane Lavender, (all from Mt. Zion and Concord Churches in Greene County), James Wrenn, Eliza Wrenn from Ebenezer Church, Thomas Moore and Elizabeth C. Moore from Bethesda Church, Mrs. Anna Elliott from Harmony Church. The next members to be added to the roll were: William and Joseph Greenlees, Mrs. Isabella Greenlees, Mrs. E. Cavert, Mrs. Liza Patton, Mr. Carder and wife Nancy from Mt. Zion, all of whom united with the church 23 August 1835. Mrs. Mary Yarbrough (wife of Alfred Yarbrough) joined the church 23 July 1837. David Gage and wife Nancy from Philadelphia Church in Wayne County, Mississippi, George W. Wrenn (who married the daughter of Mary and Alfred Yarbrough) and Jacob Shipman and his wife, Eliza, all united with the church in 1839. (From the original Minute Book of Bethel Presbyterian Church.)

The oldest home in the community is "The Cedars", built by John E. Brown. His great granddaughter, Mrs. Julia Praytor Killingsworth, lives in this lovely old home built in 1838.

The Jeremiah Brown home is about three miles west of Sumterville. It was remodeled after the Civil War by Mr. White who married Addie Brown, a daughter of Mr. Brown. It was changed to look like his old home in Kentucky. The stair case which forms a balcony facing the front dorr, is especially interesting. Mrs. James, whose home is in Virginia owns this lovely old home which is called "Louden." She is the great granddaughter of Jeremiah Brown, who was the largest slave owner in Sumter County. It is said he owned more than a thousand slaves, many of whom he did not know as he had over-seers to look after various sections of his plantations.

Each plantation around Sumterville, and in other parts of this section of North Sumter County, had plantation stores or places to store foods raised on the land and used to furnish the slaves during the year. Each plantation was sufficient unto itself as cotton was raised, ginned, spun into thread and woven into cloth by either the slaves or by the men and women of the home. Leather was tanned at home and made into shoes, harness and the like. The shoes were pegged together with wood pegs, usually made at home. Meat was killed and cured, vegetables and fruits were dried for future use.

Over the years Sumterville failed to grow, in fact it became smaller. Livingston was chosen in 1832 as the county seat instead of Sumterville, or Hickory Hill, which was just out of the town, itself; the railroad was put through or near Jones Bluff so Sumterville was left out of the main line of communication;at a later date another railroad was built six miles west at what is now Emelle; Sumterville was left off the main highways of Sumter County; the planters sold out and moved "west" after the slaves were freed; the top soil was washed off the hills so the bare lime rock was in evidence everywhere. Land in 1832 was bought from the Government from 2¢ to $2.00 per acre; by the late 1830's land land sold for $100.00 per acre and in Reconstruction days some lands were sold again from 2¢ to $5.00 and $10.00 per acre.

In 1840 the population of Sumter County was 29,937. In 1940 (or a century later), we had 2,416 fewer persons; but the amazing part is that in the last hundred years we had lost 8,231 whites and had gained 5,815 Negroes. In 1940 the percentage was 79.4% Negro population or an increase of 21% over 1840; while the white population had decreased 26%. Sumterville had lost more whites in proportion than many other parts of the county. Today there is only one small white school north of livingston as children are transported by bus to centrally located places. We have in 1959 only 46 white teachers in the entire county; but the Negroes boast of 181 Negro teachers; their schools are newer, more modern and in many cases better equipped than some of the white schools.

The once bare lime rock hills around Sumterville are now covered with grass and the Hereford cows are peacefully grazing, making more money for their owners than the slaves ever produced working in cotton fields. The village is still the quiet, easy going place of yesterday where many of the old timers still live graciously. The names "Sumterville", "Bethel" and "Old Side" are yet loved today by a multitude of people scattered to the four corners of the earth; even though the old glory has all but vanished "with the wind".

Minutes

BETHEL PRESBYTERIAN CHURCH

Sumterville, Alabama

Sumterville, Saturday 22 September 1835. On this date a meeting was called to organize a Presbyterian Church three miles west of Sumterville where the present Bethel Chapel now stands. The Charter Members of this church were:

P. B. Fleming	Sara Kerr	)
Mary B. Fleming	Margaret Kerr	) From
Jennett Dial	Robert S. Lavender	) Mt. Zion and Concord Churches
Mary Dial	Jane Lavender	) Greene County, Alabama.

James Wrenn and Eliza Wrenn from Ebenezer Church, Greene County, Alabama. Thomas Moore and wife Elizabeth from Bethesda Church, South Carolina. P. B. Fleming and Thomas Moore were elected Ruling Elders of this new church; they were ordained 23 September 1835. Mrs. Anna Elliott of Harmony Church was received as a member same day.

21 November 1835. The Church was officially named "Bethel". Signed Thomas Moore, Clerk and J. B. Adams, Moderator of Tuscaloosa Presbytery.

8 May 1836. Isabella Ramsay was received into the church from Ebenezer Church, Greene County, Alabama.

12 June 1836. Robert L. Lavender and Mrs. Jane Lavender received from Concord Church, Greene County. (Seems that their letters came at this time, joined as Charter members.)

7 October 1836. William Greenlee, Joseph Greenlee, Mrs. Isabella Greenlee and Mrs. E. Calvert received into church, Mrs. Eliza Patton received same day from Cedar Grove; Mr. Carder and wife Nancy from Mt. Zion, Greene County joined by certificate.

23 July 1837. Mrs. Mary Yarborough received by letter from Millenium Hope Church.

26 November 1837. Mr. David Gage and wife Betsey P. were received into the church from Philadelphia Church, Wayne County, Mississippi; and Mrs. Lavender from Greensboro Church.

26 May 1837. Mr. James Wrenn and Eliza Wrenn were received by letter from Ebenezer Church, Greene County, Alabama. (Letter received on this date.)

24 November 1839. Jacob Shipman and wife Eliza presented their certificates and J. W. Kerr joined church by profession of faith.

9 August 1840. Armstead, Viney, and Charlott slaves of Mrs. Mary Yarborough and Cleressa and Clary, slaves of Mrs. Jennett Dial joined the church. (These were the first recorded Black members. Later on many slaves joined the church.)

12 July 1840. Mrs. Nancy Jamison was received by letter from Courtland Church; Andrew Nevill and wife Mary along with Elenor Rix were received from Gainesville Church. Mr. Joseph McCorcle and wife Violet from Ebenezer Church: William Frierson Fulton and wife Elizabeth received from Mt. Zion, also slaves joined church at same time.

Mention was made of Mr. Thomas Moore being ill. He was absent quite a time from church.

13 December 1840. William F. Fulton and Joseph McCorcle were elected Ruling Elders.

25 April 1841. Andrew J. Laughridge brought letter from Mesopotamia (Eutaw) and William M. M. Meek from Louisville, Mississippi Church.

26 April 1841. Mrs. H. E. McLunsey received from Methodist Church, Darlington Circuit, South Carolina. On same date Mr. Jane McKenley was baptized.

7 August 1841. Mr. T. R. Kendal from Burlington, Vermont Congregational Church, and Mrs. Amanda Kindal and Mr. Robert McCorcle received on examination; Mrs. Ester Kennon by certificate from Concord Church (Mrs. Mary Ward and Mrs. Amanda Kindal were baptized.)

15 August 1841. (There must have been a powerful revival service as so many joined the church on this date.) The following joined by profession of faith: John Ward, Armstrong Kerr, David McKenley, James Linch, Jacob E. Thompson, Abraham P. Fisher, Leroy Boyett, Thomas J. Davidson, George J. Shipman, Mary Ann Hopper, Rebecca Dial, Mary L. Moore, Martha H. McCrrkle, Mary A. Fleming, Ellen E. Carder, Mary Ann Lavender, Catherine Fleming, Amanda E. McCorcle.

21 August 1841. (The revival must have lasted a couple of weeks.) The following united with the church: Andrew McCorkle, Nancy G. Porter, Margaret E. Moore, Virginia Kerr, Jane E. Moore, John Fielder, Robert &. Fleming, Mary E. Ramsay, Elizabeth C. Jackson, Catherine E. Jamison, John W. Dial and Washington Edwards.

22 August 1841. The following joined the church: Margaret Ramsay, Hester A. Greenlee, Geo. Rix, Robert Hadden, John Smith, James Fleming, Jane McDow, Martha Yarborough, Thomas Jamison, Jeremiah Dial (this was the son of Jennett Dial), James Dial (his brother.)

15 December 1841. Received by certificate Mrs. Martha B. Hadden, Miss Laura Ann E. Hadden and Nancy J. Fulton. The same day the death of Mr. D. Gage was annouced.

17 April 1842. Mrs. Effy Clark was received from North Carolina; and Wm. J. Campbell and William M. Hadden joined the church.

26 February 1843. Benj. P. Burwell was received into the church. Mrs. Shipman and John Fielder were dismissed at their request.

1st Sabbath April 1843. Leroy Boyett and wife dismissed at their request.

4 June 1843. Merritt and wife Paulina, slaves of Thomas Moore were received into the church; Charles belonging to Thomas P. Harper and Rosanna belonging to Isaac Hadden and Willis belonging to Jeremiah Dial joined the church.

6 August 1843. Mr. John Soule, Henry R. Leveret, and Andrew J. Leveret united with the church on this date.

21 January 1844. Mr. B. P. Burwell was dismissed at his request to a church in Mobile.

1 May 1844. Mr. B. P. Burwell presented certificate from 2nd Presbyterian Church in Mobile.

1 April 1844. The total membership of Bethel Church was 83 Whites, 44 Blacks.

3rd Sabbath October 1844. William Kerr received upon examination.

2nd Sabbath 1845. John McDow received upon examination as were Margaret E. Lavender; Mrs. Isabella Ramsay and daughter Mary dismissed to join another church.

15 February 1846. Mrs. Ester Kennon dismissed to join a Mississippi church.

1 April 1845. This church membership consisted of 68 Whites and 42 Blacks.

9 April 1846. No mention before this of Alfred Yarborough having joined the church but on this date a committee was appointed to see why he was not attending. He said as long as the present minister served there he was not going. He was suspended from the church. Many members were turned out about this time; some for swearing, some for drinking and for other things. Negroes were turned out for stealing, lying and breaking other commandments. Jeremiah Dial was turned out for swearing. He said he was not going to say he would stop, furthermore he did not want to belong to their church; Jesse Hutchins was turned out because he was seen drinking - these are but a few.

21 February 1847. T. R. Kendal and wife Amanda were dismissed to a Mobile Church; Mrs. Nancy Jamerson (Jamison) and son Thomas dismissed to a Tennessee church and Mrs. Lavender to Payneville.

25 April 1847. John Ward and wife Mary were dismissed to Gainesville church.

3 May 1847. Mr. William Hadden and James Hervey Fulton dismissed to Danville, Kentucky. At this time the membership was 55 Whites and 61 Blacks.

29 March 1850. Mr. Geo. Rix and wife, Rebecca, Mr. James Roberson dismissed to Gainesville.

3 June 1850. Mrs. Mary C. Burwell was dismissed to Jackson, Mississippi Church,

28 May 1853. John W. Kerr and wife Margaret and daughters Susan and Sarah Ann were dismissed to Presbyterian Church in St. Louis, Mo.

3 July 1854. Mrs. Louisiana Handley (Mrs. Peter) presented certificate from Gainesville.

1 October 1854. Mrs. Eliza N. Wrenn, Joseph R. Ramsay, Joseph D. Mitchell, Mrs. William Johnson, Mrs. Keziah E. Mitchell and Miss Susan B. Meek received into the church.

24 December 1854. Lucy Smith, Mrs. Mary Whitsett, Margaret Nevill, and Frances J. Wilson joined the church. Andrew Nevill and son William dismissed to Mobile.

14 January 1855. Mrs. Jane Roberts was dismissed to join Carrolton Church (Alabama.)

23 July 1855. Mrs. Melvira Dillard and Mrs. Josephine Fulton received by faith.

25 May 1856. Mrs. Mary Whitsett was dismissed to join church in Tuscumbia. Miss Susanna Frierson dismissed to Zion Church in Mississippi; Mrs. Martha Heddleston to join church in Greene County, Concord.

22 February 1854. Mr. Mitchell McKinley and wife Eliz. and daughters Sara, Isabella, and Mary Jane were received by certificate from a Presbyterian Church in South Carolina.

28 June 1857. Margaret Kerr was received by faith.

10 October 1857. Joseph Kerr, John Moore and John McKinley were received into Church by faith. At same time Franklin Burwell, Benj. F. Mitchell, W. T. Harwell, James D. Harwell were received by faith also.

27 March 1858. Joseph R. Dial was received by faith. Mrs. Martha McConnell was dismissed to a Presbyterian Church in Yorkville, South Carolina. B. P. Burwell, his wife Margaret Burwell and Franklin Burwell were dismissed to a Presbyterian Church in Texanna, Texas.

9 October 1858. A committee was sent to the home of Doct. B. A. Jones to examine him on faith; he was in a poor state of health so could not go to church. He was accepted as a member. Same day John W. Dial and wife Eliza were dismissed to join church at McKinley. Michael McKinley and wife Eliz. and 3 daughters Sara, Isabella and Mary Jane and son John were dismissed to join a church near Louisville, Mississippi.

12 June 1859. Mrs. Palmer and Carr Eason joined the church by faith. Mrs. Ann Clark was dismissed to Payneville. Isaac F. Kerr and Logan Kerr were united with the church, by faith.

30 September 1860. Miss Mary Hannah Fleming joined by faith. Mrs. Willie Ann Johnston asked for certificate to join church in Centerville, Texas.

30 March 1861. Mrs. Louisiana Handley asked for certificate to join church at Pensacola, Florida.

21 September 1861. Mrs. Nancy Mitchell and J. M. Joseph to Presbyterian Church in Meridian, Mississippi. Miss Lucy Nevill was received on profession of faith.

Saturday 18 September 1864. Mr. Luke Palmer received religion while in the Army and was received into the church, on this date.

2nd Sabbath October 1865. Mr. T. J. Templeton was dismissed to join a church in Mississippi.

(This brings us to the end first 30 years of the history of Bethel Churchs. The Church owns a complete record to the present day.)

METHODIST CEMETERY
SUMTERVILLE, ALABAMA

This cemetery is located on a hill just as one leaves Sumterville on the Emelle road. At one time a church stood by this cemetery. (See Sumterville history.) This old church is still spoken of in reverent tones by those who recall the many memories of days gone by. They love to tell about Henry McDaniel's vision of building a church; of William Godfrey's stroke in the church after "feeling the hand of the Lord" at Quarterly Conference; of the Godly old preacher, Rev. James M. Patton who was born in Perry County, Alabama in 1829 and who married Miss Mary Falconer, born in Eutaw, Alabama in 1843. All the children looked forward to Saturday before "meeting day" when then trudged down the road to meet Brother Patton. They considered it a great treat to unhitch his horse from the buggy and ride him bare back to the pond to let him drink.

Brother Patton buried the dead, married the young and he preached powerful sermons which were instrumental in the salvation of more people than it is possible to estimate. Not a stone is left of this old church; it was sold for a few pieces of silver and the money applied to a debt on the parsonage at Gainesville, Alabama.

Inscriptions

John Elmore Baker, born 8 August 1865, died 9 February 1944. (He was a native of Virginia, as is his wife. They are the parents of 10 children viz: Elizabeth, (Mrs. Waibel), Charlie W., Joe P., Martha (Mrs. Frank Diall, see Boyd Cemetery for this family of Dials), Mrs. Frances Bassett, John E.,Jr., who married Margaret (Peggy) Ormond, the daughter of Evan and Sallie (Burwell) Ormond - See Ormond records Old Side Cemetery.

Brown

In memory of **Milton Dozier**, son of G. A. and Sara B. Brown, died 14 March 1861, aged 2 years, 10 months. (His parents were George Alexander Brown and wife Sarah B. Godfrey. George Alexander Brown was the brother of John Evander Brown - see John E. Brown Cemetery records - and Sara B. Godfrey, daughter of William Godfrey, married 9 May 1839.)

******

Mary Alice Brown who departed this life 11 January 1847, aged 4 years

1 month.

******

Cornelia G. Brown, daughter of George A. and Sara B. Brown, died 15 August 1858 in the 16th year of her age.

******

John Lewis Brown, born November -- 1869, died January 1918. (He was William Henry Brown's son and the great nephew of George A. and John E. Brown.)

******

Infant son of George and Sara B. (Godfrey) Brown, died in 1848.

******

Infant son of George A. and Sara B. (Godfrey) Brown, died in 1847.

******

William Henry Brown, born 10 October 1839, died 22 March 1913. (He was the son of Lewis Brown, the nephew of John E. and George A. Brown, and brother of Lewis, Jr., and Emma Brown Massey.)

******

Kathleen Armour, daughter of J. D. and J. K. (Brown) Bancroft, born 30 November 1897, died 6 May 1898.

******

Julia Kathleen, wife of J. D. Bancroft, born 18 August 1879, died 29 January 1900. (She was the daughter of William H. Brown and the wife of Dr. Josiah D, Bancroft.)

******

Infant of J. D. and Julia K. (Brown) Bancroft -- (Just a slab, no dates.)

******

Mrs. Emma A. Massey, born 29 March 1844, died 23 November 1898. (She was the daughter of Lewis Brown who was brother of John Evander; she married Rev. R. A. Massey whose son Walter established Massey Business College, Birmingham, Alabama. She had a daughter Eula and son Albert also.

******

Kate (Henagan) Brown, wife of W. H. Brown, born 6 March 1842, died 16 April 1867. (She was born in Brownsville, South Carolina.)

Dial

David Montgomery Dial who departed this life 24 September 1834 in the 49th year of his age. (He was the son of John Dial of Newberry District, South Carolina, and the grandson of Jeremiah Dial, Sr., of the same place. Jeremiah, Sr., was the immigrant forebear who was a patriot. John Dial fought in the Revolution. Both men have been registered with the National D.A.R. in Washington by Nellie Mae Goggans and Florence (Kay) Dial, respectively. Jeremiah Dial, III who married Summer ---- and came to Sumter County in the 1830's was a brother of David Montgomery Dial -- See Dials in Boyd Cemetery.

******

Jennett Dial who was born 1 October 1783 and died 24 May 1855, aged 71 years 6 months and 23 days. (She was the wife of David Montgomery Dial. Jennett Dial was a Spence prior to her marriage. The inscription on this grave has been read wrong and published as read. It was very hard to read but the lettering stood out boldly after a clorox solution was brushed on the stone. The dates, as I have them here, tally with the dates in the 1850 census. See Bethel Cemetery and Land Patents for children besides those who are buried in this cemetery.)

******

William Montgomery Dial died 10 October 1840, at age of 13 years and 25 days. (He was the son of David M. and Jennett (Spence) Dial.)

******

James Dial, born 13 January 1826, died 28 April 1860. (Son of David Montgomery and Jennett (Spence) Dial.)

******

Mary (Dial) Buford, wife of Thomas N. Buford, died 6 January 1837, aged 20 years, 1 month and 14 days. (She was the daughter of David M. and Jennett (Spence) Dial. She married Thos. N. Buford 16 March 1836. By her side lies Edwin Dial Buford, their baby, who died 14 July 1837.)

Godfrey

William Godfrey, Sr., Revolutionary Soldier, married Sarah Britton 19

June 1777 in South Carolina and they became parents of at least two children: (1) William Godfrey Jr., the pioneer settler of Sumter County, Alabama, and (2) Martha Godfrey who married James Myers. (See Old Side Cemetery records for the Myers history.)

William Godfrey Jr., married (1) Elizabeth Dozier born 24 November 1781, died 28 March 1826 near Fort St. Stephens, Alabama, married 1 March 1809 in South Carolina. They had children (a) Martha Ann born 5 February 1810, died 9 October 1848, Marion County, Mississippi, married Richard Henry Herbert born 1800, died 1870, (b) Abraham Dozier born 1811, died 1843, (c) James Wilson, born 1814, died 1815, (d) Mary Jane born 12 January 1816 married John E. Brown (see John Evander Brown Cemetery records), (e) Wilson Leonard born and died 1818, (f) John Dozier born 6 January 1819 married Margaret Philips, his second cousin as she was the granddaughter of his aunt Martha (Godfrey) Myers, (g) Elizabeth Giles born 13 October 1820, married A. W. Jones, (h) Sarah Britton born 22 February 1822, married George Alexander Brown, brother of John Evander Brown who married Mary Jane Godfrey, (i) William Wilson born 5 September 1825, married Miss E. J. Paul.

William Godfrey Jr., married 25 July 1826 (2) to Mrs. Harriett Pegues (Powe) McRae born 8 August 1791, died 30 September 1845. She had two sons by Mr. McRae. She and William Godfrey had 4 children, viz: Amelia Ann born 29 May 1828, married Frederick Stewart born in New York and died in Mobile; Olivia Ellen born 16 May 1830, married William Underwood; James Myers Godfrey born 7 September 1832, married Lucy Rhodes of Demopolis, Alabama; Eliza McIntosh born 29 May 1834, died 9 February 1907, married William (Billy) Baker, buried in Mobile. Please note that William and Harriett Godfrey named one child "James Myers" the full name of his brother-in-law; note also Asberry Myers, son of James and Martha (Godfrey) Myers, married a McRae, and William Godfrey's wife, Harriett, married (1) a McRae. I believe there was a relationship between the Myers and Godfreys prior to these marriages; both families carry the name Wilson over and over, so the Godfreys must have had a Wilson line, too.

Dr. J. M. Godfrey (James Myers) born 7 September 1832, died 20 January 1890. (He was the son of William Godfrey and wife Harriett Pegues (Powe) McRae Godfrey. Graduated in medicine in Philadelphia, Penna.)

******

Lucy A. Godfrey, born 13 July 1834, died 2 March 1914. (She was the wife of Dr. J. M. Godfrey and she was Lucy Rhodes of Demopolis, Alabama prior to her marriage.)

******

W. E. Godfrey, born 14 October 1856, died 18 July 1925. He was the son of Dr. James Myers Godfrey and wife Lucy Rhodes Godfrey. (He married

(1) Cornelia Ormond, niece of "Uncle Tom" Ormond. Their children were (1) Julia who married Mr. Elliott of Carrollton, Alabama; (2) William who married Mary Julia Simms the daughter of John T. and N. Epes (Thomas) Simms - (see Old Side Cemetery records) William and Mary Julia Godfrey had children William, Cornelia, Julia, Lillian and Inistore; (3) Fannie who married a Mr. Poythress; (4) Lillian who married Mr. Little brother of the late Mrs. Rosa Meek of Panola, Alabama. He married (2) Florence Chapman the sister of Bascomb Chapman who married Odell Gee -- the Gees lived next to the McDow place on Factory Creek. The children of W. E. Godfrey and (2) wife Florence Chapman Godfrey are: (5) Earl who married Annie Simms, sister of Mary Julia who married Earl's half brother, William; (6) Ernest or "Shorty" who married Bee Payne who is descended from the Payne-Elliott family of old Payneville; (7) Mary (deceased) who never married, and (8) Florence who is married and lives in Birmingham.

******

Florence Chapman, wife of W. E. Godfrey, born 25 June 1867, died 4 February 1923.

******

Cornelia Ormond, wife of W. E. Godfrey, born 6 November 1859, died 6 December 1886.

******

Lucy Godfrey Davis 1900 - 1922

******

Lucie E. Godfrey, wife of J. R. Ramsay, born 21 April 1873, died 27 October 1902.

******

Godfrey Cameron, son of C. H. and F. G. Watts, born 19 December 1889, died 3 September 1890.

******

E. B. Godfrey -- no dates.

- Davis -

Martha C. Davis, born 10 March 1834 and died 17 April 1849. (She was the daughter of William H. and Frances Davis and the granddaughter of Brooks H. Davis, Sr. Other children of William H. and Frances Davis were: Austin, Angletta, Nicey or Penecy, Sara and Martha - the last two named were not in the census. William H. Davis lived in a large two story house between Emelle and Sumterville and today is known as the Bell house.)

- Gilbert -

William Gilbert, born in Jones County, North Carolina, 23 July 1818, died 12 January 1870. (This was William Gilbert, Jr., as his father William Gilbert patented land in the very earliest settling of the County in Township 20, Range 2 West, which is just east of Sumterville. He and his wife Susannah sold land to Seaborn Jackson the first part of 1835; a few months later he alone sold land - just his signature. This was June of the same year. Susannah probably died between January and June of 1835 and he sold land to Ebnezer Wyatt at later time. It was ca1839 when William Gilbert, Sr., died but I have not been able to locate the graves of either William, Sr. or Susannah Gilbert.

William Gilbert, Sr., left children William, Jr., Susan and James - the latter died in 1851. The nuncupative will of James Gilbert was probated 19 December 1853. William Gilbert, Jr., Susan Gilbert, John Gilbert and wife Mary E- Gilbert (nee McDaniel) swore under oath that on 28 April 1851 that James Gilbert thought he was going to die and said he wanted his daughter, Susan Frances and his wife Mary, to have the land he inherited from his father, William Gilbert, Sr., and his said daughter to have the land he owned in Texas; his son, David, not to get any of his property as he had property coming to him from an estate in North Carolina.

William Gilbert, Jr., married (1) Nancy Ann (Amason) Speight, a widow - see Old Side Cemetery records - with two little girls, Catherine and Sammy Ann. William and Nancy Ann Gilbert had two boys, Thomas J. and Eli Amason Gilbert. She and William Gilbert were divorced and she moved to Mississippi. William Gilbert, Jr., married (2) Catherine Poythress who was descended from Pocahontus and John Rolph - see Poythress family in Lavender records in Bethel Cemetery.

William and Catherine Poythress Gilbert had children: J. G., Anna B., Luvenia, William B., John Wesley, and Edward A. (Hash); his will was signed 11 January 1870 and probated 14 Febraury 1870, Will Book 2-394. Luvenia or Lena married John F. Peel 10 July 1875- Mr. Peel was descended from the famous Peel family of Bury, England. Sir Robert Peel, a close relative, founded the British police force. The English police are called "Bobbies" and the Irish police are called "Peelers" after Sir Robert. He and the Duke of Wellington led all the progressive movements in the early reign of Queen Victoria. John F.

and Luvenia (Gilbert) Peel had children: John who married Ina Gilliam and they became parents of Inez who married Walter Watson; Betty who married Dr. Tom Lawrence and they have a son Tom, Jr.; Leon married Myrtle Sheppard and they have children (1) Jackie Nell who married Richard Cobb and are parents of a son Rickie, (2) Leon, Jr., (3) Ina Mae, (4) Carolyn and (5) Jerry Lee; John, Jr. married Bobbie Bishop and they have children Pamela and John III; Albert married Ann Eldridge and they are parents of Charles and Davis; Lucile married J. C. Newberry and they are parents of Michele, Larry and Amelia; Joseph married Bettie Richie. Other children of John F. and Luvenia Peel were Josephine never married, Kate never married, Ellen married James Knighten and had children Leslie, Ernest and Herbert (killed in World War I); Annie B. never married; Fannie married Barney Rigdon and had children Evelyn, Arthur and Roberta; Sara married A. E. Cherry and had children Earl, Virginia, James, Raymond, Arnold, Wilbur, Helen, Fay and Fred; Willis married Gertrude Woods; Ruby married James Harvey Cherry and had children Ellis, Cecil, Richard, Edwin, Catherine and Ralph - both Cherry families live at Townsend, Mississippi, Kemper County. Anna Bell Gilbert married Dr. Hamet Pinson and had several children among whom was Hon. John H. Pinson who has a son Geiger Pinson (more about this family in Volume 2 as space does not permit lengthy record of this family, or the Edward A. Gilbert family which will be treated at length in Volume 2 - Professor William Gilbert of Jacksonville State College is descended from this family.) More about the Catherine Pinson Shirley (Mrs. James Shirley) family in Volume 2. The Robert Gilbert family is a large and prominent family - the present Dr. Gilbert of DeKalb, Mississippi and his late father, Dr. Lonnie Gilbert are members of this family as are the Monroe Aust family all of whom will have prominent place in Volume 2.

Hodges

Sarah Melissa, wife of J. G. Hodges, born 2 January 1851, died 11 October 1889.

Holland

John Holland, born 1766 in Prince George County, Virginia, died 1842. (John Holland was a soldier of the American Revolution; enlisted as a drummer boy at the age of about 13 in Abbeville District, South Carolina. After the Revolution he removed to Greene County, Kentucky where he received a land grant for 150 acres (#50) - recorded in Book 1-50, he lived in Caldwell County, Kentucky, also. Removed to Marengo County, Alabama in 1818 and became resident of Sumter County, Alabama where he received a pension under Act of Congress passed 7 June 1832. He served under Captain Bowie, -- John Howard and Thomas Prince were Lieutenants, and Samuel Earle, Ensign.

His wife was Jane Holland who died in Texas 11 February 1859, nearly 90 years old. Their children and grandchildren: (1) Sally Cherry (wife of Jared or Jaret Cherry who later married Susan Jenkins in Marengo, County) - their children were Ezekiel, Charlotte, Susan, Caty and Joshua, five in number; (2) Elizabeth Cherry, (3) Anderson Holland, deceased - whose children were Bluford, Thompson, F. Marion, William C., Vincent, and Dulcinea; (4) William Holland; (5) Pernica Davis, wife of Brooks H. Davis; (6) Dorcus, wife of John Le Davis; (7) Susan, wife of Henry J. Darnell.)

Hutchins

Thomas H. Hutchins born August 1763, died 27 November 1842. (Thomas H. Hutchins had children Jesse H. Hutchins, Elizabeth Phipps, James L. Hutchins, Ellen M. Stark, Amanda Simms and Washington P. Hutchins. His widow was named Mary.

Elizabeth Hutchins Phipps had children (1842): Elizabeth Jane and Thomas H. Phipps. Thomas H. Hutchins mentioned the children of James L. Hutchins as: Amanda Kendall, Jane E. Hutchins, Margaret Hutchins, and Ruth Hutchins. (Jane E. married Geo. W. Mayberry -- Ruth died in 1855.)

Thomas H. Hutchins daughter Amanda must have married (1) a Baker and (2) a Sims as her children were named in the will as Anthony Baker and John F. Baker, and Thomas H. Sims.

Thomas H. Hutchins' daughter Ellen M. Stark had children: Thomas H., Emma, Matthew and Ellen.

******

J. H. Hutchins born 11 October 1810, died 27 August 1842. (This is Jesse H. Hutchins mentioned (see above) in his father's (Thomas H. Hutchins) will. Jesse H. died three months before the death of his father; the wife of Jesse H. Hutchins, Elizabeth, died about 16 months earlier. Jesse H. and Elizabeth's children as mentioned in Thomas H. Hutchins' will were as follows: Caroline (Carolina), Virginia (who died young), Louisiana (also called Lou and Lucy Ann), Elizabeth M. (the M. was for Maryland, she was also called Mary), and Missouri -- all named for States in the Union -- Missouri married Mr. Gates of Gainesville; she, Louisiana and Elizabeth all belonged to the Presbyterian Church at Gainesville. Louisiana married Peter Handley and moved to Texas. Their granddaughter, Mrs. Louise Bard, lives in Birmingham. Peter Handley had a previous marriage - to Schaharissa Browning. They had one child who died. (See Browning Cemetery Records.)

James L. Hutchins who died in 1872 mentioned in his will, daughters: Amanda Kendall of Keokerk, Iowa; Catherine Lemmon, wife of --- Lemmon, living in New Orleans, La., and Margaret M., wife of T. J. Porter of

Sumter County, Alabama; and dower right to his widow, Sarah Hutchins. According to H. L. Landfair, Jackson, Mississippi, the immigrant forebear was James Hutchins who died 1780 in Richmond, County, North Carolina. His wife was Elizabeth ----, and they had children Jesse born 1778, married Mary French; Thomas H. born 1763 in South Carolina.

******

Elizabeth Hutchins, died 14 August 1841 aged 45 years. (This was the wife of J. H. Hutchins - she was older than her husband.)

******

William, son of J. H. and Elizabeth Hutchins, died 1855, aged 3 years.

******

Ruth D. Hutchins, daughter of J. L. and Sara Hutchins, died 25 August 1855, aged 12 years.

******

William P., son of J. L. and Sara Hutchins, died 1855 aged 12 years, 9 months.

******

Child of James L. and Sara Hutchins, died 1845, aged 13 years.

Jackson

Jacinth Jackson, born 16 October 1796 and died 5 September 1869. (He was the son of Randle Jackson, born in Brunswick County, Virginia. Jacinth Jackson was commissioner in Pike County, Alabama. (See Ala. Laws 1823 Page 141.) Jacinth Jackson married Prudence Allums and had a son Jefferson Franklin, born 23 November 1821, died 27 March 1862, married Eleanor Clark Noyes who was born 10 January 1829 and died 3 February 1867. They had a son, Charles Whiting Jackson, born 23 November 1852, died 24 August 1884, married Sara L. Hart born 27 February 1860, died 6 April 1938; they were parents of Lilian Jackson born 5 October 1879 and married Wade Hampton Coleman, born 27 August 1875 and died 7 February 1947; they were parents of children among whom are: Sara Hart, Jeff, Clayton, Wade and Nell. The will of Jacinth Jackson is in Will Book 2-392 Sumter County, Alabama and was probated 8 November 1869. Mentions the following: To grandchildren Charles Jackson, Frank Jackson, William Jackson Nelly Jackson the children of deceased son Jefferson F. Jackson. To grandson Jandax Jackson son of James Jackson, deceased. To children John R. Jackson, Jordan Jackson, Jasper N. Jackson, Jane L. McKenzie and wife Mary Jackson. The 1850 census gives Jacinth Jackson 53 born in Georgia, Prudence Jackson 52 born in Georgia, Lucinda 20 born in Alabama. Also in the home were listed others John H. Robinson 38 an trader born in Ala., Joseph W. Jackson 20 born in Alabama and a farmer, John R. Jackson 18 a farmer born in Alabama. The latter was the son of William Jackson, a brother of Jacinth Jackson, who died just after coming to Sumterville. Jacinth Jackson was his guardian and reared John R. - see Old Side Cemetery records.

******

Prudence, consort of Jacinth Jackson, born in Georgia, 20 December 1797, married 26 May 1814, died 2 October 1857.

******

Lieut. J. T. Jackson, son of Jacinth and Prudence Jackson, born in Barbour County, Alabama, 9 February 1839, wounded at Resaca, Georgia, 15 May 1864, died at Atlanta, Georgia 1 June 1864.

******

Sara E., daughter of Jacinth and Prudence Jackson, born 13 February 1827, died 8 July 1844.

******

James C., son of Jacinth and Prudence Jackson, born 29 March 1815, died 21 August 1843.

******

Randle born in Brunswick County, Virginia, 17 October 1863, died 17 July 1838, aged 75 years, 9 months.

******

Elizabeth Jackson, wife of Randle Jackson, born in South Carolina, moved to Georgia, then to Alabama in 1818, died 1854 at 78 years, 2 months 10 days. (She was nee Elizabeth Kendall born 5 April 1776.)

Knight

Paul S. Knight, died 8 April 1843, aged 28 years.

McDaniel

James E., son of H. and D. McDaniel, born 13 July 1848, died 22 September 1848.

******

William Henry McDaniel, son of Henry and Delila McDaniel, born 9 September 1847, died 28 July 1848.

******

William McDaniel, died March 1835 in the 56th year of his age.

******

Elizabeth C., daughter of William and Penelope McDaniel who died in the 10th year of her age, in 1842.

******

William Harris, son of Henry and Delila McDaniel, died 30 June 1842, aged 11 years.

******

Elizabeth, daughter of Henry and Delila McDaniel, born 28 November 1841, died 20 June 1859.

******

Margaret Jane, daughter of Henry and Delila McDaniel, born 14 January 1831, died 11 August 1860.

******

George W., son of Henry and Delila McDaniel, born 11 March 1837, died 9 October 1865,

******

Rosa Knox, daughter of John and Mary McDaniel.

******

Mary McDaniel Wilson, daughter of Henry and Delila McDaniel, born 14 February 1850, died 14 February 1880. (She had a son Asbury who lived in Texas.)

******

Delila, wife of Henry McDaniel, born 27 April 1807, died 10 March 1876. (She was Delila Harris, daughter of John and Margaret Harris of Davidson County, Tennessee, moved to Washington County, Alabama when it was Mississippi Territory, lived for a time near St. Stephens, then moved to Sumter County in 1835. The McDaniels were the first names enrolled on the Methodist Church book, with Rev. Wiley Thomas, Minister.)

******

Hulda Ann, daughter of Henry and Delila McDaniel, born 24 December 1832, died 19 August 1858.

******

John Knox McDaniel, son of John and Mary Knox McDaniel, born 28 December 1877, died 1905.

******

Belle Barnett McDaniel, daughter of John M. and Mary Knox McDaniel, born 22 January 1871.

******

Mary Knox McDaniel wife of John M. McDaniel, born in Talladega, Alabama, 29 July 1845, died in Nashville, Tennessee, 20 March 1914.

******

John M. McDaniel, died 7 July 1882, aged 48 years.

******

Pamelia McDaniel, wife of Henry McDaniel, died 19 April 1884, aged about 42 years.

******

Henry McDaniel, died 12 October 1880, aged about 83 years.

******

Henry Clay McDaniel, son of Delila and Henry McDaniel who died 26 July 1844, aged 2 months.

******

Penelope, wife of William McDaniel, died 1874, aged 84 years.

McCain

William Claude McCain, born 4 November 1879, died November 1950.

******

Adam Creed McCain, born 6 September 1859, died 9 July 1931.

******

Mary Nixon McCain, born 26 April 1880, died 21 March 1934. (Sister of W. J. Nixon who married Alice Boyd.)

******

Clarence, infant son of A. Creed and M. A. McCain, born 1896, died 1898.

Mitchell

Twin daughters of B. J. and Nancy (Dial) Mitchell, born and died 15 January 1844.

Ormond

Thomas S. Ormond, born 8 July 1808, Green County, North Carolina, died 31 August 1868. ("Uncle Tom" Ormond's record is to be found in Old Side Cemetery records -)

Nixon

Hester Ann, wife of J. M. Nixon, born 21 March 1824, died 6 September 1878.

McKinsie

Edgar J., son of John and Jane McKinsie, born 3 December 1853, died 11 October 1857.

Porter

James Lemuel, son of L. J. and M. M. Porter died 26 July 1857. (Grandchild of Jesse H. Hutchins.)

******

Sallie Bell, daughter of L. J. and M. M. Porter. (Sister of above James L. Porter.)

Mayberry

G. E. Mayberry, son of G. W. and J. E. Mayberry, died 27 December 1854, aged 10 years. (Grandchild of Thomas H. Hutchins.)

Richardson

Sarah J. wife of J. R. Richardson, born 26 November, 1843, died 21 October 1908.

******

James H., son of J. R. and S. J. Richardson, born 26 November 1866, died 6 August 1909.

Webb

Infant daughter of John H. and Mary H. Webb-- no dates.

******

Sara Ann, daughter of John H. and Mary H. Webb, died 20 April 1853, aged 16 months.

******

John Parker Webb, son of John H. and Mary Webb, died 4 March 1848, aged 6 months.

Nance

Mary Ann Nance, daughter of W. T. and Sarah Nance, born 16 August 1847, died 30 August 1848. (The father, W. T. Nance, was born ca 1825 in Virginia, and his wife Sarah was born ca 1827. The other children of this couple were James Walker (buried at Gainesville, Alabama), Wm. Hugh also buried at Gainesville, Thomas H., buried in Texas and Fannie Ella born 1852, died 1924 and is buried in Greenville, Texas.)

Prince

Sarah E. Prince, born 17 August 1837, died 9 March 1902.

Somers

George Somers, died 4 June 1861, aged 65 years, 9 days.

History

of

BETHANY or OLD SIDE BAPTIST CHURCH

Old Bethany Baptist Church was located at Sumterville, it was a Missionary Baptist Church but in 1838 those in the church who did not believe in foreign missions organized what was called "Old Side" Baptist Church, so called because the members were said to be on the "old side" instead of the new side or side of foreign missions. The cemetery is known to this day as "Old Side Cemetery" for this Baptist Church. After the Primitive Baptist Church at Emelle burned the "dyed in the wool" Baptists joined Old Bethany Baptist Church at Sumterville and buried their dead in Old Side Cemetery.

The organizing members of Old Bethany Church were: Asa Wright, Clark Crocker, Thomas Hagger, Randle Jackson, Elisha T. Thomas, P. McDaniel, Aratron Smith, James Williams, Sara Irwin, Henry Smith, C. N. Bryant, Wright Jones, Lermel Mathress, Benj. J. Richardson, Henry Richardson, Gain C. Richardson and Washington P. Hutchinson.

GRAVESTONE RECORDS FROM OLD SIDE BAPTIST CEMETERY

This cemetery is located on that part of the old Emelle-Sumterville road which in now abandoned. The only means of entrance is from a road which turns due east from James Ormand's home which is located on the road which connects the old Sumterville-Emelle road with the old Emelle-Livingston road. The road to the cemetery has recently been improved, so is now passable. This cemetery is very interesting; those sleeping here are related to each other either by blood or marriage, and most of them had their roots back in Edgecombe County, North Carolina.

-- A --

William Amason, born in Edgecombe County, North Carolina, 13 August 1798, removed to Alabama in 1835, died 6 January 1858.

(The will of Ellendor Amason was proved in Edgecombe County, North Carolina, 18 August 1829. Final settlement February Court 1832 Book F page 131. "To daughter Sally Ward; to granddaughter Eleanor Ward; to son William Amason; to granddaughter Eliza M. Amason; to sons Nathan Amason, Elbert Amason, Asa Amason; to daughters Nancy Amason, Polly Amason and Elizabeth Amason. signed Ellendor Amason ". Witnesses/ James Barnes and Colfield Ellis.

Note: Nancy (Ann) married Samuel Speight in 1831 and he died in Sumter Co., Ala., 1837, two months before his second daughter Sammy Ann was born. Sammy Ann married Emanuel Carr and his brother Abraham married Sammy Ann's sister, Catherine, on 8 July 1856 Sumter County, Alabama. This Samuel Speight family was related to the Speights and the Littles around Warsaw in Sumter County. Nancy (Amason) Speight married William Gilbert of Sumterville and they had two boys, (1) Thomas Jefferson Gilbert and (2) Eli Amason Gilbert (see "Gilbert", in Methodist Cemetery at Sumterville) born 12 January 1846, died 11 May 1911 and married Mattie E. Turner. Thomas J. died Eagle, Texas during the Civil War. William and Nancy Ann Gilbert were divorced, and she removed to Mississippi. Sammy Ann Speight, born 1837 in Sumter County and her husband, Emanuel W. Carr, born 1836, died 1880, were married 8 April 1858 and had several children, among whom was Edwin Speight Carr who married Lillie Brame Scott. They had a son Samuel B. Carr who married Velma Lewis. Their daughter Patricia Ann married DeWitt C. Black on 10 February 1958. They live in Jackson, Mississippi. By courtesy of Mrs. Black.)

******

Asa Amason, born in Edgecomb County, North Carolina, 3 December 1804, removed to Alabama, died 8 August 1876. (See Ellender Amason's will.) His first wife, Sara, is buried by his side; and his (2) wife Lydia G. Lewis Amason is buried in Livingston, she died in 1906. She was the daughter of Obedience Lewis who died 8 June 1864. Lydia and Asa Amason were married 2 October 1855. Other Lewis heirs were Eliza McLean, Sara Meadow, Martha Lewis, Thomas R. Lewis and Thomas R. Lewis, Sr., and Lewellyn Lewis (see gravestone inscription of Lewellyn Lewis in this cemetery, and Probate Record Book #20.)

******

Sara Amason, consort of Asa Amason, born in Edgecombe County, North Carolina, 1804, removed to Alabama in 1838, married 25 November 1838, died 11 February 1855. (She was the sister of William T., Jacob, Jesse, Leroy Simms, and Mary Grice, - most of whom are buried in this cemetery,- and Charity Woodard Grice who is buried at Bethel Cemetery. See Simms records.)

******

Infant daughter of Asa and Sara Amason, born and died 1840.

******

Susan, daughter of Asa and Sara Amason, born 1842, died 1848.

******

Elbert Amason, born in Edgecombe County, North Carolina, 8 June 1802, died 1872. (See will of Ellendor Amason under gravestone record of William Amason. Elbert was the father of Nannie (Amason) Gregory and her brother Eli.)

******

Elizabeth Amason, consort of Elbert Amason, was born in Edgefield District, South Carolina, 28 January 1813, died February 1886. (Elizabeth Foy was the daughter of Terry and Nancy Foy--see Foy records--She married Elbert Amason 17 December 1840.)

******

Nathan Amason, born in Edgecombe County, North Carolina, 6 June 1800, died 24 February 1877. (He married Emaline Knight, 21 March 1848; and (2) Artemisa Lacy, 25 January 1859 Sumter County Bonds. See William Amason record for relationships.)

******

Emaline Amason, wife of Nathan Amason, born in Edgecombe County, North Carolina, 10 October 1808, moved to Alabama 18 October 1836. (Nathan and Emaline were married 21 March 1848. He married Artemisa Lacy 25 January 1859.)

******

(Eli Amason, the son of Elbert and Elizabeth, lies in an unmarked grave along side of his wife, also in an unmarked grave. He married (1) Jane Gee 28 September 1870. She was a widow. (2) M. Lou Burton 15 January 1878. He had no children. The 1850 Census gives; Asa Amason 45 Merchant born North Carolina; Sara Amason, 46, born North Carolina; Laura Grice 18 born North Carolina; Mary S. Cockrell, 5 born Alabama; Catherine Cockrell 3 born Alabama. William Amason 50 born North Carolina.

Nathan Amason 47 born North Carolina; Emaline 40 born North Carolina; Martha A. Knight 17 born North Carolina; Catherine A. Knight 7 born North Carolina; Joshua T. Smith 10 born Alabama.

Elbert Amason 47 born North Carolina; Elizabeth 38 born South Carolina; Nancy A. 8 born Alabama; Eli 2 born Alabama. Elbert Amason in his will (Book 2-402) mentions his wife, Elizabeth, his son Eli, and his daughter Nancy Ann Gregory.)

-- B --

Elizabeth Goldsmith Bell, wife of William D. Bell, born in Tarboro, North Carolina 17 March 1830. She was named for her mother Elizabeth and her grandmother Sallie Goldsmith. Elizabeth Goldsmith (Bell) and her husband William D. Bell were second cousins as the father of William D. Bell was first cousin of Frederick Bell Jr. the father of Elizabeth Goldsmith Bell. William D. Bell's father was Whitmell Bell and he married Betsy ---. his will was proved 24 March 1824, Edgecombe County, North Carolina. Whitmell Bell and Frederick Bell, Sr., (father of Frederick, Jr.) were sons of Joshua and Phereby (---) Bell. Joshua's will was proved 7 April 1793. Joshua and Phereby Bell had 8 children.

The will of Frederick Bell, Jr., was proved 28 January 1844 in Edgecombe County, North Carolina and also recorded in Sumter County, Alabama as there was a dispute over some provision in the will. A son of Frederick Bell, Bennett B. Bell, came to Sumter County and settled at Warsaw. His niece and fourth cousin, Alice or Alleraner Bell came to Warsaw to live with his family. She married James T. Daniel of Warsaw -see his record in Bethel Cemetery - who was a relative of Bennett B. Bell's first wife, Susannah Turner the daughter of Matthew Turner - Alice or Alleraner (Bell) Daniel is buried at Central Cemetery--see records in this book. Bennett B. Bell married (2) to Caroline Little, daughter of Dr. Blake Little and had children (a) Margaret who was wife (2) of A. J. Arrington and had Lona who married Will Willis, and Margaret who married Odie Cathay; (b) John W. Bell whose descendants live in Chattanooga; (e) Lucy married W. R. Arrington; (d) David H. Bell whose son Bennett Bell lived in Selma.

Elizabeth Goldsmith (Bell) Bell's gravestone has disintegrated. She was visiting her daughter Alice (Bell) Daniel when she died.

******

Charles Sidney Bayless, born 7 April 1859, died 4 March 1911. (He was a native of Mississippi; married Lucy Jackson, daughter of John R. and Rebecca (Wrenn) Jackson. Both her parents are buried in this cemetery.)

******

Lucy Bayless, born 27 August 1866, died 22 July 1946. (Her mother was Rebecca (Wrenn) Jackson, the daughter of Rixie (Richardson) and Elias N. Wrenn and her grandparents were Bryant and Uney (Ray) Richardson, all of whom are buried in this cemetery.)

******

Mrs. Nancy Boyette, born 1793, died 13 October 1840. (She was the wife of Locke Boyette who came to Sumter County from Autauga County.)

******

Locke Boyette, born 1784, died 9 October 1840. (See obituaries in Sumter Democrat. The settlement of this estate shows that Zelpha was the wife of Loftin Pipen, and that Leroy, Eleanor and Thomas W. were minors. Leroy became of age the next year and married Mary S. Moore 14 May 1842. Robert a son of Locke, died a short time before his father died --Locke was shown as being administrator of Robert's estate. See "Sumter Democrat -- 1854 -" T. W. Boyette-)

******

Ellen A., daughter of Locke Boyette. Born -- 1828. (The stone is broken, we think this is perhaps Eleanor A., who is mentioned in the settlement of the estate.)

******

E. N. Bryant, born 24 June 1812, died 3 January 1876. (This is Evan N. Bryant, native of Nash County, North Carolina, the husband of Cherry Lane Bryant. He was one of the first settlers in the vicinity of Sumterville. He has some Bryant descendants in Sumter County and his daughter, Cherry Ella married John Fletcher Ormond, descendants of whom live in Sumter County, also.

******

Cherry Lane Bryant, born 1 September 1818, died 18 March 1881. (She was the daughter of Bryant and Uney (Ray) Richardson. Evan N. Bryant, her husband, was guardian of some of the minor children of Bryant Richardson. See obituary of Cherry Lane in the Livingston Journal of 1881.)

******

William T. Bryant, son of E. N. and C. L. Bryant, born 1836, died 1842.

******

Thomas, son of E. N. and C. L. Bryant, born 13 August 1839, died May 1843.

******

Mary L., daughter of E. N. and C. L. Bryant, born 6 October 1842, died the 1 September 1844.

******

Lizzie C., wife of E. N. Bryant Jr., died 2 March 1882.

******

Martha A. R. Buntin, born 21 July 1828, died 24 November 1853. (Martha was the daughter of Bryant and Uney (Ray) Richardson. She married (1)

William High, by whom she had two children, William R. and Mary High; she married (2) William Buntin by whom she had two children John S. and Martha Buntin.)

******

Reverend John Wesley Burton, born 18 November 1851, died 8 November 1926. (See Burton family cemetery records for his history. He was the 2nd husband of Nannie Amason, the daughter of Elbert and Elizabeth (Foy) Amason. -- See her tombstone record in this cemetery -- John Wesley Burton married (2) Sallie Roberts 29 August 1906, daughter of Sara E. (Selby) and John Roberts of Mississippi. He had by his first wife one child, Johnnie Burton -- see his record in Central Cemetery----He had only one child by his second wife -- she is Bessie (Margaret Elizabeth) Burton Fuller who lives in the old Eli Amason home with her mother and the two boys. Bessie married 27 November 1928 to Ed Fuller from Choctaw County. They have children: Sara Ann, Ruth Wrenn, James Burton and Howard E., Jr.)

******

Nannie (Amason) Gregory Burton, born 1 October 1844, died 4 July 1904. (She was the daughter of Elbert and Elizabeth (Foy) Amason who married (1) William J. Gregory -- see his record in this cemetery -- and (2) John Wesley Burton -- see his record above -- She had two children by William J. Gregory they were Doc and Elbert; and one child by Mr. Burton, his name was Johnnie.)

--- C ---

Cockrell Family

According to Dr. Spratt's unpublished history of Livingston in Livingston Library the Cockrell family who migrated to Sumter County, Alabama, originated in Nash County, North Carolina, the grandfather being Jacob Cockrell. He had a son Nathan who had two sons (1) William, and (2) Dempsey who came to Sumter County but settled in Greene County before Sumter County was opened for settlement. The death notice of Dempsey Cockrell's wife, Millicent, in the 1854 (January) "Sumter Democrat," stated she was the daughter of Jubal and Sara Carpenter. Millicent (Carpenter) and Dempsey Cockrell had the following children: Nathan, Augustus W., Leonidas A., Luther, Quintus, James and Mrs. William Wrenn whose brothers were James and Joe Wrenn of Sumterville. William Cockrell settled at Sumterville while Dempsey settled at McCainville. Several members of the Cockrell family are buried in Old Side cemetery.

--- C ---

Millicent Cockrell, wife of William J. Cockrell, born 15 October 1827, died 20 March 1849. She was the daughter of John and Mary (Simms) Grice; she was born in Edgecombe County, North Carolina. --See proof of relationship in record of Leroy Simms, in this cemetery. Also W. J. Cockrell married Milicent Grice 1 May 1845 - John Grice consents.

******

Infant son of William and Millicent Cockrell, born January 1846. (Notice that sometimes the name William Cockrell is written W. J. Cockrell in the inscriptions.)

******

Mary S. Cockrell, daughter of W. J. and Millicent Cockrell, born 1 June 1847, died 6 May 1865.

******

James A. Cockrell born 1 November 1847, died 2 February 1884.

******

Nathan Cockrell, Co-founder of SAE at the University of Alabama. (He was the son of Millicent (Carpenter) Cockrell and Dempsey Cockrell who lived at McCainville in Sumter County. After graduating at the University of Alabama he came back to Sumter County and was editor and publisher of Sumter County Messenger, a newspaper published in Livingston. No known copies in existence.

There was another Nathan Cockrell in Sumter County who advertised his storehouse at Sumterville for sale in the late 1830's. He was perhaps the husband of Temperance Cockrell named in the Will of Harris Horn as "My daughter, Temperance Cockrell, shall have her share beyond the reach of creditors of her husband, Nathan Cockrell." This will was written 1 April 1844 and proved 24 August 1844. Will Book 1, Sumter County. Harris Horn married a Grice. There was a Nathan Cockrell who died in Greene County, Alabama in 1832; he had a son Nathan, who was about 8 years old at the time of his father's death.

******

Louisa L. Cockrell, wife of William Cockrell.

******

Infant of Louisa and William Cockrell, born and died in 1851.

******

Joseph, son of William and Louisa Cockrell, born and died in 1855.

--- D ---

James J. Dixon, born 8 March 1848, died 22 November 1928. (He was the son of John and Mary (Ormond) Dixon of Hookertown, Green County, North Carolina, and he was the nephew of "Uncle Tom" Ormond, pioneer settler. James J. Dixon married Martha Foy, granddaughter of Terry Foy. Uncle Tom Ormond is buried Methodist Sumterville Cemetery. His will, however may be found in Will Book 2, page 378, Sumter County, Alabama. He asked that his estate be kept intact until Cornelia Ormond should arrive of age, and that it be managed by Lemuel T. Ormond. He left land to nieces and nephews, viz: Julia F. Ormond, Elizabeth Dixon, William Ormond, Cornelia Ormond, and to pay Lovey A. Dixon $100.00 annually, and to give William Ormond, Elizabeth Edwards and Margaret Alberton each $1,000.00. Lemuel T. Ormond was to have the plantation then under cultivation; the female heirs of Mary Dixon, viz: Sara Ann Hart, Emeline Susan Dixon, Frances Alberton, and Nancy Dixon $1,000.00 each in gold. He also mentioned Wesley Ormond of Mississippi, James J. Ormond, and Benjamin Franklin Ormond. Signed, Thomas Ormond. Witnessed by John E. Brown and J. M. Godfrey 13 October 1868.

******

Mattie A. Dixon, born 13 June 1856 died 6 February 1931. (This was "Martha" Foy, granddaughter of Terry Foy, who married James J. Dixon.)

--- E ---

John Thomas Eason, born in Pitt County, North Carolina, 20 November 1796, died 6 April 1864. (He voted at Sumterville, Alabama, 1841 --see Alabama Genealogical Register, Volume 1 Number 2, page 96. According to John Thomas Eason's will he named children Elias Carr Eason, Theophilus H. Eason, Mary Cecile wife of Elnathan Tartt, Emily L. wife of Enos Tartt (Deceased), Ester Lucilla Grigsby wife of Luke Grigsby, and the children of Emily L. Tartt: Thomas C. and Sara Allis Tartt.)

******

Winifred W. Eason, wife of John T. Eason and daughter of Elias and Cecil Carr, born in Pitt County, North Carolina, 14 August 1800, died 10 May 1855.

******

William H. Eason, son of John T. and Winifred Eason, born in Pitt County North Carolina in 1825, died in 1842.

******

Elizabeth M. Eason, daughter of John T. and Winifred Eason, born 15 July

1833, died 7 July 1853.

******

Henry, the son of E. C. and E. K. Eason, born 1865, died --. (Henry's parents were Elias Carr and Kessiah (Mitchell) Eason who married 12 January 1858. She was the daughter of Benjamin J. and Nancy (Dial) Mitchell. See Mitchell record in Sumter Democrat, and Dial record in Sumterville Methodist Cemetery Records. Elias C. Eason removed to Lauderdale, Mississippi soon after the Civil War. Their son Joseph Addison Mitchell died at Jones Bluff in 1881, when he was only 21 years of age.)

******

Richard J. Epes, born in Luneburg County, Virginia 25 September 1773, died 24 December 1865 - a Mason. Monument erected by his nephew Dr. J. W. Epes.

******

Martha J. Epes, wife of Dr. J. W. Epes, born 16 October 1839, died 8 July 1906.

(Dr. J. W. Epes married Martha Thomas, the daughter of Wade R. and Millicent (Horn) Thomas. John Horn who died in 1844 named in his will, Millicent the wife of Wade R. Thomas; Patience the wife of Morrison Thomas --brother of Wade R. Thomas -- wife Aseneth a close relative of William Thomas Simms; daughter Julia Ann Elizabeth Horn, who later married Bennett B. Thomas a brother of Wade R., and Morrison Thomas. A daughter of Bennett B. and Julia A. E. (Horn) Thomas, N. Epes, married John T. Simms, son of William T. Simms --see other records in this cemetery such as Simms, Cockrell, Hagood, Grice. These families married back and forth "with the greatest of ease" but in another generation or so it would take a "Philadelphia lawyer" to figure the relationship of every one buried here. See Horn Cemetery records for Horn family.)

Richard Junius Epes and John Cross Epes, sons of Rebecca (Cross) and Peter Epes, Jr., who married 15 February 1798, came to Sumter County and settled at Jones Bluff, now called Epes. John Cross Epes died prior to 1860; the settlement of his estate (Book 10, Orphans' Minutes - page 171) shows the heirs of John Cross Epes as John W. Epes, Sara L. Randolph and Epes Randolph. Richard Junius Epes never married. His nephew, Dr. John W. Epes inherited his property. John W. Epes married Martha J. Thomas, daughter of Wade Thomas 27 October 1858, and had children, (1) John Peter Epes, (2) James Vernon Epes, (3) Una Epes who married Geo. P. Kinkle and had children, (a) Una Gerald Kinkle who married Jos F. Gilbert, (b) Martha Mary Kinkle married Charlie Brown, (c) George P. Kinkle, (d) Blevens Kinkle, (e) and Raymond Kinkle; (4) Junie Wade Epes married William E. Oliver (see Oliver records in Vol. 2 "Pioneer Families of Sumter County") and had (a) Martha Oliver who married Richard M. Mendenhall and had a son Junius, (b) William Junius Oliver who married Mary Ella (known as Mary Lou) Harrison and had children William E.; Marilyn (Bunda) who married Joel B. Griswold and they had a son Joel, Jr.; Melanie and June. (5) Martha Scott Epes (Mattie) married Charles H. Whitely of Rome, Georgia - he was first cousin of Ellen Axson, wife (1) of President Woodrow Wilson. Martha and Charles H. Whitely had children: (a) Wade H. Whitely who married Goldie Thrasher, (b) Blair Whitely who married P.L. Bowling, (c) Lt. John Whitely who married Florence Jones, (d) Morrison married Margaret Thom, (e) Vernon married Annie Cox, (f) Martha (Lady), not married, (g) Fitzhugh married Janie Jackson, (h) Elizabeth married E. H. Noone.

******

Children of J. W. and M. J. Epes --Dott born 7 July 1871, died 26 September 1872, and Mamie, born 4 October 1863, died 26 September 1872.

******

Minnie Morrison Epes, born 7 August 1876, died 25 November 1951.

--- F ---

Terry (Terrence) Foy, born in Ireland in the county of Meud 25 May 1776, he died 24 August 1842. (He is the only Catholic buried in this cemetery. His descendants married into many of the old families buried here. Terry Foy landed to South Carolina directly from Ireland and stayed there for 4 years, then came to Clinton, Greene County, Alabama where he lived a couple of years before removing to Sumter County.)

******

Nancie Foy, consort of Terry Foy, born in Chester District, South Carolina, in August 1777, died June 1854. (Terry and Nancie were the parents of Elizabeth (Foy) Amason, Davis Foy and others.)

******

Robert Emmet Foy, son of Davis and Eliza Foy, born 21 August 1860, died 1873. (He was probably named for Terry Foy's brother who got to the port of embarkation with Terry, but returned home to tell his sweetheart goodbye and was killed in a political uprising.)

******

Sara K., daughter of William and Ellen Foy, born 24 March 1854, died 1855. (William Foy married Ellen Ward December 1844, license bought on the 20th.)

******

Lemuel Foy, son of William and Ellen Foy, born 1852, died 1853.

******

Mary Foy, born 19 July 1858, died 10 February 1940. (She was known as "Miss Mame", and she lived with her nieces Miss Mary Dixon and Mrs. Evelyn Little.)

******

T. T. Foy, born 21 February 1850, died 28 May 1878.

******

Eliza T. Foy, wife of Davis Foy, born in Edgecombe County, North Carolina, on 16 May 1829, died 9 April 1893. (Eliza Foy was born Eliza Amason and married Davis Foy on 28 March 1849.)

******

Davis Foy, born 1811, died 17 October 1877. (The 1850 Census shows one child at that time--Thomas T.--so T. T. Foy (above) who died in 1878 was the son of Davis Foy.)

******

James Davis Faulkner, born 11 December 1833 in Georgia, died 7 September 1810. Lived for 17 years with his nephew, Hugh Boyd Praytor, at the home of Mrs. J. B. Stewart's, Sumterville, Alabama.

--- G ---

Thomas P. Gordon, born 1881, died 1891. (He married Ella Wrenn, a sister to Mrs. King and Joe & Jim Wrenn) married a Mr. Gordon - Her father was E. H. Wrenn.)

******

Olivia Gordon, born and died 1886.

******

William J. Gregory, born in Montgomery County, Missouri, 25 October 1840. (He was the first husband of Nannie Amason, the daughter of Elbert and Elizabeth (Foy) Amason. See Nannie (Amason) Gregory-Burton.

gravestone.)

******

William Elbert Gregory, born 31 December 1868, died 17 January 1916. (He was the son of William J. and Nannie (Amason) Gregory. William (or Bud Eb, as every one called him) had a brother known as Doc. William Elbert married Margaret Alice Little and Doc married her cousin Lethia Little, both of Clinton, South Carolina. They were Presbyterians; their parents, grandparents and many other relatives are buried in the church yard at that place. William Elbert and Margaret Alice (Little) Gregory had two children, viz: (1) James Gregory who lives in Meridian, Mississippi. His wife Maggie (Blackwell) Gregory died in 9 January 1958. They are parents of three children; (2) Margaret Gregory, married Roland Epes Simms of Emelle, Alabama. They have two children, (a) Alice who married Jack Jones; and (b) Mary Louise. Col. Roland Epes Simms, Tax Collector of Sumter County, and is the son of John T. and N. Epes Simms.

******

Margaret Alice Gregory, born 27 January 1872, died 24 June 1926. (She was the wife of William Elbert Gregory; see his record for relationships. Her mother and father were first cousins.)

******

John Grice, born in Nash County, North Carolina, 27 April 1803, died September 1864. (He married Mary Simms who was a sister of William T. Simms, Leroy Simms, Jesse Simms, Jacob Simms, Charity Simms Woodard, and others. He and Mary had daughters who married into the Bell, Cockrell and Richardson families. The John Horn and Henry Horn families were related to those children as John Horn married Aseneth Simms and her sister Mary married Henry Horn (see Horn Family History, a copy of which is owned by Mrs. Sammie Webb of York, Alabama.) John Grice had a son who was 10 years old in 1850 (Census Record), his name was William T. Grice. Laura Grice married Elijah Bell of Dallas County and Susan Patience Grice married William Bell, also of Dallas County. Asa Simms, son of William T. Simms married his cousin Miss Bell of Dallas County; their daughter Miss Mary Simms lives in the old home near Browns. Another daughter of John and Mary (Simms) Grice, Mary Sarah, married Bryant Richardson (the son of Bryant and Uney (Ray) Richardson.) Their son A. T. Richardson is buried in this cemetery. John Grice was constable of Beat 6, Township 20 Range 3 West. He lived on what is now known as the Treadaway place just south of land owned by Tom Jenkins. After the death of his wife, Mary, we find that John Grice married Mary's sister, Charity (Simms) Woodard who is buried at Bethel Cemetery. See Leroy Simms' gravestone record and notes, to prove all these relationships. Ann Grice m. Thomas Horn; Betsy Grice m. Jere Horn & after her death he m. her sister Martha.)

******

Mary Simms Grice, born in Edgecombe County, North Carolina, 27 April 1809, died 17 August 1847. (See John Grice gravestone record for relationships.)

******

R. J. Hagood, son of R. Z. and Ida Hagood, born 1874, died 1876. (Thomas Z. Hagood married Ida Thomas 10 September 1868, at the home of her father, J. D. Thomas, the son of Ichabod Thomas --minor heir at the time of Ichabod's death-- married Mary High on the 6 January 1847. Mary High was the daughter of Martha A. Richardson who married (1) William High and (2) William Buntin --see Martha A. R. Buntin gravestone record in this cemetery -- James D. Thomas, the son of Ichabod and Susannah (Barnes) Thomas, had brothers Wade R. Thomas, Bennett Barrow Thomas, Morrison Thomas' Archaleus Thomas (Sheriff of Sumter County in 1836) and others. Ichabod Thomas, father was Theophilus Thomas and his father was John Thomas who married Christinola Roberts and lived in Virginia, removed to North Carolina prior to 1747 and he died 1788 in Edgecombe County, North Carolina. Courtesy of John Asa Simms as taken by him from old Bible records; and from Sumter County Court Records. Since Mr. Simms gave me the above information on the Thomas family I found in "Old Albemarle" by Ray, the following: "The first Thomas family in America was John Thomas family who came to America in 1610 in "The Sea Venture", he had sons John, Phillip, William, Richard and Marke. John Jr., was in Nasemond County, Virginia, at one time, his wife was Dorothy and they had children William, Richard, John, Elizabeth, Sarah and Catherine. John Thomas was born 1704/5 married Christiana Roberts and had children John, Jonathan, Obedience, Theophilus, Milicent, and Teresa (the latter married Theophilus Hill). Theophilus Thomas married Mary Rogers and had children Obedience, Millicent, Ichabod, Benjamin, Tabitha, Theresa, Micajah, John Rogers, Theophilus, Nancy and Elizabeth.

******

Amanda Jane Hale, daughter of R. (or H.) and Malinda Rogers, and wife of J. M. Hale born 21 May, 1839, died 27 October 1857.

******

Martha Frances, daughter of J. M. and Amanda Hale, born 1854, died 1856.

******

Elizabeth, daughter of ----- and D. D. Hale, born 1841 and died 1843.

******

Clarra, daughter of J. H. and V. A. Hendricks, born 13 May 1859, died

1800. (J. H. Hendricks married Virginia A. Drummond 19 July 1854.)

******

Mrs. T. A. High, born in Wayne County, North Carolina - dates illegible (but we know from Sumter County, Alabama records that Temperane A. Cook married William R. High 5 January 1847 - see his record in this cemetery.)

******

William R. High, born in Wake County, North Carolina 18 March 1825, died 25 -- 1866. (He was the son of William and Martha (Richardson) High. His mother was the daughter of Una (Ray) and Bryant Richardson. See Martha R. Buntin and R. J. Hagood records in this cemetery for relationships.)

******

A. H. Holcombe, born 21 July 1813, died 9 July 1852. (He was a merchant in Sumterville. The 1850 census shows that Bennett Barrow Thomas was living in the home of Alva H. Holcombe, and they both were merchants living at Sumterville, Alabama. We feel that the Thomases and Holcombes were related. Bennett Barrow Thomas bought the William S. Anderson land which he (W. S. Anderson) had bought from the administrator of the estate of Leroy Simms, and moved to Old Ramsey in 1864. This same land is now owned by Henry A. Jenkins, great great nephew of William S. Anderson.)

******

John A. Hollis, born 22 November 1866, died 4 November 1886.

******

Emily A. Hollis, born 20 March 1865, died 15 April 1933.

******

James L. Hollis, son of J. W. and A. B. Hollis, Born 1895, Died 1895.

******

Infant son of A. M. and A. B. Holloway, born 21 November 18--, died 9 February 18--

- J -

John R. Jackson, born 1831, died 1924. (He was the son of William Jackson who was the son of (John) Randall Jackson who was born in Brunswick County, Virginia. William died when John R. was only two or three years old. His uncle Jacinth was his guardian. See Jacinth Jackson gravestone record in Methodist Cemetery at Sumterville. John R. was a Civil War soldier.)

******

Isephena A. E. Jackson, 1st wife of John R. Jackson, born 8 November 1835, died 7 January 1872. (She was Isephena Holliday, the mother of Will D. Jackson.)

******

Rebecca Wrenn Jackson, born 1840, died 1912. (She was the 2nd wife of John R. Jackson, and the daughter of Elias H. and Rixie (Richardson) Wrenn, and granddaughter of Bryant and Uney (Ray) Richardson. Mrs. Lucy Bayless, Mrs. Fannie Bride and Mrs. Sara Stinson (the first Mrs. W. R. Stinson) were the children of Rebecca (Wrenn) and John R. Jackson. See Elias H. Wrenn in this cemetery.)

******

Mary A. Jackson, daughter of Mrs. R. P. Bobbitt, and wife of C. M. Jackson, born in Franklin County, Tennessee, 7 December 1854, died 27 March 1877.

******

Willie (or Will) D. Jackson, born 10 March 1865, died 22 October 1924. (He was the son of John R. Jackson and wife Isaphena Holliday Jackson. (See other Jacksons and Stinson for relationships.)

******

Mary Jacqualine Jackson, born 26 October 1864, died 24 December 1932. (She was Miss Sanders of Millville, Alabama. Will D. and Jacqualine were married 1897. They are parents of Isephena who married Melvin Joyner (see Boney Cemetery records), William Andrew, deceased; John R. who lives in Waynesboro, Mississippi and Jabe Cook Jackson who lives in Michigan.)

******

William Andrew Jackson, born 28 September 1900, died 1 January 1910. (He was the son of Will D. and Jacqualine (Jackie) Jackson.)

******

(There was a man by the name of Ephriam Jackson who died in Sumterville in 1840; he jointly owned land with Hiram Jackson so it had to be sold. The widow, Rhoda, and Seaborn Jackson were administrators of the estate. No grave stone has been found for Ephriam.)

--- K ---

John Kennedy, born in Lenoir County, North Carolina 26 October 1796, died in Lauderdale, Mississippi 18 January 1874. (See McCainville records.)

******

Harriett A. Kennedy, born in Jones County, North Carolina, 8 November 1805, died March 1849.

******

Joseph Knight, born 1806, died March 1847. (He was probably the son of Jarret Knight, for in 1835 when Jarret died, Joseph was made guardian of Lavina and Rachel--see Orphans Book 2 page 217 -- Cynthia Knight died in 1853 and named Rachel, wife of Lewellyn Lewis -- see Will Book 2 page 28. Thomas J. G. Knight died in 1840; citation issued by court to William Knight, Joseph Knight, Nancy Knight, Rachel Knight and Luvenia Knight to appear before the court -- but the above T. J. G. Knight, in his will (Bood 1, page 141), says the property to be divided among Joseph Knight, his brother, and his three sisters.)

--- L ---

Lewellyn Lewis Sr., born 12 October 1813 died 5 July 18--. (See above record and Asa Amason record.)

******

Rachel, wife of Lewellyn Lewis, born 21 August 1819, died 1 June 1909. (She was the daughter of Cynthia Knight. See Richardson records for other Knights.)

******

Mary Ann, consort of H. B. Lacy born 23 July 1823, died 27 June 1853.

******

Evelyn Little 1886-1935. (She was the wife of Martin Little, a native of Louisiana. He is buried in Livingston, Alabama. They had one daughter Martha. Evelyn was the daughter of James J. and Martha (Foy)

Dixon. See Dixon and Foy records.)

--- M ---

Nannie Foy May, born 22 October 1851, died 14 March 1933. (She was the wife of Ben May, and the sister of Martha Foy Dixon and Miss Mame Foy.)

******

Ben May, born 5 March 1852, died 12 December 1926. He was husband of Mrs. Nannie Foy May.)

******

James W., son of Wilson G. Myers, born 8 December 1830, died 1 May 1849.

******

Wilson G. Myers Jr., son of W. G. and Margaret C. Myers, born 16 April 1840, died 8 April 1855. (Wilson G. Myers Sr., was Adj. of Batt., 69 Reg. --See Alabama Genealogical Register, page 32, Vol. 1, Number 1. This was in 1836. He was county surveyer in 1839 and voted at Sumterville in 1841. James Myers, husband of deceased Martha Godfrey Myers, died in 1842 and named as his heirs Wilson G., George M., William G., John M., Asberry, Leonard L., Thomas M., Martha G. wife of John Phillips and Ann D., wife of Joseph Read. --Martha's husband John Phillips died in 1846 and left children Sara J., Ellen A. (or Helen A.), Jack, George M., Florence M., and Margaret Godfrey, widow of Dozier Godfrey whom she had married 23 March 1837 and latter married Mr. Arrington; her sister Helen also married an Arrington. William Godfrey administered the estate - Orphans Book 3 page 42.)

******

Samuel W., son of Wilson G. and Margaret C. Myers, born 18 July 1842, died 25 July 1844.

******

Richard A. Myers, born 12 August 1850, died 14 October 1855.

******

Infant son of Richard W. Myers born and died 1858.

--- O ---

John William Ormond, born 10 December 1883, died 11 May 1929. (He was son of John Fletcher and Cherry Ella (Bryant) Ormond and the husband of Mary Burwell Ormond. Their son, Will, is a Presbyterian Minister. See Burwell in Bethel Cemetery records.)

******

John Fletcher Ormond, born in Green County, North Carolina 6 October 1843, died 24 May 1924. (He was the husband of Cherry Ella (Bryant) Ormond and the father of children (a) Fletcher B. Ormond born 1870 married Frances Sugg of Mississippi, (b) infant who died, (c) Sallie Ella born 1872, married (1) George White and had one son to live - William George White, (2) W. O. Walton. She is still living, (d) Charles A. born 1875 and died an infant, (e) Blanche born 1877 lived to be 18, (f) Fannie born 1878, died 1931 married Jackson Gordon - no issue, (g) Evan born 19 March 1881 died 9 February 1955 married Sallie Burwell - see Bethel Cemetery for Burwell line. Both Sallie and Evan Ormond are buried in Livingston, (h) John William born 1886 died 1929 - see his gravestone in this cemetery, (i) Julia Cornelia born 1886, (j) Julia Olivia born 1887 Married Grover L. Lewis and had a daughter Mrs. Robert M. Jones who had two girls and two boys, (k) Infant son who died, (1) Luther Adolphus born 27 March 1892 married Flora Sims and had one child L. A. Jr., who married Marjorie Virginia McDonald and they are parents of two children, Scott McDonald and David Adolphus, (m) Carra born 1893 married Mr. Simpson and had children Samuel and Gladys, the latter married Preston Doughty and had children Kay and Ormond Ralph, a Lieut. Colonel in the U. S. Marines. He is married and has at least two children. John Fletcher Ormond was visiting his sister, Mrs. Thomas, at Gainesville when he died. The late Mrs. Vivian Ellis of Gainesville was the daughter of Mrs. Thomas.

******

Cherry Ella Ormond, born 19 October 1857 died 24 July 1897. (She was the daughter of Cherry Lane (Richardson) and Evan N. Bryant both of whom are buried in this cemetery. E. N. Bryant of York (Route), Alabama, is also a descendant of E. N. Bryant, the pioneer.)

--- P ---

Matthew Parham, born 1792, died 10 January 1859. (He was the father of Mary Ann Parham who married James Q. Yarborough, son of Alfred and Mary Yarborough - see Boney Cemetery -- James Q. and Mary Ann Yarborough had a son named Parham who inherited 77 slaves and quite a bit of real estate. J. J. Arrington was his guardian; one of the slaves owned by Matthew Parham was Hilliard Bryant who was 7 years old in 1859, according to age given in inventory of estate. He lived to be almost 100 years old. William T. Simms bought Hilliard when he was 10 and he lived with the Simms family many years after he was emancipated. He has told me many tales about his youth and about the old white families in the community.) In 1869 we find James Q. Yarborough had moved to Texas and was the guardian of Parham Yarborough, his son. They sold the thousand acres that Parham had inherited from Matthew Parham, the child's grandfather. This land lay in sections 19 and 20 and 30 in Township 20, Range 3 West and patented by Martin Simms, Malachi Nettles, William H. Lacy, Henry J. Darnell, and Benj. Talliafarro.

******

Nancy Parham, she was born in Sampson County, North Carolina, 10 July 1810 and died 18 January 1859. (She lived only 8 days after the death of her husband. Frances T. Morton and Arnold Walkings of North Carolina claimed to be legatees of the Matthew Parham estate.)

******

Matilda B., wife of J. M. Parham, born 22 April 1853 died 21 March 1871. Connie Jean their daughter born 1870 died 1874.

--- R ---

Virginia, daughter of J. P. and M. W. Ramsay, born 1912 died 1913. (John and Molly (Wrenn) Ramsay had children: John, Molly, Kate and Virginia and perhaps others.)

******

Molly E. Renfroe born 7 March 1846 and died 2 August 1868. (She was the first wife of Steve S. Renfroe, Sumter County's notorious outlaw. Mollie was buried at Bethel Cemetery but at the funeral of wife #2, Renfroe suddenly decided to exume body of wife #1 and place it by the side of wife #2. He immediately went to Bethel and by the time the grave had been opened it was night, but this did not deter him from completing the task. It was daybreak by the time the last shovel of dirt was thrown on the new grave. He placed a twin monument to memory of his wives - Ripley, in Believe It or Not, paid Mrs. B. G. Killingsworth for sending him this fact.

******

Mary M. Renfroe, wife of S. S. Renfroe, born 17 November 1849, died 11 July 1871. (She was also the sister of E. S. Sledge who later became target for many of Renfroe's vicious depredations. Renfroe was tall, dark and handsome and a "dare" among the ladies. He was found to be a scion of a Kentucky family who was always feudin' and wightin' with neighbors. He fought from Sumter County as a Confederate soldier who won the love of his comrades; he helped rescue Sumter County from Radical rule of Reconstruction Days by driving out men like Tobias Lane who turned over the rule of the county to the "Freedmen", the Carpetbaggers and the Scallywags such as Freedman Houston, Billings, Greta, Wells and Choutteux, to name a few; helped restore order for the white men who had come home from war, broken in mind, health and spirit, to find themselves paupers and with the foot of tyranny hard pressed against their necks, so he earned the respect of the best citizens; as a true Democrat he won the confidence of his party and as a reward he was elected to the office of sheriff.

This is the first picture with manliness and sparkle on its face. The second picture is as black and heinous as the first is bright. He became a corrupt official who had been a "Doctor Jekyll and Mr. Hide" while showing his bright and shining face to the citizens of Sumter County. It was found that he had sold pertinent information to the Military power in Reconstruction Days, information gained while being on the "inside", a despicable turn-coat in any language. He turned renagade as sheriff while posing as one carrying out the law; he plundered and stole from those who trusted him, even his brother-in-law, E. S. Sledge. Finally, he was stripped of his insigna and was taken to Tuscaloosa jail for safe keeping against infuriated men who had trusted him. There he burned a hole in a 16-inch beam under his bath tub and escaped jail. He left a note to the jailer bidding him good-bye and saying he was taking the first train out of town, no matter which way it went. (In another issue of the same paper an account was given of the honors bestowed on Steve Renfroe, Jr., aged 10 years, at the "Prof. Seth Mellen Institute" in Livingston.)

After his jail break, Renfroe began operating on a larger scale extending from Tennessee to New Orleans, terrorizing communities as he went, but he made the swamps of Sumter County his headquarters, slipping into town at night burglarizing stores, dwellings, and burning and plundering as he wished. He stole mules and horses and sold them in other states. People were afraid to light their lamps at night or to walk or ride alone on the streets and roads, so great was the fear inspired by this outlaw.

Posters, giving notice of rewards, were printed and sent out far and wide. Weeks went by but still he was not captured, until someone reported to farmers Ainsworth and Hinton that a white man, at regular intervals, passed along their road leading a train of horses and mules. They waylaid this man and captured him before he had time to draw his gun. He claimed to be a "Mr. Jones" but the men took him to Enterprise, Mississippi 50 miles from where they captured the suspicious looking character. As it happened, the marshall was James S. Boyd, a former citizen of Sumter County and he immediately recognized "Mr. Jones" as the outlaw, Steve Renfroe, the fact he did not deny to James S. Boyd who was the son of James Marion Boyd of Sumter County, and an uncle of J. W. Boyd who yet lives at Payneville. Not only did Renfroe have stolen stock but had Mrs. John E. Harris' silver with him when captured. A posse formed to take Renfroe from Mr. Boyd, who also ran the hotel. He had Renfroe in an upstairs room in the hotel and Zora Boyd, the wife of James S. Boyd, stood at the head of the stairs with a pistol and dared a single man to take the first step on the stairs. Finally, Mr. Boyd with the help of others, got Renfroe out of the hotel and on a train bound for Livingston in Sumter County. There he was placed in jail and the jailer went to dispatch messages about the capture. A posse found the cell key and took Renfroe, handcuffed, from jail. The men, their faces covered with handkerchiefs, marched him down the street past the Methodist Church, and homes with families barricaded behind closed doors, all except the Scruggs family who were uninformed of pertinent facts. They were sitting in the yard and heard the tramp, tramp of feet going by their gate and down the hill toward Sucarnooche River. Mrs. Tempie (Scruggs) Ennis was a small child at the time, but she says the memory of that moonlight night burns vividly in her mind, even till today. She said soon afterward that the same men who had marched past her father's gate, came back one by one from the tree where they had left Renfroe's body hanging from a limb, with a placard pinned to his back, "The fate of a horse thief".

The "Messenger" deplored the fact that men were compelled to become executioners, but stated that Renfroe had trampled under foot and disregarded every law in the land "so no man could deny that Renfroe did not merit his doom." Papers over the State condemned Sumter County and blamed the sheriff for being away from jail when the posse appeared. But the editor of the "Messenger" in the next week's paper, reiterated the dire atrocities committed by Renfroe, and stated had Rendroe escaped that he would have burned the town as he had so flagrantly threatened.

Sometime after the lynching of Renfroe, his widow appeared in court and asked that her son's name be changed from Renfroe to Reynolds. They moved away and the boy grew up to be a well respected citizen of a city not far from Livingston.)

The above was taken from "The Gainesville Messenger", "Livingston Journal", and by interviews with J. W. Boyd, Mrs. Tempie (W. L., Sr.,) Ennis, and from records of Sumter County.

******

Sallie J. Richardson, born 1885 died 1921. (She was the daughter of Arch T. and Sallie Thomas Richardson, both of whom are buried in this cemetery.)

******

Sudie B. Richardson, born 1887 died 1903. (She was the daughter of Arch T. and Sallie Thomas Richardson.)

******

A. Richardson ("A." for Apple White) died 29 October 1863, aged 34 years. (He was a son of Bryant Richardson & Uney (Ray) Richardson.

Apple White married Martha A. E. Knight 4 June 1851. He was Confederate Soldier.

******

Mary Emma, daughter of A. W. and Martha E. Richardson, died 1863, aged 11 years.

******

Almeth, daughter of William R. and Ester Richardson, born 24 July 1837, died 18 July 1842. (William R. Richardson married (2) Cynthia Knight 7 February 1857. Cynthia Knight had chosen Apple White Richardson to be her guardian. See Knight records.)

******

Arch T. Richardson, born 1857, died 1935. (He was the son of Bryant Richardson Jr., and Mary Sara (Grice) Richardson. Mary Sara was the daughter of John and Mary (Simms) Grice. Bryant Richardson Jr., was killed by a Negro during Reconstruction Days. (See Old Ramsey or Emelle History.) Arch T. Richardson married Sallie Thomas, the daughter of Bennett B. Thomas (see Thomas Records.) Sallie Thomas was a sister of N. Epes Thomas who married John T. Simms. Arch T. and Sallie T. Richardson had children to reach maturity and marry as follows: (1) Bryant who married Annie Bell Elliott, daughter of Calvin A. and Rosa Daniel Elliott (See Daniel and Elliott records at Central Cemetery.) They were parents of (a) Sara Bell Richardson who married Jack Crumpton and had children Sara Elizabeth and Bell Crumpton. (b) Thomas Richardson married Lillie Ash Jones, granddaughter of J. L. Parker Sr., of Livingston, Alabama - no issue. (c) George Edward who married Maria Marino of South America - they are parents of two sons: Bryant and Henry Andrew. (2) Arch Richardson Sr., married Mrs. Olga Boyd, widow of Grover Boyd (See Central Cemetery records.) They have one child Ina Bell who married Eugene Wheeler and are parents of one child. (3) Oscar Grice Richardson married Ruby Boyd, daughter of Robert J. Boyd and wife Susan (Davis) Boyd (See Boyd cemetery records.) They are parents of two boys: Oscar Grice Richardson Jr., (unmarried), and Walter Richardson who married Elaine Embrey. They are parents of one child, Rickey. (References: Sumter Co. Court House Records - and Bible records.)

******

Sallie T. Richardson, born 1864, died 1934. (She was the daughter of Bennett Barrow Thomas and his wife Julia Ann Elizabeth Horn the daughter of John and Aseneth (Simms) Horn. Sallie was the sister of N. Epes Thomas who married John T. Simms, the son of William T. Simms.)

******

John H. Richardson, born in Wake County, North Carolina, 5 December 1809, died 24 November 1878.

--- S ---

Harriett, wife of William T. Simms, born December 1829, died 4 March 1873. (She was born Miss Harriett Gray, aunt of the late Hon. Oscar Gray of Butler, Alabama. She was also descended from the Deane family of South Carolina; a member of this family, Silas Deane, went to France with Benjamin Franklin and Arthur Lee to seek alliance with that country against Great Britain in the war of the Revolution, according to Mrs. Em. Brothers, daughter of Harriett and Wm. T. Simms.)

******

Leroy Simms, born 15 July 1811, died 11 October 1849. (He was the brother of William T. Simms and he was a business partner of William T. in farming operations. Leroy was also a surveyor in the early 1840's; he advertised in the different issues of the Sumter County Whig. If he ever married we know nothing about it. His estate was settled in 1852 by the administrator, William T. Simms and the property divided as follows: to Jessie Simms; to Jacob Simms; to John Grice for wife Charity; to Asa Simms for wife Sally; to Bryant Richardson for wife Mary Sara (Grice) Richardson; to William T. Tureman for Mary S. and Catherine Cockrell (he was their guardian --their mother was a Grice--); to Asa Amason for Laura Grice; to W. S. Tureman for Patience Grice (see Richardson, Grice and Cockrell records in this cemetery and Charity (Simms) Woodard-Grice record in Bethel Cemetery.) Jacob Simms lived near Payneville; he voted there in 1841 and died in 1852 after the settlement of Leroy Simms' estate. Jesse Simms was born in 1800, married Mary Holland, daughter of Exum Holland, he was born in Virginia 1748 - another daughter of his, Mrs. Sykes - married William T. Horn, according to Sammie Webb whose wife is a descendant of the Hornes. Jessie Simms had children: Edy and Exum born in Tennessee, Nancy, Sidney and Jesse born in Alabama, and Emily who married James DeBerry 25 April 1840 in Sumter County. Exum Holland went with Jesse Simms and his family to Leon County, Texas. To complicate matters, family records show that Jacob Simms married Millicent Thomas soon after he came to America - their daughter married William Simms; and their (Jacob and Millicent) son John married Aseneth Simms who was born 8 April 1789 and died 10 November 1842. John and Aseneth (Simms) Horn daughters (see Thomas records) married Thomas girls some of whom married back into the Simms family. -- Where is that Philadelphia lawyer?)

******

John T. Simms, born 2 April 1865, died 13 December 1935. (He was the son of William T. Simms and Harriett (Gray), and husband of N. Epes Simms - daughter of Bennett B. and Julia Ann Elizabeth (Horn) Thomas

(Julia A. E. Horn was daughter of John and Aseneth (Sims) Horn. John T. and N. Epes (Thomas) Simms had children: (1) Mary Julia who married William Godfrey - see Godfrey records -, (2) Bennett Thomas now teaching in Ankara, Turkey, married Lillian La Londe and became parents of Tom Simms who married Mittie Jones, their children are Susan and Tom Jr., John (Jack) Donald married Jo -- and they have children Johnnie and Jane, Elizabeth La Londe (Mimi) not married, Marjorie Epes married Bob McLean and are parents of Nancy Ellen McLean; (3) John Asa Simms retired, married Ailene Brown and have children: Ailene who married Frank Creighton and have children Milton, Ailene, Edith and Susan; Betty married Bill Rheinschmidt and have children Elizabeth Ann, Alice and a son; John married Jan -- and they have a son John; (4) Annie married Earl Godfrey half brother to William Godfrey who married Mary Julia Simms; (5) Inistore not married; (6) Roland Epes Simms (Tax Collector Sumter Co.) married Margaret Gregory - see Old Side Cemetery records-- and have children Alice who married Jack Jones and are parents of Roland and Margaret, and Mary Louise Simms unmarried; (7) Leroy Simms, Managing Editor Birmingham News, married Virginia Hammell and have one daughter, Lucy Grey, who married Clifford Grubbs and they are parents of Nancy, Bill, Elaine and Leroy; (8) Leslie buried in this cemetery.

******

Leroy L. Simms, born 1 March 1863, died 12 January 1871. (Infant son of Harriett and William T. Simms.) and

******

Henry H. Simms, born 6 April 1865, died 12 January 1871, and **Ben. F. Simms,** born 29 March 1869, died 12 January 1871. (These three brothers, children of Harriett and William T. Simms, died the same night of spinal meningitis.)

******

Mary Leslie, daughter of Harriett and William T. Simms --(She married a Graham.)

******

William T. Simms was 43 years old in 1850, born in North Carolina. His wife Harriett was 20 years old and born in South Carolina. He had other children who are not buried in this cemetery, viz: Emily who married Mr. Brothers and lived in Meridian. They had children among whom are Addie MacLaurin who first married Joe Tomlinson by whom she had one daughter, Em, who married Aubrey Cobb, son of Robert J. and Nettie (McElroy) Cobb- (see Central Cemetery records.) Em and Aubrey have one daughter and three sons. Addie MacLaurin married (2) to Mr. McLeod. Another daughter of Emily Simms Brothers is Mildred Brothers, married Mr. Buck and they live in Jacksonville, Florida. A son, Alva; a son John Teeter;

a son Doc; and sons who died young. After Harriett Simms died her husband married the second time to Miss Poythress of Sumterville. They had two sons, Rich and Roland, both of whom died without issue. Mr. William T. Simms was postmaster at Old Ramsey, when in 1872 a mail route was established between that place and Livingston. See Livingston Journal, 1st January 1872 issue. Mr. Simms died of pneumonia.) Asa Simms, son of William T. and Harriett Simms went to Dallas County when he was a young man and married his cousin, the daughter of Elisha and Laura (Grice) Bell. Their daughter Mary Simms and her sister live in the old home near Browns.

****

Sara Jackson Stinson, born 17 February 1871, died 7 July 1906. (She was the sister of Mr. Lucy Bayless and Will D. Jackson, and was the 1st wife of W. R. Stinson, Sr. W. R. Stinson Jr., married Laurel Browning and they have an adopted daughter. --See Jackson & Richardson records--)

******

Lula, infant daughter of W. R. and S. R. Stinson born 1889, died 1892.

******

Lilliebeck, infant daughter of W. R. and S. R. Stinson born 1889, died 1892.

--- T ---

James Tartt, born in Edgecombe County, North Carolina, 1792, died 1857. (He married Sara Barnes who died 1847 -- Shelby Family Bible record.)

******

Penninah Tartt, born in Edgecombe County, North Carolina, 10 April 1821, died 23 November 1852.

******

E. B. Tartt (Edwin Barnes), native of Edgecombe County, North Carolina, born 26 April 1827, died 23 May 1856. (He was the son of James and Sara (Barnes) Tartt. His first wife was Josephine Bullock, and his 2nd wife was Susan F. Burton who died 4 September 1894. E. B. Tartt is the ancestor of E. B. Shelby, whose daughter Catherine married Walter Plott, son of S. E. (Dial) and James Plott -- See Boyd cemetery records.)

******

Josephine, consort of E. B. Tartt, died 1871. (She was Josephine Bullock; her twin babies are buried in the same grave with her.)

******

Emily L., daughter of John T. and Winifred Eason, and consort of Enos Tartt, born in Greene County, Alabama, 20 January 1837. (See Eason records in this cemetery. 1850 Census shows Enos Tartt 32 b N.C. Emily 23 b N.C. Thos. C. 4 Ala and Sara A. 1 Ala. Emily Eason and Enos Tartt married 24 April 1845. Thomas C. Tartt in Conf. Army in 1864 when gr. fa. Eason died. Orph. Records 20 - page 2.

******

Mary C., wife of Elnathan Tartt, and daughter of John T. and Winifred Eason, born 1 August 1823, died 20 September 1866. (See Eason Records. Elnathan and Enos Tartt married sisters. James Tartt, Thomas Tartt and Jonathan Tartt were brothers and Dr. Wiley Brownrigg and Edwin B. Brownrigg (see Sumter County Whig) were their half brothers. James and Sara (Barnes) Tartt had children Edwin Barnes, Thomas Morrison and his twin Pernina were born in North Carolina in 1821; Jonathan was born 23 September 1823, Elnathan was born 11 August 1816; Enos was born 19 November 1817, Archibald B. was born 26 April 1827 and died 23 May 1856; Mary Ann was born 5 May 1819 and married Mr. Adams; Elizabeth O. B. was born 12 January 1823; Margarette was born 15 August 1835. Jonathan married Jane Prestwood, daughter of Austin and Mary (Boyd) Prestwood and granddaughter of John and Jane or Jennett (Dial) Boyd --See Boyd Cemetery records. Jonathan was a Civil War soldier. He went to relieve Robert Boyd, son of above John and Jane or Jennett Boyd, and was killed.)

--- W ---

Matilda Ann Wilson, daughter of R. H. and Malinda Rogers, and wife of William H. Wilson of Abbeville, South Carolina, born 1834, died 1857.

******

Isaac R. Wilson, born 6 January 1838, died 24 December 1918. (He was a soldier in the Civil War who stayed in Sumterville after the surrender and married Mary Wrenn 22 January 1870.)

******

Mollie Wilson, daughter of Henry Wrenn, born 18 September 1846, died 18 October 1939.

******

Mrs. Martha C., consort of E. R. Wilson, born at Bluffport, Alabama 5 April 1838, and died 15 April 1869.

******

Infant of Martha and I. R. Wilson, born 1862; George R., born 1883, died 1888; Lucy Ella daughter of I. R. and M. Wilson 1889-1892.

******

Elias H. Wrenn, born 14 April 1810, died 21 December 1889. (He married Rixie Richardson. Children: W. B. Wrenn, Mrs. J. R. Wilson, Mrs. S. E. King, J. H. Wrenn, G. A. Wrenn, L. C. Wrenn, Mrs. Ella Gordon, E. H. Wrenn, Molly Wrenn, W. Ramsey Wrenn, Rebecca Jackson.

******

Rixie R. Wrenn, born 24 January 1821 in Jones County, North Carolina, died 10 December 1899. (She was the daughter of Bryant and Uney (Ray) Richardson who were natives of Jones County, North Carolina. See Cherry Lane Bryant record. Rixie married Elias H. Wrenn and their daughter, Rebecca married John R. Jackson, see his record.)

******

Infant son of E. H. and R. Wrenn, died 1863, aged 5 years.

******

James T. Wrenn, born 7 June 1844, died 18 December 1899. (He married, Catherine W. Cockrell 13 December 1866. See Simms, Grice Records.)

******

Catherine W. Cockrell, wife of James T. Wrenn, born 1 June 1849, died 4 September 1898. (She was the granddaughter of John and Mary (Simms) Grice, and daughter of Millicent (Grice) Cockrell.)

******

Josiah H. Wrenn, born 17 April 1852, died 16 January 1922.

******

Nannie E. Cockrell, wife of Josiah H. Wrenn, born 1865, died 1932, and daughter of Wm. Cockrell. Infant children of J. H. and N. E. Wrenn (Four of them from 1878 thru 1887.)

******

Geraldine P. wife of (illegible) died 1869 aged 27 years.

Those buried in unmarked graves

Furney Richardson, son of Bryant and Uney Richardson ca 1817 in North

Carolina, died prior to June 1860 in Sumter Co., Alabama when his estate was being settled - Orphans' Min. Book 10 page 114. All the heirs were minors and as follows: Bryant, Alexander, Andrew, William, Margaret, and John R. He had several slaves among whom was Anthony Richardson who was under 10 in 1860. He was bought by William Thomas Simms. Anthony became quite wealthy in his own right before his death in the 1830's.

Furney (W.) Richardson married (1) Margaret Ramsay, "daughter of Andrew H. Ramsay", 3 October 1845 (See Bethel Cemetery); he married (2) Margaret Bennett 8 June 1858 at the home of Mrs. Sara E. Bennett.)

Bryant Richardson, born 28 February 1782, died 19 March 1836. (He married Uney Ray in Johnson County N. C. and came to Sumter County, Alabama 1833. Before his estate was settled his wife died. Both Bryant and Uney Richardson lie in unmarked graves.)

Uney Richardson, (nee Ray), was born in Johnson County, North Carolina, 24 January 1789, died in Sumter County, Alabama 12 November 1843. (The settlement of her estate in Orphans' Min. Book 5, pages 545 through 547 names heirs: Cherry L. Bryant, Rixie C. wife of Elias H. Wrenn, Furney Richardson, John R. Richardson, and minor heirs: Bryant, William R., Applewhite, Jonathan and children of Harriett Richardson who married William Oneal, and children of Martha R. High -- (she married William High and after his death married William Buntin) --viz: William R. High, Mary High, John S. Buntin and Martha Buntin.)

Bryant Richardson, Jr., was born 1825 (according to 1850 Census) and died in 1868. (He married Mary Sara Grice, daughter of Mary (Simms) and John Grice, 17 March 1847. The 1880 census shows Mary Sara to be 50, Mary L. 27, Arch T., 22, Sallie 20, Oscar 18, Eunice 16, William 12. - William D. named in the 1850 census, probably died and the last child named for him, a custom in that day. Bryant Jr., was killed by "Freedman" Enoch Brown.

******

Mary Sara Richardson, born in 1830/31 (Census records) died after 1880, wife of Bryant Richardson, Jr., (both of whom lie in unmarked graves), daughter of Mary (Simms) and John Grice.

******

Bennett B. Thomas was born in 1818, Census record) and was living at Ramsey Station when the 1880 Census was taken, he married Julia Ann Elizabeth Horn, daughter of John and Aseneth (Simms) Horn. They were parents of two daughters, Sallie who married Arch T. Richardson and N. Epes who married John T. Simms.)

******

Julia Ann Elizabeth (Horn) Thomas, born in Edgecombe County, North Carolina 24 September 1827, she was the daughter of John Horn born 14 September 1776 - his father was Henry Horn who lived in Wayne County, North Carolina, and was a Major in the American Revolution.

******

Ichabod Thomas, the father of Bennett Barrow Thomas, Wade Thomas, Morrison Thomas, John J. Thomas, Archilaus B. Thomas, Edward B. R. Thomas, is probably buried here in an unmarked grave, see R. J. Hagood record in this cemetery. According to John Horn's estate settlement in Sumter County - Orphans' Court Book 7 we find that Wade Thomas married Millicent Horn and Morrison Thomas married Patience B. Horn, both daughters of John Horn whose wife was Aseneth Simms. Wade and Millicent married in North Carolina, Morrison and Patience married in Sumter County 28 December 1841. The 1850 Census shows Wade R. Thomas as 46, Millicent 43, Mary 22 born N. C., John H. 19 born N. C., Martha J. 10 born Alabama, Wade R. 7, Morrison 5, Sallie 2, and Julia Horn living in the family 22 born in N. C.

History

of

BETHEL MEMORIAL CHAPEL

The first Presbyterian Church at this site was called Bethel. Preaching was held a year previous to its organization on 22 September 1835. Mathematical and Classical Academy, under supervision of Benj. P. Burwell, stood a hundred yards or so just north of old Bethel Church.

The Church was in the center of a Presbyterian community extending from almost to the Mississippi State line (Alfred Yarborough family belonged to this church and they lived at the eastern edge of Range 4 West, Township 20 - Bethel Church was in the north central part of Township 20 Range 3 West) --- and south of Bodka Creek on the north, to the southern edge of Township 20 -- east to, and beyond, Sumterville at which point the settlement became Baptist.

The Fultons, the Ramsays, the McDows and the Kerrs and Dials had organized Presbyterian Churches at every place they stopped, in their migration, after landing in the Colonies not many years prior to the Revolution. So it was fitting that they should have a church of their choice in this community. Rev. Carouthers was the organizing minister and Bethel came under the auspices of Tuscaloosa Presbytery late in the year of 1835. Rev. Isaac Hadden, who served this church, lies sleeping in Bethel Memorial Cemetery along side of his wife and son.

After the Civil War so many of the old settlers moved away until the church all but died. It was finally torn down and moved to Sumterville, about three miles east of the old site. A church was built near the Fulton home for the Negro members of the old church. After the war the Negroes, themselves, withdrew from the white churches and organized churches of their own. Most Negroes were Baptist, however.

Mrs. Kate Brownson, (Catherine Fleming McDow, daughter of Alexander and Mary Adeline McDow, married John Milton Brownson) conceived the idea of a chapel on the site of the old church ground. She furnished the money to build the lovely brick chapel in which funerals are held. It was called Bethel Memorial Chapel, and was dedicated on 14 June 1908 by a former pastor, Rev. C.M. Hutton, of Ft. Worth, Texas. He took his text from the 21st Chapter of St.Matthew and the 13th verse, ''My house shall be called the house of prayer''. On the Chapel walls are hung scrolls with the names of the Confederate soldiers who went to war from the old church; the beautiful stained glass windows; the lovely pews facing a simple, dignified altar all attest the fact that this is a sacred spot. One is more impressed of the sacredness of the surroundings when the chapel is seen from the front, so silent, so dignified against the sleeping place of many saints. the ancient stones marking the places where they were laid to rest. Its doors are rarely used any more as the old grave yard is about full, but occasionally some one is buried there; I can think of about eight in the last 35 years. Most people are now buried at Central Cemetery which is used by both Presbyterians and Methodists.

Inscriptions

William Turnbull Burwell, born 13 September 1849, died 25 November 1909. (He was the son of Benj. P. and Margaret (Moore Burwell. Benj. P. Burwell married (1) Mary Ann Frierson in 1847; she is buried in this cemetery but the stone is buried in the ground or broken. He married (2) Margaret Moore, daughter of Thomas and Elizabeth C. Moore, both of whom are buried in this cemetery. William Turnbull Burwell married Margaret Ramsay, daughter of Joseph Reid and Sara (Wrenn) Ramsay. They had children (1) Mary Elizabeth who married John William Ormond, (buried at Old Side Cemetery) -- they have one child, Will, who is a Presbyterian Minister; (2) Sallie Ramsay who married Evan Ormond (both buried in Livingston) and had children: (A) James who married Jospehine Fort, they have children: Evan, Fort and Reid; (B) Eleanor who married Rev. Erskine Jackson and have two girls Sara and Lane; (C) Margaret or Peggy married John E. Baker Jr., and have two children Edith and John; (3) Margaret who married Dr. William James Wrenn the son of Josiah and Nannie (Cockrell) Wrenn, - See Old Side Cemetery records.

Margaret J., wife of William T. Burwell, born 25 September 1857, died 30 August 1895. (She was the daughter of Joseph Reid Ramsay and wife Sara Wrenn. The second wife of William Turnbull Burwell was Lillie Campbell. They were the parents of one child, Willie Evelyn who married J.D. Brandenburg of St. Matthews, South Carolina. Willie Evelyn is a half sister of Mary Elizabeth Ormond, Sallie R. Ormond and Margaret Wrenn.)

* * * * * *

Reid Ramsay Burwell, born 7 January 1871, died 1 June 1913. (He was the son of William T. and Margaret Ramsay Burwell.)

* * * * * *

Edward, son of Benj. and Mary J. Calhoun, born 1850, died 23 August 1851.

* * * * * *

James Townsend Daniel, born 1824, died 24 December 1875. (The husband of Alerena or Alice Bell - see Central Cemetery records - He was the son of Joseph Daniel and his first wife (name unknown); Joseph married (2) to Mrs. Helen York 12 April 1846. Joseph died ca 1847 leaving four grown children, (1) James T., and (2) Patience Amanda, born 1820 and married James H. Bell - their daughter Mary Bell married Mr. Paul Fulton of Warsaw, Alabama -- James H. Bell was a cousin of Alerena or Alice Bell who married James T. Daniel; (3) Monroe Daniel, son; and (4) Martha, who married a Mr. Buffington. Minor heirs: William, Robert, Redman, David and Wiley. James H. Bell was made administrator of the estate and guardian of the minor children. James T. Daniel was a Confederate soldier having enlisted at Cooksville, Mississippi.

The parents of Joseph Daniel were Rufus and Rebecca (Turner) Daniel who married 1809. The parents of Rebecca Turner were Patience (Dickinson) and Matthew Turner. She was born 18 November 1779 and married 1801. Patience Dickinson was the daughter of Keziah (Simms) and Shadrack Dickinson, who married 1771. He died 1819 and his will is recorded in Goldsboro, North Carolina. Shadrach Dickinson was the son of Daniel Dickinson (wife unknown) of Wayne County, North Carolina.

Daniel Dickinson was the son of John Dickinson who died 1749 and wife Rebecca. They were in Bertie County, North Carolina in 1719. (Reference: Coverta Georgia Chronicles.) The above Keziah Simms who married Shadrach Dickinson was the daughter of Robert Simms whose will is in Wayne County, North Carolina. Robert Simms was a Revolutionary soldier who received Army pay at Warrenton, North Carolina in 1786.

Other members of the Dickinson family married into the Hackney, Brownrigg, Barnes, Stanton, Thomas, Jernigan, Smith, Peele, Newcombe, and Fultree families -- Courtesy of Mrs. Lillie Borden of Reform, Alabama for the Dickinson history. The Daniel History is from Bell Family Bible and Sumter County records.)

* * * * * *

Slater Dozier - died in 1876.

* * * * * *

Mollie E. Dozier - died in 1876.

* * * * * *

Amanda E., daughter of Joseph and Violet McCorcle, and wife of David Drummond, born 12 October 1824, died 10 October 1853.

******

William Flemming, born 1760, died 11 November 1849. (He was a Revotionary soldier on pension pay roll of Hall County, Georgia in 1832. He was a private in a company of North Carolina volunteers in 1780. under Captain Hanna and Colonel Bratton. He was a native of Maryland.

******

Mary B. Fleming, consort of Pliny (Rutherford) Fleming, born 26 January 1792, died 25 November 1841. (He married (2) Delinda Sadler 10 August 1842. She was a member of the Gainesville Presbyterian Church; removed letter to Green Lake, Texas in 1869.)

******

Mary Fleming, born 1766, died 4 November 1849. (Wife of William Fleming.)

****

Robert H. Fleming, born 16 December 1818, died 28 March 1850. (He married Jane R. McDow 13 January 1841 - see McDow records in this cemetery.)

****

Emma, daughter of R.H. and J.R. Fleming, born 1848, died 1849.

******

James H. Fleming, born 11 March 1723, died 15 May 1847.

Margaret C. Fleming, born 24 March 1827, died 25 August 1843.

******

William Frierson Fulton, born 25 August 1805 near Franklin, Tennessee, died 3 October 1886. (His parents were Paul and Martha (Armstrong) Fulton. Martha Armstrong's parents were James and Agnes (Frierson) Armstrong who married circa 1804.

William Frierson Fulton married Elizabeth Dial, daughter of David Montgomery Dial and wife Jenett Spence. They had children: James Harvey, David Graham, Edwin Kerr, Samuel Paul, William Frierson, Mary Jennett, Martha Agnes and Julia Emaline.

Edwin Kerr Fulton married Laura Montgomery and a son. Milton married Annie Morrow of Gadsden (both are buried in Birmingham). They were parents of: (1) Annie Laura, who married Arthur Randall and live in San Antonio, Texas; they are parents of two children; (2) Edwin T. (see his gravestone record); (3) Lawrence who married Stella Ramner and have two daughters to get grown; (4) Alice who married Andrew Ramsay, son of George W. and Willie (Ramsay) Ramsay - she (Mrs. Ramsay) later married Evan Ormond buried in Livingston, Alabama, by the side of his first wife Sallie Burwell Ormond.) Alice and Andrew are parents of two boys and two girls.)

******

Mary H. wife of William Frierson Fulton, born 1812, died 24 March 1846. (She was wife #2, a Mrs. Meek, prior to this marriage, William F. Fulton married four times, and he was never without a wife at Christmas, after the death of his first wife.)

******

Mary Elizabeth Fulton, daughter of Wm. F. and Mary H. Fulton, born 1850, died 1851.

******

James Harvey Fulton, born 22 January 1860, died 18 November 1860.

******

Edwin Kerr Fulton, born 30 January 1839, died 30 September 1904. (Son of William F. and Elizabeth (Dial) Fulton.)

******

Mrs. Harvey Fulton, born 12 May 1829, died 21 March 1853.

******

Edwin T. Fulton, born 16 October 1891, died 8 April 1920. (Son of Milton and Annie (Morrow) Fulton; he married Mary Boyd, daughter of A.G. and Caddie M. Boyd. Edwin was struck by lightening while riding horse back. Later on two other people were struck while riding in this saddle. His widow married Harry Davidson of Livingston.)

******

Lawrence Montgomery, son of Lawrence and Stella (Rainer) Fulton, born and died 1923.

******

Rev. Isaac Hadden, born in Abbeville District, South Carolina, 15 August 1799, died 27 August 1847. One of Alabama's first Presbyterian Ministers.)He was the son of Mrs. Elizabeth DeFour Hadden - and Revolutionary soldier William Hadden, so '"Owens' History of Alabama' states (Vol. III page 213). He died before the family came to Sumter County. Mrs. Elizabeth Hadden died between the signing of her will 27 August 1847 and the time it was recorded on the 6 October 1846. (I have not found her gravestone.) She named in her will the following: Lewis Hadden, Jane Brewer, wife of Robert W. Brewer; Lucinda Grey, wife of Washington Grey, Isaac Hadden; William Hadden; Mary Ann Smith, (wife of Ebenezer Smith of Indiana); and grandchildren Emaline Wammel, and Martha L. Gasten.
Lewis or Louis Hadden was a physician and was born circa 1819, and married Margaret A. Harper, daughter of Wyatt and Elizabeth Harper of Belmont, Alabama. Dr. and Mrs. Louis Hadden had three children buried at Belmont, viz: Sophia Elizabeth, David Louis, and Stella. Dr. Louis was father of Mrs. T.B. Smith, and grandfather of the late Dr. Dadden Smith of Livingston whose sons Hadden, Louis or Pat, Thomas or Tip, and John Smith all live in Livingston at the present. Mrs. Chris Pinson, wife of Dr. Chris Pinson, is also a granddaughter of Dr. Louis Hadden.

******

Martha B., relict of Rev. Issac Hadden, born 17 October 1792, died 5 September 1849.

******

Rev. Robert Wilson Hadden, died 29 January 1852 in the 29 year of his ministry. (See his obituary, which differs slightly from the gravestone record. Robert Wilson Hadden married Louisa J. Bingham 10 December 1850. They had one child to survive him, Robert, as named in the settlement of his estate. May term court 1859. Other marriages of the

Isaac Hadden children were: Laura Ann Hadden married Armstrong Kerr 1 February 1843 (see Kerr records); and Martha Jane married Samuel J. Bigham 12 April 1843.

******

David M. son of J.P. and J. Hale, born 21 November 1822, died 25 January 1844.

******

Infant son of T.D. and A.L. Hansel.

******

C.C. Hodges, born 26 January 1809, died 31 October 1854.

******

Leroy Holt born Columbus, Georgia, 12 July 1853, died 19 September 1899. (He married Elizabeth C. or Bessie Burwell, daughter of Benj. P. and Margaret (Moore) Burwell. They had two sons viz: Thad Holt and Leroy Holt of Birmingham, Alabama. Both men have been outstanding in the development of Birmingham and of the State of Alabama.)

******

Janie Moore, daughter of Leroy and Bessie (Burwell) Holt, born 8 September 1893, died 15 July 1895.

******

Evelyn Jeter, born 1869, died at 2 months of age.

*****

Bessie Alberta, died 1861, aged 1 month.

******

Abigail, daughter of Thaddeus and Mary Kendall, died 1844, aged 4 years.

William Kerr, born 6 June 1803 died 15 December 1886. (He was born near Philadelphia, Pa., and came to Alabama via Campbellsville, Kentucky where a sister married a Mr. Campbell. William settled near Eutaw in Greene County, Alabama; he married 26 January 1832 to Sara Dial, daughter of Jennett and David Montgomery Dial. He died from a kick of a mule. (See Tract Book Records - Sections 3 and 4, T20)

*****

Sara D. Kerr, born 4 March 1815, died 10 April 1866. (She was the daughter of Jennett and David Montgomery Dial, and the wife of William Kerr. Her grandfather was John Dial, Revolutionary soldier and patriot from South Carolina. Her great grandfather was Jeremiah Dial, Patriot of the of the Revolution (both men accepted by the National daughters of the American Revolution - Florence (Kay) Dial registered John Dial record, and Nellie Mae Goggins registered Jeremiah Dial record, both members of Bigbee Valley Chapter of D.A.R., Livingston, Ala. Sara D. Kerr was a neat niece of Mrs. Jane or Jennett (Dial) Boyd, wife of John Boyd of Payneville and she niece of Jeremiah Dial III who married Summer —. Jeremiah III died the fall of 1841.)

******

James D. Kerr, (stone broken) born 1844. (He was the son of Sara and William Kerr.)

******

Lawrence D. Kerr, died 1871. (He was the son of William and Sarah Kerr.

******

Telemachus Kerr, born 1832, died 1911. (He was the son of Sara and William Kerr. See Section 3 Township 20, Range 3 West in Tract Book Records.)

******

Frances Elizabeth Kerr, born 29 January 1839, died February 1926. (She was the wife of Telemachus Kerr. Among their children who married were Virginia who married Mr. Murray - See Central Cemetery records; Horace-See his gravestone inscription in this cemetery; Sallie who married Mr. Briggs and had children Aaron, Ben and Dick as well as a daughter who is married; Vista who married Mr. Crum - See Central Cemetery records; and John who is buried in this cemetery.

******

John L. Kerr, born 1863, died 1947. (He married Miss Mattie Moreland and they had children Jimmie Bell and Arthur. He was the son of Telemachus and Frances Elizabeth Kerr.)

******

Horace Harmon Kerr, born 18 October 1870, died 15 July 1943. (He was the son of Frances Elizabeth and Telemachus Kerr; he married Sara Amelia Boyd (daughter of Robert J. and Susan (Davis) Boyd and great granddaughter of John and Jennett or Jane (Dial) Boyd. Horace Harmon Kerr was descended from David Montgomery and Jennett (Spence) Dial - David Montgomery Dial was nephew of Jennett or Jane (Dial) Boyd. Horace and Sara (Boyd) Kerr had children as follows: Walter Williams born 1903, married Maggie Causey - one child buried in this cemetery; Lucile born 1911 married Mr. Sanders and had one child Larry who married and has a child Keith; Elizabeth born 1908 and married (1) a Mr. Felton and had a son Joe who was adopted by his grandfather Horace Kerr; Emma born 1913 married Mr. Wade and adopted a child who was a daughter of Emma's adopted brother and also nephew, Joe Kerr.

******

Margaret Williams Kerr, born 9 September 1939, died 19 October 1989. (She was the daughter of Walter Williams Kerr and wife.)

******

Elvin Kerr, born 188?, died 9 May 1906.

******

Walter W. Kerr, born 1852, died 1929. (He was the son of William and Sara (Dial) Kerr. W.W. Kerr never married.)

******

Laura D. Kerr, died 5 October 1854, died, at the age of 5 years.

******

Mary Elizabeth Williams, daughter of James and Sinthy Kerr, born 25 March 1834, died 25 February 1852.

******

George Taylor, son of James and Sinthy Kerr, born 1840 and died 1852. (The 1850 Census shows James Kerr, 45, born in Kentucky, Cinthia, age 37, born in Alabama, Mary E. 16, Lawrence D. 13, Emma R. 13, William D. 18, John M. 12, James A. 8, Evan R. 7, Rufus L. 5, Geo. T. 4,)

******

Jane Lavender, born 27 April 1799, died 6 December 1846. (She married in Greene County, Alabama 22 September 1824, to Hugh Levi Lavender, son of Hugh Lavender, a Revolutionary War Soldier, and his wife Rebecca (Smith) Lavender who was born in Ireland 1759. Jane Lavender was the daughter of Sallie (Dial) and Hugh Hopper; Sallie Dial Hopper was the daughter of Jane Dial who married John Boyd and lived in Greene and Perry Counties in the 1820's, John David Lavender, son of Jane and Hugh Levi Lavender was born 29 February 1836 and married in 1860 to Rebecca Barlow Poythress (other Poythresses married into the Gilbert and Simms families), the daughter of Catherine Smith Preston and James Edward Poythress. John D. and Rebecca (Poythress) Lavender had several children among whom was Herbert Windham Lavender, born 20 October 1878 and died 1952, married 20 December 1902 Mary Ruth Scarbrough born 20 April 1881, died 14 October 1956, the daughter of William Henry Scarbrough and wife Sara Ann Leitch)See another volume for the history of the Scarbroughs and Leitches.) Herbert Windham and Mary Ruth Lavender had children William Alton who died, Mary Estelle who married Cecil Wilkerson, Rebecca married Fred Anderson, Ruby married James Weaver, Ruth married Philip Boyd (son of Conde and Margaret Neelly Boyd - see Boyd Cemetery records) and John David Lavender who married Janie Mae Ozment 14 September 1933 and had children: Mary Jane who married Theodore Marcus Spidle and have children Theodore Marcus, Jr., Frances Lynn and Carol Jane; Sara Estelle married Edward John Gibbs, Jr., and had a son Rock Anthony, Pearl died 10 June 1958 and W. T. has remarried; John David, Jr., and Herbert Windham II both of whom are in school. Ophans' Minute BookI (Pages 373-74) 24 April 1838 shows that Jane Lavender was the relict of Hugh Levi Lavender, and named the minor heirs of Jane and Hugh L. Lavender as follows: Robert S. aged 12, Sara Ann 11, Ruth L. 10, William E. 6, Alexander 5, Margaret Ann 3, and John D. 2.

******

Sara, wife of Robert S. Lavender, born 15 May 1817, died 3 May 1854. (Sara Strothers married Robert S. Lavender 25 January 1848, he married Mrs. Margaret (Hodges) Wiggins - see McCain Cemetery - Robert S. Lavender was the son of Hugh and Rebecca (Smith) Lavender, and a brother of Hugh Levi Lavender. Hugh Lavender's will is in Book 1, page 153, Greene County, and named children: Margaret, Sara Bennett, Robert S., John, Ruth Barbour, Mary Tolbert, Nancy McDaniel, and Hugh Levi, James Campbell and Lucy Lavender were also named in the will.)

******

Dr. John A. McConnell, born 8 October 1825, died 24 May 1855. (The McConnels migrated from Penna. to South Carolina and then to Sumter County. In each state, they lived in or near a place with ''York'' in its name, such as Yorktown, Yorkville, New York (in Sumter County). Dr. McConnell practiced medicine in the Bethel Community. After his death, his widow - the former Martha McCorcle-removed to South Carolina but her sons returned to Sumter County and became forebears of the McConnells - See Parker Cemetery records. Dr. John A. McConnell's will is in Will Book 2, pages 71-72. He mentioned his wife Martha, a sister Martha E. Miller and a brother Andrew F. McConnell. The will was signed 22 April 1855 and probated 19 June 1855.

* * * * * *

Joseph McCorcle, born 17 August 1554, died 14 September 1849. (The Mortuary Schedule of the 1850 Census of Sumter County, gave his birth place as North Carolina.)

* * * * *

Violet, wife of Joseph McCorcle, born 12 October 1890, died 25 July 1855. (The settlement of Violet McCorcle's estate is found in Orphans' Minutes Book #6, page 41 and it names Martha McConnell as her daughter and mentions Susan Meek as a grandchild.)

* * * * *

W. E. McCorcle, born 13 April 1820, died 11 August 1844.

* * * * * *

Thomas J. McCorcle, born 30 September 1830, died 1 November 1859.

* * * * * *

W.L. McDow, born 15 October 1794, died 31 March 1870. (William Loftin McDow was born in Pendleton District, South Carolina, the son of Arthur McDow born 16 March 1756, died 20 May 1839, and Margaret Loftin born 1765 and died in 1846, her mother's name was Sara Neil) and married Jane Ramsay 1819. She was the daughter of Alexander Ramsay, Sr., and sister of Alexander Ramsay, Jr., and Andrew H. Ramsay who helped organize Sumter County (also listed as Andrew Ramsay) whose daughter, Margaret, married Furney Richardson who was the son of Bryant and Uney (Ray) Richardson. Alexander Ramsay, Sr., was born in Scotland 27 July 1747 and died 27 July 1826, he married Mary Eggar who was born in Scotland 7 February 1755 and died in Clinton, Greene County, Alabama 10 October 1841, married 3 October 1788. Mary Eggar's mother was Elizabeth Orr. Alexander Ramsay, Sr., was a Revolutionary soldier who was captured but liberated at the Battle of Kettle's Creek. Alexander Ramsay, Jr., was born 30 September 1799, married Sarah Hargrove Reid and had sons Andrew Ramsay and Joseph Reid Ramsay. Andrew Ramsay married Sallie Jarrett of Jarrett Manor at Toccoa, Georgia. Their daughter, Willie, married Geo. W. Ramsay of Sumterville, Alabama. Geo. W. Ramsay was the son of Joseph Reid Ramsay, nephew of Andrew. Geo. W. and Willie (Ramsay) Ramsay had one son, Andrew who married Alice Fulton (see Fulton history in this cemetery). Mrs. Willie Ramsay married (2) Evan Ormond who married (1) Sallie (Ramsay) Burwell who was the granddaughter of Joseph Reid Ramsay. Sallie Burwell was named for her aunt Sallie Ramsay, also a daughter of Joseph Reid Ramsay, who married Mr. Smith of Epes and they became the parents of Maggie Smith who married Lewis Spratt, (See Spratt Cemetery history.)

* * * * * *

Jane R. McDow, born 21 October 1831, died 13 October 1910.

* * * * * *

Martha C. McDow, born 29 May 1833, died 13 October 1898. (She was the daughter of Thomas Moore and married W.L. McDow Jr., and lived at what is now the Roger Smith place north of Sumterville. She and her husband deeded their holdings to her niece, Bessie or Elizabeth Holt and her husband LeRoy Holt but retained a home for life. The Holt children, Thad and LeRoy were reared at the old McDow place.

* * * * * *

A. McRobinson, born 24 August 1815, died 8 May 1856.

* * * * * *

Mary A., daughter of P.R. and M. Fleming, and wife of Alexander McDow, born 24 March 1827, died 2 November 1848. (Alexander McDow was born in Greene County, Alabama 10 August 1822 and died 5 February 1891. He and Mary Adelia Fleming married 18 September 1845. He married (2) Mrs. Sara Harriett Thompson Posey, daughter of Alexander and Elizabeth Thompson of Eutaw, Alabama, died in Fayette County, Texas 1864. Catherine F. McDow, daughter of Alexander and Mary Adelia McDow born 20 August 1846, married John Milton Brownson. She gave the money to build Bethel Memorial Chapel.)

* * * * * *

Benj. James Mitchell, born in Abbeville District, S.C. 25 February 1809, died April 1857. (He married Nancy Dial, daughter of Jennett Spence and David Montgomery Dial, who was born 2 December 1812, and died in Navaro County, Texas - see her obituary. Benj. Mitchell was a hero on the river boat "Eliza Battle" when it burned on the Tombigbee River -- at the time he was living at Jones Bluff, now Epes,

Alabama. The heirs of Benj. J. Mitchell as shown on page 20, Orphans' Minutes Book 10, Sumter County as follows: Joseph R. Mitchell, Keziah E. Eason, E.C. Eason, James E. Mitchell of Sumter County, Willie A. Johnson, wife of John H. Johnson of Texas, minor heirs Benj. F. Mitchell, David M. Mitchell, Margaret J. Mitchell and Susan J. Mitchell and Nancy the relict - July Term Court 1859.)

* * * * * *

B.F. Mitchell, son of Benj. J. Mitchell, born 16 April 1840, died 4 August 1861 at Charlottesville, Virginia.

* * * * * *

Thomas Moore, born 23 July 1789, died 8 December 1852. (His will is recorded in Will Book 2, page 24, Sumter County Court House - mentions daughters Mary Louise Boyette wife of Leroy Boyette, Margaret E. Burwell wife of Benj. P. Burwell, and son James A. Moore, and younger children Elizabeth Jane Moore, Robert H. Moore, William H. Moore, Martha Catherine Moore (who later married W.L. McDow, Jr.,) and John T. Moore. See minutes of Bethel Church for more about Mr. Moore and Old Side Cemetery records for Boyetts.)

* * * * * *

James A. Moore, born 28 December 1824, died 9 May 1881. (Son of Thomas M. Moore.)

* * * * * *

S. Evelyn, daughter of J.A. and E.A. Minniece wife of James A. Moore, died 24 August 1869, aged 30 years.

* * * * * *

William H. Moore, born 9 April 1831, died 16 December 1858. (Son of Thomas Moore.)

* * * * * *

Thomas J.H. Moore, born 5 November 1836, died 21 June 1850. (Son of Thomas Moore.)

* * * * * *

Eliza Moore, born September 1873, aged 8 years.

* * * * * *

Mary Nevill, oldest daughter of Jane Ramsay and William Loftin McDow, was born 1 May 1824, died - October 1852, married Andrew L. Nevill

1836. (They had children William, James, Samuel and A. McDow; see Central Cemetery for Samuel Loftin Neville the son of James Neville, the son of Andrew L. Nevill.)

* * * * * *

J. Reid Ramsay, born 14 December 1827, died 27 June 1899. (He was born in Pendleton Dist. South Carolina near Pickens Court House. He married 4 October 1853 Sara J. Wrenn, daughter of James Wrenn who married Eliza Philips McDow born 6 July 1825. J. Reid Ramsay and wife Sara J. Wrenn were parents of George W. Ramsay who married Willie Ramsay, his first cousin and daughter of Sallie (Jarrett) and Andrew Ramsay of Georgia. Both J. Reid Ramsay and Andrew Ramsay were sons of Alexander Ramsay, Jr.

* * * * *

Alexander H. Ramsay, son of J. Reid and Sara J. Ramsay, born 7 November 1859, died 11 March 1880.

* * * * * *

George Wrenn Ramsay, son of J. Reid and Sara J. Ramsay, born 28 November 1886, died 9 October 1923. (He married Willie Ramsay, his cousin - see above - and they had one child, Andrew who married Alice Fulton - see Fulton history in this cemetery.)

* * * * * *

William A. Ramsay, born 17 December 1873, died 8 December 1907.

* * * * * *

James Wrenn Ramsay, born 27 September 1864, died 1 April 1946. (He was the brother of George Wrenn Ramsay.)

* * * * * *

Susie Bell Ramsay, born 17 November 1873, died 26 February 1955. (She was the daughter of Rev. Elijah Bell who married a daughter of John Grice, and the wife of James Wrenn Ramsay. No Issue.)

* * * * * *

William Wiley, died 8 April 1876, aged 28 years.

* * * * * *

Wiley, son of L.V. and B.J. Riley, died 1871.

* * * * * *

Willie Riley, son of W. and B.J. Riley, born 1871, died 1877.

* * * * * *

Eleanor Portor, wife of George Rix, and daughter of Calvin and Sally Skinner of Royalton, Vermont, born 20 October 1813, died 16 June 1841.

* * * * * *

Frederick and Rebecca Dial Rix, children of George and Rebecca (Dial) Rix. (Rebecca was the daughter of Jenett (Spence) and David Montgomery Dial.)

* * * * * *

Moses M. Sanders, born 14 August 1815, died 8 May 1857.

* * * * * *

Dr. C.U. Silliman, born 7 April 1833, died 3 November 1913. (He was grandson of John Silliman Sr., born in Carncastle, Ireland 1747, died 1825 in York District, South Carolina. John Silliman Jr., married Mary Campbell born 16 August 1793 and died 1866, the daughter of Alexander Campbell and wife Mary Straight in 1816 in South Carolina - the Straights came to Greene County Alabama and married into the Grantham and Shaw families - Alexander and Mary Straight Campbell had 8 children among whom was Calvin U. Silliman who married (1) Jennie Hughes, daughter of Dr. Hughes of Chunkeyville, Mississippi and had children, John H. and another child who died with the mother in 1861; he married (2) Jennie or Jeanett Mitchell, daughter of Benj. J. and Nancy (Dial) Mitchell and had children to live: (1) Carrie Silliman born 1874 and married Walter Whitfield and became parents of Annie who married Ernest Flowers (see Flowers history), and Helen born 1900 and married Russell Elliot (see his record in Central Cemetery), Calvin born 1894 married and had a son - he lives in Birmingham; (2) Mary Silliman born 1880 and married Edwin A. Harris of Meridian, Mississippi.)

* * * * * *

Jennie (Jeanette) Silliman, born 2 October 1845, died 21 December 1926. (She was the second wife of Dr. U.C. Silliman and daughter of Benj. J. and Nancy (Dial) Mitchell - see obituary of Nancy D. Mitchell, Livingston Journal 1868 and Sumterville Methodist Cemetery records.)

* * * * * *

Sterling S. Smith, born 6 July 1841, died 18 September 1856.

* * * * * *

Lucy B. Smith, born 19 August 1839, died 23 March 1857.

* * * * * *

Martha Leila, infant daughter of Enos and Mary A. Tartt, born 26 September 1856, died 1857. (See Old Side Cemetery records for Enos Tartt family.)

* * * * * *

Mary Frances Templeton, born 16 July 1842, died 14 June 1909.

* * * * * *

L.V. Underwood, died 1874. (Deed Book G., page 178 shows transfer of Negro girl to Martha W. Underwood, wife of L.V. Underwood, and daughter of F.G. Thomas Jr., Jacob S. Horn, security.)

* * * * * * *

Adelaide Randolph, daughter of L.V. and E. Underwood. (Date illegible.)

* * * * * *

William Wheeling, born 1792, died 1849. (No history.)

* * * * * *

Ester Wheeling, born 1792, died 1849. (No history.)

* * * * * *

Felix Hamilton Woodard, died 20 January 1849, aged 42 years. (He married Charity Simms, sister of William T. Simms. Felix H. and Charity S. Grice had a child named Emily who married Joseph Dial, the son of Jennett (Spence) and David Montgomery Dial, and they had a son Ed Dial of Meridian, Mississippi - Emelle, Alabama was named for his daughter, Emelle Dial.)

* * * * * *

Charity Grice, former wife of F.H. Woodard, died 5 July 1865, aged 63 years. (She married John Grice - see Old Side Cemetery records - after the death of her husband F.H. Woodard. John Grice married (1) her sister.)

* * * * * *

Eliza P. Wrenn, born 2 September 1804, died 24 October 1862. (She was the wife of James Wrenn.)

* * * * * *

James Wrenn born 2 June 1800, died 18 October 1843. (He was the husband of Eliza P. Wrenn and he was the brother of Henry Wrenn, Josiah Wrenn, Elias H. Wrenn. James Wrenn married Eliza Philips McDow and had children: George M. Wrenn who married Samantha Yarbrough, Elias N. Wrenn, Margaret J., Arthur M., Mary E., and William James.

* * * * * *

Josiah Wrenn, born 3 March 1813, died 13 June 1885. (He was the brother of James, Henry, and Elias H. Wrenn who are said to have removed to Alabama from Buncome County, North Carolina. He lived on the north banks of Bodka Creek near the Raes and Watsons. He married Mrs. Nancy Elizabeth Patton, nee Blacksher of Belmont, and the widow of Wayne who was the grandmother of the late Joe Patton, Tax Collector of Sumter County for many years. Joshia and Nancy Blacksher Patton Wrenn had children among whom is Mrs. Cora Bolton living at Brewersville in Sumter County, and is in her 90's. The widow of Josiah Wrenn is buried at Brewersville.)

* * * * * *

Elias N. Wrenn, born 31 January 1829, died 17 April 1903. (He was the son of James and E.P. Wrenn.)

* * * * * *

Margaret Wrenn, daughter of James and Eliza P. Wrenn, born 6 June 1830 and died 3 June 1854.

* * * * * *

Arthur McDow Wrenn, born 11 Mary 1832, died 2 September 1858. (Son of James Wrenn.)

* * * * * *

George M. Wrenn, (Heavy stone on ground so could not see dates.)

* * * * * *

Eliza McDow Wrenn, daughter of G.M. and M.F. Wrenn, born 1873, died 1875.

* * * * * *

Mary E. Wrenn, born 9 September 1836, died 1862.

* * * * * *

Mary George Wrenn, (Daughter of G.M. and M.F. Wrenn.)

* * * * * *

Arthur   Wrenn, 1880 – 1887. (Son of G.M. and M.F. Wrenn.)

* * * * * *

J. Walter Wrenn, born 2 February 1863, died 10 November 1894. (He was the son of Josiah and Nancy E. (Patton) Wrenn, and the brother of Mrs. Cora Bolton.)

* * * * * *

James Manning Wrenn, born 1878, died 23 January 1912.

CHAPTER III

PAYNEVILLE

HISTORY OF OLD PAYNEVILLE

Payneville, one of the oldest established towns in the county, lay in Township 19, Section 13, Range 4 West. It was named for Ranson Payne - see Acts, 1839. The town was laid off in lots which were advertised for sale in the "Voice of Sumter" 9 August 1836. The commissioners who signed the notice were: James Hodges, Alexander Campbell, R. T. Payne, James Sample, Tyrell Gorman, A. M. Griffin and J. C. Puckett. It was incorporated 19 January 1839.

There was, already, asettlement on the site chosen for the town of Payneville. It had been an "out look" after Fort Tombecbee became Fort Confederate under the hands of the Spanish and then the English rules. At this time another "out look" was near the present site George S. Gaines. Owen's **History of Alabama** tells us that the third Alabama Baptish church or mission was within the confine of the present bounds of Sumter County. The mission, established ca1810, was called "Tubby's Oak Mission".. It is the opinion of this writer that this mission was near this old out-look because there is a creek that runs near the town of Old Payneville called "Tubby's Creek". When the first settlers, ca1832, came to Township 19 there was an old Indian still living near Tubby's Creek on a piece of land received from the Government by virture of a clause in the Treaty of Dancing Rabbit Creek; the Indian's name was Tubby which is said to mean "dead man" in the Choctaw tongue. Mr. Greenlee bought Tubby's land and the Indian finally moved on west to join his kindred in their new hunting ground. (Courtesy of Mr. Charlie Burton.)

Payneville was located near the Sucarnoochee River 10 miles above Livingston and a mile or two from the Mississippi State line. James Hodges operated a ferry on this river and the Burtons had a mill near the ferry both of which were at the head of navigation. It was only during high waters that barges came up to Payneville bringing supplies of all kinds and carrying away cotton to be sent to Mobile by steam boats which plied the river during this era ("Voice of Sumter" 1837.) It was just below the ferry and the mill, that James Horn built the first steel bridge in Sumter County. Even though the road has been abandoned and the bridge is impassable the road is called Horn's Bridge Road. John Horn lived near this bridge - see Horn Cemetery records.

An Academy was established at Payneville - a two story brick building - in January 1837 - also according to the "Voice of Sumter" in which was published an advertisement for teachers and signed by trustees: John Thomas, R. T. Payne, William K. Tyler, Thomas M. Jones and James Hodges. The first teacher who taught at the old academy was Bob Farrah, brother of Susan Farrah who married (1) Mr. Silliman and (2) Matthew Boyd. Another early teacher was John W. Beavers. Reverend Isaac Hadden was Head Master at the Academy at a later date and preached in the Presbyterian Church at Payneville - see history of Hadden Presbyterian Church elsewhere in this volume.

The Methodists bought a lot and were ready to build a church when the Mobile and Ohio Railroad built just across the State line in Mississippi. Many first settlers - some of whom were Methodists - moved to Lauderdale, Daleville, Narkeeta and Porterville, towns on the railroad. The Presbyterian Church, rebuilt in 1850, absorbed the membership of the other denominations so the plans for a Methodist Church never materialized. About this time the name of the Payneville church was changed to Hadden Presbyterian Church. The next preacher was a Mr. Bingham. One of the Hadden girls married this minister and Robert Hadden married a Miss Bingham. The Haddens and Binghams contributed culture, book-learning and spiritual discernment to this and other Sumter County communities.

The first post office was established in Payneville in 1837 - see "Voice of Sumter" 18 May 1837 issue - and the first Post Master was C. J. Puckett who helped organize Sumter County and was also the first doctor at Payneville. The last Post Master at Paynevill (but at that time called "Dial") was the father of the late John Peel of that community. This post office was discontinued with the advent of Rural Free Delivery. A few years later the school was discontinued and the children were transported by bus to Livingston, and the old town of Payneville whose back was broken by the building of the M. & O. R.R. and the Gainesville-Narkeeta Rail Road, and later by the yellow fever epidemic of 1870, and by the migration west after the War Between the States, gave its last gasp and died. Not a semblance of the old town is left for the Hadden Church was recently rebuilt - a modern brick structure - but stands alone with only the manse near by.

Payneville had no central burying ground but each family or group of families buried in family plots. Very few of the first settlers who who died had tombstones to their graves, perhaps for two reasons. The first was because the Indians could count the graves and see how many or how few settlers were left, and the second was because tombstones were very expensive and hard to get. They had to be shipped down the coast from Vermont to Mobile and thence up the Tombigbee River to a river town. After which the heavy stones had to be hauled over trails and muddy roads to the cemeteries. It was easy, in those days, of hardships and long dreary days of toil, to follow the line of least resistance in cases that did not mean survival to those left to struggle on. These family cemeteries can no longer be found as the forests have closed in and covered the scars man made in the first years of settlement. We understand the Rigdons, the Burtons and the Bullocks were buried at one spot but there is not much left to tell the tale: perhaps a sunken place or two and a few slighty mounded spots which one would guess to be graves. Modern farming with tractors and bull dosers have obliterated other cemeteries while cattle have pushed over the stones in pastures and grass has grown over them. In many instances Mrs. Frank Stegall and I dug up and pieced together the broken pieces in order to record the inscriptions for posterity. In this locality we found the Elliott family cemetery and the large Boyd-Dial family cemetery the only ones to be cared for and enclosed by fences.

One of the early businesses at old Payneville was a gin making establishment owned by A. Campbell and Son. In an issue of the 1840 "Sumter County Whig" there appeared a notice that "in the future the firm would go under the name of A. R. Campbell at the old stand near Payneville" and it was signed by Alexander Campbell and A. R. Campbell.

There was a tannery near Payneville owned and operated by John Knox Elliott. Even yet one can see the old vats lined with hand hewn oak beams, where the raw hides were soaked in red oak bark juice to remove the hair and then the hides tanned to make into shoes, harness and other leather goods used by the community.

A large two story hostel called The Tavern stood near the old Academy. Travellers by stage coach west used this tavern for refreshment and rest as Payneville was a point where horses were changed and mail picked up.

Payneville boasted a battalion of soldiers to propect the town in case of trouble. 19 March 1844 there was an announcement in "Sumter County Whig" of an election to be held at "Yarborough and Daniel's Store" at Payneville on Saturday 13 April 1844 to elect a colonel to command 1st Battalion, 64th Regiment and it was signed by William Arrington, Colonel 64th Regiment, 6th Brigade, 3rd Division.

There were other stores at Payneville, among which were the ones owned by Robert and Jefferson Boyd and by Jim Boyd. There was one owned by Peter and John L. Handley for in 1852 the people of Payneville signed a petition asking "the power that was" to allow this firm to handle spiritous liquors. At that time only store keepers who did not partake of intoxicating refreshments and who were of moral repute could handle "fire water", as it was called by the Indians. But even the most virtuous in that day kept liquor in the home as it was believed by every one, if it were taken in moderation, would cure "what ailed you".

It was not all work with the early settlers at Payneville for the town boasted of a race track where the landed gentry raced their fine horses. Much money and even land changed hands on those "tournament days"; people from far and near came to Payneville to see the races, so the stores and the Tavern promoted these tournaments for they (especially

Handley Brothers) did a flourishing business on those days and the Tavern was full to overflowing. The men and boys played horse shoe and bets were made on the side. Another game was played from fast running horses with the riders holding outstretched bayonets on which they tried to catch rings thrown to them as they passed certain spots. Indian ball games were well attended - many Indians stayed in this part of the country instead of going to Oklahoma after the Treaty of Dancing Rabbit Creek - for there was sure to be a fight or two between some of the Indian bucks over some of the finer points of their game, made finer by having imbibed too often from the white man's fire water jug.

Those were "the good old days" we have heard about; but Hadden Presbyterian Church, her Elders and her Ministers held the balance wheel in that community. Almost every month some one was brought before the Session for a wrong doing such as drinking, swearing, gambling or an immoral act. Gradually the entire community life centered around the church so that today very few know anything about the sports of the early days. Even then, however, after days of festivities, if preaching day followed, the entire community would scrub behind their proverbial ears and the women would bake pies, cakes and hams - fried chicken galore would be prepared and home made salt rising bread cooked for "dinner on the ground" after Sunday School and Church service. They got a double dose of religion on those days for in the afternoon as soon as every one had eaten, the women had cleared away the tables which had been spread under the trees, and the men had taken several walks down to spring where they had drunk long, cool drinks of water and stretched their legs, the church bell was rung again for afternoon service. The Deacons and Elders sat in the "amen corners" nodding and napping while the preacher's voice droned on and on and on interrupted only from an occasional outcry from one of the infants asleep on a palate in the back of the church. Those days are gone forever.

Then war was declared and men answered the call to arms and rode away, many of whom did not return to their old homes. Union soldiers from across the Tombigbee River in Pickens County, and from Dallas and from Tuscaloosa Counties foraged all over Sumter County for food for their men and beasts. People in Payneville community hid their grain deep in the woods, drove their cattle and hogs into the swamp and buried their meat in a long trench just across the creek and west of the road which connects Highway 11 with State Highway 17. After the trench was dug they placed boughs of trees in the bottom of it and then put the meat on them. They covered the meat with planks and then with soil. It has been said that the Union Soldiers thought that the people around Payneville were on the verge of starvation while all the time they were laughing up their sleeves about how they had fooled the Damnyankees.

Many romances budded during the war one of which was that of Etta Allison and Sam Turk, a Kentucky soldier who came through Sumter County and met Etta. He could not forget her sweet face for after the war he returned to the county and claimed her for his bride. After the war many people moved West; only a few families remained. Within a radius of six miles of old Payneville the Boyds, the Dials, the Danners, the Davises, the Simmons, the Allisons, the Moores, the Tartts, the Prestwoods, the Aekins and Sledges remained. Today if you pass through this area and meet a man and say, "Good morning Mr. Boyd," and he looks at you kind of funny you should say, "Beg your pardon, Mr. Dial." There are few left except Dials and Boyds and their kin folk.

Not one thing is left of the once prosperous incorporated town of yesterday but people still speak of going to Payneville when they mean they are going anywhere within the six mile radius of the old church and academy. The old has made way for modern living; the only old homes left have been completely modernized. W. Jake Dial lives in the old John Knox Elliott home and J. W. Boyd lives in the other old house both of which are lovely to see and comfortable to live in. The modern brick church, with the manse near the old spring, is still the center of community life and in every direction, but within a mile or so of each other, one sees modern homes with all the conveniences of the day.

The glory of the past is about forgotten; the young people know nothing of it. Wilbur Dearman, our Probate Judge, recently said to me that very little is known about the history of old Payneville. I went to my notes which I had collected over a period of forty years and talked with many people who had listened to the tales of early settlers. I perused early newspapers and pieced together the history of old Payneville which I hope you have enjoyed.

TOWNSHIP 19 RANGES 3 AND 4 WEST

Many people bought land in this township for speculation so they never lived here. They lived in other parts of the county or in other parts of the state. I shall endeavor to give you something about these people who lived in other parts of the county in later volumes. Those whose histories are given in cemetery records will be merely mentioned, while in some cases I shall give you a little history of others. Range 4 West of Township 19 is in what we call the Flat Woods and was never cleared. Some of this land sold for as little as 2¢ per acre in the early 1830's. Sumter Lumber company, in Electric Mills, Mississippi, Kemper county, owned much of this land. After this company went out of business it was sold to Flintcote. Mr. Fred Rogers of Meridian, Mississippi is also a large holder of this land.

Township 19 Range 3 West

Section 1

In 1834 Joseph Rogers, Shadrach Rogers, James Parker and Elijah Price patented land in this section; in 1840 John Horn patented the last 160 acres.

Section 2
In 1834 John Horn, William Hall, James F. Tutt, John Rasser, Felix Thompson and Jacob Simms patented this land; Jacob Simms was the largest landowner, however.

Section 3
James B. Tutt Patented all the land in this section.

Section 4
James B. Tutt, Rigdon Edwards, Benj. O. Gee, John H. Gee, John E. Anderson and Jane White patented land in this section. Permilla Anderson, daughter of John E. Anderson, married Lewis L. Parham.

Section 5
Benj. O. and John H. Gee, John E. Anderson, John J. Burton, Starling

Gorman patented land in this section.

Section 6
This section was taken up by John J. Burton, S. Gorman, Geo. W. Harper and Joel Mallory.

Section 7
Those who bought the land in this section were William Straight, Geo. W. Harper and Joel H. Mallory, Dillard Payne (1835), Anna Elliott and George W. Payne. According to a record of George W. Payne family as recorded on the fly leaf of Matthew Henry Commentary of the Bible owned at the present by Mrs. R. K. Elliott we learn that William was born 15 July 1835, Laurana was born 2 November 1836, James M. Payne was born 183-, John Knox was born 3 February 1840, Victoria Ann was born 25 October 1841, Mary Almira was born 12 November 1843.

Section 8
John P. Hall, Robert Straight, William Straight, James Parker, James H. Chambers and Anna Elliott patented this section.

Section 9
Matthew Boyd, Robert and William Hall, Loftin and Norflit Pippen and Bryan Lavender patented this land in 1834.

Section 10
Those who patented land in this section were: Martha W. Cobbs, Wilson Hodges, John W. Smith and Andrew W. Hanna.

Section 11
John C. Whitsett (under Choctaw Treaty of 1830) and John Horn obtained and/or bought this land.

Section 12
Jonah Robinson, James Parker, John A. Hodges, Capt. Jerry Fulson, patented this land but the latter named obtained it under the Treaty of Dancing Rabbit Creek.

Section 13
Jerry Fulson, Isaac N. Mitchell, Edward Harper and James Parker patented this section.

Section 14
Enoch Travis, Austin Hitt and Drury McMillan bought this land. Drury McMillan is buried at Brewersville, near where he lived.

Section 15
Drury McMillan, Fulipalcha (Choctaw Indian), John P. Rhodes, Cordy Fant and Benj. Upchurch patented all of this section; along with Daniel McMillan, Geo. Pickles and Lebbens Hunter.

Section 16
This was a school section.

Section 17
John Boyd and son John M. Boyd, David Boyd (also a son of John Boyd) and Geo. Payne patented this land.

Section 18
James Payne, Dillard Payne, John M. Boyd, John C. Jones and Alexander Campbell patented land in this section. Alexander Campbell married in S. C. to Mary Straight whose people settled in Greene County. Their children were Thomas born 2 May 1787, Rosanna 6 November 1788, John 3 May 1790, Alexander 8 September 1791, Mary born 16 August 1793, died 1866, married John Silliman, William C. born 1795, Samuel C. born 1797 and Elizabeth born 1798 and married Joel Grantham of Greene County.

Section 19
This is a fraction of a section so many people patented scraps of land that happened to border on land they already had. They were as follows: George Payne, Alexander Campbell, Henry H. Jones, Stephen W. Clay, James Hodges, Charles J. Pucket, William Smith and Dillard Payne. James Hodges was the son of Robert Hodges whose will is in Book I-362 and names sons James and Allen, grandsons Amos, John P. and James Allen; grand daughters Melinda McDaniel (see Methodist Sumterville Cemetery), Karen or Cairen Anderson (see Anderson records in Township 20), Celzann J. Hodges, Elizabeth Ross, grand son Thomas Hodges, daughter Cely Hellson.

Section 20
Jacob Danner, David Boyd, George Payne, David E. Moore, Charles J. Puckett and John C. Jones and Julius Martiniere patented the land in this section.

Section 21
James Smith, Jeremiah Kendall, Anthony Seale patented this land. Anthony Seale was a brother of Buford and Eli Seale and they were sons of Jarvis Seale.

Section 22
Daniel McMillan, Israel Shelton, Geo. Pickle, Thomas H. Hutchins took up this land.

Section 23
Same people patented this land as those in section 22.

Section 24
Patented by same people, and Andrew Hanna, Elisha Mellard and Seaborne Mimms. (See Mellard and Mimms Cemeteries.)

Section 25
Hugh McCann patented half of this section; he and wife Rachel sold out

within the next few years Book A-296; and Seaborne Mimms patented the rest of section.

Section 26 and Section 27
Hugh McCann, Anthony Seale and John C. Jones took all the land in these sections.

Section 28
John Perry, Anthony Seale, William Simmons, David E. Moore, Jeremiah Kendall, W. Johnson, Nathaniel B. Drake and James White patented this section. William Simmons was the son of Robert Simmons - Probate Record Book 9-187 the Exe'r named the heirs as William Bustin and wife, J. Kendall and wife, Robert H. Simmons, William M. Simmons, John C. Simmons, B. A. Simmons, E. W. Simmons, and grandchildren R. Boyd, J. C. Boyd, and James Boyd - wife was Ann T., and Benj. Asberry Simmons was Adm'r. There was a James Simmons who died in Sumter County; moved from Giles County Tenn. to Lauderdale County, Ala. in 1814. His granddaughter Elizabeth A. Grace married Henry M. Dorman 23 March 1840.

Section 29
John Robinson, Henry Harris and John C. Jones, and M.&O. R.R. patented this land.

Section 30
Matthew Gayle, Malcom Johnson, Fergus P. Ferris, William Smith, Thomas Patton patented the land in this section.

Section 31
M. & O. R. R., Daniel Greene, Thomas Patton, John Curry, Henry H. Harris, Isaac M. Hunter, Norflit Harris patented this land. Daniel and Stacy Greene sold their land to R. Eatmen in 1836.

Section 32
Same as above.

Section 33, Section 34 and Section 35
Speculators already named patented this land. John H. Silby patente patented 80 acres here.

Section 36
Same as above.

Township 19 Range 4 West

Part of this Township lies in Mississippi. Payneville lay in the extreme western part of it.

Section 1
George Harper, Joel Mallory, Starling Gorman and James P. Pyle patented

the land in this section.

Section 10
Sections 2 through 9 lie in Mississippi. John Greenlee, Alexander Walker, Tishohomattak (a Choctaw Indian) by Treaty of Dancing Rabbit Creek owned the land in this section.

Section 11
William Brewer, Hiram Payne, Starling Gorman, Alexander Breathit, Charles J. Puckett were the ones who parented the land in this section.

Sections 12 and 13
Starling Gorman, William Payne, Daniel Payne, Ransom T. Payne and Elisha Shelton were the ones who patented this section.

Section 14
Terrell Gorman, Austin Hitt and James McCown patented this land. James McCown and wife Elizabeth sold some of their land to Eli Seales of Kemper County, Mississippi and some to William Evans in 1836. Austin Hitt's will is in Will Book 2-27 and he names wife Rebecca, children: James A., Sibell, Cornelia, Penelope, Clark, Nancy A. and Rebecca. Dated 17 June 1853.

The father of Eli, Beaufort, Anthony Seales or Seale was Jarvis Seale and his first wife was Ann Yarbrough. Anthony married Polly Bishop, Beaufort or Bufort married Mary Ann Evans, William married Jane Carr Elliott and Eli married (1) Philida—, (2) Sara Alexander. Jarvis Seale married (2) to Lucretia Oneal and they had 4 children. The Seales came from Wilkes County, Georgia but were natives of South Carolina. They first settled in Greene County, Alabama before coming to Sumter County.

Section 15
John Greenlee, Beaufort Seale, John Pyle who married Malinda Threadgill, and Julius Martiniere patented this section.

Section 22
Sections 16 through 21 lie in Mississippi. Harrison Evans and the Seale brothers patented this land. Harrison Evans and his wife Eliza sold some of this land to Archibald M. Griffin on 3 September 1838.

Section 23
W. H. Smith and Hugh McCann patented this section. Hugh and Rachel N. sold out in 1836.

Section 24
James Hodges, Jesse Ross, Ransom Payne, Stephen W. Clay, Hugh McCann and Joseph Smith patented this section.

Section 25
James Land patented this land along with some mentioned before.

Section 26
Elisha and John E. Shelton and John Smith patented land in this section.

Section 27
W. Freeland, John E. Shelton, Thaddeus McGowan and Wm. Evans patented this section.

Sections 28, 29, 30, 31 and 32 lie in Mississippi.

Section 33
This section was taken up by Francis Martin.

Section 34
Robert R. Shelton, Eli Seale, William Smith and Francis Martin patented all this land.

Section 35
Daniel Greene, John Shelton and John Hand patented this section.

Section 36
William H. Smith, Daniel Greene, Josiah Houston and John Hand patented this land.

GREENLEES CEMETERY

This cemetery is located near old Payneville but today there are no stones in this burying ground; it is said that the stones are broken and buried in the soil or that they have been carted away and used as door steps. There are signs of many graves in this cemetery.

I was very lucky to have found a book on the Greenlees family dating back to Ireland a generation or two before the immigrant came to America. The book which was so graciously shared with me is owned by Mrs. Margaret Elizabeth (Bessie) Burton Fuller. "The Greenlees of America" was compiled over a number of years and was published about 60 years ago.

Hugh Greenlees born Belfast or Lesbrum, County Down, Ireland married Isabel McGowin born in County Down. They were parents of children among whom were **John** and **Joseph Greenlees** who came to America the latter part of the second decade of the 1800's.

(1) **John Greenlees** was born 11 May 1796/97 in County Down, Ireland and

died in Sumter County, Alabama 2 September 1855. He became naturalized in Greene County, Alabama, March Term Court, 1830 and the papers were recorded in Greene County but transferred to Sumter County 7 November 1834 - Probate Records Book 1, page 88. He stated in 1830 that he had "lived in the States upward of 3 years, and in Alabama 1 year of that time." The Greenlees, Calverts and other Presbyterian Irish immigrants settled in Greene County, Alabama in what was known as "the Irish Settlement", and later came to Sumter County when it was opened to the white settlers.

John Greenlees married in Ireland 28 November 1819/20 to Isabella Dickson born 21 July 1797 in County Down, and died near Payneville, Alabama 18 May 1859. She was the daughter of David and Margaret Dickson. The children of Isabella (Dickson) and John Greenlees were: (a) Jane born 11 November 1820 married John Campbell, (b) William born 31 January 1822 died young, (c) Hugh born 26 November 1826 married Mary Elizabeth Hopper born 28 November 1838, daughter of William and Sara (Key) Hopper - see Robert Boyd record in Boyd Cemetery--Hugh Greenlees family lived at Gainesville and had children: Mary Ida born 1863 married R. J. J. (Red Head Jeff) Boyd (see Boyd Cemetery), Annie Laura born 1869 is still living in 1960, Helen Irene married Robert J. Dial both of whom are buried at Boyd Cemetery, and Addie who married Wade Hailey - their son Hugh Hailey married Ruby Waddell, sister of Lolita Waddell who married Dr. Austin F. J. Boyd. Hugh and Ruby Hailey have one son Hugh, Jr. who married Patsy   , (d) Isabella born 19 May 1829 married 26 August 1856 Joseph Eakins, born 11 May 1829 in Raleigh, North Carolina, the son of William and Ann (Walker) Eakins, (e) Margaret Ann, born 8 January 1830 married Absolom Farrar Burton -- see Burton Cemetery records, (f) Mary born 6 March 1832 married George Calvert, (g) John born 23 March 1833 married Georgie Appleby, (h) David James born January 1837 married Sallie (Hopper) Thomas - see Thomas Cemetery records - he was a member of 43 Mississippi Reg., and was killed at the Battle of Nashville, (i) Joseph Patterson born 9 December 1838 married Sallie L. Manning, (j) Charles born 1839 and died 1845.

(2) **Joseph Greenlees** or Greenlee was also a son of Hugh and Isabell (McGowin) Greenlees and died circa 1880. His wife (1) was a Miss Bushby - perhaps Isabelle - and (2) Leah Wiggins. The Greenlee family of Epes and Mrs. Bettie J. Lee of the same place are descendants of this branch of the family (more about this family in another volume).

THOMAS CEMETERY NEAR OLD PAYNEVILLE

This cemetery is deep in the woods across the road from the present Presbyterian Church at Payneville; we have Mr. W. Jake Dial to thank for acting as guide in finding this cemetery. There are only two graves with stones, but there are several unmarked graves.

Inscriptions

Fannie E. daughter of John M. and Delia J. Thomas, born 5 October 1875, died 5 September 1876.

******

Mary Isabella, daughter of John Marshall and Delia J. Thomas, born 29 January 1871, died 1871.

******

(The father of these children (John Marshall Thomas) was the son of William Grey Thomas and his wife Rosannah (Boyd) Thomas. Rosannah was the daughter of John and Jane or Jeannett (Dial) Boyd. The mother of these children, Delia Jane Burton, the daughter of Drury Langley and Ann Eliza (Oliver) Burton (see Burton Cemetery), was born 2 October 1848 and died 5 December 1933, both Delia J. and John Marshall Thomas are buried at Toomsuba, Mississippi. They had children: Eliza Rosannah born 1866, died 1888, Sara Elizabeth born 28 December 1868, married Jesse B. Phillips, Mary Isabella born 29 January 1871 (see above gravestone inscription), Amanda Deliah born 24 October 1872 married James Joseph Rigdon, Fannie Eleanor born 5 October 1875 (see above gravestone inscription), Alice Vivian born 31 October 1888 married Walter J. Owsley, Adeline Grey born 2 July 1883, married Mr. Pigford.

William Grey Thomas and his wife Rosannah (Boyd) Thomas had other children: Jane who married Richard Hodges son of Janes Hodges and his first wife (James Hodges married Rosannah (Boyd) Thomas after the death of William Grey Thomas), Amanda married John Shanahan, William Grey Jr., married Thomas Burns, Erasmus married Sarah V. Hopper (sister of Rebecca (Hopper) Boyd who married Robert Boyd, brother of Rosannah Boyd), and Caroline who married William Thomas.

The above Erasmus Thomas, son of William Grey and Rosannah (Boyd) Thomas married Sarah V. (Sal) Hopper (see Robert Boyd line for Hopper-Key history). They had children Annie who married Matt Persons; and Georgia who married Will Lavender (see "Lavender", Bethel Cemetery), the latter couple had a daughter Annie Lavender who married her distant cousin, Cliff Dial, brother of Will and Clarence Dial. Cliff and Annie (Lavender) Dial have a daughter, Valera, who married Jake Cherry (see Cherry records, Boney Cemetery.) Erasmus Thomas was killed in the Civil War and Sarah, his wife, married (2) Austin Greenlee, and (3) Mark Moore. (See Drury L. Burton - Land patents section).

BURTON CEMETERY

This family cemetery lies deep in the woods about a mile north east of, and across the road from Hadden Presbyterian Church near old Payneville. There are signs of several graves but there are only three markers standing. It was by the courtesy of Mr. W. Jake Dial that we found this burying ground. No one knows where the first generation of Burtons is buried unless it is in a burying ground long since abandoned and overgrown with brush with no sign of stones. It is said that the Bullocks, the Hodges, the Campbells, the Calverts and many more are buried there.

Inscriptions

Absolom Farrah Burton, born 19 March 1823, died 22 October 1903. (He was the son of Jane (Langley) who died 24 December 1842 and her husband Thomas Burton who was born in Virginia 1778 and died 23 February 1855 of pneumonia. Thomas Burton was the son of Allin Burton who was born in England and migrated to Virginia and later came to Caswell County, North Carolina after which he removed to Sumter County, Alabama. Jane (Langley) and Thomas Burton had following children: (a) Dianna Burton born 1803, (b) Nancy Burton born 1808, married Thomas Burton and died in Arkansas, (c) Louisa Burton born 1806 and died 1845, (d) Susan Burton born 1810, married Thomas Richmond both died in Neshoba County, Mississippi, (e) Margarette Burton born 1812 and married a Danner, (f) Francis Allen Burton born 1814 died in North Carolina, (g) David Sidney Burton born 1816 died of yellow fever in Sumter County in 1864, (h) Thomas William Burton born 1818 died 1903, (i) Drury Langley Burton born 10 November 1820 died 12 January 1850 of yellow fever married Ann Elizabeth Oliver (see Thomas cemetery records) Drury's widow married John L. Handley brother of Peter Handley, (j) Absolom Farrah Burton born 19 March 1823, died 22 October 1903 married Margaret Ann Greenlees and is buried by her husband in this cemetery.)

******

Margaret Ann Burton, born 8 January died 25 May 1906. (She was the wife of the above Absolom Farrah Burton and the daughter of John and Isabella Greenlees. They married 6 February 1849, John Greenlees, her father, gave his ronsent, - see Greenlees Cemetery for their history. Absolom Farrah and Margaret Ann Burton had the following children: (a) Andrew Jackson Burton born 22 December 1849 married Nancy Jane Davenport, (b) John Wesley Burton born 18 September 1851 -- see Old Side Cemetery records -- (c) Thomas William Jefferson Burton born 14 February 1853 married Fannie Torian and lived in Kemper County, Mississippi. Charlie Burton of Payneville is the son of Thomas William Jefferson Burton, and he is the father of several children).

******

Absolom Farrah Burton, Jr., born 16 February 1858 and died 11 May 1868. (He was the son of Absolom Farrah Burton and wife Margaret Ann.)

EXCERPTS FROM HADDEN PRESBYTERIAN

MINUTES BOOK, OLD PAYNEVILLE, ALABAMA

This church was first organized in Perry County, Alabama, 19 May 1827, and was called "Harmony Presbyterian Church". The Rev. James Hillhouse helped with the organization. The minutes of this first meeting stated, "At this time there was no public house for the worship of God, but a subscription for this purpose was procured. God, who is the Creator and Author of events and the efficient cause of all good design in his creatures hath put it into the hearts of His people to have the Gospel among them, that their children and servants might have the opportunity of attending the means of Grace, united effort was made to build a commodious house. But a few were professors of religion and still fewer of the Presbyterian Order. Numbers few and means limited when the church was organized, only 9 persons were found who were in full communion and who would be united with this branch of Zion, viz: William Cubley, Joseph P. Dowdle, Elizabeth Knox, Rebecca Bell, Jane Boyd (the wife of John Boyd), Margaret M. Bell, Elizabeth McConnell, John M. McConnell, James McConnell. William Cubley and Joseph Dowdle were chosen Ruling Elders. First pastors were Rev. James Hillhouse and Robert Holman, the latter a licentiate from Kentucky. The first Sacrament was administered 3 March 1828 by Rev. White. Mrs. Elliott, Miss Margary Bell and Mrs. Elizabeth McConnell joined the church. The first Sabbath in August 1828 Mr. Thomas L. Eskridge, Mrs. Julia Eskridge, John Knox, David Boyd, John Cameron, Mary Cameron and Maria Holman joined the church."

(At this point the minutes end for Harmony Church. The members picked up lock, stock and barrel and came in a wagon train to Sumter County and settled in and around Township 19, Ranges 3 and 4 West, and named their new town Payneville, and called their new church "Union", and headed their minutes as such with no elaboration; just continuing the minutes in the old Harmony Minute Book.)

"The Tuscaloosa Presbytery invited Rev. J. H. Grey to organize a church in Sumter County (at Payneville). Members to be found in good standing were: Thomas Campbell, Alexander Campbell, Mary Campbell, William Calvert, Francis McEwin, Ellen McEwin, John Dove, Jane Boyd, Rebecca Brown, Dorcas Brown, John Greenlees, Isabella Greenlees, Alex Brothwait, Jane Brothwait, Anna Elliott. John Greenlees and Thomas Campbell Ruling Elders.

The Church was named "Union" and came under the care of Tuscaloosa Presbytery in the Spring of 1838. When William Greenlees and J. K. Elliott presented certificates of church membership it was found that Mr. Elliott had been an Elder from where he removed, so was elected to fill that place in this church.

August 1839 Hugh Calvert and Perry Sylliman were taken into the church.

30 May 1840 Joseph P. Dowdle and Elizabeth Dowdle were received as members. 27 August 1841 Miss Ann P. Moore, Mary Jane Seale, Miss Elizabeth Campbell, Dorcas Campbell, Eliza Calvert, Alex. Brothwait, Jane Dowdle, Isabell Brothwait, David Boyd, united with the church, of this number Eliza Calvert was baptized. The following infants were baptized: John Greenlees, son of John and Isabella Greenlees, Robert Calvert, son of Wm. and A. Calvert, Elizabeth Ann McCowen, daughter of F. and E. McCowen. 16 July 1841 Elizabeth Dowdle died.

September 1843 those taken into the church were: William K. Tyler, Mrs. Ester Calvert, Sara Ann Crenshaw, Miss Elizabeth Pippen, John Boyd, Jefferson Boyd, James Boyd, Lawrence Dogerty, Martin B. Dabney and his wife Nancy, Mrs. Sara Boyd, Aron Calvert, Hugh Greenlees, Isabella Greenlees, William Greenlees, George Calvert, John Silliman.

Next members received were on 27 September 1844 and were: Austin Prestwood, Mrs. Mary Prestwood, Mrs. Daughtery, Mrs. Elizabeth Danner, Margaret Campbell, Miss Margaret Greenlees, Mary Greenlees, Mr. Francis Moore, Mr. Thomas Silliman."

(The minutes were headed "Union" until through September 1859, then suddenly without explanation they were headed "Hadden" on the 6th of November 1859; named for Rev. Isaac Hadden, an able minister and brilliant educator. (See Bethel Cemetery for more about Rev. Hadden.)

BOYD CEMETERY NEAR BOYD, ALABAMA

This cemetery is about one mile west of the little town of Boyd which is located a few miles north of York, Alabama, on Highway #17. One turns off this highway, just before getting to Boyd, on a black top road which turns due west. The cemetery is to the right of this road, one turns off of it in front of J. W. Boyd home and follows it around through a field for about one half mile back toward Boyd. The road ends at the cemetery. With the exception of one or two, everyone buried here is related to everyone else.

Gravestone Inscriptions

John Boyd, born Chester, South Carolina, 1 November 1776, died 4 September 1854. (He was the son of Hugh Boyd, Revolutionary Partriot and Soldier. Hugh Boyd was a wagon maker as mentioned in both deeds and in Revolutionary Service Records. He was born in Ireland and came to the American Colonies with his father, John Boyd, Sr., prior to the Revolution. Hugh Boyd married Mrs. Jennet Muffitt, a widow. His will is recorded in Book B, page 311, Newberry, South Carolina. He mentions his sons Mathew Boyd, John Boyd, Hugh Boyd and Robert Boyd, and daughters Jane Boyd, Rosanna Boyd, and a brother, John Boyd. It was signed 3 October 1798 and was proved 5 March 1799.

Proof of relationship may be found in Mathew Boyd's will proved 26 November 1835, Box 73, pkg. 35 #831, Newberry, South Carolina, which is as follows: "My estate to my sister's (Rosannah) lawful children, to William Muffitt my half brother, John Boyd my brother, Hugh Boyd's (my deceased brother) children, Jane Campbell my sister and Robert Boyd my brother, -witnessed by Nathan Renwick, Thomas W. Little, John H. Hatton. W. Willson, Ordinary. Signed Mathew Boyd "

Deed Book A page 199 - On the 30 December 1785 William Killpatrick, Sr., of District 96 Newberry, South Carolina sells to Hugh Boyd 100 acres of land on the branch of Indian Creek and Broad River, being part of 300 acres granted Wm. Killpatrick on 6 February 1773. Witnesses/ John Blalock, John Blalock, Jr. and William Woodall.

Deed Book A page 156 - On 7 and 8 June 1786 John Reid, a taylor of 96 District, South Carolina sells to Hugh Boyd 150 acres of 250 acres granted John Reid on 1 September 1768 between Broad and Saludy River called Gilders Creek and bounded by Wm. Cannon. Witnesses John Blalock, Sr., John Blalock, Jr. and Simon Keary.

Deed Book A page 195 - James Johnson sold Hugh Boyd Wagoner, 144 acres on 19 November 1785 - (George Eakins, wit.) on branch of Indian Creek, waters of Enoree River.

Deed Book M page 316 - John Boyd of Newberry County, South Carolina sells to Jacob Duckett land on Indian Creek, waters of Enoree River - mentions John Boyd had a brother Matthew Boyd who was willed land by their father Hugh Boyd. It was signed 5 September 1818 and witnessed by Adam Chambers, George McCreless, Young J. Harrington, J.Q. Jane or Jennett Boyd, wife of the above John (Deed Book M-316) signed her dower to the above land willed to John and Matthew by Hugh Boyd, their father, 7 January 1819.

John and Jane (she used "Jane" in signing legal papers, but she was "Jennett" to her husband) Boyd removed to Perry County, Alabama in the early 1820's and patented land in both Perry and in Greene Counties. Some of their children married and lived in both Counties. They sold land in Perry County as late as 1838 (after their removal to Sumter County) and their signatures were witnessed before Jacob G. Danner, J. P. (their son-in-law.) John Boyd and his son John M. Boyd jointly patented land in Sumter County (certificate received in 1834) and we find in Deed Book E. 652 that John and Jane Boyd sold their part of this land for $1.00 to John M. Boyd - 18 December 1840.

Now that I have proved the line of descent I will give you Hugh Boyd's Service record. "Hugh Boyd ... Revolutionary Service .. 668 wagon hire 1780 to 1782 £ 52 5s 8½p .... October 10, 1783, Rec'd by Richard Speake £ 823, signed, Hugh Boyd. Rev. Accts AA668 Acct 1703 X-Hugh Boyd,

Department of Archives, Columbia, South Carolina." I am giving you this wagon service instead of his fighting record to prove he, as wagon maker, was the same as our Hugh Boyd, the wagon maker mentioned in deeds.

John Boyd's will may be found in Will Book 2 page 50 Sumter County. It was probated 14 October 1854 -- and he names his children as follows: Hugh, Mary, David, Sara, Rosannah, Matthew H., Elizabeth, John M., Jefferson, James Marion and Robert. He mentioned "Jennett Dial Boyd, daughter of my son Jefferson Boyd".

Jennett Boyd, born in Newberry, South Carolina, 8 August 1781, died 31 March 1844. (She was the wife of John Boyd who called her "Jennett" but all her legal papers were signed as Jane. Also called Jane in her father's (Jeremiah Dial Sr.) will. We find her father Jeremiah Dial in the Newberry District, South Carolina 1790 Census. He was born in Ireland between 1719 and 1720. According to pension application of Jeremiah Dial Sr., W - 14 Nat'l Archives, Washington, D. C. his father removed from Ireland to Charleston 1772. He and his sons Jeremiah Jr. (whom we call the II), John and William obtained land on south side of Enoree River.

Jeremiah Dial Sr., was a patriot in the Revolutionary War. Reference for Jeremiah Dial Sr., in Books W-W p 260 No. 436 Libr W - issued 19 August 1785 for 88/12/9 and passed by Commissioners of Accts. ... 88/12/9½ and interest.

There are indents showing that Jeremiah Jr. or II, William and John Dial were soldiers. Indent showing that John Dial served 63 days service militia duty 1782 for 4/10/0 approved 20 May 1785; and another entry for 93/19/7½ stg. for duty as Sgt. in Militia as audited .. Books O and R-T pages 257 no. 290, Libr. Q. and p. 175 Libr. respectively.

John Dial's will is in Newberry S.C. Book A-142 Mary Doyle (Dial) admr. Same book p-149 Mary, the widow is called Mary Dial. Sales bill shows that Mary Dial, the widow, and Jeremiah Dial were large purchasers. John Dial left his estate to his widow.

The will of Jeremiah Dial, Sr., Newberry, S.C. -- File 6 p 13, Est #129, Bk. H-114 dated 1 January 1805, proved 4 Nov. 1805, Wit/ Archibald McMillan, John Hopper and Alexander Hopper. Exers. "my beloved wife Margaret, David Montgomery, William Lavender. Signed by Jeremiah Dial (this was "Senior"). He made bequests to wife Margaret, to sons William and Jeremiah (II), to daughters Margaret Ingram and Jane Boyd, wife of John Boyd. To grandsons David Montgomery Dial and Jeremiah Dial (III). to daughter Sallie, wife of Hugh Hopper.

Margaret, widow of Jeremiah Dial Sr., sold her land to David Montgomery Dial and Jeremiah Dial (III) 17 January 1808 - Deed Bk J p-220 Newberry, S. C. Jeremiah III then sold his share to David Montgomery Dial 1811. Deed Bk L-268, who then sold to Jacob Duckett M-292. Jennett Dial, wife of David Montgomery Dial signed dower.

According to Sam T. Boyd, grandson of John and Jane (Dial) Boyd, in a sworn statement March 1960, David Montgomery Dial and Jeremiah Dial who came to Alabama in the same wagon train with Jane or Jennett (Dial) Boyd were her nephews, the sons of her deceased brother, John Dial, Revolutionary soldier.

Here, I will give the history of Jeremiah Dial III as his grave has not been located. He patented land in T 19 R2 W. He voted in Livingston March 1841 and died the fall of the same year. Orphans Bk 11 p-222 shows widow Summer Dial. Heirs: John Dial, Mary wife of John Johnson, Davis or David M. Dial, James P. Dial, William H. Dial, Margaret wife of E. Johnson, Geo. W. Dial, Jeremiah Dial, and granddaughter Mary J. Campbell. (She was the daughter of Nancy Dial (dec'd) who married James W. Campbell 25 December 1839.) The 1850 census shows Summer as 57 born in S. C., Wm. H. 24 born in Alabama, George W. 20 born in Alabama, Jeremiah 16 born Alabama.

Mrs. Summer Dial married Calvin Johnson, after death of Jeremiah Dial III; she died 1857 and notices issued to James Dial, Wm. H. Dial, Mary Johnson, John W. Dial (who resides in Pickens County) and David M. Dial minor heir - estate consisting of 1181 67/100 acres.

I give you the children of John and Jane (Dial) Boyd not buried in this cemetery. The numbers by their names correspond to the numbers by names listed in the will of John Boyd. They are as follows:

(1) Hugh Boyd was born in South Carolina, married late in life, a widow, Mrs. Elizabeth Nelson who had a daughter by her first husband. This family left Sumter County and was lost sight of.
(2) David B. was born 1805 in South Carolina; he married Sara Clark 26 May 1836. He was dead in 1854 for John Boyd in his will deeds property "to children of my son David B. Boyd."

(10) James Marion (buried at Enterprise, Miss.) son of John and Jane or Jennett (Dial) Boyd born 1819 in South Carolina and married Susan H. Simmons 30 July 1844 as his second wife. (See her obituary in Sumter Democrat.) His first wife was Caison Hodges. His 3rd wife was Margaret Jane Powe born 29 August 1828 and married James Marion Boyd 26 June 1855; Margaret Jane Powe Boyd had a brother William Thrashley Powe who married Susan Lightsey in 1845; their daughter Clara Jane married Robert Clay Boyd, son of James Marion and Susan (Simmons) Boyd.

Because the Powes are so muchly intermarried with other families in Sumter County, I stop here to give a little about this family. William Powe and wife Elizabeth Marcia Pegues had a son William Henry Pegues Powe who was born 27 April 1799 and died 1865, he married Sara Harry Chapman the daughter of Thrashley Chapman and wife Catherine Edwards. They had children (1) William Thrashley born 1822 who married Susan Lightsey in 1845, (2) Charles Edward born 1824 married Elizabeth Chapman in 1855, (3) Catherine Thrashley born 1826, married David H. Williams in 1848, (4) Margaret Jane born 1828, married James Marion Boyd, son of John and Jane (Dial) Boyd, in 1855, (5) Allen Chapman born 1830 married Josephine George (daughter of Sara Boyd who was daughter of John and Jane (Dial) Boyd) in 1855), (6) Mary Eleanor born 1832 married Newton Prestwood (son of Mary (Boyd) and Austin Prestwood -- see their history in Boyd Cemetery, (7) Elizabeth Mariah married Rev. Milton J. McClain, (8) Sarah Olivia born 1839 married John Turnipseed.

Alexander Craig Powe, brother of above William Henry Pegues Powe, married Mary Allen Chapman who was a sister to W. H. P. Powe's wife.

They had a sister, Harriett Pegues Powe who married (1) Mr. McRea and (2) William Godfrey. Mrs. Fannie Bell Boyd, wife of J. W. Boyd is a descendant of William and Harriett Pegues Powe, Fannie Bell married J. W. Boyd the son of Robert Clay Boyd who was the son of James Marion and Susan (Simmons) Boyd -- Robert Clay (see above) married Clara Jane Powe. (See Robt. Clay Boyd gravestone records).

James Marion Boyd and his third wife, Mary Jane Powe, had three children: William Henry, Susan Silliman and Cordelia all of whom died young.

(8) John M. Boyd (buried elsewhere) born 1816, the son of John and Jane or Jennett (Dial) Boyd, married (1) Louisa Jane Moore, 20 January 1837. (2) Louise L. Holm 26 December 1867. Louisa Jane was born in Alabama 1823, the daughter of Robert and Theodosia or Leodosia (Hamilton) Moore. (See Rachel Moore Obituary in Sumter County Whig.) The children of John M. and Louisa Jane Boyd were: Lucy J. born 1839, Robert born 1841, Mary C. born 4 April 1843 died 6 October 1882 married Robert T. Simmons 6 March 1862, John C. born 1846, Hugh L. born 1848 married February 1871 to Missouri Payne, Matthew H. born 1850. Robert Moore age 14 was living in this family in 1850 census.

The children of John M. and his wife (2) Louise L. Holm were: Theodosia or Leodosia who married Mick Dove, Thalby, and Thomas - have no history on the last two named. Descendants of John M. Boyd went to Texas. Tradition says that Louise L. Holm was a niece of his first wife.

Matthew H. (born 1809 in South Carolina, the son of John and Jane or Jennett (Dial) Boyd; he is buried in an unmarked grave by the side of his son John Jeames Boyd in Boyd Cemetery. Matthew H. died 15 January 1877. He married (1) Eliza Amanda Key born 28 October 1812, the daughter of James and Rebecca (Grizzle) Key. James Key was born 20 July 1788 the son of William Bibb Key and his wife Morning Key. He was born 2 October 1759 and she was born 12 August 1764. William Bibb Key was the son of Martin and Nancy (Bibb) Key and should have shared in the Robert Edwards' estate which has never been settled and is said to be of tremendous value today. The children of James and Rebecca (Grizzle) Key were: (1) Eliza Amanda, (2) Sara Pavey (or Sallie), (3) David Marshall, (4) Hubard, (5) Joel Marion, (6) Charlotte Earley, (7) George Henry, (8) James Thomas, (9) Susan and (10) Mary.

Matthew H. (arper) Boyd married Eliza Amanda Key 24 April 1832. She was born in Georgia and died in Sumter County, Alabama 1857. Their children were: Mildred born 1833 married a Mr. Howell; Rebecca Jane born 1835 married William D. Richmond, John James born 1837 married Eliza Frances Hopper; Joel Marion born 1839 married Queen Victoria Davenport; Marshall born 1841 died 1864; Mary born 1845 married Benjamin F. Rushing; Thomas born 1847 married Mary Augusta Silliman daughter of Matthew H. Boyd's second wife; Susan Virginia born 1849 married John L. Wilkerson; Louisa M. born 1852 married Will B. Davenport; Emily Eliza.

Matthew H. Boyd married (2) Mrs. Susan Maria (Farrar) Silliman, the widow of Thomas N. Silliman (see Silliman in Bethel Cemetery Records.) She had three daughters by Thos. N. Silliman: Martha Jane, Mary Augusta and Susan Pauline. Matthew H. Boyd and his second wife Susan Maria (Farrar) Silliman (born 13 March 1827, died 31 May 1911 in Anderson County, Texas -- and whose mother was Martha Carlisle who married John Absolom Farrar --) married 5 October 1858 in Sumter County, Alabama, had two children: (1) Absolom Farrar Boyd born 22 January 1860, died 5 August 1948, married Lulu DeWitt 23 December 1886. The daughter of Joel L. DeWitt and wife Mary Ann (McGowan) DeWitt. They were parents of (a) Tom Bordeaux Boyd, born 9 January 1889 and married Ruth C. Sexton 30 March 1921 and are parents of Mary Lou who married Howard N. Andreola; Nancy who married Richard Weldon Gibson. Mary Lou and her husband have at least one child, Nicholas Brock born 8 August 1954. Nancy and her husband have at least one child, Richard Weldon Jr., born in Shreveport, Louisiana; (b) William Robert Boyd born 13 June 1891, married Mary V. Early on the 16 August 1943. No issue; (c) Bettie Maud Boyd, born 5 January 1894, married James Drake Kirk 5 May 1913. They are parents of two children: Robert Langford Kirk born 8 May 1915, married Mary Catherine Swigert 5 June 1939. In 1949 they had a child born to them, Roberta Jean. (2) Chellie Rosanna Boyd, whole sister of Absolom Farrar Boyd, was born 25 March 1862 and died 7 July 1942 in Texas, she married John Thomas Prestwood, grandson of Austin and Mary (Boyd) Prestwood - see Prestwood records in this cemetery. Mary Boyd, born 29 May 1845, the daughter of Matthew H. Boyd and his 1st wife, Eliza Amanda Key, married Benjamin F. Rushing who was born 17 March 1842. They are buried at Elmo, Texas. Their children: Bob, Connie, Bennie. It is said that Bob became a doctor and removed to Louisiana; Connie never married as he was badly burned when a child so could not walk. Bennie is buried by her parents. She died when her son was born, he was adopted by Mr. and Mrs. King of Tyler, Texas.

Other children of Matthew H. Boyd are buried in this cemetery, the histories of whom I will give as I come to them.

According to a citation in the settlement of Matthew Boyd estate - Probate court 8 September 1881, the 28 October 1881 was set for a hearing and application for the following heirs: Susan M. Boyd, Absolom Boyd and Chellie Boyd who reside near Livingston, Alabama, Mildred A. Howell who resides at Union, Mississippi, John J. Boyd and Louisa V. Davenport who reside in Kemper County, Mississippi, Thomas J. Boyd and Mathew P. Boyd

P. Boyd who reside in Terrell, Kaufman County, Texas, Susan V. Wilkerson, wife of John Wilkerson of Kemper County, Mississippi, Thomas Boyd, Laura Boyd and James Boyd of Lauderdale, Lauderdale County, Mississippi, Rebecca Richmond wife of W. D. Richmond residing in Neshoba County, Mississippi -- all heirs of Matthew H. Boyd, deceased. Signed by W. R. DeLoach, Probate Judge.

James Thomas Boyd, son of Matthew H. and Eliza (Key) Boyd, born 3 March 1847, died 27 February 1890, married 10 February 1867 Mary Augustine Silliman, born 18 January 1850 and died 30 April 1870. Her parents were Susan Maria (Farrar) and Thomas N. Silliman. James Thomas Boyd and wife Mary Agusta were parents of Mary Ernest born 15 October 1869 in Sumter County, Alabama. At the death of her mother 30 April 1870 she went to live with her grandparents, Susan Mariah (Farrar) and Matthew H. Boyd who reared her with their two children Chellie and Absolom. Mary Ernest married Dr. Charles Walter Goddard 5 June 1892 -- he was born 24 March 1867 and died 14 March 1927. They were the parents of children: Raymond Boyd Goddard born 28 November 1895 married Ilsa Underwood 23 December 1916; Walter Crosswaite Goddard (M.D.) born 30 June 1901 married Blossom Wooten 11 September 1925; Erwin Silliman Goddard born 30 January 1904 married Eleanor Roeck 13 June 1925. The above Ramond and Ilsie Goddard have one son Raymond, Jr., born 28 January 1931 and married Betty Ann Allen 1 September 1951. They are parents of Susanne born 16 December 1952 and Betsy Elaine born 7 July 1955 at Weisbaden, Germany.

******

Jefferson Boyd, born in Newberry District, South Carolina, 18 December 1817, died 19 January 1894. (He was the son of John and Jane or Jennett (Dial) Boyd. He married three times. (1) Sara M. Hudson 29 August 1839, (2) Virginia Godfrey, (3) to Mrs. Emma Faulkner Lewis. The children by Sara Hudson were: (1) Austin Gambrel who is buried in this cemetery; (2) Robert Jefferson who is buried in this cemetery; (3) Mangus who was born 18 September 1860, died 21 January 1934 in Lubbock, Texas; he married Nannie Josephine McClain, born 11 November 1875 in Georgetown, Texas. Their children: Thomas Edward, Miller Robert, Morgan Clendon married Effie Miller no issue, Hugh Mangum, Jr., and Jay Woodson married Reba P. Charley, one child Reba Fay born 1937; (4) Molly; (5) Cora; (6) Jennett Dial who married T. H. Turnipseed 26 July 1866 and removed to Pickens County; the children of Virginia and Jefferson Boyd were: (7) Maggie buried in this cemetery; (8) Leila who was living in 1959; (9) Hattie; (10) Blanche; (11) Samuel Tilden born 12 June 1885 who married Mamie Adams daughter of J. R. and Mary (Narze) Adams 20 December 1908: their children are: Erline Estell born 20 April 1911, married Tad Lidikay, their children are Betty Jo (Elizabeth Josephine) who married James Kennith Daniel, Tad Jr.; and Mack Boyd. The second daughter Bonnie Jean born 2 April 1914 married John L. King, no issue. Samuel Tilden Boyd living 1960. Jefferson Boyd had only one child by his third wife, Mrs. Emma F. Lewis, viz: Austin Grover Boyd who is buried at Central Cemetery which see for his descendants.

******

Sara M. Boyd, wife of Jefferson Boyd, born 17 July 1829, died 7 October 1865. (She was Sara M. Hudson, who was a relative of Louise Jane Moore who married John M. Boyd. Both girls and Louise L. Holm, 2nd wife of John M. Boyd are descentants of Loderwick and Rachel Moore. Sara A. Boyd was the mother of Austin Gambrel Boyd, Robert Jefferson Boyd and others. See above.)

******

C. Virginia Boyd, wife of Jefferson Boyd, born 17 July 1846, died 10 February 1885. (She was the mother of Samuel Tilden Boyd and others. Several of the girls died young. She was said to be the daughter or granddaughter of William Godfrey and was living in Arkansas at the time of her marriage to Jefferson Boyd.)

******

Robert Jefferson Boyd, born 29 December 1856, died 5 November 1928 (son of Jefferson and Sara (Hudson) Boyd. He married his second cousin, Susan Davis 5 December 1877 - Marriage Book IV page 177, Sumter County. Their children: (a) Jeff Boyd (see Central Cemtery records), (b) Beulah Boyd, born 23 November 1878, died 4 August 1960, married 12 December 1907 Walter Allen Motes, born 26 June 1878, died 28 June 1947, issue: (ba) Stanton Boyd Motes, born 14 December 1909, married September 1950 Maggie Smith Pettet, (bb) Nellie Mae Motes, born 2 September 1911, married 14 April 1940 Louis Leon Goggans, born 14 October 1906, son of Kim Buck and Mary E. (Coefield) Goggans, issue (bba) Barbara Nell Goggans, born 25 November 1946, (bbb) Joe Goggans, born 14 January 1948; (c) Ada Boyd married Harold C. Wood, Lives (1961) in Washington, D.C., issue: (ca) Vivian; (d) Arch S. Boyd married Jeanette Jenkins, daughter of Thomas L. and Annie (Andrews) Jenkins, they had two children, Dorothy who married Paul Jones and they have one child, Johnnie; and Audrey - see Central Cemetery records; (e) Scott Boyd who married Joe Dobbins, both deceased - they had one child Linnell who married Noble Frank Greenhill and they are parents of Scott, Deborah Lynn and Noble Frank, III; (f) Walter Boyd, who died young; (g) Sara Boyd who married Horace Kerr (see Bethel Cemetery records); and (h) Ruby Boyd who married Oscar Grice Richardson (see Old Side Cemetery records.)

Nellie Mae (Motes) Goggans established her DAR membership through Jeremaih Dial, the father of Jane or Jennette (Dial) Boyd, who was the great great grandmother of Nellie Mae (Motes) Goggans. Her National DAR number is 456,079.

******

Mrs. R. J. Boyd, born 17 September 1858, died 2 June 1946. (She was Susan Davis, the daughter of William R. and Mary Amelia (Danner) Davis. (See Davis Cemetery Record).

******

Austin G. Boyd 1850-1932 (He was the son of Jefferson and Sara M. -- Hudson -- Boyd and grand son of John and Jane or Jennett (Dial) Boyd. Austin Gambrel Boyd was born 23 October 1850, died 19 January 1932, married Harriett Cadmus (often called Caddie) Moore 21 December 1872 - Sumter County marriage Book 4 page 57 - Children of this union were (1) Conde C. who was born 11 November 1873, died 24 May 1936, married Margaret Neely (the daughter of Mary Elizabeth (Peterson) Neely who is buried at Boney Cemetery, and her husband Henry Frankin Neely) who was born 19 July 1874 and died 10 August 1957. Their children are: 1. Grace Catherine Boyd born 30 May 1898, married James Leland Aust (his history will be in another volume) on 27 October 1926, their children are (a) Betty Bell born 3 November 1929 and married a distant cousin, Jim Allen Dial on 8 June 1947. Children of this union: Jim born 10 October 1948, Lee born 29 December 1949 and baby Jerry Lynn who is buried in this cemetery; (b) Jo Ann born 27 October 1927, married Malcolm G. Larkin Jr., (also called Jimmie), whose history will be in another volume, children of this union: Malcolm Kenneth born 9 October 1948, Michael Eugene born 28 October 1950 and Joyce Katherine born 21 January 1952; (c) George Neely born 30 September 1936, married Madge Glass and they have one child Catherine Wingate; (d) James Leland Jr., born 17 November 1932. (2) Ralph Franklin Boyd born 3 May 1900, died 19 February 1922. (3) Philip Marshall Boyd born 24 February 1902, married Ruth Lavender 24 January 1930 - see Lavender history in Bethel Cemetery records - she was born 10 July 1908, the daughter of Herbert and Mary Ruth (Scarbrough) Lavender -- see Scarbrough history in another volume - children of this union (a) Ruby Ann born 19 October 1933 and married Thomas H. Baty 1 November 1952, their children are Richard Wayne and Terri Lynn Baty born 24 March 1955 and 29 May 1957, respectively; (b) Herbert Marshall born 17 December 1937; (c) Jacqueline born 19 July 1939, married Carl G. Hosty 6 October 1956; (d) Mary Ruth born 9 June 1944 in Birmingham, Alabama, all the other children were born in Livingston, Alabama.

(4) Ruth Caldwell Boyd born 21 March 1904, married George Chappell, Children of this marriage are (a) Margaret Neely who married Preston Copeland and they have children Karen and Terri, (b) Betty Ruth married Allen Lumpkin, no issue; (c) Bruce married a German girl Agnes -----, and they have two children Boyd and Peggy. (5) William Austin Boyd born 20 November 1906, married (1) Louise Aust by whom he had children Dorothy Jean who married J. B. Baty, Sara Frances who married Eugene Baty, Patricia who married Bill Smith, Leonard Caldwell Boyd who married a Miss Baty, cousin of J. B. and Eugene Baty, and William Jr., married   . William Austin Boyd's wife (2) is Viola --- whom he married in Mobile; they are parents of one child May Ann; (6) Margaret Hazel Boyd born 19 November 1908 married William T. Brannon; (7) Sara

Boyd born 16 September 1910 married W. O. White; (8) Ernest Moore Boyd born 18 June 1912 married Telitha Land 4 October 1935 -- her father is Luther Land the son of Elaza Land both of Tallapoosa County, Alabama, her great grandfather was James Doster Land of North Carolina. Ernest and Telitha Boyd are parents of (a) Mary Kay born 19 July 1936 who married George Thomas Cooper in 1957. They are parents of Charles Anthony and William Christopher Cooper, and (b) Ernest Land (Lanny) born 16 June 1947. (9) Hattie Mary Boyd born 26 May 1914 married Cephas R. Holliman on the 6 August 1938 (he was born 17 August 1904 the son of Joseph R. and Mary Elizabeth (Parks) Holliman). Hattie Mary and Cephas Holliman have 2 children: Linda Boyd Holliman born 25 February 1941 married George Stewart 2 April 1960; and Cephas Robert Holliman Jr., born 3 September 1944. (10) Conde Caldwell Boyd born 18 August 1916 and died 22 January 1927. Conde Boyd, Sr., and his wife Margaret Neelly are buried in the Livingston Cemetery.

******

Caddie M. Boyd 1854 -- 1937 (Her real name was Harriett Cadmus Moore, wife of Austin Gambrel Boyd married 21 December 1872. She was the daughter of Frank B. Moore and wife Ann Pauline Silliman, the daughter of Mary (Campbell) and John Silliman, Jr., married ca 1837 (see Campbell record in Land Patents -- see Silliman in Bethel Cemetery records) -- Frank B. and Ann Pauline (Silliman) Moore had children: (a) John William born 1840 married Miss Coit; (b) Mary A. Moore 1812 married Newton Prestwood -- see Prestwood in this cemetery -- whose first wife was Mary E. Powe buried in this cemetery; (c) Susan C. Moore married Mark Sledge who died and then her sister (d) Sara Pauline Moore married Mark Sledge; (e) William Rutledge Moore; (f) Harriett Caddie Moore and (g) Addison Perry Moore who went to Tyler Texas.

Addison Clarence Boyd, born 29 November 1878, died 8 December 1955. (He was the son of Austin Gambrell and Caddie (Moore) Boyd, and great grandson of John and Jane or Jennett (Dial) Boyd, and he was the grandson of Jefferson and Sara Hudson Boyd. Addison Clarence Boyd married Amelia Cobb, the daughter of Frank and Molly (Barbaree) Cobb. Children of this marriage were: (1) Clarence who married Virginia Murray 12 April 1920. They had children (a) Add who married Eloise Metzger and they are parents of Pierce and Smith Boyd; (b) Rachael who married Kenneth Strumquist and they have 5 boys. (2) Frank married Glennie Hutcherson of Geiger. They are parents of Frank Jr., and Ilsie. (3) Velma married Joe Robert Miller and they are parents of (a) Alice Amelia Miller, (b) Kate Marie Miller who married Bob Smith and are parents of Terry DeLyn (c) Robert David Miller married Joe Ann Doss and have children David and Tonyann, (d) Joe Frank Miller. (4) Amelia married Davis Burton (see Central Cemetery records for Burton record) and they are parents of (a) Johnnie Jean who married Irvin M. Commander Jr. and they have Dave Steve and Amelia (b) Davis Burton Jr., who is married. (5) Mattie married J. B. (Jim) Stegall (see Central Cemetery for Stegall), and they have the following children: (a) Glenda Carol who married her distant cousin, Bobbie Boswell (see R. J. Dial record in this cemetery)

(b) James B. Jr., (Jimmie), and (c) Annie Lou.

Amelia Boyd born 29 November 1878, died 23 October 1915. (She was the wife of Addison Clarence Boyd, and daughter of Frank and Molly (Barbaree) Cobb, natives of Cedartown, Georgia, but died in Sumter County, Alabama.)

Pauline Boyd, daughter of Austin G. and Harriet Cadmus (Moore) Boyd, married T. M. Panky and had children: Paul who married Marline Estes and they became parents of Betsy, Marline, Tommie, Harriett and Paul; Mildren is not married; Violet married David C. Peebles and they are parents of Bill, David, Paul, Mary Jo and James; Paige married Whit McSween and they have three boys, viz: Whit, Mike and Pat; Austin Bennett is not married.

Betsy Panky, daughter of Paul and Marline (Estes) Panky, married Allen Head of Birmingham. Pauline (Boyd) Panky is living with her daughter, Mildred, who teaches in Mobile. T. M. Panky died several years ago.

Mary Boyd, daughter of Harriett Cadmus (Moore) and Austin G. Boyd, married first Edwin Fulton (See Fulton records in Bethel Cemetery) who was killed by lightning, she married (2) Harry F. Davidson, brother of Mrs. Thomas F. Seale of Livingston. They are parents of one child, Mary Elizabeth who married (1) Mr. Davis and became parents of a son Bill, she married (2) James Vernor Park of Aliceville, Alabama and they are parents of a son James Vernor Park, Jr.

Eva Boyd, the daughter of Austin and Caddie (Moore) Boyd, is buried in another cemetery. She married Oscar Cobb, brother of Robert C. Cobb who is buried at Central Cemetery. Eva and Oscar Cobb were the parents of (a) Eugene Austin Cobb - see Central Cemetery for his record - (b) Fred Lamar Cobb born 7 March 1913, married 23 October 1940 Mary Brewer, the daughter of Bettie Florence (Harris) and C. W. Brewer of Cuba, Alabama. They are the parents of Harrell Lamar Cobb born 15 January 1941, Judy Davis Cobb born 18 July 1943 and Cathy Lou Cobb born 3 August 1953; (c) Marvin Cobb unmarried; (d) Smith Cobb killed in an automobile wreck when about grown.

Austin Frances Jefferson Boyd, M. D., was born 14 July 1887 living in 1960, son of Austin Gambrel and Caddie (Moore) Boyd, grandson of Jefferson and Sarah (Hudson) Boyd and great grandson of John and Jane or Jennett (Dial) Boyd; he married (1) Irma Pittard 9 November 1917. Her immigrant forebear came to America with Lafayette and fought with the Colonists to attain their freedom from the British; Irma is a native of Mobile but was living in New York when they married in "The Little Church Around the Corner". One daughter Mary Virginia born 23 September 1918, she married 7 March 1936 T. O. Howell, the son of Thomas O. and Mattie (Earl) Howell, his grandfather was Thomas Jefferson Howell, and his great grandfather was Benjamin Howell. T. O. and Mary Virginia (Boyd) Howell are parents of an infant born and died in 1942, a daughter Mary Christopher Howell born 23 October 1943, and a son T. O. Howell III, (Thomas Orr), born 8 February 1947.

After the divorce of his first wife Dr. A. F. J. Boyd married Lolita Waddell 6 January 1926. She was born December 1903 and died 10 November 1950 and buried at Boyd Cemetery. Lolita Waddell Boyd was the daughter of Rufus Alexander and Sally (Bishop) Waddell who were parents of other children: Mattie, Samson, Mary Ellen, Frank, George, Edna, Ruby, Elsie and Mamie Laura. George married Gillye Simmons and they live in Sumter County and are parents of Wayne and Barbara Waddell. (See Greenlee Cemetery for Ruby (Waddell) Hailey.)

Austin Francis Jefferson Boyd and his (2) wife Lolita were parents of: William Calvin Boyd, II, born 8 November 1926, married 10 June 1952 to Julia Knox Elliott, daughter of Clyde and "Jack" Reynolds Elliott (see Central Cemetery records); they are parents of Gail Boyd born 11 June 1953, William Calvin Boyd III, born 30 May 1955 and Clyde born 8 February 1957.

(2) Austin F. J. Boyd Jr., was born 21 December 1928, married 18 August 1949 Ruby Nell Allison who was born 4 September 1931. They are parents of Gloria Boyd born 1 January 1951, John Jefferson Boyd born 12 December 1952, and Gambrel Boyd born 14 July 1954.

(3) Anita Lolita Boyd born 15 August 1932, died 23 February 1955, married Henry Andrews Jenkins 11 June 1950 - (see Jenkins' records in Central Cemetery.)

******

Walter, son of Robert Jefferson and Susan E. Boyd, born 16 January 1884, died 21 October 1909.

******

Clara Helen Boyd, born 8 March 1921 died 8 October 1925. (Child of J. W. and Fannie B. Boyd.)

******

Robert Bruce Boyd, born 25 December 1927 died 17 January 1928. (Brother of Clara Helen's.)

******

James Clifton Sutton, born 28 March 1888 died 4 July 1947. (Husband of Susan Boyd.)

******

Susan Boyd, wife of J. C. Sutton, born 10 April 1888, died 29 April 1917. (She was daughter of Robert Clay Boyd, and sister of J. W. Boyd.)

******

Robert Clay Boyd, born 25 July 1845 died 8 December 1920. (Son of James Marion and Susan H. (Simmons). Robert C. Boyd married Clara Jane Powe, daughter of William Thrashley and Susan Lightsey Powe.)

******

Clara Jane Powe, wife of Robert C. Boyd, born 14 July 1860 died 4 April 1910. (See Robert C. Boyd for her parents. Robert C. and Mary Jane (Powe) Boyd had children: "J. W." or James William born 29 May 1891, he married Fannie Bell (Whitfield) daughter of Helen (Stewart) born 30 January 1861 and Le Grande Whitfield born 9 April 1858. J. W. and Fannie Bell Boyd are parents of: Frances who married Ray Essary - one child Sidney Ray; Kate married Lloyd Adams and they have one child Carol Ann; James William, Jr., married Ruby N. Hudnall and they are parents of Ruth Frances, Barbara Nell, James W. III, Newton Whitfield and Edward Leon; Jane married (1) Hodges Wheeler and they had children James Irvin and Hodges Glenn, she married (2) Fred Holmes. Other children of R. C. and Clara Jane (Powe) Boyd: Mary, Robert, Kelly and Clara who married William Treadaway by whom she had two children (a) Dolly who married R. Newell and (b) Tommie Treadaway. Mr. Treadaway married (1) Dolly Wise and they had a son Tracy - stepson of Clara (Boyd) Treadaway.)

******

Mary Eleanor Powe, consort of Newton Prestwood, and daughter of W. and S. Powe, born 25 September 1832 died 15 October 1868. (She was the daughter of William Harry Pegues Powe and his wife Sara Harry Chapman. Mary E. Powe was sister of Allen Chapman Powe who married Josephine George and she was sister of Margaret Jane Powe who married James Marion Boyd and niece of Harriett Pegues Powe who married William Godfrey and became ancestors of Fannie Bell Whitfield who married J. W. Boyd, grandson of James Marion Boyd whose wife (3) was the niece of Harriett Pegues Powe. I need the Philadelphia lawyer to tell me who is related to whom. Austin and Mary (Boyd) - daughter of John and Jennett (Dial) Boyd - were parents of Newton Prestwood born 1832 and died in Tyler, Texas 1901. Mary Eleanor (Powe) and Newton Prestwood were parents of (a) John Thomas Prestwood born 24 September 1861, died 4 November 1914, married Chellie Roxanna Boyd, daughter Matthew Harper Boyd - buried in this cemetery - and Susan Maria Farrar. Children of this union (maternal side descended from Matthew H. Boyd and the paternal side descended from John Boyd, father of Matthew H. Boyd) are as follows: (1) Hubbard Lee Prestwood born 31 August 1866 in Sumter County, married in El Paso, Texas to Constance Macias, daughter of Constance (Delgade) and Joseph Macias - their children, Edw. Lee born 16 September 1930, Wendell Cody born 8 October 1931, Constance Pauline born 23 September 1932 and married William P. Cassidy, Howard Baine born 24 September 1933, John Thomas born 23 June 1935, Donna Lee born 19 September 1938 - his wife (2) was Dottie Lee Fants, no issue.

(2) Austin Farrar Prestwood, son of John Thomas and Chellie Roxanna (Boyd) was born 26 May 1888 in Sumter County, Alabama, married 25 January 1907 to Lucile Walker McIntyre born 31 July 1890, daughter of James Robert and Mary Elizabeth (Walker) McIntyre. Children of this union were Mary Elizabeth Prestwood born 26 January 1908, married 27 July 1927 to Owen C. Savage born 1898, son of McIver (Cross) and William H. Savage. Their children: Caroline Lucile who married James I. Jordan, Jr., Owen Cross married Shirley McLean and are parents of Owen C. III, Austin Boyd born 13 March 1910 married Marguerite Beard 19 August 1944, Paul Duane born 12 April 1914 married Jaunita Montague 19 September 1953, Chellie Pearl born 9 September 1916 at Drew, Texas, married (1) Bruce R. Parrish 24 July 1940 - he was born 21 June 1876 - died 28 February 1954 son of Nancy Elmira (---) and William E. Parrish, one child born of this marriage, Chellie Elizabeth born 4 March 1942 and married. After the divorce of Chellie Pearl and Bruce R. Parrish she married (2) 18 August 1945 Donalson Amyl who died 11 February 1949 and she married (3) 24 January 1950 James Amos Garoutte who died 1959.

(3) Carrie Paulina, daughter of Chellie Roxanna (Boyd) and John Thomas Prestwood, was born 1 July 1893, died 1927, unmarried, (4) Clyde Haynie, also son of C. R. and J. T. Prestwood, born 6 August 1895, died 1952 married Adelyn Brown 7 April 1918, one child Clyde Lee married Ruth Jo Dacy 1942.

Newton Prestwood who married (1) Mary Eleanor Powe, married (2) Mary Ann Moore, daughter of Francis B. and Ann Pauline (Silliman) Moore 15 February 1869, Sumter County, Alabama, she died 13 January 1911 in Tyler, Texas, children of this union were Annie Paulina born 1870 died 1921 married W. L. Watkins, Carrie Cadmus born 1872 died 1933 married C. H. Rice, Emma Newton born 1875 never married, Newton Jr., born 1877 died 1938 married (1) Belle Riviere, (2) Jesse Wilder, Mary Moore born 1886 died 1940 unmarried.

Jerry Lynn, infant son of Betty and Jim Allen Dial, born 13 September 1951, died 29 September 1951. (See Conde C. Boyd and James P. Dial for Bettie Bell's and Jim Allen's lines.)

William Erwin Moore, born 6 August 1881, died 26 August 1952. (He was better known as Cub Moore, and he was not related to anyone in this cemetery.)

Danny Aust, son of Margie (Aust) and Grady Dial, 31 October 1947. (See Clarence Dial record.)

Betty Sue, daughter of Jake and Mildred Dial, 30 October 1953, 3 December 1951 (Jake Dial is the son of Robert Jeff Dial and great grandson of Jacobus Jeremiah Dial.)

Edward Wayne, son of Robert Mitchell and Lucile Dial, 19 November 1934, 4 October 1935. (See Clarence Dial record in this cemetery.)

Mary, consort of Austin Prestwood, and daughter of John and Jennett or Jane (Dial) Boyd, born 23 August 1802, died 10 December 1867, married Austin Prestwood 18 October 1821.

Austin Prestwood, born 9 March 1797, died 9 December 1873. (He was the son of Thomas and Elizabeth or Polly (Swilla) Prestwood of Georgia. Austin Prestwood and Mary Boyd married, they had children: Elizabeth born 1825, died 1870 married James R. Turner, John born 1827, died 1862, married Mary Dabney, Jane born 1830 married Jonathan Tartt who was born in Edgecombe County, North Carolina 23 September 1823 and was brother of Thomas Morrison Tartt, Enos Tartt, Elnathan Tartt, Pernina Tartt, Elizabeth and Margaret Tartt, Jane married (2) William Eakins; Newton born 1832 married Mary Eleanor Powe (See their history under her gravestone record in this cemetery; Mary Clay 1839 married Arch C. Walker 1859.)

Ella Dial, wife (2) of James Dial, born 6 December 1882, died 21 November 1908. (She was Ella Campbell, the mother of Kelly and Coleman Dial. Kelly Dial married Miss Bond, Coleman Dial married a Miss Wilder).

James Dial, born 14 May 1858, died 7 January 1935. (He was the son of James P. and Catherine (Danner) Dial, and the brother of Robert Jefferson Dial and Jacobus Jeremiah Dial. He was married three times, but had children only by his second wife, Ella Campbell.)

Maggie B. wife (1) of James Dial, born 28 October 1859, died 29 December 1882. (She was Maggie Eakins and had a daughter Ethel Dial who married Mr. Tucker.)

Margaret B. Dial, wife (3) of James Dial, born 1867, died 1927. (Daughter of Jefferson Boyd.)

Parks Oliver Key, born 25 January 1852, died 26 October 1929. (He was related to the Keys who married Hoppers and Boyds; he was a crippled person and lived with Mr. Sem Sledge.)

Ella Key McCain 1854 - 1926 (She was the wife of George W. McCain and sister of Parks Key.)

George W. McCain, born 1849, died 1932. (Husband of Ella Key McCain.)

Susan E. Plott, born 23 March 1895, died 19 November 1947. (She was the daughter of Jacobus Jeremiah and Marietta or Mary Etta (Prestwood) Dial, and the wife of James L. Plott.)

James L. Plott, Jr., born in Aliceville 7 June 1890, died 15 December 1947. (He was the son of James L. Plott of Aliceville, and the husband of Susan Elizabeth "S. E." (Dial) Plott. Children of this union are: Walter who married Catherine Shelby, daughter of E. B. and Tamsy Hannah (Weathers) Shelby, and have children Eugene born 4 July 1950, and Anthony Allen born 24 December 1959. Other children of E. B. and Tamsy

Hannah Shelby are Helen Ruth, Dorothy Jean, Nina Mae and Marcus Eugene. E. B. Shelby's parents were Joseph Alexander and Anna G. Tartt (see Old Side Cemetery records). The Shelbys are descended from Moses Shelby and wife Mary Anna Knox, and on the maternal side from Eli and Margaret (Alcorn) Alexander. Margaret Alcorn was born in Ireland 1782, the daughter of Jeremiah and Rebecca Alcorn. Catherine Plott, sister of Walter Plott, married Ed Baggett, Martha Sue Plott is not married, and Jimmie Lee, or James L. Plott III is not married, and lives in the old home near Payneville.

Margaret Ann, infant daughter of Susan E. and James L. Plott, 19 March 1930.

Henderson Dial, born 14 January 1918, died 3 November 1951. (He was the son of William R. and Mamie Florence (Henderson) Dial; he married Geneva Powell and they had one daughter, Barbara.)

Geneva Powell Dial, born 21 November 1925, died 20 July 1950. (She was the wife of Henderson Dial.)

William R. Dial, born 8 January 1880, died 2 August 1947. (He was the son of Jacobus Jeremiah and Mary Eleanor or Etta (Prestwood) Dial, and grandson of James P. and Catherine (Danner) Dial, great grandson of Jeremiah III and Summer (---) Dial, and great great grandson of John Revolutionary soldier and Mary Dial, and great great great grandson of Jeremiah Dial, Revolutionary Patriot and immigrant. William R. Dial married Mamie Florence Henderson of Preston, Mississippi (living in 1960), descended from Thomas Henderson who came to Jamestown 1607. Her grandfather was Lindsey Henderson who first settled in Alabama and then went to Mississippi, he married and had a son Robert Wilson Henderson who married Queen Victoria Callicoat - their daughter Mamie Florence married William R. Dial and had children William Hodges Dial who was born 9 September 1905, married Clara Bell Buchanan and became parents of Florence (Kay) Chaworth Dial and William Buchanan (Buck) Dial; Lindsey Winyard Dial married a distant cousin, Inez Hopper, descended from Sally (Dial) and Hugh Hopper (Sally and Jennett or Jane (Dial) Boyd were sisters), Winyard and Inez are parents of Lindsey Winyard, John William and Larry Hugh Dial; Henderson Dial is buried in this cemetery.)

Headley Davis husband of Mary J. (Dial), born 30 June 1834, died 14 July 1907. (They had no children but reared Susan E. (Davis) Boyd after the death of her parents. Headley Davis was the brother of William R. Davis.)

Mary J. Davis, wife of Headley Davis, born 16 April 1848, died 13 July 1930.

George H. Dial, son of James and Maggie Dial born 26 January 1883, died 27 December 1883.

George H. Dial, born 14 May 1867, died in Tyler, Texas, ----. (R. J. Dial's brother.)

James P. Dial, born 8 August 1820, died 20 March 1870 (the mortuary Census shows a different date for his death - He was the son of Jeremiah Dial III and his wife Summer (---) Dial. -- I have an idea that Summer Dial was Summer Hopper prior to her marriage as there was a Summer (Hopper) Spinks who lived at Payneville at the same time that Summer (--) Dial lived there; she was an aunt of Rebecca (Hopper) Boyd. Among some old papers belonging to Lizzelle Nixon, deceased, she had a notation that John Spinks, the son of Summer (Hopper) Spinks was a Confederate soldier from Payneville, and stated that "aunt Summer (Hopper) Spinks was an aunt of grandmother Boyd," that made her a sister of William and Hugh Hopper. James P. Dial made his will 7 September 1863 and left everything to his wife Catherine Danner Dial. It was probated 8 August 1870 and the estate was settled in 1873 and the following children named in the citation: Josephine, Robert, Jake (or Jacobus Jeremiah), George, James, Susan and Margaret Dial, and the widow Catherine.)

Catherine G. Dial, born 15 January 1826, died 16 June 1905. (She was the daughter of Jacob G. Danner and wife Mary (Boyd) - see their gravestone records.)

Lexena Elizabeth Rigdon, born 27 January 1846, died --, (daughter of Jacobus Jeremiah Dial.)

Miss Jo Dial, born 11 January 1853, died 20 February 1930. (Sister of Lexena Dial Rigdon.)

J. G. Danner, born 15 March 1871, died 2 September 1913. (Father of Grace Dial, wife of Robert Jeff Dial - See Jacob G. Danner and Elizabeth (Boyd) Danner for relationship between Grace and Robert Jeff.)

Eula Danner, born 19 June 1875, was the daughter of John James Boyd and his wife Lyde (or Liza) Hopper, the sister of "Uncle Jim Hopper" who is buried in this cemetery. Eula Boyd married J. G. Danner who was a grandson of John and Jennett (Dial) Boyd.)

Hugh G. Danner, born 27 May 1834, died 26 April 1927. (He was the son of Jacob G. and Elizabeth (Boyd) Danner.)

Joe M. Boyd, born 10 August 1839 died 3 March 1877. (Joel Marion Boyd was son of Matthew H. Boyd - see his record in this cemetery - Joel Marion married 1860 in Kemper County, Mississippi to Queen Victoria Davenport (Kemper County Court House burned so could not get exact marriage date) who was born 11 November 1844 in Marengo County, Alabama, died 18 December 1917, daughter of Benj. Franklin and Jane P. Davenport. Joel M. and Victoria Boyd became parents of (1) Thomas Marshall Boyd born 5 February 1865 died 15 December 1948 married Cornelia Ann Bailey born 3 May 1870 and died 16 October 1924. They were parents of (a)

Stella Alda Boyd born 9 January 1881 and married Andrew Lee Ramsey, they are parents of Stella Beatrice born 4 December 1911 and married L. C. English and are parents of Malcolm Lewis English born 26 January 1933; and Madelyn Frances born 21 February 1934 and married Mr. Bond of Hattiesburgh. (b) Adelia Boyd born 22 January 1891 - still living - married Walter Earl Rogers of Porterville, Mississippi, he died 5 February 1950, they became parents of Frederick Marshall born 30 March 1916 and married RoSelle Turner born 28 January 1919, daughter of RoSelle (Kirkpatrick) born 1895 and William Durden Turner born 1888. Fred and RoSelle Rogers are parents of Frederick Marshall Rogers, Jr., born 11 September 1946, Walter Turner Rogers born 4 July 1949 and William Turner Rogers born 24 June 1952. Eugene Willard Rogers, also son of Adelia and Walter E. Rogers, was born 7 June 1918 and married 10 December 1947 Ethel Eleanor Suto - children of this union are Thomas Boyd Rogers born 17 September 1948, Jon William Rogers born 9 April 1951, Mary Dianne Rogers born 4 December 1952 and Robert Allen Rogers born 25 April 1955. Howard Rogers, the third son of W. E. and Adelia (Boyd) Rogers, is unmarried and lives at home with his mother. (c) Laura Ethel Boyd was born 24 February 1893, died 1894. (d) Nona Boyd born 26 September 1895 - still living - married (1) Mr. Graham and had a daughter Willie Mae Graham born 14 December 1916 married (2) 29 May 1958 to Keith Simpson. Willie Mae had a daughter, Terry born 1940, by a former marriage. Nona Boyd married (2) on 11 March 1939 to Harold Marchant born 31 July 1878 - they live in St. Louis. (e) Cervera Boyd born 30 January 1895 (living in 1960) married Ernest Graham. (f) Jaunita Boyd born 5 February 1900 (living in 1960) married Leon J. Hudnall of Porterville, Mississippi. No issue. The other children of Thomas Marshall and his wife Cornelia Ann (Bailey) were Laura Jane, Ida Florence, James Matthew and Stella.)

E. G. Danner born 1842 - died 1895. Next to this were two graves with inscriptions illegible.

******

Mary A. Davis, daughter of Jacob and Elizabeth (Boyd) Danner, born 3 August 1835, died 27 January 1861,' married 29 October 1857 and became the parents of Susan E. Davis - see Susan E. Boyd gravestone in this cemetery.)

******

Robert Getson Danner, son of Jacob and Elizabeth (Boyd) Danner, died 6 February 1858, aged 15 years.

******

Jacob Getson Danner, born in Union District, South Carolina, 11 December 1798, died 1 March 1856. (He married Elizabeth Boyd, daughter of John and Jennett (Dial) Boyd 28 March 1825. They had children Thomas Danner, Jane Danner born 1830 married Jonathan Lancaster, Hugh Getson Danner born 1834 died 1927, married Ellen Davis sister of W. R. Davis - see Davis Cemetery records -- Mary Amelia Danner born 1835 married W. R. Davis; Sara E. who married John Hopper; Robert Getson who died before the estate was settled; Leonidas; Catherine who married James P. Dial; and Eliza who married George H. Key brother Eliza Amanda Key who married Mathew H. Boyd who was uncle of Eliza Danner, and brother of Sara P. Key who married William Hopper, and uncle of Rebecca Hopper who married Robert Boyd. Estate settlement is in Orphans' Minute Book 9, pages 47, 48 and 538. The children of Jane Danner and Jonathan Lancaster were William Thomas born 1849 died 1923, married Anna Swain; Benjamin born 1851 married Laura Swain; James J. was born 1853; Lewis J. was born 1855; Mary Virginia was born 1857; John A., was born 1859; Sallie was born 1861. Jonathan Lancaster, Confederate soldier, died of small pox in camp during the War Between the States.

******

Elizabeth G. consort of J. G. Danner, born 1810 died 1873. (The stone has been broken and mended so part of the dates could not be read. She was the daughter of John and Jennett (Dial) Boyd - see John Boyd records.)

******

D. A. F., daughter of Joel and Victoria Boyd, born 1870 and died 1871.

******

Stella R., daughter of Joel M. and Victoria Boyd, born 1875 and died 1881.

******

Infant son of James and Bettie (McGowen) Dial, born and died 23 April 1907.

******

James Dial, born 7 November 1877 (living 1960), double stone with his wife, Bettie. Bettie McGowen Dial, born 2 October 1876 and died 26 September 1955. (Wife of James Dial). They are parents of (1) Robert Jeff Dial who married Grace Danner (see Eula Danner record), and had children: (a) Mildren who married J. M. Dearman and they have children Constance Sue, Mary Faith and John Andrew; (b) Mary Douglas married J. O. Gentry and they have children Patricia and Scarlett; (c) Ruby Helen married L. L. Fuller; (d) Bryant married Mary Lou Long and they have Gail, Bob Bryant and Tommie; (e) Jake married Mildred Gordy and they have children Marilyn and Marshall; (f) Thelma married Jim Hutcherson and they have Nanette and Kenneth; (g) Betty Jean married James Chandler and they have James Allen and Earl; (h) Shirley married Ellis Coleman and they have Harlan Kent; (i) Janice married H. B. Rozelle and they have one child Melanie; (j) Jim married Margie Simpson and they have children Lynn and Ann; (k) Joe is not married and (m) Annie Kate is deceased. (2) W. Jake Dial married Alline Hopper, the daughter of John Allen Hopper and wife Nannie Katherine (Barfield) and granddaughter of William Albert who was the son of John Hopper who is buried in this cemetery. Jake and Alline are the parents of (a) Billie Dial who married Ernestine or "Teenie" Harry and became parents of three daughters Fay, Lynda and Sandra; (b) Jim Allen Dial who married Bettie Bell Aust - see Conde Boyd record under Austin A. Boyd - and they have children Jim and Lee. (3) Vivian McLean married Mr. Edmonds and they have children Bettie Frances who married Lee Davis, Ruth Ann married Jimmie Stone, and a son who is "Junior". (4) Pearlie Mae Dial married (1) Ed Dollar and (2) John Darling. (5) Ouida Ruth Dial married G. A. Hyngue, they have a daughter Ouida Mae who married Vester Yeats and are parents of a son Gregory; (6) Clyde Dial married Lucile Harris, their daughter Eddie Mae Dial married Jeff Stokes, (7) Clyde E. Dial and (8) Claude E. Dial are twins.

******

Clarence E. Dial, born 9 July 1885, died 19 June 1953. (He was the son of Jacobus and Mary Etta or Marietta (Prestwood) Dial and married Betsy Thomas. They were parents of: Robert Mitchell who married Lucile Brayer and have children David Mitchell and Thomas Allen; Bessie married D. B. Love and they are parents of Samuel and Lowery; Nila Nell married Francis Hopper and they have Ruby Ann and Frank; Mary Helen married (1) Turner McLean and they had Turner and Bobbie, (2) Marvin Ruehl; Dorothy Jean married Herman Brown - see Boney Cemetery record for Cherry - and are parents of Alfred; Annie married Carl A. Vollrath and they have Mary Carol; Irma married J. D. Herndon and they have Jeanette and J. D. Jr.; Grady married Margie B. Aust and they have children Steve and Randy; Fred married Dorothy Jean Simmons and they have Betsy, Doris and Fred; Oscar married Virgine Clark and they have children Judie and Susan.

******

Betsy Dial, born 15 May 1886, died 26 October 1957. (She was the wife of Clarence E. Dial and daughter of Ed and Augusta Thomas.)

******

Irma Dial (date illegible) -- By this grave was another with inscription illegible.

******

Eva, daughter of Clarence and Betsy Dial, born 9 October 1911, died 23 January 1931.

******

Ike David, son of J. W. and Nettie Hopper, born 28 September 1902, died 11 October 1904.

******

Mary Etta Dial, born 21 November 1854 and died 1 November 1927. (She was the wife of Jacobus Jeremiah Dial and the daughter of John and Mary M. (Dabney) Prestwood. John Prestwood was the son of Austin and Mary (Boyd) Prestwood. Mary Boyd was the daughter of John and Mary (Dial) Boyd. Mary Etta Prestwood had brothers and sisters Susan E. who married Jesse R. Brown, Nancy Jane who married J. M. Williams, Alabama who married Bryant Richardson in Texas, John Duncan and Austin G.)

******

Dr. W. P. Kelley, died 25 January 18-7, aged 56 years, 1 month and 20 days. (He was the husband of Sallie Eakins.)

******

J. J. Boyd, Co. A-7 Alabama Cav. C.S.A., born 3 August 1837 died 19 October 1915. (He married Elida Frances Hopper who became the grandparents of Grace Danner who married Robert Jeff Dial - see Eula Danner record. J. J. or John James - called John Jeames - was the son of Matthew H. Boyd who is buried in an unmarked grave by the side of John James. 5 July 1860 John James married Elida Frances Hopper (also called Eliza Francis) who was a sister of Rebecca Hopper who married Robert Boyd - Elida Frances Hopper and John Hopper, forebear of Alline Hopper Dial, were probably first cousins. John James Boyd was constable in his beat in 1866.)

****

J. J. Dial, Born 13 November 1850, died 25 September 1928. (He was Jacobus Jeremiah Dial who was named for his two grandfathers, Jacob Danner and Jeremiah Dila III. He was the son of Catherine (Danner) and James P. Dial; he married Marietta or Mary Etta Prestwood 7 December 1876 and had children William R. who is buried in this cemetery; Clarence also buried here; James still living -see his descendants under Bettie McGowen gravestone record; Annie who married Will Hailey and moved to Texas, they are parents of four daughters Mary Clifton, Catherine, Christine and Doris all of whom are married; Kate married Herbert Hopper of DeKalb Mississippi and they are parents of three daughters, viz: Mrs. McRae, Mrs. Brown and Mrs. Stuckett; Cliff born 14

August 1887 died 28 April 1959 and were parents of William Jeremiah Dial who was born and died in 1915, and Velera who married Jake Cherry - see Boney Cemetery records for this line - and had children Bessie Ann Cherry who married James Madison Briggs and have children Annie Laurie, Dottie Sue, and James Edgar; Sue Cherry married Oddie Tubberville; Mamie Clifton Cherry married John H. Lunceford. Annie (Lavender), widow of Cliff is the daughter of William H. and Georgie Lavender, (daughter of Sara V. Hopper and Erasmus Thomas) and granddaughter of W. Urias Lavender who was the son of David S. Lavender who was the son of Robert S. Lavender, the son of Hugh and Rebecca (Smith) Lavender - see Bethel Cemetery records; Susan E. Dial married James L. Plott - see their gravestone records in this cemetery.

******

John Prestwood, born 15 January 1927, died 1 June 1952. (Son of Mary (Boyd) and Austin Prestwood. See Marietta or Mary Etta Prestwood Dial gravestone for John's record.)

******

Thomas Davenport, born 19 February 1856, died 20 April 1881.

******

Cora Davenport, daughter of Jefferson and S. M. Boyd, born 21 July 1853, died 23 September 1882.

******

C. Virginia Boyd, wife of Jefferson Boyd, born 15 June 1846, died 10 February 1885. (She was the wife (2) of Jefferson Boyd and became the mother of Samuel Tilden Boyd still living in 1960 - see Jefferson Boyd records. C. Virginia is said to have been a Godfrey who was living in Arkansas when she married but had once lived in Sumter County.)

******

Sara M. Boyd, wife (1) of Jefferson Boyd, born 17 July 1819, died 7 October 1865. (See Jefferson Boyd for their children.)

******

Uncle Jim Hopper, died 1897, aged 80 years.

******

John Hopper, died 1857, aged 47 years, 7 months, 14 days. (He was the grandfather of Alline (Hopper) Dial, wife of W. Jake Dial and either an uncle or cousin of D. J. M. Hopper.)

******

D. J. M. Hopper, husband of S. E. Hopper, born 1835 and died 1885. (According to a scrap of paper in the belongings of Lizzelle Nixon, D. J. M. Hopper was born 16 December 1835, the son of William and Sarah Peavey (Key) Hopper, and was a brother of Lizzelle Nixon's grandmother, Revecca Hopper who married Robert Boyd.)

******

Elizabeth, wife of D. J. M. Hopper, born in Sumter County, Alabama in 1839, died in Kemper County, Mississippi in 1897.

******

Cornelia B. daughter of D. J. M. and S. E. Hopper -- 1879 - 1883.

******

Allen C. Powe, Company C, Jeff Davis Legion, Mississippi Cav. C.S.A. (See Powe records.)

******

Willie Ann Hopper, born 14 February 1865, died 15 June 1907.

******

Susan Amelia Hopper, wife of Harvey P. Thompson, 1870 - 1899. (Harvey P. Thompson married (2) Jennie Hopper, sister to Susan Amelia. She is still living 1960).

******

Dr. Harvey P. Thompson, born 6 November 1858, died 11 October 1909. (He married two Hopper sisters - see above - He and his first wife had a daughter, Gennn who married I. D. Gordy and their daughter, Mildred, married Jake Dial the son of Robert Jeff and Grace Dial.)

******

Roddie, wife of J. O. Boyd, born 10 February 1883, died 10 April 1908.

******

James O. Boyd, born 13 May 1885, died 17 February 1917. (He was killed by Bob Hopper.)

******

Roddie Estell, daughter of J. O. and Roddie Boyd, born 1915 died 1917.

******

James A. Hopper, born in Greene County, Alabama, 9 December 1833, died 23 December 1869 (?). (He was the son of William and Sara Peavy (Key) Hopper and the brother of Rebecca Hopper who married Robert Boyd. The other brothers and sisters of Rebecca (Boyd) Hopper and James A. Hopper were John D. M. Hopper born 1835, Mary E. Hopper born 1838, Eliza (or Elida) F. Hopper, Sara V. Hopper (Sallie), born 1843, William Hopper born 1845, Susan Hopper and Georgie A. Hopper born 1850.)

******

Melvin S. Boyd, born and died 8 June 1950.

******

Mother: **Maggie Dial Hopper**, born 5 March 1863, died 21 August 1941.

******

Father: **Eli Hugh Hopper**, born 8 October 1853, died 24 August 1928.

******

(11) **Robert Boyd**, born 1823 in Alabama (see 1850 census) and died at Camp Chase, Ohio during the War Between the States. He is not buried in this cemetery. He married Rebecca Ann Hopper 16 October 1849. Rebecca Ann Hopper was the niece of Eliza Amanda Key who married Matthew H. Boyd, a brother of Robert Boyd, and she (Rebecca Ann) was the daughter of Sarah Peavey (Key) and William Hopper. Sara Peavey Key's parents were Rebecca (Grizzele) and James Key born 1788; James Key's parents were Morning, (--) born 12 August 1764 and William Key born 2 October 1759; William Key's parents were Nancy (Bibb) and Martin Key. Rebecca Ann (Hopper) Boyd's parents were, as stated before, were Sara Peavey (Key) and William Hopper; William's father was the son of John Hopper, said to have been a brother of Hugh Hopper who married Sallie Dial, the sister of Jenett (Dial) Boyd. (See Lavender record in Bethel Cemetery.) Rebecca Ann Hopper and Robert Boyd were married in Greene County, Alabama 16 October 1849 and became parents of (1) William Ellery Boyd born 4 February 1851 - see his gravestone record in this cemetery; (2) Ella Cornelia Boyd born 24 February 1853 and died 2 January 1916, in Miss. She married John E. Boyd and were parents of (a) Lena born 1870, married Mr. McConnico, (b) Maud born 1874, married Mr. Lyon; (c) William Edward born 1880; (d) Ella May born 1883; (e) Adah born 1871, (f) Susie Rebecca born 1878 and Robert Wilson born 1878; (3) James Jefferson (Red Head Jeff) born 1864, married a Miss Greenlee and is

buried in this cemetery. They had children: Mabel, Lillian, Jesse, Robt. Hugh, Annie May. (4) Alice married J. W. Nixon (see record under "Nixon".)

******

(3) **W. E. Boyd**, born 4 February 1853, died 30 March 1877. (William Ellery Boyd was son of Rebecca (Hopper) and Robert Boyd. He married Alice Rhyne and had one daughter who married a Mr. Vick and lived in Hattiesburg, Mississippi.)

******

(4) **Alice Boyd Nixon**, born 11 May 1859, died October 1939, (She was the daughter of Rebecca Ann (Hopper) and Robert Boyd, and married J. W. Nixon 2 December 1879. -- See Robert Boyd record - and J. W. Nixon record in this cemetery.)

******

J. W. Nixon, born 16 November 1858, died 31 December 1934. (John William Nixon was the husband of Alice (Boud) Nixon and the husband of Hester (Howard) and James M. Nixon; the parents of Hester Howard were Hulda (McDaniel) and Captain John Howard. John William Nixon was born near Wilmington, North Carolina and belonged to Scotts Hill Methodist Church; he came to Sumter County when he was about 13 years of age --his relatives, the McDaniels had already come to Sumter County, - see Sumterville Methodist Cemetery rrcords. John William and Alice Boyd Nixon became parents of: (a) J. W. Nixon married Ella Patton 29 December 1908; (b) Annie Vera Nixon born 5 February 1880 married Jim Mitchell of Bluff Port and had children: Aubrey who married Ruth Mitchen and had 3 girls; Merlin married Eva May and had children; Royce married and had children Christin and Lydia; Onis married and had a boy and a girl; Doris married and had three children; Avinelle married a Breitling, (c) Robert Bascomb Nixon born 30 June 1882, married Missouri Grimes and had children Bascome Nixon married a Miss Marlow of Demopolis and had children; and Grimes Nixon married and has children; (d) Lizzelle Nixon born 16 February 1886 and died September 1958; (e) James Moreland Nixon born 14 September 1889, married Helen Anderson and had children: Moreland Jr., who married Kitty Pope and became parents of Dianne and Lynda; and a daughter Alice who married Bill Carroll and had Billie and Jimmie; (f) Allie Bell Nixon born 3 January 1892 married (1) Mr. Angle and had daughter Helen (2) John Craddock and had children: John, Juliette, Bascomb, Jimmie, Edward and Alice - most of this family lives in Mobile; (g) Percy Nixon born 9 August 1894 married Nettie Almon and had children: Jo who married Joseph Reed of Coatopa, Alabama and had children Jaryll, Donner, Karen and Melner; John William (Billy) Nixon married Carol Hush and have children Debora and John; Percy Nixon Jr., married Sara Farmer and they have children Susanna and Don; (h) Leslie Creed Nixon born 5 February 1897 married Edna Ratcliff and had children Marjorie who married Frank Campbell and they are parents of Marsha,

Frances and Sandra; Leslie (Bud) Nixon Jr., married Alleen Lang daughter of Hunter Lang buried at Bethel Cemetery, and they have children Louise and Peggy. Alleen and Bud are related as she is descended from David Montgomery Dial and his wife Jeannett (Spence) Dial; and Bud is descended from John and Jenett (Dial) Boyd, and aunt of David Montgomery Dial. (i) Leland Jefferson Nixon born 5 February 1897 (twin of Leslie's) married Hermie Lou Boyd, the daughter of Mary (Key) and Jeff Boyd --see Central Cemetery records - so Leland and Hermie Lou are related through the Boyds, the Keys and the Dials: they have children Pete who married Miss Powell of York and had one child Cathy Jean; Jean Nixon married and they live in Texas; Harry Nixon is unmarried. (j) Cameron B. Nixon Born 20 December 1899 married Valley Maud Ratcliff, sister of Edna who married Leslie Nixon, and had three children: Breezie who married Marie Pritchard and had children Rose Marie, James and Cameron; Carolyn Nixon married Bob Dillard - no issue; Annette Nixon married Bill Durant and they are parents of Joy, Jan and Angeline.

(4) **Sara** (Not buried here), daughter of John and Jennett or Jane (Dial) Boyd, married Thomas J. George 24 July 1835. They had at least one daughter, Josephine who married Allen Powe, son of William Henry Pegues Powe and his wife Sara Harry Chapman - Allen's sister married James Marion Boyd and a sister married Newton Prestwood. Josephine had children: Richard, Julia, Alice, William and Charles.

(5) **Rosannah** (Not buried here) daughter of John and Jennett or Jane (Dial) Boyd, married (1) James Hodges and had children Joe who married Julia ----, Sudie who married a Mr. Armour and a baby who died at birth. Sudie married (2) Mr. Festervan - had sons, Bus and Joe. Julia ---- and Joe Hodges had children: Jerusha, Leona who married Floyd Daniel, Hoyt, Fannie died young, Lilly May, Mont died young and Delmar called Drew. Rosannah married (2) William Grey Thomas -- see Thomas Cemetery records. Rosannah died and was buried near Camden, Arkansas.

CHAPTER IV

EMELLE

LIBERTY CHURCH AND BONEY CEMETERY

BONEY CEMETERY is located about two and one half miles due west of the Village of Emelle, Alabama. It is really on the edge of Township 21 Section 36 Range 4 West. However, because so many of those who sleep there lived in Township 20, we decided to include it in the records of that township.

At one time old Liberty Primitive Baptist Church stood at the edge of this burial ground. Mr. Richard Newton and Mr. Wimbeck Boney were two of its founders. Later on, after the death of Mr. Boney, others came into possession of his lands. A dispute arose over the location of the cemetery. The new land owner claimed the cemetery was on his land instead of the land across the road where it was supposed to be; so he cut the timber from the cemetery and church grounds. A law suit followed. In the meantime one of the leading citizens in the suit was brought before the church with a charge of gambling and he was finally turned out of the church. The community took sides in the "rippet" which had now progressed to a heated pace, -- so heated till the church went up in flames.

The Liberty Baptist Association helped the community build another church but instead of putting it back at the old location, it was built near the station, Ramsey, on the Gainesville-Narkeeta Rail Road. By that time families of other denominations had moved into the community and some of the Primitive Baptists had moved away. When a vote was taken the "old timers" found to their utter consternation that the Methodists had out voted them, so the new church became Methodist. Many Baptists removed their letters to the Baptist Church at Sumterville and buried their dead at Old Side Cemetery.

Beginning at this time the cemetery was no longer called Liberty Church Graveyard but gradually became known as Boney Cemetery in honor of the man who helped organize the church. Many years later, Ripley in "Believe It Or Not", said this burying ground was the only one in the world that was called "Boney Cemetery".

RAMSEY STATION (NOW EMELLE)

The community of the present Emelle was known as Liberty Church community in the earliest settling of this part of Township 20 Range 3 West, and a little later became known as Ramsey Station when the Gainesville-Narkeeta Rail Road was built.

The first settlers voted at Sumterville but later two voting places were established in Beat 12: one at Sumterville and one at Ramsey Station. A great deal of the trading of the pioneer families in this section was done at Sumterville. The cotton was shipped from Gainesville, however. I have heard the second generation from those pioneers say that in the fall of the year droves of turkeys were driven to Gainesville to be shipped to Mobile.

There was no academy at old Ramsey but the children were educated elsewhere after getting what education they could at Professor Burwell's school at Bethel which was about half way between Ramsey and Sumterville. Some of the families had governesses or tutors for their children and for those children of their neighbors. Later on, after public schools were established, when John Anthony Winston was Governor of Alabama, Ramsey had a small school from which several men went forth into the world and made high marks for themselves. This section of the township was different from the section around Sumterville as it is more rolling or of a flat nature. It, too, was covered with hard wood trees interspersed with switch cane which grew ten feet tall on high land and about twenty feet tall in creek bottoms.

Mrs. Vincent Anderson has been quoted as saying, "We came to Sumter County when my Catina was a baby, and this country was a howling wilderness." Her Catina was one of twins and a drunken Indian tried to kill them because they thought it was bad luck to have twins.

After the forests were cleared and the cane cut, strawberries sprang up around the edge of the forests. They said that the cows came home at night with their udders stained red from the juice of the berries. This region was the natural habitat for wild pigeons. It has been said by old timers that in time of their migration that they would black out the sun in their flight.

William Thomas Simms had the first store at old Ramsey, Captain Winston and William Maurice (Reuben) Thomas were partners for a number of years in the mercantile business. Squire Folsom, a little later, opened a third store, all of which were built around the station at the rail road. The station was called Ramsey Station for Mr. A. K. Ramsey, a promoter of the rail road, but he lived about one and one half miles west of the station.

In 1872 the mail came from Livingston by star route and William T. Simms was the first post master. (See the 1872 file of Livingston Journal.) T. L. Jenkins was the next post master, he was followed by John T. Simms who kept the office for the next three decades or until just before his death.

The 1850 census shows seven slaves in this county were born in Africa. Most of them belonged to a man by the name of Poole who bought them from a man by the name of Jones in North Carolina. The mother was Betty and one of her daughters was named Elsie. Betty became civilized enough to do real well, but Elsie would have none of the white man's ways. She would not wear clothes provided for her, nor would she eat the fare of the other slaves, she wanted uncooked food. She would not work in the fields with the other women but liked to clear the forests. At night time she would sleep under the trees disdaining the comforts of a dwelling and a bed. She died some time in the seventies when her nephew, Ors Jones (they took the name of the former master when emancipated) was about 25 years old. Ors lived to be about 103 years old and he told me many things about his grandmother Betty and his aunt Elsie. These "Jones" Negroes were powerfully built. Henry could pick up a bale of cotton and walk off with it. One peculiar thing about them was as a family they did not believe in God; most Negroes are very religious. Ors said during the Reconstruction period that he lived on the Trimble place and that a white woman by the name of Sally McCarty came there from the North and taught the Negroes. She boarded with a Negro named John Inge. She never mixed with the white people. A man by the name of Poe did the same thing about three miles west of Ramsey.

The second generation of the "landed gentry" of this section was noted for their gambling, a trait said to have been prevalent among the gentlemen of the Black Belt. They bet on anything and everything. Mr. Frank Watson, Mr. Trimble and Mr. Walter Kerr were fording Bodka Creek when the horse Mr. Trimble was riding got from under him. As he could not swim he was about to drown. Mr. Watson bet Mr. Kerr a dollar that "Trim" would not make it and Mr. Kerr took the bet. Mr. Kerr called, "Come on Trim, You can make it." Mr. Watson yelled, "Give up, Trim, you'll never make it."

During the War Between the States much corn was raised in this part of the county. Log bins were built along the rail road and the corn stored until it could be picked up by the trains and taken to mills to be ground into meal for the Confederacy. Only foraging Union soldiers entered this county but the grain was protected by the home guards. Once a small band of these foragers was reported to be around the bend of the road from the John R. Jackson place. He was home on furlough when a runner told him of the soldiers being in his community. He knew if they found him they would take him prisoner. His granddaughter, Isaphena (Jackson) Joiner, told me he ran around the house looking for a place to hide. The most likely place was the bee hives which were alive with bees. He scraped the bees out of one of them and into the hive he crawled. She said, "The bees were a-humming and the Yanks were a-coming but they could not find Grandpap."

Even tho this section did not see any action during the war, the people were plenty plagued by the Carpetbaggers and a Scallywag during Reconstruction Days. Billings, a lawyer from the North, was the most prominent Carpetbagger around Ramsey. His collaborator (or Quisling, as he would be called today) was Dr. Choutteau who lived in sight of Ramsey Station. Their plan was to steal the wealth of the country through the Negro vote. They incited the Negroes against the whites, promising them 40 acres of land, a mule and their franchise to side with them against the whites. They held big meetings, sometimes attended by as many as a thousand "Freedmen". The Negroes took to the meetings their buckets and sacks in which, they hoped to be able, to take home their franchise.

The Livingston Journal of 9 October 1868 gives a distorted account of the stabbing of Mr. Bryant Richardson, Jr. (he married Mary Sara Grice, niece of Mr. William T. Simms) who was disemboweled by the Negro, Enoch Brown, with a butcher knife which he took from Mr. Richardson's kitchen. The paper said Enoch was apprehended by a couple of Negroes and was turned over to the authorities. This was told to soothe a rabid unrest in the county. Anyway in the search for Enoch he was traced to Choutteau's home where he was asked to surrender. Yankee Ben, a Negro body guard of Choutteau's was mistaken for Enoch. Yankee Ben was so scared he ran up the chimney and jumped to the ground and did not stop running when called to. He was shot. This infuriated the Carpetbaggers and the Scallywags and they would not let an inquest by authorities be made. The body lay where it fell, for several days, during which time hundreds of armed Freedmen milled around. Later the doctor moved to Livingston where Dr. John Bailey Browning (native of Ramsey and a cousin of Catina Anderson) was killed by another body guard of Choutteau's. The Carpetbagger, Billings, was killed; the Negroes quieted down and peace reigned where terror once strode rough shod. It was suggested at the time to use the following epitaph on Billings' gravestone:

> "Pause, gentle reader, lightly tread!
> For God's sake let him lie;
> We live in peace since he is dead
> But Hell is in a fry."

The wood burning engine was taken off the Gainesville-Narkeeta Rail Road after the war and the cars were drawn by mules. One of the most famous mules was named Morgan and was said to be gray. When the engines were used the train stopped at Ramsey Station to take on water from the "Gee well"; a well which never went dry but would fill up to the top over night after the engine had quenched its thirst. William Maurice (Reuben) Thomas, who married Narcissa Anderson, had a steam mill and gin near the well. He sent one of his colored workers to fire up the engine and put water in the boiler. He did it in just that order and when he let the water into the hot boiler it blew everything sky high, killing five persons, one of whom was never found as he must have been blown to bits. The back of Marcus Ramsey's head was taken off and the cavity was filled with shelled corn. A long splinter was thrust through another Negroe's neck between the windpipe and the spine the splinter showing on both sides of the neck. Mr. Asa Simms, son of William Thomas Simms, pulled the splinter from the man's neck and applied kerosene. The Negro lived to a ripe old age.

Old Ramsey Station gave up the ghost and died when the Alabama, Tennessee and Northern Rail Road was built through this section about 1910/12. Mr. Ed Dial gave the railroad a number of lots in the new town and other consideration in building the depot if the town were named for a daughter, Emelle Dial. She was named for two of her aunts, Emma and Ella Dial. The two merchants at Ramsey at the time, were John T. Simms and T. L. Jenkins who picked up, lock stock and barrel, and moved to the new town a mile away. J. W. Burton put up a store, someone opened a drug store. Dr. Swain, physician who married Olive Jenkins, did a thriving practice for miles around.

Today we have paved roads in all directions; people live in modern homes with all the conveniences of the day. The fields are no longer cultivated but white face cattle (they do not dip snuff, nor do they have to be bonded out of trouble) peacefully graze in pastures which are green most of the year. Today we have sans boll weevil, sans row crops, sans Saturday night cuttings among tenants, sans strife - sans everything except quiet, peace and gracious living.

BONEY CEMETERY
formerly
-Liberty Church Cemetery-
Gravestone Inscriptions

-- A --

1. **Vincent Anderson** died 7 April 1833, in the 34th year of his age. (He lies in an unmarked grave near his wife, Sara (Jenkins) Anderson. The exact date of his death may be seen in the Bible of Brooks H. Davis, a cousin of his, who went to Texas. Court records show that Judge William G. Anderson, also a cousin, ordered the Vincent Anderson estate in Marengo appraised and sold on 24 August 1833. Alexander Anderson and Holland Jenkins the administrators; Mason L. Anderson and Albert G. Anderson securities. Thomas Anderson, E. D. Hester and Anderson Holland to appraise the property in Marengo County, while John E. Anderson, William Bruton and David Warren to appraise the Sumter County property.

Vincent Anderson, so Brooks H. Davis Bible stated, "Died in the triumph of Faith of a better world and exhorted his friends and relatives to try to prepare to meet him in the world where parting is no more." Vincent Anderson left children: John Alexander Anderson, Melvira Anderson, William S. Anderson, Narcissa Anderson and Catina Anderson (her twin brother died an infant.) See other tombstone records for more of the Anderson history.

******

2. **Sara Anderson**, wife of Vincent Anderson, and daughter of J. and S. Jenkins, born 15 July 1801 in Kentucky, and died 24 December 1880. (Upon the death of her husband, Sara Anderson wrote her brother in Springfield, Missouri to send one of his sons to her. He had several sons among whom were Wilford, Winifred, William, Washington, and Dominico. He sent Dominico to Sumter County to look after his sister's estate. When Melvira (see children of Vincent Anderson) grew up, she and her first cousin Dominico Jenkins married 25 January 1844, Wm. T. Simms, security. They bought land in Alabama on the Mississippi State line, and later moved to Kemper County, Mississippi. Their son, Thomas Leonidas, stayed with his grandmother Sara Anderson nearly all his life; and remained in Sumter County for good when his aunts needed him, about the time he was 20 years of age. See T. L. Jenkins gravestone record, and the Thomas records in this cemetery.

******

3. **William S. Anderson**, son of V. and S. Anderson, born 22 May 1833, and died 23 September 1862. (He was born about 6 weeks after the death of his father, Vincent Anderson. William S. Anderson died in the War Between the States. The settlement of his estate is as follows: Book 20 Orphans' Court Records, his sister Narcissa F. Anderson stated in court that William S. Anderson, her brother, died in Mobile, Alabama, while serving in the Confederate Army; his brother John Alexander Anderson, whose home was in DeSota Parish, La., was then serving in the Confederate Army in Arkansas; Melvira, the wife of Dominico Jenkins lived in Kemper County, Mississippi; her sister, Catina Anderson lived in Sumter County, Alabama. So Narcissa F. Anderson was appointed as administrator of the estate, her mother Sara Anderson and her cousin's husband, John Browning, made bond for her, for $25,000. William S. Anderson's brother John Alexander Anderson, married Susan Cherry the daughter of Ezekiel Cherry who was the son of Jared and Sally (Holland) Cherry --Sally Holland was the daughter of John Holland, Revolutionary War soldier. Ezekiel Cherry's grandfather Cherry was Joshua Cherry, also a Revolutionary War soldier. (See Cherry gravestone record in this cemetery.)

John Alexander Anderson's family moved to Kerens, Texas after his death in Kechi, Louisiana in 1878. John Alexander Anderson and his wife, Susan (Cherry) Anderson had three sons: William Harvey, born 1866, Ezekiel V. born 1876 and John Alexander Jr., born 1878. (1) William Harvey married (1) Emma Smith and they had one daughter, Doris who married Luther J. Westbrook and their children are Jack, Luther and Margaret. Wife (2) Vetia McConico and had two children: Eva who married Mr. Walker, no issue; and William Harvey married Laura Lee Kirk and had children Judy and Kirk, (2) Ezekiel V. Anderson married Bertha Williams and had two daughters: Evelyn married Charles Lunceford, no issue and

Velma married Harry Hargrove and had three children: Harvey, Nona and Jack.

(3) John Alexander, also son of John A. and Susan (Cherry) Anderson, married Lucy Berry and had three children: Lucile married Charles E. Reese and had three children Jacqueline who married Richard J. Marshall and had one boy, R. J.; Charles Anderson Reese married Gayle Smith, no issue; John Alexander Anderson III married Helen Hemphill and they have 7 children, viz: Pam, Pat, Peggie, Priscilla, John A. IV and twins Jean and Joan.

******

4. Ann, wife of G. Anderson, born 27 March 1812, died 12 January 1887. (No history. However, the "G." might have been for "Garrison" Anderson.)

-- B --

5. **Wimbeck Boney**, died 25 June 1845, aged 56 years. (He was born in North Carolina ca 1788. His first wife was named Ann (according to signature on deeds.) The 1850 census gives his widow as Nancy, aged 56, born in North Carolina, and in the Boney household, Elizabeth Harper 23 born in Alabama and her daughter Emma age 1 year. (Wimbeck Boney married Nancy Lacy 24 April 1834.) Same census gives Wm. G. Boney as 26, born Alabama, wife Nancy C. 25 born in Alabama and daughter Caroline age 1, born Alabama -- he married Nancy Lacy, daughter of Elisha and Caroline (Anderson) Lacy 11 June 1845. Nancy Boney's nuncupative will, Book 2, page 59, 10 March 1855 and sworn to by A. K. Ramsey and Richard Newton stated her daughter, Elizabeth Harper nor her servant be charged board against the estate, and that son William G. Boney to have her watch.

Wimbeck Boney's land which he patented took in the Choctaw town "Quilby", the largest Indian village in North Sumter.

Orphans' Book 6 p 66 shows the heirs of Wimbeck Boney, viz: (1) Richard, (2) William G., (3) Martha Lacy, wife of William A. Lacy, (4) Elizabeth, wife of James C. Harper (they married 18 June 1846, the father James Harper gave consent), (5) Margaret A. wife of William C. Foster, (6) Kitty J. Hollingsworth formerly Kitty Boney, (7) Susan C. wife of Charles D. McCall. (Most of the children went to Lauderdale County, Mississippi. Kitty Hollingsworth had children: Thomas Richard, Jacob, William Robert and Simons. Martha Lacy had children: Elisha W. and Richard T. (Orphans' Book 7 pages 162 and 164.)

******

6. **Rev. Jared W. Cherry**, son of Joshua and Martha R. Cherry, was born in

Tennessee 26 May 1796 --- stone broken in this place but according to settlement of his estate he died in 1871. (As stated above his father was Joshua Cherry who was born 5 February 1769, enlisted in the Army when he was 17 in Pitt County, North Carolina. The 1840 Census shows Joshua a pensioner living with Jared Cherry in Marengo County, Alabama. Joshua and Martha R. Cherry had several children among whom were Ezekiel, Jared and Robert, Elizabeth and Margaret. The father of Joshua was Jesse whose wife was Julia ---. Jesse's father was John -- John had a brother Samuel whose second wife was Clary--, according to Mrs. Arthur Smith, Yanceyville, N. C., they had a son named Dr. Thomas D. Cherry who married Emily Bell who came to Alabama, too -- John and Samuel's parents were Samuel and Gatsey Llewellyn Cherry, daughter of George Llewellyn. Samuel Sr., died in 1754, his will is in Beaufort County, North Carolina. Samuel who died 1754 was the son of Samuel and Frances Ballentine Cherry of Norfolk, Virginia. Dr. Blake Little's father, Gray Little married Sylvia Cherry, the sister of Samuel and Jesse Cherry -- the Cherrys and Littles were intermarried with the Thigpens who also settled around Warsaw in North Sumter County -- (see volume #2 of Sumter County Pioneers, to be published later.)

Ezekiel Cherry, the oldest son of Joshua Cherry, was born 6 September 1792, and was a soldier in the War of 1812 and became a 2nd Lieut. under command of Col. Wm. Hall and Capt. John Wallace - he enlisted 11 November 1812 - having married Jane Wilson in Sumner County, Tennessee on the 5 November 1812. She was born 24 August 1792. Ezekiel Cherry died 5 December 1854, Mansfield, La., soon after leaving Sumter County, Alabama where he had patented land. -- His daughter Martha K. Cherry and her husband Ezekiel Cherry II, son of her uncle Jared Cherry, lived on this Sumter County land until they removed to La. ca 1860.

Children of Ezekiel and Jane Wilson Cherry were Elizabeth W. Cherry born 1814, Martha K. Cherry born 24 December 1816, (she married her 1st cousin Ezekiel Cherry II, son of Jared and 1st wife, Sallie Holland Cherry), Sara L. Cherry born 1818, William L. Cherry born 1820 and died single, John K. born 1822 died single, Samuel Cherry born 1824 died single, Mary J. born 5 October 1827 was the 2nd wife of her dead sister's husband, Ezekiel Cherry II and is buried in Kerens, Texas, Matilda Cherry born 1829 and died single, Albert A. Cherry born 7 April 1832 married Sarah F. Walker, Ezekiel Cherry Jr., born 1834 died young.

Jared W. Cherry who is buried in this (Boney) Cemetery and brother of above Ezekiel I was born in Sumner County Tennessee (see gravestone for date of birth), married (1) Sally Holland, the dau of John Holland, also a Revolutionary War Soldier, -- (see William Holland and Brooks H. Davis records in this volume) -- Jared W. and Sally Holland Cherry were parents of: Ezekiel, Charlotte, Susan, Cathy and Joshua. The will of John Holland proved in Sumter County, Alabama, names the above children of "my daughter Sally Cherry - Will Book 1 p 253 in 1842. Marengo County records show that Jared and his wife Susan Cherry (wife no. 2) signed receits for money from the Holland Estate to the minor heirs, Joshua and Cathy.

Jared Cherry married (2) Susan Jenkins -- who was the sister of Sara Jenkins Anderson, wife of Vincent Anderson both of whom are also buried in Boney Cemetery. They married in Marengo County, Alabama, 13 October 1827. -- See Susan Cherry's gravestone record in this cemetery--Rev. Jared Cherry removed to Sumter County, Alabama from Marengo County after his father's death. Jared Cherry married (3) to Mrs. Martha Pollard. The Cherry place was what is now known as the Leland Aust place. At Martha's death she left her estate to her step daughter-in-law, Eliza (Parker) Cherry - (see her gravestone record in this cemetery -.)

According to the settlement of Jared Cherry's estate, Orphans' Record Book 29 p 122 Sumter County, 8 August 1871, the following (then living) heirs were named: Martha Cherry, widow, Sumter County, Alabama; William J. Cherry, Sumter County, Ala.; Henry F. Cherry, Sumter County, Alabama; Margaret W. Sanders wife of James L. Sanders, Perry County, Alabama; Lucinda L. Ware, wife of Henry A. Ware, Kemper County, Mississippi; Elizabeth Cherry Sumter County, Alabama; Ezekiel Cherry who resides in Louisiana; Robert L. Cherry who resides in Texas; Joshua Cherry's children who reside in Texas but whose names and addresses we know not; Margaret J. Anderson wife of B. Anderson, and Milton Small, both of whom live in Louisiana, and Mary Campbell over 21 who resides in the State of Florida. (The last three are grandchildren.) The above child, Lucinda Jane Cherry born 28 November 1834 died 22 February 1888, daughter of Jared and Susan Jenkins Cherry, married Henry Allen Ware born 1823, died 1895. Their daughter Sudie born 20 April 1872, died 20 February 1940, married Bunyan R. Brown - all of whom are buried at Lockhart, Mississippi--Children of Sudie (Ware) and B. R. Brown: Ernest Brown born 1887, Herman Brown born 1892 died 1942, Willard Brown born 1898, Sudie May Brown born 1902 married H. Bowles, J. B. Brown born 1909. Ernest and Willard are living and have children. Dr. Brown, daughter of Ernest, is a physician in Meridian, Mississippi. (Ernest Brown Bible Records.)

William J. Cherry is buried at Toomsuba, Mississippi.

Henry F. Cherry, a soldier in the War between the States, married Eliza Parker 11 April 1859. Henry is buried at Biloxi, Mississippi, in the Cemetery for Confederate Soldiers. See Eliza Parker Cherry gravestone record in this cemetery for the Henry Cherry descendants.

Ezekiel Cherry II, son of Jared and his first wife Sallie Holland, married his first cousin, Martha K. Cherry when she was only 13 years of age (see Ezekiel Cherry, son of Joshua); they were the parents of J. W. Cherry born 1838 married Mary Ann Johnson, Susan born 1841 married John Alexander Anderson -- (see Vincent Anderson record in this cemetery) --, John Holland Cherry born 28 August 1846 married Ann Early Johnson, William Fayette Cherry born 2 August 1851 married Willie Johnson, Caroline Cherry born 1843 married Thomas Adams no issue, Margaret Cherry born 1843 married Calvin Scruggs. Miss Willie Fayette Montgomery of Ft. Worth, Texas is a descendant of Ezekiel Cherry.

After the death of Ezekiel (II) Cherry's wife Martha K. he married her sister Mary J., and they became parents of 2 children: Bernard who died an infant, and Kathryn who died single. Martha K. and Mary J. who married Ezekiel II Cherry, were the daughters, as before stated, of Ezekiel I, the uncle of Ezekiel II. Their father patented land in T 21, Ezekiel II and his wife Mary J. sold this land to Mr. Patton in 1859, and removed to Caddo Parish, La., where he later sold some land to John Alexander Anderson. --Book T p 41 Caddo Parish -- of De Sota Parish (John A. Anderson married Susan, the daughter of Ezekiel II and Martha K. Cherry). Ezekiel moved to Kerens, Texas where he died 7 April 1900, and his second wife Mary J. died 9 September 1900 -- see Anderson in this cemetery (Boney).

******

7. **Emma Eliza Cherry**, wife of Henry F. Cherry, born 8 August 1837, died 26 May 1929. (She was Miss Parker daughter of Gilford Parker of Preston Beat, Sumter County, Alabama. She married Henry F. (called Hence) Cherry 11 April 1859 and they were parents of (1) Mary Etta who married Bert Joyner -- see her gravestone record in this cemetery -- (2) Josh who married Dolly Todd and had children: Lida, Wilbur, Nannie, Madie, Ruby - (3) Will who married Minnie Dawkins (See Soule Cemetery Records) and had children: Hugh, Andy, J. D., Gray, Bob (Minister), Mattie, Ola, Emma, Mary K., and Eva - (4) Lee married Mamie Parker and had children: Gray who lives in Mobile, and Jake who married Valera Dial - (see Dial records, Boyd Cemetery.)

******

8. **Caroline**, wife of W. J. Campbell died 3 April 1852, aged 23 years, 5 months, 13 days. (She was the daughter of Jared W. and Susan (Jenkins) Cherry. She left a daughter, Mary J. The 1850 Census of Sumter County shows her in the home of Jared Cherry along with her parents William Campbell, carpenter, age 30 born in Ky., Caroline 22 born in Alabama, and Mary J. 6 months, born in Alabama. Mary J. is mentioned in Jared Cherry's will.)

******

9. **A. V. Clark**, son of L. V. and R. J. Clark, born 18 May 1846, died 5 May 1882.

******

10. **Louisa C. Cobb**, wife of J. J. Cobb, died ---- (illegible).

-- D --

11. **Minnie T. Davis** 1866 - 1940. (She was the daughter of Mrs. Annie (Folsum) Treadaway and wife of Ben Davis. No issue. She had been

married to Mr. Portis before her marriage to Mr. Davis.)

******

12. **Zula Day**, wife of J. W. Davis, born 1867 died 1922. (This Davis family is not related to the Ben Davis Family. Zula was half sister to Annie Andrews Jenkins, buried in this cemetery. No issue. J. W. Davis married (2) May Compton of Calif.)

-- F --

12. **Squire Folsum** born 18 October 1819 died 21 September 1904. (He was born near Niagara Falls, New York and married Frances Powers of Hale County and they were parents of Annie E. Treadaway and Ida McCrory -- see their gravestone records in this cemetery. Squire Folsum was an early merchant at Old Ramsey.)

******

13. **Willie T. Fortner** born December 1870, died 12 September --- (illegible).

******

14. **Richard N. Fortner**, born 29 January 1856, died 30 April 1879, (he was the son of Lucinda (Newton) and Gilford J. Fortner, Jr.)

******

Mrs. **L. B. Fortner**, born 10 April 1831, died 12 February 1892. (She was Lucinda B. Newton, and she married G. J. Fortner, Jr.; 26 December 1854, J. B. Massangile, security. Her father was Richard Newton -- see his gravestone record in this cemetery.)

-- H --

Leila Caroline Harry born 22 January 1870 died 30 October 1879.

******

Daniel Y. Harper born 18 May 1829, died 4 January 1850 (He was a school teacher - see 1850 Mortuary Schedule.)

-- J --

William Bert Joyner born 13 February 1857, died 29 December 1945. (He married Mary Etta -also called Molly - Cherry, the daughter of Henry and

Eliza (Parker) Cherry, 18 September 1884. The father of William Bert Joyner was Giles Joyner who married (1) Mary A. B. -- (?) on 13 November 1834. When he came to Alabama she remained in Nash County, North Carolina. They obtained a divorce (see 18 November "The Whig", Sumter County, Ala.) Giles Joiner married Elvira Watson in Sumter County, Alabama on 5 February 1856. After the death of Giles Joyner, his son William Bert went to Preston Beat to live with his uncle Orrin Joyner.)

William Bert and Mary Etta (Cherry) Joyner had the following children: (1) Giles married Ione Slayton, (2) John married Rosa Knight; (3) Bill married Pearl Knight; (4) Porter married Jewell Anderson (no relation to the Andersons buried in this cemetery); (5) Mamie buried at Scooba, Miss., married Rufus Cobb (cousin of Robert L. Cobb who is buried at Central Cemetery), they had children among whom was Virginia. After her parents' death she was adopted by her father's sister, Mrs. Lucy (Cobb) Jackson of Bellamy, Alabama. Virginia Cobb-Jackson married Austin Grover Boyd (Buck) whose father was Grover Boyd (see Central Cemetery Records in this volume); (6) Clarence married Katie Mae Anderson (no relation to Andersons buried in Boney Cemetery); (7) Winston married Kelly Paul: (8) Melvin married Isaphena Jackson 4 April 1928 (see Old Side Cemetery Records for the Jackson Records), they have children Clifton Jackson born 21 August 1929 and Sara Marie born 5 March 1932, married James Ellis 4 August 1951. They have a boy and a girl; (9) Bessie married C. A. Leonard and they have three children Ted, Lydia and Rose Mary. Lydia is married and has at least 2 boys, Ted is married and has at least three girls, Rose Marie works in Charleston, South Carolina where her mother now lives.)

******

Annie Andrews Jenkins, wife of Thomas Leonidas Jenkins, born 22 January 1856, died 23 February 1926. (She was the daughter of Sara Ann (Smith) born at Centreville, Alabama, 14 July 1832 and William Penn Andrews, the son of Joel Andrews born 29 December 1787 and his wife Ann Lewis who died ca 1836. William Penn Andrews was a Quaker and was born in Medina, Orleans County, New York, 1 September 1825. (from Andrews family Bible). A letter in my possession states that George W. Andrews, brother of William Penn Andrews, assumed the birth year of William Penn, as he hoped to be President of the United States but happened to be born in Canada in 1821 while his parents were there for a short time, "a fact hid from his biographers". The "Auglaize County Atlas, Ohio, 1880" says that General G. W. Andrews was the son of Joel and Ann Lewis Andrews and that Ann was the daughter of Major John Lewis, Revolutionary War soldier from Rhode Island; Joel Andrews was a Quaker and a farmer. G. W. Andrews was a Union Soldier and a Senator, and a lawyer in Wapakeneta, Ohio - Auglaize County. From old letters in my possession from General or Senator G. W. Andrews to his brother William Penn Andrews, Editor of a Newspaper in Marion, Mississippi, we learn that William Penn was Editor of a newspaper in Wapakoneta, Ohio before coming to Mississippi; I have the demit to William Penn Andrews from the

Masonic Lodge in Wapakoneta, Ohio. George W. was a General in Union army and his brother William Penn, Captain in the Confederate Army, was killed in the Battle of Corinth. The old letters written before 1860 stated their maternal grandfather, John Lewis fought in the Revolutionary War, he stormed Stoney Point and fought on the Plains of Saratoga. Old letters stated, also, that their father was living in the home of John Mosher in 1857 - John Mosher married their sister Deborah Lewis; another sister, Jane, married a Sylvester; there was a brother John who died in 1857; and a brother Richard who "went west."

From "Rockwell-Keeler Genealogy," Library of Congress, we learn that Joel Andrews born 29 December 1789 was the son of Eli Andrews (Danbury, Conn. records were burned by the British so date of birth is unknown) and wife Ruth Rockwell who was born 13 October 1769 - they married 1789. Eli Andrews was the son of Captain Abraham Andrews, (Revolutionary War soldier), and his wife, Sara (Taylor) Andrews. Abraham was born 1721. Sara, his wife, moved her church letter from Bethel Parish, Danbury, Conn. to Winchester, Conn. November 1774. Abraham was Moderator of Winchester School Society 6 December 1774; Moderator of Town Meeting in 1783; he died 29 October 1805 at the age of 85. According to the "Olmstead History," Library of Congress, Abraham Andrews was a Revolutionary soldier and fought in New York, Long Island and Horse Neck. It went on to say that the parents of Abraham Andrews were Robert Andrews born 1693, posthumous, and his wife Ann Olmstead born 1695; they married 1720. Robert Andrews was the son of Abraham and Sara (Porter) Andrews; he was born 31 October 1648 and they were married 1682. Robert Andrews was the son of John and Mary Andrews or Andrus who came from England to Conn. on 1640. John made his will 14 January 1681, and she, calling herself "Ye aged wife of John Andrews," made her will in 1683 and died in 1694.

Distaff Lines: "Annals of town of Dorchester, Conn.," William Rockwell of Dorchester, England came to New England 30 May 1630; had a son Ensign John Rockwell who married Elizabeth Weed whose father was Jonas Weed came to New England in the Ship Arobella, sailed from the Isle of Wight and arrived at Salem, Mass.; 12 June 1630.

Ralph Keeler was born in England 1613, first wife unknown; 2nd wife was Sara, widow of Henry Whelpley of Norwalk. Ralph was a Puritan. His will dated 20 August 1672 mentions his daughter Elizabeth who married John Rockwell, who was the father of Daniel Rockwell who married Abigail Smith and became the parents of Ruth Rockwell who married Eli Andrews. In 1743 Joseph Keeler deeded John Rockwell land for "love and fatherly affection ... my son-in-law". He was chosen Deacon 8 March 1770. Page 22 Whitney Genealogy states "Daniel Keeler was the son of John and Hillabel Keeler and grandson of John Rockwell, Sr., who died at Rye, New York 1676. Page 1259, "Daniel Keeler's wife was possibly Elizabeth Weed." (This shows all these genealogies go back to the same people, same dates, etc. In 1630 Winthrop's Fleet of 17 ships left different ports in England for America. The Arobella was the one that sailed from

Cowes, Isle of Wight; arrived in Salem, Mass., 12 June 1630. Jonas Weed was one of the passengers, one of the founders of Watertown Congregational Church 26 July 1630; a founder of Wetherford Church 29 May 1635; was one of the 4 voting members at Stamford 1641. He left a wife and 9 children; 3rd daughter Elizabeth married John Rockwell.

Richard Olmstead came over in the ship "Lyon" 16 September 1632 settled in Cambridge, Mass. He was one of the original proprietors of Hartford, Conn., 1639. In 1631 purchased a township from Roger Ludlow (page 32, Dr. Hall's work on Norwalk); was 1st in Military Command. In 1676 he was Representative to General Assembly, May Session and so on to 1676; he was Comm. of Peace (town Judge). John Olmstead was the son of Richard Olmstead, and married Mary Benedict daughter of Thomas Benedict (page 185 Norwalk Records). 3rd generation was Ann Olmstead born 1695 and married Robert Andrews born 1693, resident of Danbury. 4th generation was Abraham Andrews who was born 1721, married Sarah Taylor 1748.

James Benedict was the son of William Benedict of Nottingham England, born 1617; came to N. E. 1638, died 1690; Deacon, Magistrate; Conn. Colonet; Deputy to Hempstead Convention 1665; Lieut. Foot Company; Deputy to Conn. Legislature May 1670 and one to plant Danbury, Connecticut 1684. His wife was Mary Bridgman. He died and left wife Mary, sons David and John and grandsons Thomas and James Benedict whose mother was nee Elizabeth Slawson. The daughter of Thomas Benedict married John Olmstead whose daughter Ruth Olmstead born 1695 married Robert Andrews. (Courtesy of Mrs. Minerva Rockwell of Norwalk, Conn.)

Other brothers and sisters of Annie Andrews Jenkins were: (1) Joel born 1853, died 1853; (2) Fred, died infant; (3) William Penn, Jr., born 13 December 1853, married Ursula Brogan 12 December 1877 in Marion, Miss. They had children Annie C. born 22 November 1878, married Hugh Chappell 14 January 1902 in California; William Penn III born 1883, never married. Children of Annie C. and Hugh Chappell are Hazel who married Joe Lowery and are parents of Joanne who married Mr. Thompson and Catherine who married in 1959. A son, Kenneth Chappell is married and has at least one child; (4) Henry Parker Andrews born 4 May 1861 married Lily Gay and had children: Henry Gay Andrews who married Edna Marie Fardel 8 October 1958 in Van Nuys, California, (he had an adopted daughter by a prior marriage); and two daughters Zula and Dorothy Andrews, neither of whom is married; there was a daughter of Sarah Ann Andrews by a second marriage to William C. Day - (5) Zula Day Davis, see here gravestone in this cemetery.

*****

Thomas Leonidas Jenkins, born 7 November 1852, died 19 December 1936. (He was the husband of Annie Andrews Jenkins, they married 19 November 1882, to this union were born: Sadie Lee born and died 1883; Bertram Andrews Jenkins born 19 January 1885 (See Central Cemetery records for his history); Mary Olive Jenkins born 27 April 1887 (see Swain in this cemetery for her family record); Willie Irene Jenkins born 6 August

1889, married Lawrence Rainey - they live in Louisiana - no issue; Louise Jenkins born 23 March 1891, died 16 August 1912; Annie Lee Jenkins born 5 July 1893, married William Percy Chapman 9 September 1919 and are parents of Helen Chapman born 12 August 1920 and married Paul C. Hoyt 8 April 1943, they are parents of William Chester and Patricia Ann; Mabel Andrews Chapman 11 August 1922, not married; Mary Olive Chapman born 29 January 1924, married John Elmer Bower, Jr., 19 August 1949, they are parents of Margueret Ann, John Eric and Robert David; Virginia Lee Chapman born 23 September 1925, unmarried; William Percy Chapman, Jr., born 5 December 1927, married Alice ORear 24 August 1952, and became parents of Cynthia Lee and Linda Alice; Jeanette Eugenia Jenkins born 30 June 1895, married Arch Strickland Boyd 1 June 1916 - son of R. J. and Susan (Davis) Boyd - (See their gravestone inscriptions in Boyd Cemetery for this family); Meddie Maurice born 10 February 1898 died 26 April 1960, married Bruce L. Jones in Washington, D. C. 16 March 1920 - he died 1921, they were the parents of one child James Bruce Jones born March 1921, he married Sue Abbot and have two adopted children.

The parents of Thomas Leonidas Jenkins were Dominico Jenkins who was born 13 July 1811 and married his first cousin Melvira Anderson, daughter of Sarah (Jenkins) and Vincent Anderson (see their gravestone inscriptions in this cemetery), Melvira was born 8 December 1821. Children of this union were Susan born 1845, Elizabeth born 1846, Wm. Vincent born 1848 died 1852, Thomas Leonidas born 1852, Sara V. born 1854, Narcissus born 1885, Wilford born 1857, Clara Mason born 1857, Ella Eugene born 1863, Geo. W. born 1865, died 1897 and Catina born 1870. Dominico Jenkins' father went to Springfield Ky., from Greenville County, South Carolina with the wagon train on their way west. The Andersons, Hollands, Cherrys, Mitchersons, Chapmans, Walkers, Jenkins and others left Kentucky and came to Marengo County, Alabama while members of the same families went on to Missouri and then to Texas. Dominico Jenkins' parents went to Springfield, Mo., but Dominico came to his aunt Sara (Jenkins) Anderson after the death of her husband Vincent Anderson. The father of Dominico Jenkins is said to be William Jenkins and his mother was said to have been a Holland - there was a Dominico Holland, a Revolutionary soldier. Dominico Jenkins had brothers Wilford, Washington, Winifred, Wesley, John and a sister Caroline. Washington Jenkins was living in West Plains, Mo., as late as the 1880's and corresponded with the family in Alabama. Dominico and Melvira Jenkins are buried at Hope Well Cemetery near DeKalb, Mississippi.

Brothers and sisters of Thomas Leonidas Jenkins, as named above had families as follows: Three of the girls (Susan, Sara and Elizabeth Jenkins) married Robinsons, Elizabeth's husband was born 22 April 1839 died 1901, and they had children: Ora born 1869, died 1950, Florence born 1866 died 1952, married Mr. Pollock and had no children; Meddie born 1873 married Dodson Cox, she is living (1960), no issue; Annie born 1882, living 1960, married 21 April 1923 to Mr. Henry and had one daughter, Ann born 7 December 1925 married 2 June 1950 to Houston Evans II and they have at least one child born 1954; Sallie Maurice born 1868 and died 1901; Charles Dominico born 1872 died 1889; Mamie Sue born 1877 and died 1904; Lambreth Chappell born 1885 and died 1918, James Franklin (Judge) born 1879 and died 1946, George Oscar born 5 February 1876 died 27 August 1949 married Alma Gay and had two children George Oscar Jr., who married Billy Bailey and Elizabeth Ahn who married Gordon Renard; Susan Jenkins and Sara Jenkins both married I. R. Robinson and they had a number of children some of whom live around Brandon, Mississippi and others moved to Texas, (Sara's children were Nannie M., Sara Geneva, Edward D., Richmond and Ira Virginia); Ella Jenkins married (1) a Chislom and had one daughter Lodie who married a Kinard and had a number of children among whom was Eloise, -- after the death of Mr. Chislom, Ella Jenkins married (2) a Mr. Terry; Clara Jenkins born 1859, died 1935 married (1) Billie Lyle and had one child Narcie who married a Mr. McGraw, after the death of Mr. Lyle, Clara married (2) to William M. Rush and had children Roger born 1893 married Mattie Mitchell 1929 and had children Barbara Rush who married Billy Rose and had children Nancy Dell and Joseph Cary; and Joseph Bernerd Rush married Dorothy Nell Henderson and they have children Sharon Kay, Carol Ann, Treca Gail; Maurice Rush was born 1895 and had a daughter Mildred Clarice who married (1) a Stotts and (2) Van Ellinger of Hot Springs, Arkansas, she has three children; Lonnie Rush was born 1897 and Algie Rush was born 1903, neither of whom is married; Wilford Jenkins married Emma Pollock and had children Enos, Eva and Mae. Mae married a Mr. Graham and Eva lives with them in Meridian, Mississippi, Enos is dead.

******

Susan Jenkins, wife of J. Jenkins, born in Virginia 1761 and was still alive in 1850 when she was living with her daughter, Sara Jenkins Anderson (see 1850 Census). She lies in an unmarked grave; her great grandson Thomas L. Jenkins told me she died Christmas Day 1850, (her daughter, Sara Anderson died on Christmas Eve 1880). Susan Jenkins patented land in Marengo County, Alabama in 1824, (NE 1/4 Section 14 Township 15 Range 4 East) and sold to John Finch 9 June 1927. Wit/ Holland Jenkins, Edward Jenkins and Ed F. Dunn. Her son Edward Jenkins removed to Texas, Holland Jenkins came to Sumter County and later went west.

******

Louise, daughter of Thomas L. and Annie Andrews Jenkins, born 23 March 1891, died 16 August 1912.

-- K --

E. H. Kent born 1856 - 1912 (The Kents lived across the line in Mississippi. Kemper County records were burned so nothing could be found about this family.)

******

Martha Anderson Kent wife of E. H. Kent 1854 - 1929. (A relative of the Kents told me that Martha Anderson lived around York, Alabama.)

******

Mary Annie and Sara Kent 1888 - 1892. (Nothing on these children.)

******

Marilou Kennon, daughter of John and Martha Kennon, born 29 December 1853, died 13 November 1858. (Martha A. Lacy, daughter of Elisha Lacy, married John F. Kennon 14 June 1843. See Lacy records in this cemetery.)

******

S. Evans Kennon, son of John Kennon --(date was not readable -- and another Kennon gravestone with name and dates too dim to read.)

******

Elizabeth, wife of D. L. Kirkland, died 19 September 1868. aged 33 years, 5 months, 8 days. (Elizabeth Newton, daughter of Richard Newton, married David L. Kirkland 16 December 1861. The Kirklands came from Butler County, Alabama.)

-- L --

W. A. Lacy, died 1 July 1846, aged 21 years, 7 months, 6 days. (This was not William L. Lacy who married Martha Boney as he was alive in 1850.)

******

Captain Elisha Lacy, died 9 July 1862, aged 70 years -- so was born 1792. (Elisha Lacy's will is in Will Book 2, page 245, Sumter County, Alabama and he names his children Martin V. Lacy, Thomas H. Lacy, William Lacy, Charlotte Gay, wife of Isaac Gay, Celestina Buchanan, wife of John O. Buchanan, Nancy Boney, wife of William G. Boney, Dorcas Eakin, Martha L. Kennon, Elizabeth Roberts, wife of Charles M. Roberts, Amanda N. Roberts, wife of John S. Roberts. Signed Elisha Lacy and witnessed by T. Reavis, J. B. Browning, and R. F. Woodward, dated 17 February 1860. Probated 5 August 1862.

When the Elisha Lacy estate was settled we find that Thomas H. Lacy was in Grimes County, Texas; William Lacy was in Caddo Parish, La.; Nancy Lacy wife of William G. Bony was in Caddo Parish, La.; Dorcas Lacy Eakin was in Caddo Parish, La.; Charlotte Gay wife of Isaac Gay was in Rankin County, Mississippi; Celestine Buchanan wife of John O. Buchanan was in Rankin County, Mississippi; Elizabeth Roberts wife of Charles M. Roberts was in Sumter County, Alabama; Martha L. Kennon, wife of John T. Kennon was in Sumter County, Alabama; Amanda U. wife of John S. Roberts was in Greene County, Alabama; and Martin V. Lacy was in Sumter County, Alabama but later went ot Texas.

Elisha Lacy has another daughter Elizabeth A. who married Landon J. Morris of Gainesville 20 January 1840. Elisha Lacy was guardian of her children after their parents death. Dorcas divorced her husband, Samuel S. Eakin; Dorcas was 33 in 1850 and her child Martha E. Eakin was 1 month. Amanda married John S. Roberts 24 May 1848. William A. Lacy married (1) his cousin Elizabeth Anderson and (2) Martha Boney, daughter of William Boney. Charlotte married first a Mr. May and after his death she married Isaac Jesse Gay on 22 February 1844. Martin V. Lacy married Nannie Williamson, daughter of Maj. Williamson of Gainesville, Alabama, 14 April 1857. He moved to Texas, in Grimes County.

Other Lacy records in Sumter County: 1850 Census - William A. Lacy 29 born Alabama, Martha 29 born in Georgia, Sara C.A.D. 9 born Mississippi, Elisha 7 born Alabama, Richard 5 born Alabama, Virginia C. 1 born Alabama.

1850 Census shows Thomas H. Lacy 30 born Alabama, Eliza J. 21 born South Carolina, Elisha 1 born Alabama and Clara 1 born Alabama.

William H, Lacy married Helena Bruton 6 April 1836; Matilda Lacy married William C. Bruton - the Brutons lived near Nicholas Lacy in Township 20 R 3 West. Henry B. Lacy married Mary Wardlaw 3 November 1841. Angelet Lacy married Edw. L. Penn 4 April 1839. Rosetta Lacy married William C. Turner 28 April 1843 - she was the daughter of Stephen F. Lacy. David S. Lacy's wife was Sara - they lived in Sec 7 T 20 R 3 W. Stephen F. Lacy married Mary Jane Watts 5 October 1858; his first wife was Martha --. William H. Lacy and wife Martha sold land to Sara Murry 11 March 1845. Artemisa Lacy married Nathan Amason 25 January 1859. 1850 Census - Henry B. Lacy 26 born Alabama, Mary A. 25 born Alabama, William A. 4 born Alabama, Mary L. 2 born Alabama, John C. 4 mo. born Alabama, Susan Wright 16 born Alabama. Orphans' Records Book 4 pp 456-56: Charlotte, relict of Austin H. Lacy, "now wife of Isaac Spinks," asked for settlement of Austin Lacy's estate (near Elisha Lacy's home). The heirs were John J. Lacy aged 12 years, Thomas J. Lacy aged 10, Stephen F. Lacy aged 8, Mary Ann Elizabeth Lacy aged 5. Elisha Lacy and Thomas Lacy were in Clarke County, Ala., in 1816. They were in Marengo County in the early 1820's, as was Nicholas Lacy.

******

Caroline M. Lacy, consort of Elisha Lacy, born 22 February, died at the age of 55 years, 5 months. (She was the sister of William G. Anderson, first Probate Judge in Sumter County. The Lacy lot in this cemetery is at the foot of the graves of the Vincent Anderson family. Caroline Anderson married (1) Henry Walker and had a son Franklin Walker, she married (2) Elisha Lacy.)

******

Mahulda J. Lunceford born 25 August 1843, died 27 November 1913. Mother.

******

Benj. Lunceford born 7 May 1826 - died 6 January 1923. Father.

******

J. W. Lunceford born 7 May 1826, died 29 December 1910.

******

S. O. Lunceford 1862 -- 1918.

-- M --

James Bird McCrory born September 1853, died 17 November 1939. (He was the son of Robert McCrory who was the son of James McCrory, Revolutionary Soldier who is buried at Bethany Cemetery near Vienna which is south of Aliceville, Pickens County. The tombstone inscription reads: "James McCrory, who departed this life 24 November 1840, aged 82 years, 6 months and 9 days. He was a soldier in the Revolution and was at the Battle of Brandywine and Guilford Court House. He was one of Washington's life guard at Valley Forge and served his country faithfully during the war. Peace be to the soldier's dust."

The James McCrory Family Bible is owned by his great grandson, Arthur Kipling McCrory, Ardmore, Oklahoma. This Bible was published in 1813 by Matthew Carey, Philadelphia. The family record section shows that James McCrory was born 15 May 1758 in County Antrim, Ireland near the town of Portlanore, and that he sailed from Belfast in 1775, landed in Baltimore 1 July 1775, enlisted in the Continental Army for duration of the war, was at the Battle of Brandywine, Germantown and witnessed Valley Forge.

Jean or Jane McCrory, wife of James McCrory, was born 1766, died 1 January 1840, aged 74, married 28 February 1782. She is buried by the side of James McCrory. The Bible records the following children: Thomas born 9 May 1783, died 22 October 1783, Margaret born 16 September 1784, died 10 March 1798, John born 4 January 1787, died 9 August 1840, James born 9 February 1789, died 1 August 1844, Poley born 19 January 1791, (died an infant probably), William born 13 October 1793, died 1848,

Elizabeth born 13 January 1796, died 13 May 1838, Robert born 9 October 1800, died 28 May 1870, Aalen W. born 5 December 1802, died ---.

James McCrory had three or four brothers, one of whom was killed by Indians; others lived for a time in North Carolina and then removed to Alabama. A brother, Thomas, was also a Revolutionary War soldier, a Captain in 9 Regiment, N. C. Line with his brother James. The pension records show that John McCrory was agent for James and that James received $240 per annum by Act of Congress 15 May 1828. The 1840 Census shows that James McCrory, Rev. Veteran, made his home with Robert McCrory in Pickens County.

Robert McCrory, son of James and Jean or Jane McCrory, was born 9 October 1800, died 28 May 1870 in Kemper County, Mississippi, buried just north of DeKalb at Spring Hill, Mississippi. He married 20 December 1832 to Catherine Trease who was born 26 August 1807, she died 23 July 1845. They were parents of twin daughters born 16 January 1843 (a) Sarry (Sarah) Elmira married at DeKalb, Mississippi 1859 (Bible record does not say to whom - Kemper County court house was burned so cannot get this record), (b) Jane E. married a Mr. Treadaway circa 1859.

Robert McCrory married (2) Leslie Adcock - a widow - She and Robert were parents of James Bird McCrory born 14 September 1853, died 17 November 1939 in Ardmore, Oklahoma and buried in Boney Cemetery, Emelle, Alabama. He married Ida Frances Folsum, daughter of Squire Folsum (see his gravestone inscription in this cemetery). Children of J. B. and Ida Frances McCrory: (a) Robert F. McCrory born 16 August 1879, died August 1950, married Montie Ray Poole 8 July 1906 in Ardmore, Indian Territory and they became parents of at least two children and 3 grandchildren, (b) Albert Hulbert McCrory (see his gravestone record in this cemetery), (c) James Farris McCrory born 16 October 1883 (living in 1959) married Josie Margaret Thomas in Cameron, Texas 1908. One son, James Land, died an infant, (d) Frances Ruby McCrory born 23 December 1885 (living 1959, but an invalid), (e) George Webb McCrory born 18 June 1888, died c. 1948, married Louise M. Brant 25 May 1911 and were parents of 2 sons and 2 daughters one of whom died, the others live in Houston, Texas, (f) William Powers McCrory born 26 April 1891, died 25 September 1911, (g) Carrie Annie McCrory born 19 June 1895, married Harry A. Darling and they became parents of Ida Frances who married William Delhaut of Staten Island, New York and Carrie Annie who married H. Molter of San Diego, California, (h) Arthur Kipling McCrory born 30 November 1898 (a twin, the other of whom died at birth), married Almeida Jean Ledbetter 16 May 1922 and became parents of a son Robert Horrace born 13 January 1924 and married Suzanne del Pucci of Nice, France 17 October 1950 and they are parents of James Albert Steven McCrory born 8 January 1952 and Stacy Jean McCrory born 27 January 1956. The other child of A. K. McCrory and wife, was Norma Jean who died when she was 8.

******

Ida Frances Folsum, wife of James Bird McCrory and daughter of Squire Folsum born 7 January 1860, died 7 May 1922. (She was sister of Annie Treadaway buried in this cemetery and a niece of Carrie Powers Willingham also buried in this cemetery. --- See Squire Folsum gravestone inscription.)

******

Ethel V. Wilson, wife of Albert H. McCrory, born 14 September 1893 died 15 May 1934.

******

Albert Hulbert McCrory born 31 May 1881, died 19 June 1930. (He and his wife Ethel V. McCrory adopted a son, Albert Jr., who was in the U. S. Army in 1959.)

******

Robert Allen, son of Martha and J. B. Massangale, born in Kemper County, Mississippi, 1859, died 1860.

******

Glenie Vera, daughter of W. M. and Ida Murphy, born 1902 - died 190-. Another Murphy child buried by this one - inscription illegible.

-- N --

Mary Elizabeth, wife of Henry Franklin Neely, born 19 November 1841, died 22 April 1918. (She was the mother of Rosa Willingham the wife of Philip Willingham Jr., and of Birdie Elliott the wife of Henry Elliott buried at Central Cemetery, and of Margaret Boyd the wife of Conde Boyd buried in Magnolia Cemetery in Livingston, Alabama.)

******

Richard Newton, born in Dulpin County, North Carolina, 11 May 1790, died 27 July 1878. (He was drowned when he accidentally fell into his well while trying to bail out a bucket which had come loose from the well chain. He bought his casket a few years before he died and hung it from the rafters in his attic. The Newton estate was not settled for several years after Richard's death. Mary Rea petitioned for settlement in special Term of Court 26 November 1881. The Livingston Journal carried an ad in the 9 December issue of 1881 giving names and addresses of out-of-State heirs as follows: "Lucy Rea and her husband John Rea of Kemper County, Mississippi; William Newton who resides in Columbia County, Arkansas; Lucinda Fortner who resides in Kemper County, Mississippi; Jenny and Martha Newton who reside in Louisiana; John Newton, William Newton, Nora Newton and Martha Newton who reside in Nevada County,

Arkansas. Another daughter, Elizabeth Kirkland, died prior to her father's death - see her gravestone inscription in this cemetery.

Mary Newton was born 26 July 1823 and died 26 October 1900. She married Hilliard Wilson Rae 17 September 1843 in Sumter County, Alabama; Lucy Newton married John H. B. Rae brother of Hilliard W. Rae, 22 December 1846, also in Sumter County; John Newton was born 10 May 1825 and died 23 June 1873; Joseph Newton born 14 December 1827 never married; William Newton was born 13 September 1829; Lucinda Newton was born 10 April 1831, died 12 February 1892, married Guilford Fortner 26 December 1854; Richard was born 18 November 1832, died 18 July 1864; Elizabeth (Pat) was born 11 April 1835, died 19 September 1868, married D. L. Kirkland 16 December 1861 in Sumter County, Alabama; Margaret was born 18 December 1837; Thomas was born 4 August 1839, died 6 April 1864; Martha was born 27 August 1841, died 5 February 1889; Isaac born 17 March 1843, died 8 April 1865; Naomi born 12 January 1847 died 26 October 1853. (Birth and death dates were given me by Mrs. Mace Jackson of Camden, Mississippi. She is the granddaughter of Mary Newton and John H. B. Rae.) Richard Newton fought in the War of 1812, was of English descent and is said to be of the Sir Isaac Newton line. All of the Newton boys fought in the Civil War and three never returned while one died soon after the war from wounds received in battle. Richard Newton settled first in Monroe County, Alabama and then came to Sumter County. Mrs. Mace (H. W.) Jackson's parents are Charlotte Mae (Holmes) and Ransom Lane McElroy. Charlotte Mae's parents were Lucinda (Rae) and Miles Blanton Holmes. Lucinda was the daughter of Lucy (Newton) and John H. B. Rae.

******

Mary C. Newton, born in Edgefield District, South Carolina, 3 November 1803, died 5 July 1877. (She was the wife of Richard Newton whom she married 16 March 1822. She was a Miss Burt prior to her marriage.

-- O --

Lavina Owens born 22 October 1837, died 1 March 1913.

-- P --

S. P. Parrish, born 4 April 1832 - died 26 March 1894.

******

Elizabeth, wife of S. P. Parrish, born 4 December 1839 - died 28 May 1871.

-- R --

W. H. Richardson, of Rusk County, Texas. Soldier of 10th Texas Regiment. Died in Kemper County, Mississippi 24 May 1862.

******

William R. Ramsey, born 16 May 1836, died 26 June 1874.

******

Ella D. Ramsey, wife of J. M. Ramsey, born 5 September 1835, died 28 January 1873.

******

Nancy Graves Yancy Ramsey, born in Caswell County, North Carolina 19 August 1798, died 18 January 1859; married A. K. Ramsey 7 October 1817. (Captain A. K. Ramsey married the second time and lived near this cemetery until circa 1880, after which he removed to Meridian, Mississippi. Old Ramsey was named for this Ramsey family.)

-- S --

Simeon S. Swain 1878 - 1921. (He was the son of Jerry M. Swain, and was related to the Swains and McGowans of Sumter County whose history will be given in a later volume. Simeon S. Swain was a practicing physician at Old Ramsey Station which later became Emelle. He married Olive Jenkins, daughter of Thomas Leonidas and Annie Andrews Jenkins--both of whom are buried in this cemetery--on 24 February 1904. Their children: (1) Leon was born 2 April 1905, he married Clara Lloyd of Sanford, Florida, 2 June 1928, (a) Leon Swain Jr., was born 4 August 1929 and married Betty Jo Holloway and they have children Pamela Gail and Leon Milton; (b) Lloyd Swain married Denese Stevens 25 November 1952, Susan Lynn was born 28 December 1954; (2) Louise Swain married Tommie Orr and they have one child, Bob. (3) Olive Mae Swain married George Mackey and are parents of two children, Kay and Mike. Kay married Robt. N. Weigant and has one child. Olive Swain, the wife of Dr. S. S. Swain lives with her daughter, Mrs. Mackey, in Birmingham.

******

Ann Elizabeth Folsum Treadaway, born 1851 - died 1932. (She was the daughter of Squire Folsum and mother of Minnie Treadaway Davis, buried in this cemetery, also mother of Will Treadaway who went to Texas, married there and had at least two sons, and of Julia T. Willingham - who is buried in this cemetery. Mrs. Treadaway was a sister of Mrs. Ida McCrory, and a niece of Mrs. Carried Willingham.)

******

William Maurice Thomas, born Charlotte County, Virginia 13 July 1814, died -- stone mended so date illegible but he died circa 1897. (He married Narcissa Anderson, daughter of Sara and Vincent Anderson; they reared Sallie Robinson, niece of Narcissa's, who died unmarried. William Maurice married just in time to get the Anderson slaves enumerated in his name in 1866. William Maurice was blind several years prior to his death.)

******

Narcissa F., wife of William Maurice Thomas born 19 September 1821, died 25 December 1885. (She was daughter of Vincent and Sara Anderson, and aunt of Thomas Leonidas Jenkins.)

******

Catina A. wife of William Maurice Thomas, born 25 April 1832, died 22 January 1913. (Catina was sister of Narcissa (Anderson) Thomas - no issue.)

******

-- W --

Philip Willingham, Sr., born 2 March 1809, died 3 April 1876. (The 1850 Census shows he was born in North Carolina and he was 41, his wife Frances L. born in Virginia and she was 37, Thomas W. born in Tennessee was 15, Margo (Mary) was born in Alabama and she was 13, Claudius born in Alabama was 12, William A. born in Alabama was 10, Amelia born in Alabama was 8, Usetha (?) B. was born in Alabama and was 4, **Winona** R. (probably (Reid) born in Alabama and was 1, Sara (twin) was born in Alabama and was 1.

The following is an extract from Mr. Willignham's obituary and from other records belonging to Mrs. Philip Willingham, II who is still living (1960): "Mr. Philip Willingham was born in 1809 in Person County, North Carolina but moved to Bedford County, Tennessee where he married Miss Frances L. Brown in 1834. He moved to Greene County, Alabama in 1836 where his second child was born. His wife died 9 March 1863 and he married (2) Miss Carrie Powers of Hale County in 1863 and he died in 1876."

Amelia Willingham died 30 January 1873. Thomas and Claudius Willingham joined the Cinfederate Army. Thomas was sent to Ft. Morgan and later to Accotink Creek, Virginia, where he died 12 October 1861; Claudius died at White Sulphur Springs Hospital 23 January 1863.

Reid Willingham (who was probably Winona R. in the census) married Mr. John Harris and had several children among whom was Eunice who never married, Loulie who married Mr. Love, Dora married Mr. Smith, Lee married Mary,--, and had two children, John married Aline -- and had one child, Dorothy who married Hugh Morrow, Sr., of Birmingham, Alabama. Mary Willingham married Mr. Ramsey.)

******

Carrie Powers, (2nd) wife of Philip Willingham, Sr., was born 3 June 1836, died 8 June 1909. (She was an aunt of Mrs. Annie Treadaway and Ida Frances McCrory all of whom are buried in this cemetery.)

******

Philip Willingham, Jr., born 25 October 1870, died 13 August 1931. (He was the son of Philip Willingham Sr., and his 2nd wife Carrie Powers Willingham. He married Rosa Neelly -- see Neelly records in this cemetery - and they had children Philip who married Louise Tidmore, no issue; Robert P. who married Atta Peck, no issue; Mary Neelly Willingham not married; Edwin Lee (Pete) married Ellen (Sauls) Williams and they have one child, Philip Lee. Mr. Willingham had one full sister who married Rev. Rogers. Their daughter, Edna, married Mitchell Jarman. They had one daughter, Edna who is married and lives in Chattanooga, Tennessee. They have three children.)

****

Julia Treadaway, born 9 February 1872, died July 1900, the (1) wife of Philip Willingham (son of the first Philip) and daughter of Mrs. Annie (Folsum) Treadaway.

****

James White, born 10 March 1865, aged 6 years.

-- Y --

Alfred Yarbrough, born 12 December 1792, died 26 February 1857. (He came to Sumter County from Marengo County in 1852. - See Land Patents for more about this family -)

****

Mary, wife of Alfred Yarbrough, born 31 November 1798, died 27 June 1853. (She joined Bethel Presbyterian Church 23 July 1837. This church was located where the present Bethel Chapel and Cemetery are located.)

****

Mary Ann Yarbrough, daughter of Matthew and Elizabeth Parham and wife of James Q. Yarbrough, died 27 May 1852, aged 19 years. (She left a son named Parham, he is mentioned in Matthew Parham's will. See Old Side Cemetery records.)

****

Samantha A., wife of George M. Wrenn and daughter of Alfred and Mary Yarbrough, born 24 March 1836, died 26 October 1863. (George Wrenn was the son of James and Eliza Wrenn of Sumterville.)

****

Neil Smith, son of Alfred and Mary Yarbrough, born 6 March 1835, died 17 January 1861. (He married Sara A. Manley 19 June 1857, by a Catholic Priest. After the death of Neil S., her husband, she married George W. Bales 26 October 1864 by D. P. Bester, M.G. According to the settlement of the estate of Neil S. Yarbrough (he died intestate), he left two minor heirs, Neil S. Jr., and Mary.

Alfred Yarbrough had a close relative, Elizabeth Yarbrough, who was born in North Carolina, 27 September 1792 and married Randolph Hester in Georgia 4 February 1812. He was a soldier in the War of 1812 from Morgan County, Georgia and was discharged 6 May 1815. He served in the Seminole Indian War 1817-1818 (Georgia Archives, Atlanta, Georgia and National Archives, Washington, D.C.) He and his family moved to Monroe County, Alabama in 1818 - we find him there in the 1820 Census. He removed to Sumter County, Alabama in the mid 1830's and bought land from Bemj. and Hannah Lewis in 1837, and from Joseph and Sarah Nelson in 1845 and secured lands from Gaines Whitfield. Deed Book E page 585 shows a $40,000 transaction between him and Matthew A. Marshall of Sumter County, Alabama and James W. Marshall of Tolbert County, Georgia. The indenture was witnessed by B. Seale and Edw. McCord.

Randolph Hester sold out in 1845 and went to Louisiana and he died 7 April 1851 (marker says 3 April 1851). Elizabeth Yarbrough Hester died 11 February 1873. They were parents of (1) Joseph Tapley Hester born 1821, died 1907 and married Mary Brewster in Sumter County, Alabama, 23 December 1842. They had children James Wesley, George Washington, Jane, Martha, Hodge, J. Lee, Lizzie, John R., and Josephine; (2) Robert Stephens Hester born 1824, died 1883 married Elizabeth Ann Custis of Sumter County, 7 November 1844, and they had children:

John Randolph, Elizabeth Ann, Ciscelia L. T., Mary or Molly, and Alice A. The oldest child, John Randolph Hester married Zilphia Ann King 3 September when he was 23 years old and they became parents of Walter Stephens Hester born 13 August 1871 - he married Curmeler Lawrence 19 November 1893. They had a son Earl Randolph Hester born 1 October 1897 and married Clover Feazel 4 December 1924 and had children Dorothy Claire who married David H. Bell and had children Cathy and David H. Bell IV. (2) Clover Beth who married Bobby Lee Wallace 14 November 1930, their children are Linda nad Susan.

Other children of Walter Stephens Hester and wife Curmeler Lawrence: Herman Stanerford Hester, married Myrdie Vining; Jewel Dee Hester married Joseph F. Ballard 1931 and had James Franklin and Virginia Ruth who married Cleve Hammonds, Jr.; Alice Virginia Hester married Ona Graves and had one child Curmeller Suzanne; Mary Adrienne Hester married Geo. M. Strickler; John Marvin Hester married Valerie McIntosh and had children: Barbara Carol, Edna Virginia, and Valerie; Ziphia Burlyn Hester married Dermont Louis T. O'Conner and had children Michael, Mary Doreen, Patricia, Timothy Taaffe and Dermont Taaffe.

All of Randolph Hester's sons served in the Confederate Army in the War Between the States. (3) Stephen Thompson Hester born 1826 married (1) Angeline E. W. Dyson, and had children Mary Elizabeth and Cavasso, he married (2) Mrs. Caroline Reynolds and had Regina and George; (4) John W. Hester born 1829 married Emily Pipes and had children: Susan, Cinderella, Loretta, Jerusha, Lafayette, Caldwell, Pascel W., Landrum died young, Gertrude, Quincy Adams and Ira; (5) Mary Hester born 1834 married Benj. Frnaklin Farmer and had children: Isabella, Leah Dr. Calvin Davis, William Newton married Sallie Acre Staples, Benj. F. married Mary E. Hartness, Eliza married James A. Auld. (Courtesy of **Mr. E. R. Hester,** Arcadia, La.)

CENTRAL CEMTERY

This cemetery, located about three and one half miles south east of Emelle on the old Emelle-Livingston road, serves as a burying ground for the families who once buried at Boney, Old Side and Bethel Cemeteries. It is centrally located between Boyd, Sumterville and Emelle. The descendants of the Presbyterians who once belonged to Bethel Presbyterian Church, before it was moved to Sumterville, built a church by this cemetery. There was an interlude, however, when they were united with the Methodist Church at Old Ramsey -- see Ramsey Methodist Church records -- After Central Presbyterian Church was blown down by high winds, it was rebuilt at Emelle.

INSCRIPTIONS

Austin Eugene Cobb, 1895 - 1956. (He was the son of Eva (Boyd) and Oscar Cobb, and grandson of Austin Gambrel and Harriett Cadmus (Moore) Boyd on maternal side, and the paternal grandson of Frank and Molly (Barbaree) Cobb.--See Boyd Cemetery records for Boyd line. Eugene Cobb married Fannie May Murray - see Murray records in this cemetery, - and became parents of (1) Martha who married A. C. McDade and they are parents of one child, April; (2) Edith married Tom Meek Ware, they are parents of an adopted child - see Vol. 2 for Ware line; (3) Billy married Evelyn Johnson and they are parents of Ty, Mike and Tommie; (4) Jeanie is married and has three boys and a girl.)

******

Joseph Douglas Edmonds, born 8 October 1872, died 21 April 1937. (He was the son of Joseph and Mary Edmonds of Louisiana, Missouri, an old town on the Mississippi.)

******

Frances Edmonds - no dates - double stone with Joseph Douglas Edmonds. (She was born in Pike County, Missouri, the daughter of Susan (Vermillion) and Samuel Wasson, and the wife of Joseph Douglas Edmonds. They were the parents of (1) Mary Sue Edmonds, not married, and (2) Wallace P. Edmonds; the latter married Martha Neville -see S. L. Neville record in this cemetery - and they are parents of W. P. Jr., Frances Lynn and and Mary Neville. Frances is married to Charles Leverett.)

******

Samuel Loftin Neville, born 29 January 1873, died 16 October 1949. (He was the son of James A. and Charity Neville - more about this family in Vol. 2 - and great grandson of Andrew L. and Mary Neville - See Bethel Cemetery for Neville, Ramsay and Loftin records.)

******

Stella Lynn Neville, born 28 October 1877, died 13 January 1938. (She was the wife of S. L. Neville, and the daughter of Mose F. Ramsey - see Vol. 2 for Ramsey records. S. L. and Stella Neville had two children: Martha who married W. P. Edmonds, and Sam Loftin, Jr., who married Edna Ogburn - no issue to live.)

******

J. W. Burton, born 27 September 1881, died 26 August 1943. (He was the son of John Wesley Burton (who is buried at Old Side Cemetery) and his first wife, Mrs. Nannie (Amason) Gregory.)

******

Johnnie Maude Burton, born 23 April 1883, died 19 February 1937. (She was the wife of J. W. Burton Jr., Miss Davis of Troy, Alabama prior to her marriage. They were parents of two children: (1) Davis, who married Amelia Boyd - see Boyd Cemetery records for A. C. Boyd - and they became parents of Johnnie Jean who married Irvin Commander, Jr., and they are parents of several children; (2) Davis, Jr., is married, also.)

******

Nannie Louise Wooldridge, born 6 March 1913, died 18 March 1955. (She was the wife of Travis Wooldridge and the daughter of J. W. and Johnnie Maude (Davis) Burton. Nannie Louise and Travis Wooldridge had children: (1) Patsy who married Joe Holland and (2) Johnnie. Travis has remarried to Mrs. Annie Holder Armstrong.)

******

William Jefferson (Jeff) Boyd, born 4 April 1881, died 10 November 1935. (He was the husband of Mary Eliza Key born 19 October 1889 and married 1 January 1906; and the son of Robert J. and Susan (Davis) Boyd - see Boyd Cemetery records. Wm. Jefferson and Mary Eliza Boyd had children: (1) Clara Elizabeth born 16 November 1906 and married Elisha Walter Halfacre 4 January 1937 - no issue; (2) Hermione Lou born 19 August 1908 at Stoneburg, Texas and married her cousin Leland Jefferson Nixon - see Nixon at Boyd Cemetery - also related through the Keys - Hermie Lou and Leland Nixon had children (a) Leland Jefferson Nixon, Jr., (Pete) who married Madge Powell and they have one child, Cathy Jean; (b) Sidney Nixon born 6 April 1928 and died an infant, (c) Dorothy Jean Nixon married (---) Strobough of Texas, and (d) Harry Nixon not married; (3) Marguerite Boyd married Everett Pearson - no issue; (4) Robert Sidney Boyd d

Boyd, deceased; (5) Della Eunice Boyd married Alton Smith, they have children Dewey Alton, Thomas Weldon and Mary Evelin; (6) William Jefferson Boyd, Jr., married Naidine ---, and became parents of June Marie and Wm. J. III; (7) Woodrow Wilson Boyd, deceased; (8) Parks Oliver Key Boyd who married Joan ----, and became parents of Kenneth and Floyd Dale; (9) Thomas Earle not married.)

******

Beulah Motes, born 23 November 1878, died 4 August 1960. (She was the daughter of Robert J. and Susan (Davis) Boyd, and the wife of W. A. Motes who was the son of Clabourn Right Motes and his first wife Mary Elizabeth Smith. Clabourn Right Motes was the son of John Wesley Motes born 28 December 1829 and his first wife Loucinda Rainey; the father of John Wesley Motes was Bob Motes. The Motes family were early settlers from around Athens, Alabama.. W. A. Motes and wife Beulah Boyd had children (1) Nellie Mae who married L. L. Goggans and had children

Barbara Nell and Joe; (2) Stanton who married Maggie (Smith) Pettit (see Pettit in Vol. 2) - no issue. Beulah and W. A. Motes are buried in Livingston. Motes history from family Bibles and by courtesy of Mrs. L. L. Goggans.)

******

Grover C. Boyd, born 20 November 1892, died 4 July 1930. (He was the husband of Olga Swearingen, who later married Arch T. Richardson, Jr. Grover C. Boyd was the son of Jefferson Boyd and his third wife Emma (Faulkner) Boyd, (see Boyd Cemetery records.) Grover and Austin Boyd were parents of (1) Cliff Willard who married Margaret Estes, daughter of R. T. and Maud (Sims) Estes, and they became parents of Peggy who married Fred Killion and had children Kimberly Dianne, Frederick William III and James Willard; (2) Pauline who married T. J. Kitchins - no issue; (3) Austin Grover, who married Virginia Cobb, the daughter of Jasper Rufus and Mary Virginia (Joyner) Cobb. Jasper Rufus was the grandson of Frank and Molly (Barbaree) Cobb; Mary Virginia was the great great granddaughter of Joshua Cherry, Rev. War soldier who is buried in Marengo County, (see Cherry records in Boney Cemetery.) Austin Grover is the great great grandson of Hugh Boyd, Rev. War Soldier. Austin Grover and Virginia Cobb (she was also adopted by her aunt, Mrs. Lucy (Cobb) Jackson, after her parents' death) were parents of Grover (Skip), Janice, Dianne and Jerry; (4) Billy Morgan Boyd married Ruth Hutchinson, daughter of A. H. and Era (Black) Hutchinson. Billy and Ruth are parents of Billy Willard and Ruth Elaine.)

******

Grover C. Boyd, Jr., born 11 April 1922, died 31 April 1922. (Son of G. C. and Olga Boyd.)

******

Minnie Elliott, born 10 July 1869, died 28 March 1933. (She was wife (2) of Matthew Henry Elliott and sister of Alice (Little) Gregory buried at Old Side Cemetery. Their forebears are buried at Clinton, S. C.)

******

Matthew Henry Elliott, born 3 March 1867, died 20 September 1939. (He was the son of John Knox and Elizabeth (Eakins) Elliott - see Elliott family Cemetery and "Elliott" in Township 20, Range 3 West. By his first wife, Lillie Berdie (Neelly) Elliott - see Boney Cemetery Records for Neelly - he had children: Florence who married Murray Flowers - see Flowers under Township 20 - Henry Russell buried in this cemetery married Helen Whitfield and had children Leon, Howard and Doris; Gladys buried in this cemetery; John married Goldie --, no issue; Clyde married Andrea Jackson Reynolds and had children among whom is Julia who married Calvin Boyd - see Boyd Cemetery records; Bessie married Sam Neilson and they have two boys; Elsie married Elbert Kidd and they have children;

Bruce married Margaret ---.

******

Henry Russell Elliott, born 24 March 1891, died 8 September 1957. (He was the son of Matthew Henry and Lillie Berdie (Neelly) Elliott, and husband of Helen Whitfield - see Matthew Henry Elliott records.)

******

Mary Gladys Elliott, born 3 May 1900, died 20 October 1918. (Daughter of Matthew Henry and Berdie (Neelly) Elliott.)

******

Annie Bell Richardson, born 18 August 1895, died 3 April 1937. (She was the wife of Bryant Richardson and daughter of Rosa (Daniel) and Calvin A. Elliott both of whom are buried in this cemetery. This stone is double, or a place for her husband's inscription - he was born 31 August 1889 - still living. Bryant is the son of A. T. and Sallie (Thomas) Richardson - see Old Side records.)

******

Infant daughter of Bryant and Annie Bell Richardson, born and died 6 November 1918.

******

James Soloman Stegall, born 25 March 1872 in Pontotoc, Mississippi, died 22 October 1945. (He married Matilda Ennis Daniel, daughter of Alice or Alerena Bell and James Townsend Daniel - see Records in this and Bethel Cemeteries - on 8 June 1896. He was the grandson of J. D. and Margaret Clementine (Morrison) Stegall - Margaret C. was a relative of Stonewall Jackson - and the son of Columbus Ware and Sara Elizabeth (Ward) Stegall. The mother of Sara Elizabeth Ward was Miss Taylor who married Tom Ward, the son of Tom Ward, Sr., who married Sara Love at St. Paul's, London, England. The children of Columbus Ware and Sara Elizabeth Stegall were W. T., John S., James Solomon, Columbus, Jerry, Jesse, Edna, Beulah, Lottie. The children of James S. and Matilda (Daniel) Stegall are Herman, Joe, Frank who married Elizabeth Bell and they have Joe, Hugh, John and Carl; Fred married Ted England and they have Mariola, James Calvin, Herman and Rosa Lee; Louise married Hunter Lang, buried in this cemetery; James B. married Mattie Boyd and they have Jimmie, Glenda Carol and Annie Lou - see Boyd cemetery records for Mattie Boyd, daughter of A. C. Boyd; Calvin married Catherine Saucier and they have Lona Kay, C. W., Patsy and Judy.)

******

Matilda (Tillie) Stegall, born 26 November 1871, died 5 April 1946. (She was the wife of James Solomon Stegall, and daughter of Alice or Alerena (Bell) and James Townsend Daniel - records in this and Bethel cemeteries.)

******

J. D. Daniel born 25 February 1876, died 26 April 1929. (Son of J. T. and Alice B. Daniel.)

******

Alice A. Daniel born 25 August 1840, N. C. died 19 September 1919. (She was the wife of James Townsend Daniel buried at Bethel, and was the daughter of William and Elizabeth Goldsmith Bell of Edgecombe County, N. C. - see Old Side Records.)

******

Rosa Daniel Elliott, born 27 January 1870, died 23 January 1937. (She was the wife of Calvin Andrew Elliott, and daughter of Alice A. (Bell) and James T. Daniel.)

******

Andrew Calvin Elliott, born 8 June 1865, died 18 December 1936. (He was the husband of Rosa (Daniel) Elliott and the son of John Knox and Elizabeth (Eakins) Elliott - see Elliott family cemetery and Township 20 records - He and Rosa Elliott were parents of Annie Bell who married Bryant Richardson; Rosa Knox who married Dr. J. B. Davis (deceased) and had 2 children, (1) Alice Ann who married Oscar Charles Davenhauer and they have children Anna Elizabeth and David Elliott and (2) J. B. Davis Jr., not married; Elizabeth Ann Elliott daughter of C. A. and Rosa died an infant.

******

Hunter A. Lang, born 9 February 1871, died 26 August 1949. (He was the son of Alonza and Sue! (Kerr) Lang and husband of Louise Stegall, daughter of J. S. and Matilda D. Stegall. They had one daughter, Aileen, who married Leslie (Bud) Nixon, Jr., who is her very distant cousin - she is descended from David Montgomery Dial and he is descended from David M.'s aunt, Jane or Jennett (Dial) Boyd. They have two little girls.)

******

Dan Stegall, born 28 June 1947, died 15 May 1951. (He was the son of Frank and Elizabeth (Bell) Stegall.)

******

Infant twins of Charles and Margaret (Elliott) Poole. (Grandchildren of Robert Knox and Annie (Slaton) Elliott. They died 26 September 1953 and 28 September 1953.

******

Robert Knox Elliott, born 3 October 1890, died 11 January 1949. (He was the husband of Annie (Slaton) Elliott and the son of Margaret (Bond) and William M. Elliott - see Elliott family cemetery and Township 20 records.)

******

Audrey E. Boyd, born 23 May 1920, died 26 June 1937, (daughter of Arch S. and Jeanette (Jenkins) Boyd, sister of Dorothy (Boyd) Jones and granddaughter of R. J. and Susan (Davis) Boyd and of Thomas L. and Annie (Andrews) Jenkins - see Boney and Boyd Cemetery records.)

******

Scott Dobbins, born 5 April 1896, died 21 October 1938. (She was the wife of Joe Dobbins of Ft. Payne, Alabama, and the daughter of R. J. and and Susan (Davis) Boyd. -see Boyd cemetery records. Scott and Joe were parents of Linnell who married Noble Franklin Greenhill Jr., and they have Dianne Scott, Debora Lynn, and Noble Franklin III.)

******

Anita Boyd Jenkins born 15 August 1932, died 23 February 1955. (She was the wife of Henry Andrews Jenkins who is the son of Bertram Andrews and and Nelle (Morris) Jenkins; and the daughter of A. F. J. and Lolita (Waddell) Boyd - see Boyd Cemetery for paternal lines. Anita and Henry parents of 2 children: Bertram Austin and Lolita Boyd Jenkins.)

******

Bertram Andrews Jenkins, born 10 January 1885, died 19 October 1948. Capt. 52nd Artillery Argonne, France. (He was the son of Thomas L. and Annie (Andrews) Jenkins and great grandson of Vincent and Sara (Jenkins) Anderson - see Boney Cemetery records. He was the husband of Nelle (Morris) Jenkins. They had Thomas Elbert and Henry Andrews Jenkins.)

******

Robert L. Cobb, 1886 - 1938. (He was the husband of Nettie (McElroy) Cobb, and son of Frank and Molly (Barbaree) Cobb. Robert L. and Nettie Cobb had children Leslie; Louise who married Mr. Horton; Maurine who married Woody Reeves; Aubrey who married Em Tomlinson granddaughter of Em (Simms) Brothers who was the daughter of W. T. Simms and his first wife; Allie who is married and lives in Texas; Virginia who married P. M. Norwood, and Roger who married (1) Mary Lou Greenhill, sister of Noble Frank Greenhill, Jr., (2) Ada Lee Schaff).

******

Nettie M. Cobb - 1889 (Double stone with her husband R. L. Cobb - living 1960).

******

Vista Kerr Crumm, born 3 January 1878, died 8 January 1949. (She was the daughter of Telamachus Kerr and granddaughter of William and Sara (Dial) Kerr - see Bethel records.)

******

William L. Murray, born 19 January 1864 - died 20 August 1949. (He was the husband of Birginia (Jennie) Kerr Murray who was the daughter of Telamachus Kerr. Wm. L. and Virginia Murray had children, Ovid who married Beth Long; Clyde who married Dan Trawick, Virginia who married Clarence Boyd son of A. C. Boyd, Fannie May who married Austin Eugene Cobb, and Vista not married.)

******

Virginia Kerr Murray, born 16 January 1866, died 6 July 1956. (She was the wife of William L. Murray and the daughter of Telamachus Kerr who is buried at Bethel.)

******

Helen Whitfield Elliott, born   , died 31 August 1960. (She was the wife of Henry Russell Elliott - see Bethel records for her maternal line - under Silliman. No stone at this grave because of such recent burial.)

******

Calvin Andrew Elliott, II, born 9 April 1920, died 16 May 1941. (He was the son of Laura (Slaton) and James Luther Elliott, and grandson of Calvin A. and Rosa (Daniel) Elliott - Laura (Slaton) Elliott and Annie (Slaton) Elliott are sisters and married first cousins, J. Luther and Robert Knox Elliott.)

******

Lillie Berdie Elliott, born 20 August 1872, died 11 May 1919. (She was the first wife of Matthew Henry Elliott, and daughter of Mary Elizabeth and Henry Franklin Neelly - see Boney records.)

******

CHAPTER V

FAMILY CEMETERIES

McCAINVILLE, ALABAMA

The town of McCainville was a prosperous town in the early settling of the county but today there is not one thing to mark the site of the town itself except, probably, an old cistern; this is said to have been in the Mount Moriah Academy yard. The town itself was located about four or five miles west of Livingston but the community of McCainville extended to the road which leads to Hornes' Bridge toward the south and toward Old Side Cemetery on the north. Families in the vicinity of McCainville included the Brownrigg, Freeman, Cockrell, Hopper, Hadley, Kennedy, Lavender, Martin, McCain, Jeremiah Dial, Parker, Spratt, Thomas, Travis and Horne families.

There are at least eight cemeteries in this community. After the Civil War the families moved either to Livingston or to distant states so the cemeteries have long been neglected or are included in pastures. Some of the stones are leaning against trees, some are buried in the ground, having been knocked over by cows, and some are in thickets so dense until it is almost impossible to get to them - These are not isolated cases but it is true of almost every part of the county. This is the main reason which prompted my collecting tombstone inscriptions, I realized that within a few years these stones would be gone, and information on them would be lost to posterity.

McCAIN CEMETERY

This cemetery is located about a mile west of old McCainville near a Negro Church. One has to walk over muddy, impassable roads (if it drizzles rain). It is about three quarters of a mile from the old McCainville-Payneville road on the north, after one crosses

McCainville-Payneville road on the north side, after one crosses a branch, about 200 yards or more. One would have to have a guide to find this cemetery.

INSCRIPTIONS

Adam McCain died 24 April 1841, aged 61 years. (Mr. McCain was born circa 1780 and came to Sumter County, Alabama from South Carolina in 1831. He had children Weldon, George, William and Adam Jr., Weldon taught school; the other boys were in the Confederate Army, and William was killed.)

****

Elizabeth, consort of Adam McCain, born 13 March 1798, died 11 March 1867. (She was Miss Elizabeth Marshall).

****

Adam S. McCain, born 23 July 1835, died 3 June 1870. (He was the son of Adam McCain and his wife Elizabeth Marshall McCain. He married Frances Lou Hodges and they became parents of A. C. McCain, Dr. C. M. McCain, Dr. W. J. McCain and Mrs. W. L. Kern. A. C. McCain married Miss Nixon, and had children: Clarence, who married Miss Henton, (he was sheriff at one time of Sumter County), Mrs. John Neilson, Mrs. Frances Turner, and Mrs. David White. Dr. W. J. McCain married Julia White and they became parents of Ada who married Dr. James of Virginia, Louise, Mrs. Evans wife of R. L. Evans who was principal of the Livingston High School for many years, Mrs. Reynolds, Julia, David, Mattie and Adfield who married Maude Mellen of Livingston. (More about these families in another volume.) The mother, Frances Lou (Hodges) McCain, had brothers Marion, Newt and Jasper, who served in the Confederate Army; Marion was killed in battle.)

****

Lelia Marion, daughter of A. S. and F. L. McCain, born 5 May 1863, died 4 September 1868.

****

Keyezia, wife of William Kennedy, born 25 November 1874, died 10 June 1902. (It is said that in the early settling of the county that this family spelled their name "Kanady". There were two men in this family, one was John Kennedy who lived where Ernest Boyd now lives, and Tom Kennedy who lived at the R. L. Giles place.)

****

Margaret (Hodges) Lavender, born 22 May 1815, died 28 June 1871 (wife of Robert Lavender. See Bethel Cemetery records for Lavender history.)

****

There were several other old graves in this cemetery, unmarked and sunken. There are new graves which seem to be Negroes - their church is near by.

(References: Sumter County Court records and unpublished History of Livingston by Dr. R. D. Spratt.)

SPATT CEMETERY

This cemetery is located about three quarters of a mile on the Sumterville Road which turns north off the Livingston-Emelle road near Leslie Nixon's. A crepe myrtle grove has taken over this cemetery which is on the left hand side of the road just before one gets to the Colored church on the opposite side of the road.

There are only six graves in this cemetery, all of them are Spratts. Three little graves in a row are marked "Infants" and are at the foot of a large marker with the name "Spratt" on it. One stone is marked "Walter, son of R. D. and Lillis Spratt"; another is marked "Mary, daughter of R. D. and Lillis Spratt, 1842-1845"; the third is marked "John B. son of R. D. and Lillis Spratt 1845".

According to Dr. R. D. Spratt, grandson of R. D. and Lillis (Barnett) Spratt, they came to Sumter County circa 1839. They had several children to live, viz: Susan who married A. W. Cockrell, James P., a Confederate Soldier who saw the bombardment of Ft. Sumter. He married Mattie Beggs and their children were Robert D., Helen who died young, Lewis B. who married Maggie Smith, daughter of Sallie (Ramsey) and T. L. Smith, granddaughter of Thomas and Anne (Berlin) Smith and great granddaughter of William Smith of Virginia. Sallie Ramsay was the daughter of J. Reid Ramsay (see Bethel Cemetery records.) Mr. and Mrs. Lewis B. Spratt are parents of two daughters, Louise and Lillis, the latter married Andy Allison - more about these families in a later volume.

Dr. R. B. Spratt, brother of Lewis B. Spratt was an authority on historical events around Livingston. In the Public Library is an unpublished history - typed, (and a photostatic copy in "Local History", a loose leaf book, in the vault of the Probate Judge's office), of Dr. Spratt's historical recordings. He was, also, an authority on the Choctaw Indian of this locality.

PARKER CEMETERY

This cemetery is also located in the McCainville area and is about a quarter of a mile from the south side of the Livingston-Emelle road in a pasture directly in front of the Frank Campbell home. The cows have knocked some of the stones down, some are broken and some leaning against trees some distance from the graves, others were on the ground and half buried.

INSCRIPTIONS

James Parker born 30 January 1788, died 28 November 1855. (Captain Parker was one of the largest landholders in this section and considered one of the richest men. He and his wife Mary (Mitchell) Parker were parents of Mrs. Lewis S. Brown, Mrs. Robert L. Brown, Socrates, Dave, Christine, Volney, Amoranth who married John R. Campbell, Philander W. and possibly others. Marcus Parker married Sarah E. Hines 14 September 1850. Their only child was Mary Elizabeth who married (1) Mr. Gibbs and (2) Joseph McConnell who was the son of Dr. John McConnell who is buried at Bethel Cemetery. Hon. Marcus E. McConnell, former Probate Judge of Sumter County, is the son of Mary Elizabeth and Joseph McConnell. Judge McConnell married Julia Lawrence and they became parents of Hon. Marcus McConnell, Jr., County Solicitor, John McConnell and Mary Emily McConnell.

Socrates Parker married (1) Sarah J. Brown 16 August 1842, (2) Elizabeth Lake 29 June 1848 and their son James L. Parker married Lillie Ash and became the parents of James L. Parker, Jr., who married Annie Little Oliver of Panola, Alabama. They are parents of Lake, Oliver and Ed Parker, (more about this family in Volume 2.) Ella Gaines Parker, daughter of James L. and Lillie (Ash) Parker married Sidney Jones and they became parents of Bradford Jones who married Frankie Cooper - they have a girl - and Lillie Ash Jones married Thomas Richardson son of Bryant and Annie Bell (Elliott) Richardson - see Old Side Cemetery records and Central Cemetery records.

****

Adaman W. Parker, daughter of James and Mary W. Parker, born 20 September 1838, died 30 September 1847. (This was the granddaughter of Captain James Parker.)

****

Osceola Parker, son of James Parker, Jr., and wife Mary Parker, died 21 June 1842, aged 1 year.

****

Infant daughter of Marcus and Sarah Hines Parker, died 15 July 1853.

****

Mary Parker, wife of Captain James Parker, died 25 December 1841, aged

86 years. (She was Mary Mitchell, great aunt of Mr. Dan Mitchell who lives in his ancestral home between Emelle and Gainesville.)

****

Mary W. Parker, wife of James Parker, Jr., born 28 June 1804, died 17 September 1848.

****

Amaranth M. Parker, wife of H. W. Killen, and daughter of Mary W. Parker, died 10 October 1851, aged 29 years, 4 months, 28 days. (See Horn Cemetery records.)

****

Ann Perry, wife of Josiah Perry, born 1784, died 28 June 1840.

****

James P. Brown, son of Robert and Amazon Brown, died 7 June 1852, aged 16 months, 2 days.

****

Bell Floyd, infant daughter of McDuffie and Mattie Greene.

******

Pamelia Ann, daughter of Daniel and Stacy Green, died 11 April 1846, aged 16 years.

******

Daniel Greene, native of Greenville District, South Carolina, died 21 August 1842, aged 49 years, 7 months and 20 days. (The settlement of his estate shows heirs as follows: James McCown and wife Elizabeth, James McMillan and wife Nancy, Robert B. Gunn and wife Frances, Radford M. Gunn and wife Stacy, Louise the daughter of Charlotte and Jerome McCown, David W. Fields and wife Louisa, Burwell H. Greene, McDuffie Greene, Martha Greene, Melvira Greene, Susan Greene, James M. Greene and Ezekiel Greene. (Sumter Court Records.)

****

The stone at the head of Captain James Parker's grave is very fine and is said to have been imported from France. It was shipped to New York and then by coastal boat to Mobile. There it was transferred to a river steamer to Jones' Bluff on the Tombigbee River where it was put on an ox cart and brought over a dirt road to this cemetery. It is a tall but a substantially erected monument. The history of this gravestone shows how hard it was to obtain monuments so no wonder so many graves are unmarked.

TRAVIS CEMETERY

The Travis Cemetery is located on the next plantation just west of the Parker place. It is a few steps from the house which was a lovely old home in its day. It has not been occupied in years so it is about gone. The graves are fenced off from the pasture which surrounds them.

INSCRIPTIONS

Enoch Travis, born 9 July 1797, died 20 March 1841. (A daughter married Ed Bell who was killed in the Civil War. She then married Dr. Matthew Turner of Bladen Springs. He was the son of Benj. D. Turner and Margaret Andrews Turner. Benjamin D. Turner was the brother of Rebecca Turner who married Rufus Daniel. (See James D. Daniel record Bethel Cemetery.)

****

Harriett Travis, born 25 December 1819, died 23 August 1843.

****

Ellen L. Travis, daughter of Enoch Travis, born 25 December 1839, died 3 March 1843.

****

Wiley Coleman Travis died 1916.

****

Elizabeth Coleman Travis died 26 April 1896.

****

Amos Travis -- Nothing else.
(Amos Travis married a Miss Coleman and moved to Gainesville, Alabama. After the Civil War he and family removed to Los Angeles, California. They later returned to Alabama and purchased the place known as the present Travis place near McCainville.)

******

HORN CEMETERY

This cemetery is near Horn's Bridge on the Sucarnoochee River. The road has been abandoned and the bridge has fallen in - it was built by James Horn (Acts 1835, page 102; Virginia Foscue, Place Names Sumter County - a Thesis U. of A. - page 35.) This cemetery could never be found without a guide; it was by the kindness of Mr. Jake W. Dial that we were able to finally, after much search, to find it deep in the woods. There are several sunken unmarked graves; cows have knocked the stones over and they became covered with the loam of the forest.

INSCRIPTIONS

Mary, consort of Harris W. Killen, and daughter of John and Asenath Horn, born 15 September 1811, died 4 May 1848. (John Horn's wife was Asenath Simms. See Old Side Cemetery records for other Horn relationships.)

****

Aramenta, daughter of Harris W. and Mary Killen, born 1 October 1843, died 17 October 1844.

****

Infant son of Harris W. and Mary Killen, who was born 22 July 1840, died 24 July 1840. (See Parker Cemetery records for H. W. Killen's 2nd wife.)

(According to the Thomas, Simms and Horn families there were four Horn brothers who moved to Alabama circa 1836, viz: John, Henry, Josiah and Jere. Josiah, a doctor, settled near Mobile; the others came to Sumter County, Alabama. Henry Horn had children: Jacob, Zillah, John, Jere, Henrietta, Nancy, Millicent, Patience and Martha. Jacob married Polly Amason and moved to Texas; Zilla married Orson McDaniel of Sumter County 30 January 1845 and moved to Leon County, Texas; Jere married Mary Watson of Greene County, Alabama, after her death he married her cousin Bessie Coffield of Greene County, near Boligee.

Henrietta married George W. Bryant and moved to Louisiana; Nancy married Henry Holland; Millicent married Irvine Barnes and went to Leon County, Texas; Patience married W. R. Ellis; John married Patience Simms.

Isaac W. Horn of Brewersville, Sumter County, was a son of Thomas (Tony) Horn, brother of William Horn - their father was Jacob Horn, the immigrant who married Millicent Thomas, the sister of Theophilus Thomas, just after coming to America. Other children of Jacob Horn were: (1) John Horn born 14 September 1776, died 28 September 1841, who married Asenath Simms, born 8 April 1789, died 10 November 1842. Their children were: Sarah born 3 December 1803, died 25 November 1822, married Robert Simms; Patience born 24 May 1805, died 1847, married Morrison Thomas (brother of Bennett B. Thomas), buried at Grenada, Mississippi; Millicent born 23 May 1807, died 14 September 1891, married W. R. Thomas (brother of Bennett B. Thomas) died in Meridian, Mississippi; Mary born 15 September 1811, died 4 May 1848, married H. W. Killen; Nancy born 1813, died 1885; Eliza born 4 February 1816 married (1) B. F. Bullock, (2) Albert Sledge; John born 1820, died 1827; Julia A. E. born 24 September 1827, died 19 September 1894, married Bennett B. Thomas. (See Simms, Richardson, Hagood, Epes records Old Side Cemetery.)

(2) Henry - already given; (3) Josiah who went to Mobile; (4) Thomas who had son, Harris, (5) Edie, (6) Millicent, (7) Mourning and (8) Patience.

William Horn died in Choctaw County, Alabama circa 1855 at the age of 65 or 70 years of age; he married Nancy Holland in North Carolina. Nancy Holland had a sister Mary and a brother Exum, (whose daughter married Jesse Simms--see Simms records in Old Side Cemetery); William's wife Nancy died in N. C. in 1829 and he married Nancy's sister, a widow, Mrs. Mary Sykes.

Harris Horn's daughter, Martha, married Alfred Bunn in North Carolina - had two children Kate and Fannie.

(References: Horn, Simms, Thomas Bible records, from Mr. Sammie Webb, and Sumter County Court records.)

THE ELLIOTT CEMETERY

This cemetery is located near Payneville, Alabama, within a few steps of the old John Knox Elliott home. This place is now (1960) owned by Mr. Jake Dial.

INSCRIPTIONS

Henry M. Elliott, born 4 June 1894, died 5 December 1946. (He was the son of William Melangthon and wife, Margaret Bond Elliott. He was known as Heck - never married.)

****

Margaret Bond Elliott, born 9 March 1870, died 10 September 1946. (She was the wife of William Melangthon Elliott, who was also her first cousin. John Knox Elliott's third wife was Elizabeth Jane Eakins. Their son William Melangthon Elliott married Margaret Bond whose mother was Sue Eakins and father was Bob Bond. Sue and Elizabeth Jane Eakins were sisters.)

****

William Melangthon Elliott, born 8 February 1861, died 9 June 1919. (He was the husband of the above Margaret Bond Elliott, and the son of John Knox Elliott and wife, Elizabeth Jane Eakins. They married 1 June 1857. They were the parents of John Luther, William Melangthon, Anna Margaret, Calvin Andrew, Matthew Henry and Mary Elizabeth. See Central Cemetery for Calvin Andrew and Matthew Henry Elliott families.)

****

Infant son of William M. and M. E. Elliott. (Stone was broken so could not read date.)

****

Susane, daughter of W. M. and M. E. Elliott born and died 1896.

****

The next grave was of an infant.

****

John Luther, son of John K. and Elizabeth Jane Elliott, born 28 May 1859, died 21 September 1878. (The Elliott family records show that he died in Livingston 4:30 A. M. of yellow chills of 34 hours duration.)

****

Annie M., daughter of J. K. and E. J. Elliott, born 18 March 1868, died 23 October 1878. (The family record says that she died of "yellow disease after being sick from Saturday morning 19 October to Wednesday morning at 1:00. Died very easy.")

****

John Knox Elliott, born at Pulaski, Tennessee, 1 March 1813, died 13 February 1892. (He was the son of Andrew and Anna Knox Elliott -- see section #32, Township 20 Range 3 West.)

****

Elizabeth Jane Elliott, wife of John Knox Elliott, born in Hanover County, North Carolina, 16 November 1826, died 14 February 1893. (See Margaret Bond Elliott gravestone inscription.)

****

Bessie, daughter of C. A. and R. B. Elliott, born 25 March 1898. (She was the daughter of Calvin Andrew and Rosa Daniel Elliott - both buried at Central Cemetery.)

****

John Knox Elliott was married two other times; (1) to Nancy T. Payne 21 April 1836. She was born 4 March 1815. In her husband's hand writing the following is recorded: "She died at 6:30 on the Sabbath 25 August 1850. She had 10 chills and fevers, her head was the seat of her trouble at the last. She was an affectionate wife and mother and I feel greatly her loss on this 5 September 1850. She died with but one struggle; I hope she went home to her Saviour to praise her Lord forever more. She was not in her right mind for two days before she died. She did not leave any directions about her children. Her children Harriet A. V. was born 1844, Susannah, Roxanah Missouri Elliott born 23 October 1846, Nancy Louisiana Elliott was born 1849, died 1857 of "inflamation of the brain" (the above Roxanah Susannah Elliott died 1872 at her Uncle's, D. Elliott at Tuscaloosa City, buried at Hardwick Graveyard. She married T. Ormond 1869.) Wife (2) was Nancy Oliver Nowlan. They married 20 December 1854. She was born 29 February 1830. Her child was Martha Cornelia and was born 17 September 1855; Nancy O. Elliott "departed this life 7 January 1856 after a months sickness with pneumonia."

RHYNE CEMETERY

This cemetery is located near the Mississippi-Alabama line on the Payneville-Lauderdale road, now abandoned. The road followed the old Indian trail used in pre-historic times. It leaves the present used road near the state line and runs due south west. This cemetery lies at the edge of the woods where the old road becomes impassable except as a trail.

When the Choctaw Indians started their long trek west they followed this trail as far as Daleville, Mississippi. There they congregated in preparation for their journey of blood and tears to their new home in Oklahoma.

I located this cemetery too late to do any research on the families buried there. It was by the kindness of W. Jake Dial that this cemetery was located.

INSCRIPTIONS

John E. Rhyne, born 27 May 1858, died 20 September 1862.

Sarah A. Rhyne, born 23 August 1845, died 20 January 1863.

Mary H. Rhyne, born 23 August 1845, died 20 January 1863.

Jabez A. Rhyne, born 3 March 1848, died 21 July 1870.

James Griffin, born 22 December 1820, died 11 December 1851.

J. W. Thedford, born 2 July 1825, died 7 April 1885.

DAVIS CEMETERY

This cemetery is located across Sucarnoochee River from old McCainville; and was considered part of that community. W. R. Davis owned this land; and the Danners, the Mimms and the Mellerds were neighbors along the south side of Sucarnoochee in the Horn's Bridge community.

It would be impossible for anyone to give directions to this cemetery. It is deep in the woods on the very bank of the river in a thicket of trees and brambles. We tried to find it by directions but failed so had a Negro who had worked land on that place years before to guide us to it; even then it was hard to find. At one time there were several graves with stones but today there are only three stones left.

INSCRIPTIONS

William R. Davis, born 8 October 1831, died 11 December 1871. (The Sumter County Journal 1871, 27 October, gives his obituary as follows: "Mr. W. R. Davis was a well-to-do planter ... leaves a daughter circa 13 years old -- (note: see Boyd Cemetery for Susan Boyd records) -- and a large circle of friends; he was a generous hearted friend, obedient son, kind father and true friend." He had married Mary Amelia Danner, the daughter of Jacob Getson Danner and wife Elizabeth Boyd (daughter of John and Jane or Jeanett (Dial) Boyd), 29 October 1857. William R. Davis was the son of Samuel Davis who married (2) Susannah Campbell in Greene County, Alabama 11 November 1830. Samuel was in the War of 1812, Private in Capt. Griffin's Company, S. C. Militia - received land certificate #12321 for 80 acres in Alabama. Samuel's will or settlement of the estate is in Probate Records' Book 8 p-113 Sumter County, Alabama. Names James T., as a non-resident. Other children were: John W., Rachel Walton wife of Richard Walton, William R., Headley, Hugh M., (he was captured at Petersburg in Civil War, and he was born 5 March 1836), Mary, Ellen, Amanda C., and Pernicey. Samuel's wife, Susan, was living at the time of his death. According to the 1850 Census William R. was born in 1830, Headley 1834, Hugh M. in 1836, Mary in 1838, Ellen in 1840, and Penny (Pernicia) in 1844. The marriage records show that Headley married Mary Dial 29 July 1869 - no children, but reared Susan daughter of William R.; Hugh M. married A. T. Johnson 6 December 1866;

Ellen married Hugh Getson Danner, brother of Mary Amelia Danner who married William R. Davis; and those who married prior to their coming to Sumter County were Rachael who married Richard Walton, and James T. who married Margaret Waine.)

The father of Samuel Davis and grandfather of William R. Davis was Chesley Davis, a Revolutionary Soldier, who died in Abbeville District, South Carolina in 1827. His will may be found at Abbeville Court House, Abbeville, S. C. He named in his will "my children (1) Samuel, (2) Daniel, (3) Littleberry, (4) Gabriel, (5) Jesse, (6) Beulah, (7) Nancy Hepziah, (8) Augustus. After the death of Chesley Davis certain members of his family came to Greene County, Alabama between 1829 and 1831. (Wesley Davis son of Gabriel Davis is said to have been born in S. C. in 1829 and died in Green County Alabama in 1831 -- Family Bible records). Chesley Davis was a soldier in the 3rd South Carolina Regiment, commanded by Col. Thompson - see Folder 14 page 19, Department of Archives, Columbia, South Carolina.

The second wife of Samuel Davis was Susannah Campbell of Greene County, the daughter of David Campbell who was a Revolutionary War Patriot and Soldier as per record A A 1018 acct. 1392-B, Department of Archives, Columbia, S. C. "Mr. Campbell supplied a steer to the miltia in 1782 - curr. £15-0 Int. £2/2/10."

According to Snedecor's Directory of Greene County published about 1855, Davis Campbell came to Greene County, Alabama 1817 and became the first settler in the north west corner of the county at Havana. The Indians held possession at that time to the hills of that part of the county and committed acts of depredation and murder, page 60 of Directory. David Campbell's will is recorded in Book C p-119 Greene County, Signed 7 January 1846 and probated 3 May 1846. Wills possessions to wife Lucretia, to daughter Margaret Aubrey; to daughter Susan Davis wife of Samuel Davis of Sumter County; to son William Campbell of Sumter County; to daughter Jane Fields wife of Elias C. Field; to daughter Cynthia Hall wife of A. J. Hall, to daughter Margaret Aubrey wife of Mr. Aubrey of Itawambee County, Mississippi, to daughter Mary wife of Thomas Elliott, to daughter Elizabeth wife of John Elliott (Elizabeth became the second wife of B. H. Elmore).

The family Bible gives the birth date of Susan or Susannah Campbell who married Samuel Davis as 14 March 1814.

Lucretia, wife of David Campbell, died prior to 1856. Will probated in Book 3 p-426 Greene County and mentions in will "my daughter Susan Davis - to whom she willed her carriage, - my son William Davis, and my daughter Mary Autrey."

****

Robert G. Danner, son of H. G. and E. G. Danner, born 1860, died 1863.

****

Susan Emmer Danner, daughter of H. G. and E. G. Danner, born 2 February

1864, died 1868.

(The above children were the son and daughter of Hugh G. Danner - son of Jacob Getson Danner and his wife Elizabeth Boyd Danner -- See their gravestone records at Boyd Cemetery -- and his wife Ellen Davis the sister of William R. Davis. These children, Robert G. and Susan Emmer were double first cousins of Susan Davis, daughter of William R. Davis and wife of Robert J. Boyd who was her second cousin also.) References: Sumter County Court records, family Bible records.

MIMS FAMILY CEMETERY

This Cemetery is located north of the Livingston-Horn Bridge road in the woods. It lies to the west of the Fluker place. One would have to have a guide to find it. There are only two marked graves in this cemetery. One can see partially covered up stones in a big brush, briar tangled heap. It looks as if a bull dozer pushed up the stones in a pile and the brambles grew over them. Neighborhood Negroes have taken over part of this cemetery and keep their part fairly well cleaned off.

INSCRIPTIONS

Seabourn Mims, died 17 December 1842, aged 55 years 8 months 4 days.

Elizabeth Hubbard Mims, died 14 October 1842, aged 50 years, 6 months, 23 days.

Orphans' Record Book 7 page 809 - The heirs of Seabourn Mims are as follows: Nancy wife of Robert A. Baker, Elizabeth J. wife of Elisha A. Mellard, Caroline wife of William A. Willis, Sarah H. wife of Johnson C. Williams, Alexander T. Mims, William A. Mims, and minor heirs: Seaborn D. Mims, Alabama F. Mims and Robert L. H. Mims.

Notice in the "Voice of Sumter" 1840, as follows: "Miss Augusta Fletcher of Barton Academy, Mobile, will open school at the home of Mr. Seaborn Mims -- a Female School -- Board may be had in several families of the community at $8.00 per month, including washing. Tuition will be $10.00 per session for Reading, Writing, Orthography; Geography, Arithmetic, English and Grammar will be $15.00 per session; Astronomy, Rhetoric, History, Geometry and Menmonics $25.00; Music $25.00; use of instruments $5.00.

******

MELLARD CEMETERY

This cemetery is south of the Sucarnoochee River on the Horn Bridge Road and just a few steps east of Mr. Carl Turk's barn. This place was known as the Ladocia or Theodosia Moore place in the early settling of the county. Theodosia Moore was the widow of Robert Moore; she later married Mr. Allison.

INSCRIPTIONS

Elisha Asbury, son of E. A. and E. J. Mellard, born 16 January 1843, died 5 September 1854.

****

Frances C. Willis, daughter of W. A. and C. M. Willis, died 11 August 1849 (?), aged 4 years 11 months, and 4 days. (The child's mother, C. M. Willis, was the daughter of Seabourn Mims.)

******

Elizabeth J. Mellard, consort of E. A. Mellard, daughter of Seabourn and Elizabeth Mims, died 5 September 1852, aged 36 years, 11 months and 26 days. (See Mims' Cemetery record.)

Seabourn Mellard married Martha D. Howie. Elisha A. Mellard married (1) Elizabeth Mims, (2) Jane P. Simmons. It is said that Susan (Simmons) Boyd is buried in an unmarked grave in this cemetery. She was visiting at the Mellard home and died. The waters were too high to carry her body back to Boyd Cemetery for burial.

WATSON CEMETERY

This cemetery is located on the Watson place on the banks of the Bodka Creek. As there is a close relation of this family to the community and old Liberty Church near Ramsey I will include them in this book. At one time there was a ford on Bodka just behind the Newton place which connected the Newton, Watson, Rae and Lacy families with the Liberty Church-Ramsey community. (See Boney Cemetery and Old Ramsey histories.)

INSCRIPTIONS

Mattie B., wife of Tom Watson, 22 November 1872, aged 33 years of age.

******

Floyd Watson, died 22 March 1926, aged 58 years. (He was born 1866.)

******

Grover Watson, died 18 April 1931, aged 51 years. (She was the wife of Floyd Watson. He married Grover Aust in 1906. They had two sons, Floyd and Frank, and Alice who married Jimmie Foresman; and Ann who married Guy Purvis. Floyd married Irene Bell - See Bell family in another volume. Frank married Mary Lou Wall of Scooba.)

******

Infant son of Floyd and Grover Watson, born 18 September 1908.

******

Martha Jane, wife of William Ashford born 8 February 1829, died 17 August 1850- (Martha Watson married William Ashford 31 January 1849 - Marriage Book 2 page 51, Sumter County.

(I have not been able to locate the graves of Jaret and Judy (Holt) Watson, the pioneer forebears of this family.

The Watsons, the Newtons, the Reas, the Wrens and others were travelling through in a wagon train for points west when Mr. Watson fell from his wagon and broke his leg. This band of travellers decided to camp on the spot for the winter. They liked the place so they made their permanent homes on the banks of Bodka.

Jaret Watson came to Sumter County from Marengo County where he married Judy Holt 6 February 1821, page 14 Book 1, Marengo County, Alabama. Cader Holt was Judy's father and James Holt was perhaps her grandfather. James Holt died prior to 1824. The estate was settled 16 May 1825 - Misc. Records page 48, Marengo County, Alabama

Jaret Watson (also spelled Jared, Jarret, Jeared) died ca 1861. His son, Thomas F. Watson, was administrator of the estate, (Orphans' Record Book 20-330, Sumter County.) The heirs named as follows: Thomas F. Watson, residing in Greene County, Alabama; Elizabeth Pollard, Sumter County, Alabama; Samuel T. Watson residing in St. Laudie or Laudry Parish, Louisiana; Samuel L. Ashford, Kemper,County, Mississippi; William T. (or J.) Watson of St. Laudie Parish, Louisiana; Judith Louisa Cade of Holmes County, Mississippi. They were all of age except Samuel L. Ashford who was 12 years old in 1862/64.

Louisa Watson married William Ashford 31 January 1847, Jaret Watson consents. When the estate was finally settled in 1864 we find William J. (or T.) Watson living in Sumter County; Thomas F. Watson was a physician.)

JOHN EVANDER BROWN FAMILY CEMETERY

"The Cedars", Sumterville.

This cemetery is located on the right side of the drive, leading from the old Sumterville-McCainville road, to the John E. Brown home now occupied by his great granddaughter, Mrs. Burton G. (Julia Praytor) Killingsworth. This lovely old home, built in 1848, is known as "The Cedars" as the drive way was lined on either side by stately old cedars imported into the community from old Jones Bluff. A cyclone in the 1950's uprooted all these trees and took the roof off the old house but did not destroy the lovely heirlooms which have been handed down in the family for generations.

INSCRIPTIONS

John Evander Brown, born 5 September 1809, died 17 March 1868. (He was the grandson of Rev. John Brown, Revolutionary War patriot, of Burlington, New Jersey. Reverend Brown was born 20 August 1714 and died in South Carolina in 1801/02. He had 5 daughters and 2 sons. The sons' names were Sam and Jesse. Sam married (1) Miss Newberry and they had 2 sons, viz: John and William; he then married (2) Miss Murphy and had a son Jeremiah. The above John Brown, son by his first wife, married Julia Ann Windham 1 September 1808 and they became parents of 10 children - 7 boys and 3 girls - among whom was John Evander Brown. The father of these 10 children was drowned in Pike County, Alabama after which tragedy John Evander Brown, along with his "kith and kin" came to Sumter County, Alabama. Some of John E.'s brothers settled near him and his half uncle, Jeremiah or Jere Brown, settled a couple of miles east of him. John Evander and George Brown, brothers, married Mary Jane and Sara Godfrey, daughters of William Godfrey - see Godfrey records in Sumterville Methodist cemetery. John E. Brown served his county in the State Legislature and is said to have been instrumental in getting the name of his town changed from "Patton Hill" to "Sumterville". John E. and Mary Jane (Godfrey) Brown had children as follows: Mrs. Julia Stewart, Mrs. (Dr.) R. M. Harris, Mrs. (Major) J. G. Harris, Mrs. Nettles, Mrs. Lurton who married (2) Dr. Randall, Mrs. Reynolds (her son married a daughter of Dr. McCain's - and Dr. McCain married a granddaughter of Jere Brown, so Mr. Reynolds and Miss McCain were distantly related).

****

Mary Jane, wife of John Evander Brown, born 12 January 1816, died 6 March 1883. (She was the daughter of Harriett Pegues (Powe) and William Godfrey. Harriett P. Powe married (1) a Mr. McRae and (2) William Godfrey - see Methodist Cemetery at Sumterville for Godfrey line. See Boyd Cemetery for Powe history.

****

John E. Brown, Jr., died 3 March 1866, aged 22 years, 8 months. (He was born in 1843.)

****

Arthur Godfrey Brown, died 9 October 1866, aged 12 years, 10 months, 6 days. (Born 1854.)

****

Julia Brown, wife of Lt. Col. C. S. Stewart, C.S.A., born 11 December 1836, died 1 March 1928. (She was the daughter of John E. and Mary Jane (Godfrey) Brown; her husband was a brother of Frederick Stewart who married Amelia Godfrey, a sister of Mary Jane (Godfrey) Brown - both daughters of Harriett Pegues (Powe) and William Godfrey. Col. Stewart was accidentally killed by an explosion of a shell from his own cannon during the War Between the States.

****

Mary Jane Stewart, wife of Hugh Boyd Praytor, born 17 April 1857, died 17 March 1929. (She was the daughter of Julia (Brown) and Lt. Col. C. S. Stewart.)

****

Hugh Boyd Praytor, born 1 April 1856, died 15 May 1942. (He was the son of Middleton Praytor - see his obituary - He and his wife, Mary Jane (Stewart) Praytor had two children to get grown, viz: Stewart who married Annie Laurie Freeman, and Julia who married Burton G. Killingsworth of Aliceville, Alabama. Julia (Praytor) and B. G. Killingsworth had children: Burton Killingsworth, not married; Hugh Killingsworth who married Madelyn Holp and they have children Lynn and Paul; Lillie Marie Killingsworth married James E. Williams and they have children Louise, Jim and Mike; Julia Killingsworth married William L. Ivey and they are parents of one child Martha House. Julia (Praytor) and husband, B. G. Killingsworth living 1960.

****

Charles Stewart Praytor, born 5 November 1883, died 13 October 1918. (He married Annie Laurie Freeman, whose grandmother was a Miss Clay, a cousin of Henry Clay, married Nathaniel Nuckols who was descended from John Nuckols the immigrant forebear who settled at Jamestown in 1607. Laura Caroline, daughter of Nathaniel Nuckols, was educated in New York City - going to Charleston by stage from Georgia, thence by boat to New York. She married George Fouche Freeman and they were parents of a son, Harvey Hawkins Freeman, after they removed to Alabama; he married Ettie Alice Harwell and they became the parents of Annie Laurie who married Charles Stewart Praytor. After Charles Stewart's death she married Oliver Reuben Chafin son of Laura Prescott (Gilliland) and James Madison Chafin, both buried at Salem Church Cemetery, Crossville, Alabama. Children of Annie Laurie and Oliver Reuben Chafin are: Oliver Reuben Chafin Jr., and Roger Stewart Chafin. The Chafins live at Panola. Charles Stewart Praytor and Annie Laurie had no children.)

****

Hugh E., son of H. B. and M. S. Praytor, born 25 July 1899, died 16 July 1890.

****

Two little graves marked "Infant" children of R. M. and E. D. Harris.

****

Ella F., daughter of R. M. and E. D. Harris, died 19 February 1864, aged 2 years, 10 months. (The above children, Infants and Ella F. were grandchildren of John E. and Mary Jane Brown.)

****

Charles Stewart Herring, born 18 March 1887, died 1 April 1922.

****

Julia Ada Herring, born 11 July 1892, died 16 October 1918. (Charles S. and Julia A. Herring were grandchildren of Julia (Brown) and C. B. Stewart.)

****

JONES FAMILY CEMETERY

This cemetery is located about 2 miles north of Emelle and west of Hughway #17 about a mile. It is on an impassable plantation road except in very dry weather. And it is almost impossible to find it except by guide. There is a high brick wall around this cemetery - in perfect condition; the bricks made by slave labor. After the death of Dr. Jones and his wife, and two of his sons dead, Mr. Philip Willingham had charge of this plantation with its 106 slaves. At the present Mr. R. H. Darrah, a relative, has it in charge. Several of the descendants of the old Jones slaves still live on this place. See Township 20 for more history of this family.

INSCRIPTIONS

Dr. Benjamin A. Jones born 10 June 1791, died 29 June 1859.

****

Mary J. wife of B. A. Jones, born 27 August 1798, died 20 June 1858.

****

Addison Ward Jones, born 6 October 1831, died 15 June 1857.

****

Benjamin A. Jones, Jr., born 11 September 1838, died 29 August 1852.

(See Vol. 2 "Pioneer Families of Sumter County" for more of the history of this family, Jones-Giles-Neville-Brown.)

****

DILLARD FAMILY CEMETERY

This cemetery is located north of old Ramsey Station about a couple of miles, and near the south bank of Bodka Creek. It is very hard to get to as one has to go through pastures. The roads are rough in dry weather and like goo in wet weather. The first time I saw this cemetery it was well kept by Osborn Jones, a colored man. Since his death the stones are knocked over, and buried in the ground. My son, Henry Jenkins, had to dig them out of the soil. They were hard for us to locate even we thought we knew exactly where to look.

Dr. Dillard was one of the first doctors of his section, along with Dr. B. A. Jones. He married a sister of W. O. and J. M. Winston, so the Dillard history will be given in Vol. 2. "Pioneer Families of Sumter County," along with the Winston history.

Inscriptions

John J. Dillard, born in Amherst County, Va., 7 March 1797, died 10 October 1850.

******

Eliza, daughter of Dr. J. J. Dillard and N. C. Dillard, born 31 October 1829, died 17 October 1851 aged 21 years. - Slab erected by her husband.

******

Watson W. Dillard, born 22 June 1843, died 14 August 1856.

(I believe there were other stones in this cemetery but they could not be located. Perhaps they are buried quite deep as it looked as if a bull dozer had pushed trees over the graves and then burned.)

****

NICHOLAS LACY CEMETERY

This cemetery is located about a mile in front of the A. G. Boyd place on the old Emelle-Livingston road. The Lacy place is now owned by Mr. Jake Dial. The old cemetery is in a pasture. We had to walk about to get to it and even then could find only pieces of two stones which were partially covered with sod. We had to have a guide to show us where the graves were. There are signs of perhaps a dozen graves.

Inscriptions

Nicholas Lacy, born 4 October 1790, died 20 July 1858.

******

Mary Lacy, born 1793, died 26 June 1843.

(The 1850 Census gives Nicholas Lacy as Family 344, and he was 59 born in South Carolina, Asta M. Lacy was 26 and born in Alabama, Carline Lacy was 19 and born in Alabama, Sara Lacy was 17 and born in Alabama, Feriby Darden was 24 and born in Alabama (Feriby Lacy married John Darden 9 May 1843 in Sumter County, Alabama. Benjamin Bustiant was 10 and born in Alabama, Frely Jones was 30 and born in North Carolina.)

******

BROWNING CEMETERY

This Cemetery is located about 2 miles north of Emelle on the right side of the road, not far from where the Hamner road leaves High Way #17. It has grown up in bushes; some stones have fallen down and one of them is broken. One would have to have a guide to get to this cemetery because the growth is so dense the graves would be hard to find. There is part of an old picket fence still leaning against the brambles after the passing of a century since it was put there.

Inscriptions

John Bailey Browning, born 21 November 1831, died 12 August 1869. (He was the son of John and Clary (Classie) Browning. He attended the University of Alabama and graduated in Medicine in Philadelphia. He fought in the Civil War and afterward he practiced medicine with a doctor in the neighborhood, Dr. Chouteux. Later Chouteux became a scallywag, cohort of Billings, the notorious carpetbagger. The two of them incited the Freemen against the whites; the situation became so acute until the white people under the leadership of Dr. Browning, Mr. Sledge, the Richardson brothers and many more attempted to stop their dastardly, insidious acts of depradation on the whites. The outcome of which was the murder of Dr. Browning by Coblintz, body guard of Dr. Chouteux after Yankee Ben (Chouteux' former guard) was killed. (See Richardson history.)

Elizabeth C. Browning, born 1829, died 1853.

J. H. Handley, born 24 November 1846, died 3 September 1853.

Schaharrissa B. Handley, born --- dates not readable .. (Schaharrissa Browning married Peter Handley 13 May 1845. After her death Peter Handley married Miss L. S. --Louisiana or Lou -- Hutchins od Sumterville - see Methodist Cemetery records.

Classie - Clary - or Schaharrissa Anderson married John Browning in Marengo County, Alabama 25 December 1823. Bailey W. Anderson was bondsman. She was a cousin of Catina (Anderson) Thomas - see Boney Cemetery records - my late husband, Bertram Andrews Jenkins, has told me many times that his great aunt Catina used to tell him about "Cousin Clary Browning" and related to him the killing of John Bailey Browning; she said also that when the Brownings left here some of Dr. Browning's medical books were left with "Aunt Cat". These books were burned about 50 years ago, however. Clary Browning was closely related to William G. Anderson, Sumter County's first Probate Judge.

The 1850 Census shows the Browning family as follows: John Browning age 50 born in Georgia, Clary Browning age 47 born in Kentucky, John (Bailey) Browning aged 18 born in Alabama, Martha J. aged 15 born in Alabama, John H. Handley age 3 born in Alabama.)

For your personal notes

CHAPTER VI

DEATH NOTICES FROM EARLY NEWSPAPERS

DEATH NOTICES PUBLISHED IN THE

"THE SUMTER COUNTY WHIG" 1840 - 1845

Died 27 October 1843, Mrs. Elizabeth Anderson, consort of William Anderson, Sen., Esq., in the 73rd year of her age. She was born in South Carolina in 1770; she was married to Mr. Anderson at the age of 16; a Baptist. She left many children, grandchildren and great grandchildren to mourn her death. At the time of her death she had seven little orphan children in her home. (The orphan children she had in her home at the time of her death were those of her daughter Dorcas (Anderson) and Eli Davis who married in Clark County, Alabama 25 September 1819 - see Alabama Genealogical Register, p. 57, Vol. 1, number 2. The Andersons left North Carolina early in the 1800's and joined other members of their families in Kentucky. They came to Clark and Marengo County about the time Alabama became a State; and when Sumter County was opened for settlement many of the kith and kin came to the newly formed county while others went on to Texas, followed later by many who stayed awhile in Sumter County. Elizabeth Anderson was born Elizabeth Easley the daughter of John Easley (1st Lieut. in the Revolutionary War and his wife Ann Gowen. John's father was John, and his mother was Joyce ———; this John's parents were Warham Easley and wife Sara Barnes; Warham's father and mother were Ann (Parker) and Robert Easley.)

* * * * * *

Died Mr. William Anderson, Sen., 80 years of age, Friday night, 11, February 1845. He had been to Livingston that day attending to business. He went home with half dozen friends, ate a hearty supper and soon after without a sigh, moan or a groan he dropped to the floor a helpless corpse. He was a zealous and devoted friend; a kind and affectionate husband, father and master; he was emphatically an honest man. He had children, grandchildren and great grandchildren to mourn his death. (Mr. Anderson's son, William G(owen?) Anderson was Sumter County's first Probate Judge; helped to organize the county and also helped to decide the location of the county seat. A letter published in 1836 Voice of Sumter Newspaper from John B. Stevenson, headed San Augustine, Tex., 24 March 1836, stated that he, Judge W.G. Anderson and R.W. Caldwell were ''travelling West'' together and that Geo. W. Mason was with main army under Houston. William and Elizabeth Anderson's children were: 1) John Erwin Anderson who married Cynthia D. Harper in Clark County, Alabama 10 August 1816; 2) Caroline N. Anderson who married (1) Henry Walker (2) Elisha Lacy (See Boney Cemetery Records); 3) Dorcas Anderson who married Eli Davis 24 September 1819 Clark County, Alabama; 4) Mary Burns Anderson who married Alexander Birdsong in Marengo County, Alabama 18 February 1819; 5) Bailey W. Anderson who married (1) Olive Cook in Marengo County 18 January 1823. (2) to Louisa Burton 17 March 1832 in Sumter County, Alabama; 6) Huldah Anderson who married Stephen Lacy Davis 12 February 1821 in Marengo County, Alabama; 7) William G. Anderson who married (1) Isabel Corzine in Sumter County, Alabama 20 August 1833, (2) to Mrs. Elizabeth Taylor ca 1846 in Texas; 8) Albert Gallatin Anderson (Sumter County's first Tax Collector) married (1) Mary Ann Moore the niece of G.W. Harper's wife--she was a descendant of Hance Hamilton, Rev. Soldier, and (2) to Mary Develin Drummond, a wealthy widow, both in Sumter County in 1834 July 23, and 1844 February 9, respectively. The Eli Davis children, grandchildren of William Anderson were: Huldah married 23 January 1845 to George M. Vandyke; Amanda Davis married Jackson Ward (See her obituary in Sumter County Whig); Franklin W. Davis; John E. Davis; William B. Davis; Elisha L. Davis; Jane Davis who married Gray E. Scales; Eli Davis; and Dorcas Davis.

William Anderson was first cousin of Robert Anderson for who Anderson County, South Carolina was named; William's parents were John and Ann (Erwin) Anderson--Ann's parents were Matthew Erwin and wife of Augusta County, Virginia; John Anderson's parents were James and Jean Anderson who immigrated from Scotland to Philadelphia, Penn., thence to Augusta County, Virginia. William Anderson was closely related to John Anderson of Greenville County, South Carolina, who was killed along with his sons Joshua and Scarlett and from whom Vincent Anderson, who died 7 April 1833 in Sumter County, was descended.

* * * * * *

Drowned in the Sucarnachie (sic) River on 16 April 1844, Frank Attkison, near Payneville.

* * * * * *

Died 11 April 1845 in his 33rd year, Joseph P. Allen, born in Mecklenburg Co., Va.

- B -

Died the infant son of James L. and Rebecca D. Bachelor, 9 October 1844. (James L. Bachelor married Rebecca Bradford.).

* * * * * *

Died 14 October 1843, Mr. Robert Bell in his 50th year; a native of

Wayne County, North Carolina. He had resided in Sumter County for 8 years.

* * * * * *

Died in Gainesville in this county, 16 March 1845, Col. Andrew Beirne of Virginia. He was ca 70 years old.

* * * * * *

Died 16 February 1845 after a long illness, Mrs. Ann W. Bragg, aged 33 years. She was the consort of Alexander J. Bragg and the daughter of Harry Southall, Esq., of Warren County, North Carolina. She leaves a husband and two infant children.

* * * * * * *

Died Mr. Edwin Brownrigg, 10 miles west of Gainesville, on 10 May 1843. He was kicked by a mule on his temple and lived only a few minutes. (See Old Side Cemetery--Mary C. Tartt record.)

* * * * * *

Died of congestive fever on 13 July 1843, Mr. William Blackburn ca 28 years, employed by Mr. Andrew Glassell - Not known where his relatives are.

- C -

Died on this County on Wednesday last (1843). Major John Coats, ca 60 years of age.

* * * * * *

Died 25 September 1843 in Mobile, Clementina Georgiana, daughter of Col. E.B. Colgin, formerly of near Jones Bluff.

* * * * * *

Died Saturday, 2nd of September 1843 at the home of Hon. Reuben Chapman of Blount County, Alabama, Alexander Chapman, Esq., a native Caroline County, Virginia. For several years past he has resided in Sumter County.

* * * * * *

Died 14 October 1843, James Croom, infant son of Richard Croom, Esq. (The Crooms were natives of Newbern, South Carolina. Richard's brother, Hardy B. Croom of Florida, his wife and two daughters went down on the ''Home'' when wrecked in Florida waters in 1837. Richard Croom's wife was named Winifred - Deed Book B - Page 167.

* * * * * *

Died in Sumter County 11 February 1845, Mr. William H. Clark aged ca 58 years. Truly a good man. He left a large family of helpless or- to lament his death. (His daughter Jane married William Batton.)

* * * * * *

Died in Livingston 23 March 1844, Charles Henry, the eldest son of Willie Crenshaw, aged 9 years, 14 days. (Willis Crenshaw married Amanda H. Chiles in Greene County, Alabama 15 October 1825 (Book 1 Page 35) We find him on the Committee for Arrangements for 4th July Celebration 1836, Livingston, Alabama. (See Alabama Genealogical Register Volume 1, Number 1.) At one time Willis Crenshaw owned 1,480 acres of land 6 miles east of Livingston and 7,000 acres of land in South Sumter. He was president of the proposed Moscow-Livingston Rail Road, a project which never materialized.)

* * * * * *

Died October 1843, infant daughter of Tully R. Cornick. (See wife's obituary in Sumter Decocrat 1852. Tully R. Cornick married Sophia H. Mason 8 November 1838, in Sumter Co.)

* * * * * *

Died in this County 24 June 1844, Miss Elizabeth Boon Cobbs. She was born in Raleigh, North Carolina, 22 November 1828.

- D -

Died in this county Friday night, 18 November 1843, Captain William Drummonds, aged 50 years.

- E -

Died Henry Edwards, son of Captain William S. Edwards, near Sumterville, September 1844. (W.S. Edwards advertised in the Voice of Sumter that one of his negroes had escaped; he had purchased the Negro from W.H. Kirkland; he was believed to be on the Jeremiah Brown plantation as the negro had a wife there. This was in 1836.)

* * * * * *

Died Mr. Caldwell Estis of Belmont, on the 12 October 1843, about 90 years old. (Jemima Estis was executor of his estate. Orphans' Min. Book 4 - Page 392.)

- F -

Died Mr. Baldwin Foard at his residence at Midway, Georgia. He was a brother of Major Francis Foard of this county.

- G -

Died Burrell H. Green 17 July 1843 in Wakelock, Mississippi of congestive fever; he was 17 years old and the son of the late Mr. Daniel Green of Sumter County. (Those named as heirs of Daniel Green were: Elizabeth wife of James McCown; Nancy wife of James McMillan; Frances wife of Robert B. Gunn; Stacy wife of Radford M. Gunn; Louisa daughter of Charlotte and Jerome McCown; Louisa wife of David W. Field; Burrell H. Green; McDuffie Green; Martha Green; Melvira Green; Susan Green; James M. Green and Ezekiel Green. See "Parker Cemetery")

* * * * * *

Died Hollan Ann, 6 month old infant of William H. Green, Esq., 26 February 1844.

* * * * * *

Died John Dozier Godfrey on the 26 April 1844 at the residence of his father at Jones Bluff. (His father was William Godfrey--see his obituary, Sumter Democrat. John Dozier Godfrey married Margaret C. Phillips, 23 March 1837 the daughter of John and Martha G. Phillips, the latter was a Miss Myers. See Old Side Cemetery Records. Mrs. Margaret G. Godfrey later married Mr. Arrington.)

* * * * * *

Died in Eutaw 5 April 1845 of hemorrhage of the lungs, Mr. Greer of this county in the 25th year of his age.

- H -

Died Mrs. Nancy Heard, wife of Mr. Joel Heard, in her 59th year, on 12 October 1843. (She was Nancy Gilmore of Georgia, her father died around the turn of the century but her mother died in the 1820's or 1830's in either Clark or Sumter County. Joel Heard remarried to Elenor Knox, widow of John Knox.)

* * * * * *

Died on the 15 October 1843, John Heard, 2nd son of Joel and Nancy Heard in his 27 year.

* * * * * *

Died 1843, Mr. Allen Hodges of Payneville, Alabama. (Sumter County--

the old Payneville cemetery has no tombstones; they have either been carried away or perhaps there were no stones at the graves.)

* * * * * *

Died Mrs. Jane Green Handcock, consort of J.B. Handcock of Daleville, Mississippi, 4 February 1844.

- J -

Died Mr. William Johnson, formerly of Sumter County, in Mobile on 9 October 1843.

* * * * * *

Died Mrs. Elizabeth Jackson, consort of Cornelius S. Jackson, 10 October 1843. She was born in New York City; came to Sumter County in February 1840. She died of congestion of the brain. Left two small children.

* * * * * *

Died 27 May 1843, Mr. John S. Johnson in the 31st year of his age.

* * * * * *

Died Friday 11 August 1843, Mr. John S. Jemison in his 31st year, a Methodist. He left a wife and one small son. (Funeral preached 17 March 1844, by Reverend James O. Williams.)

* * * * * *

Died at Clinton, (Greene County), 20 September 1836, Mrs. Mary Jane Jordan, consort of Burwell P. Jordan, in her 20th year. Native of Louisburg, North Carolina.

* * * * * *

Died 12 April 1845, Mr. Reuben Jones, a Baptist. He left a wife and several children.

- K -

Died in Trinidad, Cuba, 24 March 1844 of consumption, Isham H. Kelly of Pickens.

* * * * * *

Died at the home of Dr. Sidney Smith of Marengo County 20 March 1844, Miss Mary F. Lawrence, daughter of William H. Lawrence of Green County.

* * * * * *

Died last Sunday night 21 May 1843, Mrs. Margaret G. Lake, consort of Joseph Lake, aged about 40 years.

- M -

Died in Mobile, Tuesday 28 January 1845, Judge James Martin, formerly of Salisbury, North Carolina.

* * * * * *

(16 August 1845 issue of the Sumter County Whig): Died Mr. Ansel May in his 25th year; he was a native of Tennessee.

* * * * * *

Died 20 October 1843 in Sumter County, Mrs. Sara P. Marr, aged 50 years, 8 months. She was born in Rowan County, North Carolina, a Presbyterian.

* * * * * *

Died 30 October 1843, Mrs. Rachel Moore, aged 78 years, 1 month and 26 days; a native of North Carolina, from whence she emigrated to Kentucky and thence to Tennessee and thence to Alabama. She has been a Methodist for 20 years. (She was the wife of Loderwick Moore and had several children among whom was a daughter who married G.W. Harper who became the first sheriff of Sumter County, later founded Hatpersville, Mississippi. A granddaughter, the daughter of Robert and Theodosia (Hamilton) Moore, married Albert G. Anderson, the first tax assessor in Sumter County. Other members of her family married into the Boyd and Elliot families, to name only a few.)

* * * * * *

Died at the home of M.E. Gray on the 22 July 1844, Mr. James A. Moore.

- Mc -

Died the Reverend Norman McLeod in Livingston in the 41st year of his age. He was born in North Carolina 1803. (An 1844 issue of Sumter County Whig)

- N -

Died the infant daughter of Preston G. Nash, on 8 October 1844.

- P -

Died Mrs. Julia Parent, consort of Lewis Parent, 6 October 1843 of bilious-pneumonia. She left one small child. (Lewis Parent remarried

24 March 1845 to Miss Mary Little, Lauderdale, Mississippi. He was a wheel wright and made all kinds of farm machinery. His slogan was "Do not pay if not satisfied."

* * * * * *

Died in Huntsville, Alabama 14 May 1844 Col. Leroy Pope, a Revolutionary soldier and a resident of Huntsville for 34 years.

* * * * * *

Died Mrs. Margaret Parker, consort of K. Parker. Esq., in her 45th year. She was a native of Edgecombe County, North Carolina. She left a husband and 4 small children.

* * * * * *

Died General John C. Pickens in Greene County, Alabama 19 April 1844. He had bilious fever.

- R -

Died Mr. Stephen Rushing of Belmont, Alabama. He was between 55 and 60 years old. (There are many Rushings buried at Belmont but I did not find the grave of Stephen Rushing. The oldest records on standing stones of the Rushing family were J.M. Rushing born 1804; Shephere Rushing born 1806. There was a buried stone which was found to be broken in several pieces but when pieced together we deciphered: "Mary Rushing born in South Carolina 1758, died 22 August 1837.")

* * * * * *

Died on the 10 June 1844 infant son (one of a twin) of James Rhodes, aged 6 weeks.

* * * * * *

Died Mrs. Lucy Roberts, wife of Captain William H. Roberts, on 25 April 1844, aged 26 years. She left a husband and 3 small children.

* * * * * *

Died 12 November 1843, aged 41 years, 7 months, 11 days, Mrs. Elizabeth S. Ryon consort of Mr. Jason Ryon.

- S -

Died in Fayette County a few days ago, Mrs. Jane Elizabeth, consort of William R. Smith Esq., formerly of Tuscaloosa--(1845 issue of Sumter County Whig).

* * * * * *

Died Mr. Edward H. Strother, 10 June 1844, aged 46 years.

* * * * * *

Died Mrs. Eviline Smith, consort of Mr. Robert H. Smith in Tuscaloosa October 1844. She was a resident of Sumter County. (Her husband was a lawyer with the firm of Robert H. Smith. William H. Green and Murray F. Smith. He was appointed to defend Negro Collins, a slave who killed Bethel Howard.)

* * * * * *

Died Mrs. Ellen Sherer, consort of W. Waldo Sherer, Esq., in the 18th year of her life, October 1843 -- a native of Lincoln County, Tennessee. Her mother died when Ellen was a child.

- T -

"The Marengo Patriot" of 15 March 1845 says that "Mr. James B. Tutt of Sumter County who owns a plantation near Woodville in Perry County was shot by his brother-in-law, Mr. Horton. (Note: Mr. Tutt died a few days later)."

* * * * * *

Funeral service for Mr. Morrison Thomas' children will be preached at the residence of Mrs. Eliza Ann Bullock's next Sabbath by Rev. O.L. Nash. (Sumter County Whig 1844 issue. Mr. Morrison Thomas married daughter of John Horh as did Mr. Bullock. See Old Side Cemetery Records for relationships to many Sumter County families.)

* * * * * *

Died Bennett Thompkins, Esq., of a congestive chill on 3 September 1844 at Kemper Springs, Mississippi. He had removed from Sumter County only a few days before his death. He was born in Caroline County, Virginia, 29 August 1810; he came to Sumter County 1836, where he practiced law. He left a widow and 2 children. (His widow was Margaret B. --)

- U -

Died John Gano Ustick, 4 September 1844 in his 61st year. He was born in Philadelphia, Penn., 24 January 1784. Before coming to Sumter County he was editor of a newspaper in Virginia.

- V -

Died Mrs. Mary Verell, 17 October in her 49th year of age, at the home of James R. Rhodes, Esq., she was born in Johnson County, North Carolina in 1795.

- W -

Died 26 September 1843, James Madison, infant son of Mr. and Mrs. Price Williams.

* * * * * *

Died 29 September 1843, Preston, the 2nd son of Mr. and Mrs. Price Williams. (According to the June issue of Sumter County Whig the funeral of the above children was preached June 1844.

* * * * * *

Died Mrs. Amanda Ward, wife of Mr. Jackson Ward, aged 23 years, 29 September 1843, also their infant daughter, Hully Caroline, aged 9 months died at the same time. (Jackson Ward married Amanda Davis 17 August 1837; her parents were Eli Davis.)

* * * * * *

DEATH NOTICES FROM
"SUMTER COUNTY JOURNAL" IN THE 1850s

Died in Livingston 10 May 1853, at the residence of her father, Annie, the second daughter of J.A. and S.T. Abrams, aged 8 years.

* * * * * *

Died 12 February 1854 in Yalabusha County, Miesissippi, Mary Archelas, daughter of James G. and Caroline E. Ashford, aged 1 year, 11 months.

* * * * * *

Died suddenly 11 January 1854 of cramp colic, while on a visit to his son, William Altman at Newton, Mississippi, John Altman of this county. He was 68 years old and was a native of Marion District, South Carolina.

- B -

Died in Leona, Texas, 16 March 1854, in his 22nd year, Dr. T.W. Boyette, born in Autauga County, Alabama. His parents immigrated to Sumterville in this county. (See Old Side Cemetery Records.)

* * * * * *

Died near Payneville in this county after a lingering illness, on Wednesday 2 June 1852, Mrs. Susan H. Boyd, wife of James M. Boyd and daughter of Robert Simmons, Esq. She was born in Georgia 1825; leaves a husband, 4 small children and an aged father to mourn their loss. (James M. Boyd was the son of John and Jennett (Dial) Boyd, and the grandfather of J. W. Boyd who now lives near Boyd, Alabama.)

* * * * * *

Died 29 April 1852 in her 27th year, Mrs. Pamelia Blackman, consort of Mr. R. Blackman.

* * * * * *

Died at the Female Academy, Mrs. Jerush L. Bradford, daughter of Rev. H. Loomis, Presbyterian Minister. She was born in Wellington, Conn., 21 November 1806. She had been in charge of the Academy prior to her death in 1852.

* * * * * *

Died at the home of his son-in-law Hon. S.B. Boyd, Sunday last, Mr. John Mason aged 68 years, late of Sumter County. He had been a Methodist for 40 years. (Published in the 10 July 1852 issue of ''The Sumter Democrat''. The Hon. S.B. Boyd, one of Sumter County's lawyers, is said to have moved to Knoxville, Tenn.)

* * * * * *

Died Jennett Ann, only daughter of James M. and the late Susan H. Boyd, born on the 11 February 1847; died 24 July 1852. (She was the granddaughter of John and Jane or Jennett (Dial) Boyd, Her great grandparents were Jeremiah Dial (Patriot) and Hugh Boyd (Patriot) both of South Carolina.)

* * * * * *

Died on the 25th of June 1852, Mrs. Eliza J. Bester, wife of Rev. D.P. Bester, aged 43.

* * * * * *

Died William Brewer, aged 76 years. (27 March 1852 Issue of Sumter Democrat.

* * * * * *

Died in this county 15 October 1852 Mr. Thomas Blackwell aged 38 years. He leaves a young wife.

* * * * * *

Died at James Bluff, Choctaw County, Alabama, on the 19 April 1853, Mr. Matthew H. Brewer, aged 80 years. He was a native of South Carolina.

* * * * * *

Died 22 June 1853 at 7 a.m. Sallie McGill Beck, aged 12 months, 12 days.

- C -

Died in Sumter County 5 January 1854, Mrs. Millicent T. Cockrell. Daughter of Jubal and Sara Carpenter. She was a Primitive Baptist. (She was the wife of Dempsey Cockrell and mother of Nathan Cockrell, Co-founder of the SAE Fraternity at the University of Alabama- this Nathan Cockrell is buried at Old Side Cemetery.)

* * * * * *

Died 21 January 1854 William Crenshaw lately of Livingston, formerly of Lauderdale County, Mississippi, in his 39 year. Death caused by a fall from a stage coach; the wheels ran over his head. (William Crenshaw married Elizabeth Shelton, daughter of Elish Shelton, 19 March 1840.)

* * * * * *

Died recently in Livingston, Mr. C. Coon, 45 years of age. (Published in the 15 October 1854 issue of the Sumter Democrat.

* * * * * *

Died at Capan Grey, Mississippi, 31 December 1851, Mrs. Sophia, consort of Tully R. Cornick, Esq., formerly of a Sumter County, ca 30 yrs. of age. (Tully R. Cornick married Sophia H. Mason 8 November 1838. See 1843 ''The Whig'' death notices.)

* * * * * *

Died at the residence of James L. Hainsworth, 18 October 1853, Miss Margaret J. Cravens, aged 28 years, of consumption at Brewersville, Alabama, Sumter County. (See Brewersville Cemetery in another volume.)

* * * * * *

Died at the residence of his brother-in-law, R.J. Allison, in this county, Dr. William Henry Coleman, in his 42nd year. (October issue of 1853 paper) Huntsville papers please copy. (He owned property in Livingston prior to 1836. He was on the committee, "for suitable toasts to be drank" at the 4th July Celebration in 1836 at Livingston. He made a speech at that dinner. See Alabama Genealogical Register, Vol. 1, Number 1.

Died near Livingston 21 November 1853, Frank, the youngest son of Augustus A. Coleman, aged 6 months, 12 days.

- D -

Died in Livingston 8 March 1852, William Duke, aged 19 years.

* * * * * *

Died in this vicinity 13 September 1853, Mr. Samuel Davis in his 63rd year. (He was the son of Chesley Davis of South Carolina.--See the will of Chesley Davis in Vol.2 page 294, Abbeville District, South Carolina. It is as follows: To son Daniel, to son Littleberry, to son Gabriel, to son Jesse, to daughter Nancy Hepzebah, to daughter Beulah, to Frances Harris property which would have gone to Susan had she lived, the rest of the property to be equally divided among his sons and daughters Samuel, Daniel, Littleberry, Nancy Hepzebah and Beulah.
Samuel, Daniel and Gabriel Davis Executors
27 August 1827   signed, Chesley Davis

Chesley Davis was a Revolutionary Soldier. #8 in a list of those who served in the 3rd S.C. Regiment commanded by Col. Thompson.--See Folder 14 page 19 South Carolina Archives Department, Columbia, S.C.

Samuel Davis' will of settlement of estate is in Orphans Book 8 page 113, 20 February 1854 Sumter County. Mentions James T. Davis as a non-resident heir of Samuel Davis. Others mentioned were: John W., Rachel Walton, wife of Richard, James P., William R., Headley, Hugh M., Mary, and Susan. Minor heirs were Headley, Hugh M., Mary, Ellen, Amanda C., and Pernicey. Guardian was W.S. Turman. The 1850 Census of Sumter County gives them as:

Samuel Davis	60	born	S.C.
Susan Davis	34	"	Ala.
William Davis	19	"	"
Headley Davis	16	"	"
Hugh Davis	14	"	"
Mary Davis	12	"	"
Ellen Davis	10	"	"
Amanda Davis	8	"	"
Pennecia Davis	6	"	"

Samuel was married twice. (See Boyd Cemetery Records for descendant of William (R.) Davis who was 19 in 1850.)

- E -

Masonic funeral for John Thomas Eason, M.D. will take place 2 miles west of Sumterville on Sunday 19 June 1853, commencing at 11 A.M.

* * * * * *

Died in Tuscaloosa 12 October 1853, Dr. Earl, aged ca 60 years.

* * * * * *

Died in Mobile of yellow fever, William Earbee, Sr., of this county on 1 December 1853. He had left his family here and started to Texas to look for a new home. (Mr. Earbee was one of the first settlers of Sumter County. He was one of the planners for the first big 4th of July Celebration to be held in Sumter County -- See Alabama Genealogical Register Vol. 1 Number 1, page 34. Also see Death Notices in Voice of Sumter. Earbee Beat in Sumter County was named for Mr. William Earbee.)

* * * * * *

Died James Harvey Fulton 28 March 1853 aged 23 years. He settled here February last.

- G -

Died in Livingston on the 22 June 1852, Matilda Louise, aged 1 year, 10 months, the only daughter of William H. Green. (William H. Green was a law partner of Murry F. Smith. He made a speech at the notable 4th of July celebration 1836. 150 persons ''sat down'' at this dinner, and speeches were given ''in thoughts that breathed and in words that burned.'' -- See Voice of Sumter Newspaper; also Alabama Genealogical Register, Vol. 1, Number 1, page 34.

* * * * * *

Died at Jones Bluff of this county on 29 April 1853, General William A. Gibson, in the 40th year of his age. (He was Post Master at Jones Bluff in 1849.)

* * * * * *

Died William Godfrey 21 January 1854 at Sumterville, Alabama, 79 years of age. One cold day he went to the Methodist Quarterly Meeting and during the sermon he seemed to enjoy ''the love of God shed abroad in his heart''. A short time afterward he was taken with an apoplectic fit and remained insensible until his death 15 hours later.

(He was a French Hugenot who became a Methodist. He ran for the office of County Commissioner in 1836 -- See Voice of Sumter Newspaper. See John E. Brown Cemetery Records; Boyd Cemetery Records and Sumterville Methodist Cemetery Rerords and John Dozier Godfrey in Sumter County Whig Death Notices.)

* * * * * *

Died in Sumter County Daniel Gould aged 37. (He married Eliza A. Langham 28 July 1837.

- H -

Died of congestion of the bowels at his residence in this county 29 July 1851, Mr. Richard Harris aged 64; a native of Abbeville District, South Carolina. He moved to Sumter County in 1836.

* * * * * *

Died at Mrs. Bingham's at Gaston on 5 January 1852, Rev. Robert W. Hadden in the 28th year of his age and 3rd year of his ministry. He received his education at Nassau Hall (Now Princeton) and his theological education at Columbia, South Carolina. (He is buried at Bethel Cemetery by the side of his parents. There is a difference between data on tombstone and that in this article. See history of Hadden Church, Payneville, Alabama and Bethel Cemetery Records.)

* * * * * *

Died in this county 17 December 1853, Nimrod W. Hilman in his 46th year. He has been a citizen of Sumter County for 15 years;a native of Orange County, Va. (Should this be Orange County, North Carolina? He married Sara Ann May, 6 March 1848.

* * * * * *

Died in Livingston 27 August 1853,James Ferrel Harris, son of J.W. and Mrs. Harris, aged 2 years and 18 days.

* * * * * *

Died near Intercourse in this county on the 18 June 1853, Austin Hitt in his 42nd year.

* * * * * *

Died in Livingston 14 June 1853, John William, infant son of H.H. and Mary S. Harris, aged 17 months and 4 days. (Mr. Harris is mentioned in the Voice of Sumter - 1836 - as being a property owner in Livingston at that time.)

* * * * * *

Died in the neighborhood of Jones Bluff 1 June of dysentery, Mr. Joshhua W. Hilman in his 45th year.

* * * * * *

Died at the residence of his brother-in-law, Mr. Parker, David Hines aged 14 years. He was the only son of Charles and Elizabeth Hines. (Two daughters, Julia and Rebecca Hines, minor heirs of Charles Hines who died soon afterward.)

* * * * * *

Died at the residence of her father, 5 November 1852, Temperance Caroline, daughter of Bryant and Flewella Harrell, aged 19 years, 1 month 25 days.

* * * * * *

Died at the residence of Samuel Halsel in this county on 29 April 1852, Mr. Samuel M. Halsel in the 20th year of his age, of typhoid fever.

- J -

Died in Noxubee County, Mississippi, 31 October 1853, Mr. Jabel Jones formerly of Warsaw in this county, of typhoid fever, in the 43rd year of his age. (Jabel Jones was listed in the Poll List at Warsaw, March 1843 as #8.)

- K -

Died on the 14 June 1853, Benjamin Franklin Kennedy, son of B.F. Kennedy, who recently lost his wife. (B.F. Kennedy married Sally Ann Summerline 28 January 1852.)

* * * * * *

Died near Sumterville 10 October 1851, Amarnath Mary, wife of Harris W. Killen and daughter of Captain James Parker, aged 29 years, 5 months and 27 days. (See Parker Cemetery Records.)

- L -

Died Vernal Loweryn near Jones Bluff, 28 October 1851 from injuries from a fall. (His widow was named Prudence. He had a daughter Jane who married Thomas Kennard. Other children were: George, Vernal, Elizabeth, Prudence Ann and Catherine Kennard.) Will Book 2 page 13.)

* * * * * *

Died at Cottage Hill of dropsy, Charles Francis, son of Charles and Sara Labuzan, aged 4 years, 4 months. (1853 issue of the paper.-- There was a Mr. B. Lubazan who was manager of the 22 February ball given at the Planters' Hotel in Livingston in 1838. See Voice of Sumter.)

* * * * * *

Died 1 June 1853 infant daughter of Meredith and Agnes Lynn.

* * * * * *

Died near Brewersville, in this county, 21 June 1853, Mrs. Mary Ann Larkin, widow of the late Hon. R. Larkin. (This family will be mentioned at length in another volume of Pioneer Settlers of Sumter County.)

- M -

Died at Gainesville 22 May 1852, Mrs. Jemima, consort of A.L.D. Moore, 26 years of age. (Alfred L.D. Moore married Jemima Mitchell, 23 October 1848.)

* * * * * *

Died at the residence of her mother, Mrs. Jones of this county, on the 3 June 1852, Mrs. Mary, consort of Wesley A. Mundy aged 20 years. (Wesley A. Mundy married Harriett Blackwell (2), 24 September 1854.)

* * * * * *

Died in this county, 15 September 1852, Mrs. Elizabeth J. Mellard, aged 36 years, 11 months and 26 days. She was a Methodist; married E. A. Mellard 9 February 1832 and was the mother of 7 children.

* * * * * *

Died in Smith County, Texas 17 April 1854, Frank Marsh, Esq. He recently buried his son-in-law, Frank Bell.

* * * * * *

Died at Downieville, Forks of Yuba, California, Major Jeremiah Manasco, of Alabama. He was 39 years of age. (He married Miss Phoebe Hill 11 February 1846, in Sumter County, Alabama.)

* * * * * *

Died Mr. George M. Mallory, a native of Virginia, lately of Mobile.

* * * * * *

Died 30 July 1851, Robert Randolph, infant son of James W. and R.K. Maury, aged 2 months and 14 days.

- Mc -

Died 9 January 1854, Isadore McElroy, only daughter of William H. and Nancy McElroy, aged 1 year, 11 months and 11 days.

* * * * * *

Died in Livingston 25 July 1853, Martha Harriett, youngest child of Marie and the late Dr. William P. McRae, aged 8 months, 18 days. (Dr. McRae married Mary or Marie E. Hunter 14 October 1847.)

* * * * * *

Died on Sunday night 11 June 1853 after a protracted illness, Mrs. Mrs. Jacqueline S., consort of C.S. McConnico.

* * * * * *

Died in this place 4 October 1852, Maggie, the only daughter of C.S. and J.S. McConnico.

-N -

Died at his father's residence in Livingston, 12 May 1853, Frank, infant son of J.E. and M.A. Newman.

- O -

Died at the residence of E.N. Bryant, Esq., 10 January 1854, Miss Cherry Lane Oneal, 17 years of age. She was a Baptist. (The Richardsons and Oneals intermarried prior to the marriage of Harriett Richardson (Bryant and Uney Richardson's daughter) to William Oneal. E.N. Bryant married Cherry Lane Richardson (sister of Harriett) so Cherry Lane Oneal was the Bryant's niece.

- P -

Died 9 April 1852 at her home. Mrs. Azubak Post, wife of Mr. A. Post of Westbrook, Conn. (More about this family will be given in a later volume.)

* * * * * *

Died 21 February 1854, resident of this county of disease of the liver, Middleton Praytor, in his 61st year. (He is a forebear of Mrs. Julia (C.B.) Killingsworth -- see John E. Brown Cemetery records.)

* * * * * *

Died in Quchita Parish, La., 1 Septembef 1853, L. Decatur, age 3 years, 11months. 9 days, son of Col. L.D. and Harriett M.M. Phillips. (L.D. Phillips was the son of John and Martha G. (Myers) Phillips.)

* * * * * *

Died at her residence in Sumterville, in this county, Mrs. Martha G. Phillips, widow of Capt. John Phillips. (Shw was Martha G. Myers prior to her marriage. See Old Side Cemetery Records.)

* * * * * *

Died 21 September 1853, Benjamin Lucus, infant son of Benj. P. and Susan J. Portis.

* * * * * *

Died on the 25 Christ Mass (sic) Day 1853, Matthew B. Park, at Gaston in this county in the 22nd year of his age.

* * * * * *

DEATH NOTICES FROM
"LIVINGSTON JOURNAL " 1870s - 1880s

January 17, 1873 Issue.

Died Mrs. Eva Nash Cockrell, wife of W. A. Cockrell, on the 26 December 1872, in her 23rd year. She was the daughter of P. G. and Mrs. Lampeter Nash.

******

Died 22 November 1872, Mrs. Martha Watson, wife of Thomas F. Watson, Gainesville, Alabama. (Thomas F. Watson was son of Jarred Watson of Township 21.)

******

Died on 30 December 1872 Mr. Joseph Rogers, circa 63 years of age.

******

Died James I. Windham on the 26th December 1872, at his home at Warsaw.

******

Died at Warsaw on the 21st of December 1872, A. Irby.

******

Died at Warsaw on the 14th of December 1872, Mrs. Mary Ann Cunningham.

January 24, 1873 Issue.

Died 2 November 1872, Patrick Bogen May, Sr., born in Anson County, North Carolina, 3rd April 1799; moved to Alabama in 1817 and settled near St. Stephens and then to Greene County, Alabama; from there to Belmont in Sumter County where he lived for 30 years.

******

Died 23 January 1873 Henry Hooks Rogers, son of George W. and Mary S. Rogers, aged 18 months 12 days.

******

Mr. Bryant Richardson belonged to Hermon Lodge #106 F & A. M. Resolutions were passed at last meeting on the death of Mr. Richardson, signed by C. S. Henagan and J. D. McInnis.

******

Died at Ramsey's Station on Sunday February 16, 1873 of meningetis (sic) W. O. Simms, aged 20 years 2 months, 2 days. (He was the son of W. T. and Harriett (Gray) Simms.)

March 21, 1873 Issue.

Died near Gaston in Sumter County, Alabama, of paralysis, Martin Rumley on 11 March 1873, aged 66 years, 1 month, 22 days. He was a native of Beaufort, North Carolina; moved to Greene County, Alabama in 1835 and married and lived there until 1856 when he came to Sumter County. He leaves a wife and 4 children.

******

March 28, 1873 Issue.

Died Mr. Harriett Pipkin on the 27 February 1873, aged 68 years.

******

April 4, 1873 Issue.

Died Mrs. Patience A. Arrington 22 March 1873 of bronchitis, widow of the late Robert Arrington, in her 65th year.

******

Died Mrs. Tempie M. Scruggs, daughter of General Joseph and Mrs. Mary J. Arrington; born in Nash County, North Carolina 29 September 1817, moved to Sumter County when a child and married Josiah L. Scruggs 17 March 1838; died of pneumonia 31 March 1873.

******

April 11, 1873 Issue.

Died Hon. William Taylor of Sumter County, Alabama, born in Powhatan County, Virginia, went to West Virginia where he lived for 30 years; migrated to Belmont in 1857. He was a Presbyterian; member of the House of Representatives 1869 to fill unexpired term Benj. Inge; elected in 1872 by 800 majority.

******

Died at Gainesville on the 2nd of March 1873, Mrs. Henrietta Mobley, wife of Green B. Mobley, Esq., aged 73 years.

******

Died near Livingston on the 26 March 1873, Mrs. Edna M. Rhodes, wife of James Rhodes.

******

May 23, 1873 Issue.

Died near Intercourse on the 5th of May 1873, Mr. Lemuel B. Hale, born in Marion District, South Carolina October 1809. He came to Alabama in 1824.

******

Died Mr. Jabal Praytor in Birmingham, Alabama 27 April 1873. He was born in Sumter County, Alabama, 30 December 1849; was engaged by the Southern Express Company at time of his death.

******

May 30, 1873 Issue.

Died Mr. James P. Kennard at the residence of his son-in-law, Dr. M. C. Kinnard in Livingston, Alabama, 3rd May 1873. He was born 27th November 1801 in Williamson County, Tennessee. Moved to Sumter County the fall of 1832 and was clerk of Circuit Court in 1838 - 1842 - 1846. He was a member of the Presbyterian Church.

******

July 4, 1873 Issue.

Died the 23rd June 1873 in Tuscaloosa where he went to attend the graduating exercises of Tuscaloosa Female College where his three daughters went to school, Mr. J. McKerrall. One year ago he lost his wife, the former Miss Monette of Hale County, Alabama. He was circa 41 years of age.

******

Died 28 January 1881, Mrs. W. H. Goodloe of Lake Station, Mississippi, who had been visiting Livingston for some months for her health. She died at the residence of Mr. J. W. Jenkins.

******

Died Mrs. Susan Ramsey, near Ramsey Station 18 January 1881, wife of Captain A. K. Ramsey. Her death was a blow to her husband who is about 90 years old.

******

Died suddenly in Gainesville, Mrs. E. W. Monroe, mother of the editor of the Eutaw Whig, aged 69 years, 8 months.

******

Died Mr. John R. Barnes at the home of his son, Mr. A. G. Barnes, on the 11 January 1881.

******

James A. Abrams, born in Buckingham County, Virginia, 12 November 1804, died 6 January 1881 in his 77th year. He left his native state and settled in Georgia where he married. He lived in both Newman and Macon but removed to Livingston in 1835. He was appointed Probate Judge in Sumter County in 1867, and reappointed in 1868, then elected in 1874.

******

Died Lula Gillespie, daughter of Joseph and Sarah Gillespie, on 4 February 1881.

******

Died Dr. J. D. Johnson at his home near Sumterville 14 February 1881. His remains were taken to Pickens County for interment.

******

Died 2 February 1881 the 11 year old son of Mr. James Armstrong near Belmont from a tree falling on his head.

******

Died Mr. W. A. Brunson, son of Captain Thomas M. Brunson, Tax Collector, suddenly at the Battle House in Mobile, from the mumps.

******

Died in Gainesville 13 February 1881, Mrs. Sallie Roberts, aged 83 years; a native of North Carolina, moved to Gainesville in 1838 and joined the Presbyterian Church same year.

******

Departed this life 11 March 1881, Mrs. Ann Mason, wife of Mr. R. S. Mason and daughter of James P. Kennard, one of the first Deacons in in Livingston. She first married C. S. McConnico who died a few years after. In 1871 she married Mr. Mason.

******

Died a few miles west of Gainesville, Mrs. Joiner, 14 March 1881 aged 59. She was the wife of Mr. O. R. Joiner.

******

Died at the residence of J. F. Dill near Kinterbish, Alabama (in Sumter County) Mrs. Adah Fulford Dill, 76 years 2 months and 2 days of age. She was born in Beaufort County, North Carolina in 1834, removed to Gaston, Sumter County in 1835.

******

Died of typhoid fever, Prof. Andrew A. Armstrong, Principal of York Academy.

******

Died Mrs. Emma Faires of York on 7 April 1881, daughter of Mrs. Rebecca Faires who died a few days before.

******

Memorial Service at Zion Church on the 4th Sunday in March in memory of W. Adrian Brunson.

******

Died near Midway in this county 23 April 1881 of a gunshot wound accidentally inflicted by himself Mr. Samuel E. Smith, aged 25 years, 4 months and 8 days. He had been married only 2 months. (He married Beulah C. Parker granddaughter of Capt. James Parker.)

******

Died 20 April 1881 Mr. D. R. Kirkland of Livingston in Prescott, Arkansas. He was the son of the late William Kirkland.

******

Died Mrs. Cherry Lane Bryant near Sumterville 24 March 1881. Mrs. Bryant was born in Johnston County, North Carolina 24 March 1818, immigrated to Alabama with her husband and her father's family - the Richardsons - December 1833, among the first settlers near Gainesville. She married at the age of 14 and settled in Alabama near Mr. Richardson, her father, who was soon taken. Mr. Bryant discharged his duties as a son and Mrs. Bryant as a daughter and a sister. Mr. Bryant's health failed in 1864 and she cared for him for 12 years until the silver cord was loosened.

******

Died near Gaston Mrs. J. P. Carr, on 6 June 1881, a most excellent lady.

******

Died 18 April 1881 near Belmont Mrs. Bettie A. Tutt, daughter of A. D. and Nancy Newell, born in Greene County, Alabama 15 June 1833, married 29 May 1853. She has been Presbyterian at Pleasant Ridge since 1864. She leaves a husband and 4 children.

******

Died Mr. J. L. Shelby, a very old citizen, near York on 19 June 1881. He was a long time member of the Presbyterian Church.

******

Died near Gaston in Sumter County 5 June 1881, Mrs. A. J. Carr, wife of Mr. J. P. Carr, born in Duplin County, North Carolina 12 October 1831 and with her father Rev. J. Larkin came to Alabama 1839. She was a Methodist.

******

Died near Jefferson in Marengo County, Alabama, Mrs. Barbara Simmons, widow of Lewis S. Simmons, aged 64 years of age.

******

Died Mr. Z. R. Williams a few miles south of York 30 June 1881 of relapse of measles, aged 30 years.

******

Died Mr. J. B. Williams 23 May 1881, the father of Captain J. B. Williams, aged 77 years 8 months and 21 days. He had been a Mason for 50 years.

******

Died at York Station 6 June 1881 Elizabeth Curl, infant daughter of A. J. and M. L. Garrison, aged 2 years.

******

Died at the home of his mother near Kenterbish, Alabama (Sumter County) 10 August 1881, of dropsy, Mr. William J. McCann, aged 44 years 4 months 16 days.

******

Died 22 August 1881 little J. P., infant son of Jo J. and Emma K. Hilman, aged 9 months.

******

Died at York Station 12 September 1881 at 5:50 P.M., "Buckie", daughter of R. D. and Cornella E. Hoof, aged 2 years.

******

Died Mrs. Tisdale 1 September 1881, and Mr. John M. Bobnett 4 September 1881. The above Mrs. Tisdale and Mr. Bobnett were children of Mr. and

Mrs. Bobnett who are preparing to return to Kentucky, home of his childhood.

******

Died at the residence of her son, Mr. H. T. Williamson, 12 September 1881, Mrs. Elizabeth Williamson aged 74 years.

******

Died in Livingston 31 August 1881, Samuel Sprott McKnight, infant son of Mr. and Mrs. W. T. McKnight, aged 3 years 8 months 11 days.

******

Died in Livingston, Sumter County, Alabama, 20 September 1881, Joseph Addison Eason (called "Addie"), aged 21 years. He was the son of Mr. E. Carr and Keziah (Mitchell) Eason and grandson of Mr. J. T. Eason and Benj. J. Mitchell, both old and respected citizens of Sumter County. After the late war "Addie" moved with his father to Lauderdale, Mississippi. Four months prior to his death he returned to Jones Bluff.

******

Died at Sumterville on the night of 12 October 1881, Mr. Henry McDaniel. He came to Alabama as a young man; he was a member of the Methodist Church.

******

The 4th November 1881 Issue of the paper published from a copy of 24 June 1864 issue of Mobile Evening News owned by Captain Sprott the following "War News which will be of interest to some of our readers": List of casualties in the 40th Alabama Inf. - Col. John H. Higley Commanding, 15 June 1864. Company A 1st Lieut. S. H. Sprott Commanding. Killed Pvt. John Anderson; wounded Pvt. M. E. Bolding, head slt.; W. S. Daniels arm slt.; T. S. Green loins mor.; missing Sgt. M. S. Lowery, Corps. A. E. Beavers, L. Lancaster, Pvts. W. T. Jarman, A. N. Jenkiles, W. C. Lewis, H. S. McKenzie, James Pullium, John Roberts, R. Wideman. Killed 1, wounded 3 missing 10.

******

Died Captain R. M. Campbell, 29 October 1881 at the residence of Captain A. J. Derby, near Gaston, Sumter County. He was a native of North Carolina but spent a greater part of his life in Sumter County. Practiced law at Demopolis the beginning of the war; went into the Confederate Army as Captain of an Alabama Battalion garrisoned at Ft. Morgan until it was captured by the Federals spring of 1865.

******

Died in Livingston 29 October 1881, Ida K., infant daughter of John W. and Bettie Moore.

******

Died in Gainesville, Alabama 27 October 1881, John Childress, youngest son of C. D. and Clair Woodruff, aged 2 years, 16 days.

******

List of Sumter County Physicians in 1881 from Nov. 18, 1881 Livingston Journal: J. C. Houston, R. H. Arrington, R. D. Webb, E. H. Sholl, J. C. Parham, W. H. James, H. B. Ward, T. D. Bourdeau, J. B. Harvey, William A. Mobley, D. S. Brockway, R. H. Hale, J. M. Henson, S. H. Estell, John F. Allison, Darby Henagan, Calvin U. Silliman, James M. Godfrey, W. T. Abrams, A. E. Moore, J. N. Gilmore, J. W. Crocker, W. B. Washington, J. G. Foster, J. B. Marshall, J. T. Nash, W. H. Sledge, E. C. Reid. 28 in all.

Licensed to sell and compound drugs: J. L. Scruggs, M. F. Goodloe, T. C. Bourdeau, H. B. Ward, J. O. Scruggs, Parham and Brother, D. S. Brockway, R. H. Hale.

******

Licensed to sell medicines only: Ward and Company, Cuba, Alabama; William Edwards, York.

******

Died in Gainesville 7 November 1881, daughter of T. F. and Laura B. Ramage in the 3rd year of her age.

******

Died 7 November 1881 little Lorence Hodges, son of R. B. and F. Melton. He was born 20 May 1880.

******

Died 11 November 1881, Mrs. S. W. Taylor aged about 70 years.

******

Died 12 December 1881 at the residence of S. P. Hand, Mrs. Elizabeth Ratcliffe, aged more than 70 years.

******

Died 3 December 1881 Susie, infant daughter of Mr. Julius Barr of York,

Alabama.

******

Letter from A. R. Scarbrough of Dresden, Texas dated 14 December 1881, published in the Livingston Journal 23 December 1881 - in which he mentioned David William and David Maggard as living in Nevarro County, Texas where A. R. Scarbrough's sons lived. He mentioned Sumter County man, Dr. N. B. Kennedy in Hillsboro, Texas, and Dr. B. B. Seale, a dentist, at Cleburn, Johnson County, Texas, and Col. Hall formerly of Eutaw.

******

Died in Gainesville on 2 January 1882 Mrs. Mary Cravens, aged 70 years; deceased was a sister of the McMahon brothers of Gainesville.

******

A letter from Miss Mattie L. Ramsey near Gainesville, Alabama saying that William B. Gilbert died 26 January 1882, at the home of his brother-in-law, Dr. H. Pinson. He was 19 years and about 6 months of age. Funeral was preached at Soules' Chapel by Rev. John Peterson.

******

Died 2 February 1882 near Livingston of angina pectoris, Mrs. Mattie I. McDonald, wife of M. B. McDonald, in her 34th year of her age. She was a member of Elizabeth Presbyterian Church.

******

Died at Gaston 8 February 1882, Mrs. Willie Ann Gilmore, wife of Dr. J. N. Gilmore, aged 48 years, 11 months and 8 days.

******

Died of heart disease at New Iberia, Louisiana, 26 February 1882, Dr. G. J. Colgin, aged 63 years of age. The deceased practiced medicine in Sumter County for 20 years and was surgeon in the 40th Alabama Regiment in the late war.

******

Died Park McClellan Harris, a citizen of Wyandotte, Kansas, born in Livingston 20 February 1846 and died in Livingston 1 March 1882. His father, H. H. Harris who died 1862 was wealthy prior to the Civil War. The deceased went to Waverly, Mo., and became a successful merchant. Here in 1871 he married Miss Loula Gordon, who with two sons, five and seven years old survive him. He removed to Wyandotte in 1879 when his health failed. He went to El Paso seeking health. Returned to Livingston where he died.

******

Died in Lauderdale, Mississippi 18 November 1881, Mrs. Mary G. McConnell, daughter of the late Edwin and Louisa Gibbs of Sumter County and wife of John A. McConnell of York Station. Mrs. McConnell was born in Livingston, Alabama 4 May 1854, married Mr. McConnell 16 July 1879. She was a Presbyterian.

******

Died at Macon Station (note - said to be near Faunsdale, Ala.), Mrs. Mary L. Farres, wife of J. W. Farres on 21 March 1882. Her remains were brought to York for interment. She was about 40 years old.

******

Died on 8 April 1882, Mr. Albert A. Bedell, son of Mrs. B. S. Baker, of pulmonary affection.

******

Died near New Prospect in Bluff Port Community 23 April 1882 Mr. J. M. Cook aged 35. He was a brother of Thomas L. Cook who died on 5 April same year.

******

Died 14 March 1882, Mr. Sam Ezell, a very aged man in the vicinity of York. He was found dead at his plow by his son.

******

Died Mrs. Eveline Cunningham in Livingston 21 March 1882. She was born in Baltimore 2 May 1808 in her early life she moved to Knoxville, Tennessee with her father Mr. John Mason where she married Mr. Robert Park in 1825. They removed to Tuscumbia, Alabama, in the fall of 1835 where Mr. Park died. She married Mr. William Cunningham in 1837. She was a Presbyterian.

******

Died George Lawrence Brunson, second son of G. E. and Julia Brunson at the age of 23 years and 5 months. He was buried Tuesday 2nd June 1882 in Zion Church Yard in the Southern part of the county.

******

Died Hon. Reuben Chapman 17 May 1882. He came to Huntsville about 62 years ago and studied law with his brother, the late Samuel Chapman in about 1821; removed to Somerville in Morgan County; elected Governor in 1847 for 2 years. He was sent to represent the Democratic Party in National Democratic Conventions. He was born in Caroline County, Virginia.

******

Died Mrs. Sallie Wilkinson at the residence of her son Mr. J. B. Wilkinson in Mobile 23 May 1882, of typhoid fever. She was a long time resident of Sumter County. Her husband came from Edgecombe County, North Carolina in 1837. After her husband's death she removed to Mobile in 1869 to be with her son.

******

Died Mr. Boyd McDonald's daughter, Maggie, aged 3 years of typho-malaria on 17 May 1882.

******

Died Elisha Dearman, resident of Intercourse Beat, quite an old man. Found dead in a field. He left home the morning of the 28 May 1882 to visit a neighbor. He was not found until the next evening.

******

Died 25 June 1882 at the residence of his brother-in-law Mr. John W. Moore in Livingston, Robert E. Harper age 27 years: son of Mrs. Bettie Harper, nee Harewood. His father, Mr. James W. Harper died when Bobbie was an infant.

******

Died Mrs. Amanda T. Lockard 2 July 1882, aged 67 years. Her maiden name was Brewer, born in South Carolina; came to Perry County and joined the Presbyterian Church. In 1835 she married Mr. Lockard who died 1854. From 1845 to 1855 she lived in Mississippi. She was the sole surviver of the little band who organized the Presbyterian Church in this town. (Livingston).

******

Died in Sandflat, Johnson County, Texas on 26 June 1882, Mrs. Mary E. consort of Thomas F. Seal. She was born in Greene County, Alabama in 1836 and moved to Sumter County where she married and lived until 1881.

******

Died 7 June 1882, Rev. J. E. Foust at his home in Livingston in the 47th year of his age. He had been in the active ministry of the M. E. Church

South for 25 years.

******

Died Miss Mattie Lindsay about 18 years of age of a congestive chill on the 7th July 1882. She lived near the Sumter County line in Choctaw County.

******

Died John M. McDaniel 7 July 1882, graduated at LaGrange College 1854, practiced law in Livingston before he went into the army with the first volunteers and formed a company, part of the 5th Alabama Regiment and joined Morgan's Calvalry; married Miss Mary Knox of Talladega. Joined the Presbyterian Church in 1871.

******

Old Citizen gone. On Sunday 9 July 1882 at his home in Meridian, Mississippi, died Wade R. Thomas, aged 79 years of age. He was a native of North Carolina, Edgecombe County from where he migrated 50 years ago into the wilds of Alabama where he arrived in 1832 and located near Sumterville, Alabama.

******

Died suddenly 11 August 1882, Mr. David Lewis who came to Alabama from Connecticut last spring. He purchased Mr. Robert Greenlee's place. He was between 65 and 70 years. He leaves a young wife to mourn his loss.

******

Died Mr. Dan Osborne White, former citizen of Sumter County, (brother of Mr. Ben White), but for 8 years a citizen of Florida, died at the residence of Mr. J. W. Jenkins in this place 23 August 1882; born in Dallas County in 1826, moved to Sumter County in 1856 and to Florida in 1874. He left a wife and a brother.

******

Died Manasseh Lisle, infant son of D. U. and Alice Patton, born 9 October 1882, died 5 August 1882.

******

Died of yellow fever in Brownsville, Texas, William M. Winston, son of Col. W. O. Winston of this county on the 28 August 1882.

******

Death of Z. M. Hoit, Tuesday afternoon 19 September 1882, shocked the community. He was one of our Representatives elect. He married the daughter of Rev. A. R. Scarbrough.

******

Sad death of Mr. Felix G. Wimberley at Bluff Port about noon last Friday. He died in the pasture while looking for his horse.

******

Died of apoplexy, Dr. W. H. Bennett on 2 October 1882. He was formerly of Bennett's Station, but of late years a resident of Meridian, Mississippi.

******

Died 25 September 1882 in Montevallo in the 7th year of her age, Nellie, daughter of William and Alice Edmonds of York Station, Alabama.

******

Died Mrs. Julia Jackson 27 September 1882, member of the Baptist Church at Hickory Hill in Sumter County. She was born 11 November 1851.

******

Died Tuesday 21 November 1882 at the home of her son-in-law, W. T. McKnight in Livingston, Mrs. Mary Sprott in the 75th year of her age. She was a native of Scot-Ireland, but of Scotch and Irish descent. Her maiden name was Bothwell, a name well noted in Irish history. Her ancestors were from Bothwell's Bridge where the celebrated battle of that name was fought in 1679. She was a Presbyterian. In 1838 she, her husband and two children immigrated to America and settled in Sumter County in 1840. She contributed her husband (in 1862) and her 3 sons (all sons she had) to the Confederate cause leaving two helpless children dependent on her.

******

Died in Houston, Texas 3 December 1882 Samuel J. Arrington, son of the late Dr. Samuel Arrington of this county, aged about 21 years.

******

Died Mr. Samuel Flowers, many years a resident of this county in the vicinity of York, the night of the 8 December 1882. He was born in Marion District, South Carolina 1 May 1799. In 1825 he married Easter Brown. In 1835 he moved to Sumter County. He left a son, William and his family.

******

Died M. V. David 4 December 1882, member of George Wilson Lodge of F and A M.

******

Died Mr. George W. Mason of consumption at the residence of his father 6 miles north of Livingston on the 15 January 1883.

******

Died in Tuscaloosa 28 December 1882, Mr. C. H. Mellen, son of Prof. S. S. Mellen.

******

Died Miss Helen Baldwin 4 February 1883 at the Female Academy (where she taught) of pneumonia. Her mother had come from New York to be with her in her illness. She was buried at this place from the Episcopal Church.

******

Died Judge P. G. Nash one of the most respected citizens of Gaston, on the 20 February 1883.

******

Died 9 March 1883, Samuel A. Hale, Esq., at the residence of Col. I. James Lee. He was a native of New Hampshire - at one time publisher of "The Flag of our Union", in Tuscaloosa about 50 years ago. He removed to Sumter County about 1843.

******

Died Mr. S. C. Coleman of Coatopa, 6 March 1883 in Monterey, Mexico. He was buried near his old home on the 12th. He was the victim of consumption at the age of 40 years.

******

Died near Belmont, Alabama of congestion of the brain, Sadie Louise, daughter of Frank and Mollie Davidson, aged 3 years.

******

Died at his home on the 18 March 1883, "Honest John Harris". He was buried at Siloam.

******

Died Mrs. Lucinda Hitt, of pneumonia at her residence in South Sumter

County on the 16 March 1883. She was buried at Siloam.

******

Died at her home near Belmont on the 21 March 1883, Mrs. Mary Melton, aged 73 years.

******

Died 9 March 1883 near Intercourse, Sumter County, Alabama, Mrs. Della Alexander, wife of J. M. Alexander; she was born near Gaston in Sumter County, 1847; married Mr. John M. Alexander in 1870; joined Siloam Baptist Church at the age of 15.

******

Died at Lexington, Mississippi on 13 April 1883, Mrs. Ann H. Ayres, widow of a former sheriff of Sumter County - Daniel L. Ayres - born in Georgia, August 1810; her maiden name was Stuart.

******

Died at her home near York 6 May 1883, Mrs. M. C. Praytor, wife of James Thomas Praytor and daughter of Jabel Falkner, born 30 January 1826. She leaves 6 sons and 1 daughter.

******

Died at the residence of his brother, J. C. Swann, on the 10 May 1883. Matthew Peyton Swann, aged 25 years, 1 month and 2 days.

******

Died at Cuba Station, Alabama, Mrs. A. S. Ward, wife of D. S. Ward aged 43 years. She was born near Gaston, Alabama on the 26 April 1840, died 21 May 1883. She was a Methodist. She leaves an aged mother and 5 children to mourn her loss.

******

Died near Brewersville on the 28 June 1883, Dora, wife of Felix G. McMillan and daughter of the late Robert Gillespie.

******

Died on the 9th July 1883, Thomas, infant son of James B. and Susie B. Cobbs of Birmingham at the residence of Mrs. Laura J. Little.

******

Died in Jacksonville, Florida on the 25 June 1883, Helen Emerson, daughter of James P. and Mattie A. Spratt, aged 2 years, 3 months. She was buried in Livingston on the 26th.

******

Died 1 June 1883, J. R. Watts, aged 72 years, 11 months 1 day; born in Greene County, Georgia, removed to Alabama in 1838 - was a member of Western Star Lodge Number 222.

******

Died Miss Mary Coats of Sumter County, born 8 February 1853, married Ed Carroll 8 February 1870; died 18 July 1883. By W. Mixon, Norwalk, Putnam County, Florida.

******

Died Willie Wright, daughter of Mrs. Margaret Tutwiler Wright and Captain J. W. A. Wright at Greene Springs, Alabama on 1 August 1883, aged 21 years 6 months.

******

Died John A. McConnell as the home of his brother Joseph A. McConnell, on the 28 August 1883, of consumption.

******

Died Charles T. Johnson, 7 October 1883, Mrs. E. H. Johnson, 2 miles east of Livingston, aged 14 years, of malaria.

******

Died in Gainesville on the 2 October 1883, Mrs. Lizzie McMahon, widow of Col. R. G. McMahon, aged 74 years.

******

Died on the 20 October 1883 in Cotohaga Beat in this county, Mr. Ashley Alvis aged 94 years. He was a soldier under General Jackson at the Battle of New Orleans.

******

Died 17 October 1883, Mrs. Minerva Fluker age 74 years, at the home of her daughter, Mrs. C. B. Miller - wife of Dr. T. K. Miller, near Itasca, Hill County, Texas. She was a native of Statesburg, South Carolina. At the age of 19 she married Dr. H. N. Wheeler who soon died. She came to Alabama with her father, William M. Brooks, in the fall of 1847. She married Dr. William Fluker and was soon left a widow again and went to Texas in 1881. She has two sons in Alabama. She was the last of 7 sisters; she has one brother living, William M. Brooks, of Selma, Alabama.

******

Died Mrs. Sallie Graham, wife of T. R. Graham (and daughter of William T. Simms), at her home at Shuqualak, Mississippi, on the 14 September 1883, aged 26 years.

******

Died Mr. L. C. McCormick, long time resident of Belmont, but late of Forkland, Alabama, on the 21 October 1883.

******

Died in Mobile on the 2 November 1883, Allison R. Wilson, aged 40 years, son of Mr. George Wilson of Livingston.

******

Died 27 October 1883, Mrs. Lucy Snedecor, wife of Maj. F. P. Snedecor of Gainesville.

******

Died 8 November 1883, Joe Clint Houston, of Meridian, formerly of Sumter County, in his 20th year; he was killed by a train accidentally. He was buried in Livingston by his sister; son of J. C. Houston.

******

Died, Alama, daughter of E. B. and M. E. Hern, about 16 years, on the 6 December 1883.

******

Died, Allen Gowdey on the 2 December 1883, aged 7 years, 6 months.

******

Died in Gainesville on the 9th of December 1883, Mr. Young W. Harris, an old and honored citizen.

******

Died at his residence in Sumter County on the 22 January 1881, Col. James M. Lee, aged 61 years. He was born in Conecuh County, 29 December 1819; removed to Sumter County as a lad.

******

Died Mr. Ben Allen, 8 December 1882 at Kinterbish. He was buried at Siloam. The remains of Octavia Poole of Cuba, buried the same day.

******

Died Mrs. Sara Gillespie of Belmont last week. She was the mother of Miss Minnie Gillespie who attended school at this place last year -- 1 June 1883 Issue of the paper.

******

Mrs. Nancy Henagan, born in Marion District, South Carolina, 22 March 1801, died at the residence of her son, Maj. C. S. Henagan near Epes Station, Sumter County, Alabama, on 10 January 1884. She married E. L. Henagan in 1820 and became the mother of 13 children, 12 of whom lived to see their majority. Four died during the late war. Mrs. Henagan was a Methodist.

******

Mary Isabell Hale, daughter of Josephus and Eliza Wallace, was born 1 September 1861, married Joseph H. Hale November 1880, died at Gaston 26 February 1884. "Izzie" was a member of the Methodist Church.

******

Ezekiel Abner Powell, Jr., died at the residence of his father-in-law, Col. I. James Lee near Livingston 17 August 1883. He was the son of Hon. E. A. Powell of Tuscaloosa, born in North Port, Alabama, 1855 and married Miss Alabama Lee November 1877.

******

Bessie A., infant daughter of J. A. Tutt, died of Spinal infection 20 March 1884.

******

Allen Mortimer Gowdy, aged 7 years died 2 December 1883; Elmer Merit Gowdy aged 9 years died 2 April 1884; George Clarence Gowdy died 12 April 1884 - all children of George C. and Fannie M. Merritt of Livingston, Alabama.

******

Mrs. Agnes McMillan, sister of Mrs. Jennie McRee, was buried at Belmont on 26 May 1884.

******

Died at his home in Livingston, Alabama on 25 July 1884, H. D. Fellows, in his 50th year of life. He was a member of Livingston Lodge #41 FAM.

******

Died 29 July 1884, Frank Llewellyn Lewis, son of Joshua and Fannie L. Lewis, aged 4 years.

******

The 22 August issue of the paper carried the notice that Mary Lee, daughter of James A. and Sallie E. Shamburger had died recently.

******

Col. Isaac R. McElroy died at Cuba, Sumter County, Alabama 23 July 1885. He was born 1 May 1805.

******

Died Mrs. M. J. Reid, wife of W. R. Reid and daughter of Nancy and A. M. McElroy, 11 September 1884; she was born 28 July 1854.

******

Mrs. Carrie Adele Caldwell died at her home in Belmont on 2 October 1884, aged 23 years.

******

Spottswood G. Williams died near Curls Station 11 October 1884 of typhoid fever. The remains were buried in Choctaw County.

******

DEATH NOTICES FROM
" THE GAINESVILLE REPORTER "

Died Mrs. Emily W. Monroe aged 69, at the residence of her son-in-law, E. C. Meredith of Gainesville, on 19 January 1881. She was born in Athens, Georgia May 1811; removed with her husband and family to Greene County, Alabama in 1846; mother of 11 children, four of whom and her husband, John Monroe, preceded her to the grave. Mrs. Monroe was a Methodist; she had a sister (deceased) Mrs. Whitman of Chattanooga.

****

Died Mrs. Sara B. Roberts 13 February 1881 born in Mecklenburg County, Virginia 4 November 1797. In 1838 Mrs. Roberts came from Raleigh, North Carolina to Gainesville where she joined the Presbyterian Church the same year.

******

Died in Livingston, Alabama 2 March 1884 Mrs. Elizabeth W. Hopkins, wife of Devereux Hopkins and daughter of Rev. Joseph Ryan. She was born in Greensboro, Alabama 13 December 1821, married 8 February 1838. Member of the Baptist Church - (Stockton Herald California and Alabama Baptist please copy.)

******

Died in Gainesville, Mrs. Nancy Nance, sister of Mr. M. F. Goodloe of that place, on 9 March 1881.

******

Died in Gainesville at the residence of Captain W. H. Child, Mrs. Nellie C. Kelsey of Manchester, Iowa.

******

CHAPTER VII

TRACT BOOK RECORDS

Township 20N., Range 3 West

Sumterville is in the extreme eastern edge of this township, in section 13. The sections begin with 1 in the extreme north eastern corner of the township, and of course the sections are one mile square; there are six sections east and west, so section #7 is directly under section #6 and section #12 is just below section #1. There are 36 sections in a township. Keeping this in mind, one may make a chart showing just where each person settled.

Section #1

John Chambers, Jesse H. Hutchins, Thomas H. Hutchins and Matthew Newton patented land in this section; they received their certificate numbers in the fall of 1834 as did those who were in the first wave of immigrants. Some of these people had been on the land since 1831. Matthew Newton and his wife Leah sold their 160 acres to Thomas Ormond, or Uncle Tom, as all the young people called him. He never married but reared a number of nephews and nieces. At his death, caused by a fall from a wagon, he left each kinsman some land (See Old Side Cemetery Records). The history of Thomas H. and Jesse H. Hutchins may be found in the Methodist Cemetery Records, Sumterville.

Section #2

Brooks H. Davis, Elizabeth Darnell, John L. Davis and Reuben Davidson each patented 160 acres in section #2. The two Davis men married sisters of Elizabeth Darnell, they were daughters of John Holland, Revolutionary War soldier, who patented land in section #6 of Township 20, Range 2 West which was a little more than one mile due east of where his daughters lived. Brooks H. Davis and John L. Davis were sons of Brooks H. Davis, Sr., and his wife Sara Lacy Davis. Brooks H. Davis, Sr., was a Rev. war soldier who died in Kentucky in 1814. He is believed to have been a brother or close relative of Chesley Davis who also had children in Sumter County. They both were in South

Carolina during the Revolution, both soldiers, and they had children and grandchildren with the same names. (See Campbell and Susan Davis Boyd for Chesley Davis line.) Sara Lacy Davis wife of Brooks H. Davis, Sr., is buried in Centennial Cemetery, near Carthage, Texas. Inscription reads: born in Virginia 4 February 1777, died in Texas 29 January 1859. She is thought to be the daughter of William Hughes Lacy and granddaughter of Stephen Lacy of Goochland County, Virginia. The other children of Brooks H. Davis, Sr., were William H. Davis who married Frances --. Stephen Lacy Davis born 1798 and married Huldah Anderson, Sara Davis born in Kentucky 16 October 1803, died in Texas 1866, married William Holland, Eli Davis died before 1840, married Dorcas Anderson, in Clark County, Alabama 1819, Avarilla Davis born 1808 in Kentucky and married William Pearson, Archibald B. Davis born in Kentucky, married Charity Thompson, and Austin L. Davis born 1815 (posthumous) in Kentucky and died 1833 (Bible record of Brooks H. Davis, Jr. Bible is owned by Miss Miriam Dozier of Austin, Texas.

The mother of the above children ame to Marengo County, Alabama with her kith and kin where she reared her family but in the meantime she married James Murray, also a Rev. War soldier. They removed to Bluff Port, Sumter County, Alabama. She after the death of James Murray, followed her children to Texas.

Brooks H. Davis Jr., born 20 October 1804, died August 1894, his wife Penecy Holland was born 27 February 1804, died 6 December 1873. They were parents of: (1) Avarilla Davis born 10 February 1827, died in Gainesville, Alabama, (See Odd Fellows' Cemetery in another volume), married (1) Mr. Haden of Panola County, Texas and (2) William Thomas Nance born in Va., 24 September 1824, (see Odd Fellows' Cemetery, Gainesville, Alabama in another volume). Their daughter, Ella Nance, was born 17 March 1859, died in Avin, Texas 1897, married 25 December 1879 to William Allen Ward Dozier who was born in Cathage, Texas 21 February 1856, died in Harrisburg, Texas 27 September 1911. They had children: Robert, Henry, Thomas Bailey, Algernon Brooks, Fannie Lucie, Whittie Miriam, Willie Avarilla, Ward Allen and unnamed twin, Earl Vernon and Ella. (2) John L. Davis born in Marengo County, Alabama 1826 and died 1842; (3) William H. Davis born in Marengo County, Alabama 1829, buried in Mansfield, La., married Willie Ann Anderson daughter of John E. and Cynthia A. (Harper) Anderson; (4) Martha Jane Davis born 1830 died 1833; (5) Sara Davis born 1833 died 1892 married W. J. Rogers who was born 1831 and died 1892; (6) Austin L Davis born 1834 and died 1912, married (1) Caroline Rogers, (2) Rachel Anderson daughter of Holland L. Anderson and his wife Elizabeth English; (7) Elizabeth Davis born 1836 and (8) Tabitha Susan Davis born 1838.

John Le Davis, brother of Brooks H. Davis Jr., married Dorcas Holland, daughter of John Holland, Rev. War soldier, 1 February 1829. John Le Davis was born 1811 in Kentucky. The children of this union were: Arch M. Davis, Sara C. Davis, William C. Davis, Celestine Davis, Asbury M. Davis, Margaret Davis. This family was in Panola County, Texas as shown in the 1850 Census. Also living with this family at that time were Dorcas Davis, daughter of Eli and Dorcas (Anderson) Davis, and Jane Holland the widow of John Holland. Jane was 80 years old at the time.

Section #3

William W. Kerr, Benjamin J. Mitchell, Thomas Harper, and Reuben Davidson patented all the land in this section. Reuben Davidson soon sold his land to J. C. Whitsett, no other name but his on the deed. Thomas Harper sold his land to Peter M. Roberts. He was not married, evidently, as no one signed the deed with him.

William W. Kerr received his certificate, #2458, 17 October 1834, but he was certainly here two years prior to that date, as were all the others who settled in this township. All the early settlers received their certificates the fall of 1834, and they got the deeds from Washington in 1837, signed by Martin Van Buren. William Kerr married Sara Dial, daughter of Jennett (Spence) and David Montgomery Dial, 25 January 1825 in Greene County, Alabama, in a double ceremony with her sister Nancy Dial and Benjamin J. Mitchell whose land cornered the land of William Kerr's in Township 20 Range 3 West in Sumter County. The 1850 Census for Sumter County shows this family as:

Name		Age	Born	
Kerr,	William W.	46	Kentucky	
	Sara	35	South Carolina	
	Telemachus	17	Alabama	(Student)
	Elizabeth	14	"	
	Margaret M.	11	"	
	James D.	9	"	
	William J.	7	"	
	John L.	5	"	
	Susan J.	3	"	
	Laura L.	2	"	

Both William W. Kerr and his wife Sara died in 1866. William was kicked by a mule and Sara died of Kidney trouble.

(See Bethel Cemetery Records.)

(See index for other Mitchell records.)

Section #4

John W. Kerr and William W. Kerr patented all the land in this township. John's share was 480 acres and William took up 160 acres. John W. Kerr was a half brother to William W. and Armstrong Kerr. Their father came to Campbellsville, Kentucky from Penn. One of the Kerr girls married a

Mr. Campbell after coming to Kentucky.

John W. Kerr married Margaret Dial, sister of Sara Dial who married William W. Kerr. This family lived in Sumter County until 1853 when they removed to St. Louis, Missouri. The 1850 Census gives this family as:

Name	Age	Born
Kerr, John W.	52	Kentucky
Margaret	41	South Carolina
Jane	17	Alabama
Susan A.	12	"
Roberts, Virginia	21	"
Virginia	1	"

Note: Virginia Kerr married Elbert G. Roberts 3 May 1853.

Armstrong Kerr, half brother of John W. married Laura Ann Eliza Hadden 1 February 1843. See Hadden family. Armstrong Kerr family removed to Clarendon, Arkansas where he became a judge. This family transferred their church membership to La Grange, Texas 28 May 1867, where they went from Arkansas.

Section #5

William Brown, James McCown, John Hamrick and Jennett Dial, widow, and children, Margaret Kerr, Elizabeth Fulton, Joseph R. Dial, Nancy Mitchell, Sara Kerr, Mary Dial, John Dial, Rebecca Dial, Jeremiah Dial, James C. and William Dial patented the land in this section. David Montgomery Dial, husband of Jennett (Spence) Dial died in the early fall of 1834, so the certificate was made to his widow. The 1850 Census of Sumter County shows this family as follows:

Name	Age	Born
Dial, Jennett	67	South Carolina
Jeremiah	27	Alabama
James C.	24	"

Jennett (Spence) Dial and Summer Dial were sisters-in-law, as their husbands David Montgomery Dial and Jeremiah Dial III were sons of John Dial who was the son of Jeremiah Dial of South Carolina. The two brothers and their families settled in Sumter County; their aunt, Jane or Jennett (Dial) Boyd married John Boyd. The three families are remotely related, today after 130 years since leaving South Carolina they still claim relationship and know their lines of descent. (See Dial and Boyd in Boyd Cemetery and Dial in Sumterville Cemetery.)

Jennett (Spence) and David Montgomery Dial's son, Joseph R. Dial, married Emily A. E. Woodard, daughter of Charity (Simms) Woodard (See Bethel Cemetery Records) and her husband Felix H. Woodward 27 August 1845. It was E. Dial (son of Joseph R. and Emily Dial) who gave the land for the depot at Emelle; and the town was named for his daughter, Emelle Dial.

The 1850 Census shows: Joseph R. Dial as 39 born in South Carolina, Emily A., 20 born in North Carolina, and Emma 3 born in Alabama.

The 1850 Census shows:

Name	Age	Born
Dial, John	31	South Carolina
Elizabeth	26	Alabama
Sara F.	7	"
Mary J.	4	"

Rebecca Dial married 31 January 1843 to George Rix. (See Bethel Cemetery Records.)

Julia Emaline, granddaughter of David Montgomery Dial, married Dr. Wm. Webb and his daughter Betty married Hon. John Sharp Williams, a noted U. S. Senator from Mississippi.

William Brown who settled the E 1/2 of the NE 1/4 of section 5 sold to Thomas Long, with only his signature on the deed.

John Hamrick sold his part of this section to John Long, with only his signature.

James McCown patented land in several townships. He married Charlotte Greene, daughter of Daniel Greene, 27 July 1841. (See Parker Cemetery Records and Daniel Greene land patent.)

Section #6

Julius Kirkland, John J. Burton and Mrs. Sara Anderson, patented land in this section. Julius Kirkland and Mary, his wife, sold his land to Benjamin A. Jones (Doctor) of Franklin County, (Va.). This was on 13 January 1837. Dr. Jones acquired a large acreage in Township 21 Range 3 West. As this was about the first land he bought I will give you his record here. He died in the late 1850's (See Jones Cemetery Records.) and named his son John Cross Jones and his son-in-law Simmons H. Giles as the administrators of the estate. He left money to the University of the South, (Gainesville Presbyterian Church received $1,000, according to their church minutes). He asked that three of his slaves, Clark aged 55, Moley aged 15 and Manson aged 42 be given the "privileges of freedom without the disadvantages of being free" so provided for their welfare. He provided for his son John Cross Jones but stipulated that at the death of the son the property would go to Maria F. Giles, his daughter for whom he also provided for. He further stipulated his desire to always keep the land in the family, and if ever sold to be sold to members of the family either by blood or by marriage as he had buried his wife in the family cemetery and expected to be buried there himself. The will was signed 27 September 1858 and probated 11 April 1859, Will Book 2-161. Mr. Philip Willingham took over the management of this large plantation after the death of Dr. Jones. The 1866 Census shows there were 107 slaves on this Jones place. Mr. Giles, the husband of Maria F. operated large holdings across the line in Mississippi from the old Ramsey area. Their daughter married Mr. Shep Neville of Giles, Mississippi between Scooba and the State line. Mr. Shep Neville had two children, Maria who married Mr. Brown of Meridian, Mississippi and they live in Texas. Spencer married Margaret ---- of Texas and they live at the old Giles place near Scooba, Mississippi.

John J. Burton bought much land in several different Townships. An indenture in Deed Book A in 1836 shows that John J. Burton owed William Burwell of Franklin County, Virginia, so certain slaves were assigned him through Armisted Burwell and John Taylor Lomax of Marengo County, Alabama. This was about the time or just after John J. Burton's death. The estate of J. J. Burton was finally settled in 1838 and it shows he had only two children, viz: James C. Burton and Lucinda Burton Carter, wife of Churchwell Carter. His wife Nancy must have died in 1835 as she was not mentioned in the settlement; but she signed a deed along with John J. Burton, her husband, when they sold their land to Allen Harrison on 28 September 1835 - John Long and his wife Elizabeth were co-signers of this deed as they were joint owners of this land.

Sara Anderson, widow of Vincent Anderson, received the certificate for her land, in place of her husband who died soon after their removal from Marengo County. See Boney Cemetery records.

Sara Anderson patented land in Sections 6 and 35 in Township 20 Range 3 West. Her husband, Vincent Anderson, died in 1833 after they came to Sumter County from Marengo County in 1832, (see Sumter County Orphans' Minute Book 1 pages 54, 60, 66), when his cousin, William G. Anderson was Judge of the Probate Court of Sumter County. Vincent's brother, Alexander Anderson, and Sara's brother, John Holland Jenkins, were administrators of the estate. The Andersons, brothers and cousins, left Greenville District, South Carolina about 1799 and went to Kentucky and even to Missouri. In this wagon train were other relatives, viz: the Hollands, Jenkins, Darnells, Lacys and others. They did not like the climate of Missouri so came to Marengo County, Alabama. One the way back they picked up the Cherrys and others. They settled in Marengo and Greene Counties Alabama about 1819. We find records of them in Marengo County in 1820. Vincent's and Sara's first child was born in Alabama in 1821.

Vincent Anderson's grandfather was John Anderson who was killed in the Revolutionary War. John Anderson's wife was named Sara. They had several sons, two of whom, Joshua and Scarlett, were killed in the war along with their father.

Family tradition says that some of the Anderson cousins went from Kentucky to Texas. Some of the Jenkins families stayed in or near Springfield, Missouri. We do know that after the death of her husband, Vincent, Sara Anderson wrote her brother in Missouri to send one of his boys to her to look after her holdings. Dominico Jenkins came to his aunt and later married her daughter, Melvira Anderson. (See Jenkins records Boney Cemetery.) Sara (Jenkins) Anderson's mother, Mrs. Susan Jenkins, came to Marengo County and on to Sumter County with some of her children. She lived with her daughter Sara Anderson in Section 6. Mrs. Susan Jenkins' son, John Holland Jenkins, settled in Section 7, which land joined hers. Other members of the Anderson and Jenkins families went to Texas when they left Marengo County, Alabama.

Vincent and Sara (Jenkins) Anderson had the following children as shown in the 1850 Census of Sumter County, Alabama: Narsissa 29 born Alabama, William S. 20 born Alabama, Catina 18 born Alabama. It shows Sara 49 born Kentucky and her mother Susan Jenkins 89 born Virginia. The family Bible shows a son John Alexander Anderson born 182-.

Section #7

William Thomas Simms, Holland Jenkins, Austin Lacy, Jacob T. Bridges and Mason Tyson patented the land in this section.

Holland Jenkins' land joined the land of Mrs. Sara Anderson, and it was directly south and across the road from her. They were brother and sister. The record on their sister's gravestone states that she (their sister, Susan Cherry) was the daughter of J. and S. Jenkins. So Susan, Sara, Holland, and at least one brother who went on to Springfield, Mo. about the time the rest of the family came to Marengo County, Alabama were brothers and sisters. Edward Jenkins in Marengo County is thought to have been a brother, also. He had a son John Holland Jenkins who went to Texas with his parents when very young. He wrote or kept a diary during the frontier struggles of early Texas. His great grandson, John Holmes Jenkins recently published a book taking the diary as the basis for his work. The Hollands, Jenkins and Andersons had intermarried for a generation or two prior to their removal to Marengo and Sumter Counties. There was a Dominico Holland, a Revolutionary Soldier in South Carolina. The Jenkins brother who went to Missouri had a son, Dominico, who came to Sumter County and married his cousin, Melvira Anderson. Holland Jenkins married Letty Anderson in Marengo County, Alabama 6 August 1827, by John Holland Jenkins, and with Vincent Anderson security. This Holland Jenkins land is now owned by Nelle Morris Jenkins.

William Thomas Simms patented the land lying directly to the east of the Holland Jenkins land. He was born in Edgecombe County, North Carolina in 1807 and died of pneumonia at his home at Old Ramsey, Alabama. He received his land patent certificate in the fall of 1834 (see Tract Book, Sumter County.) His grandson, Roland Epes Simms, lives on the land his grandfather patented. William Thomas Simms married (1) Harriett Gray, aunt of the late Hon. Oscar Gray, ex-congressman from the Mobile-Washington-Choctaw District. W. T. and Harriett (Gray) Simms were the parents of (1) Mary Leslie, died infant, (2) William who died young, (3) Asa, (4) John, (5) Sallie who married a Mr. Graham and died soon afterward, (6) Emm, (7) Edith who died young, (8) Leroy, (9) Henry and (10) Benjamin - the three last named little boys died the same night of meningitis. A couple of years later the mother, Harriett, and another son, William, died of the same disease, but two nights apart. Asa married his second cousin, Mary Bell, of Dallas County, Alabama. She was the daughter of Rev. Elijah and Laura (Grice) Bell who married 19 October 1853 (Marriage Book 2 page 208). Asa and his wife Mary (Bell) Simms had the following children: Leslie who never married died in 1956, Mary not married, Julia who married Mr. Hamilton and are the parents of two girls, Susan is Mrs. Spain, no issue.

It is thought that Mason Tyson never lived in Sumter County but bought land here. He married Elizabeth Pate in Marengo County, Alabama 30 March 1830.. He and his wife sold their land in this section to Alfred Yarbrough February 1836.

Austin Lacy patented land in this section also. (See Lacy history in Boney Cemetery records)

Section #8

Joseph R. Dial patented land in this section adjoining the land of William Thomas Simms in section 7. He was the son of David Montgomery Dial and his wife Jennett (Spence) Dial. (See Methodist Cemetery Records, Sumterville). He married Emily A. E. Woodward, daughter of Felix H. and Charity (Simms) Woodward - see Bethel and Old Side Cemetery Records. Emily was the niece of William T. Simms. Joseph R. Dial was one of the earliest surveyors in North Sumter County. The records shows he surveyed the Sara Anderson land in 1837. Joseph R. Dial was the father of Ed Dial who gave land for the depot at Emelle, and the town was named for his daughter, Emelle Dial. The 1850 Census shows him as head of family 376 and shows him as 39 and born in South Carolina. Emily was 20 and born in North Carolina. Their baby was Emma aged 3 years.

Sara White patented 80 acres of land next to Joseph R. Dial.

Jason Watson patented the land in South East Quarter of this section.

John Anderson patented the SW¼ of Section 8. He was in Marengo County prior to his removal to Sumter County; it is believed that he was the brother of Vincent Anderson. He and his wife Cassa Anderson sold this land to John Jackson in 1835, and prior to that they sold some of the land to John J. Burton. There was another Cassa Anderson who married Furney Manley in Marengo County, Alabama 23 March 1830.

Section #9

This section was taken up by John W. Kerr (see section #3), Jeremiah Horne and William Darnell.

Jeremiah Horn is said to have married twice, to two Grice sisters. It is a known fact among all the Grice, Thomas, Simms, and Horn relatives living in Sumter County today that they are related through intermarriage. See Horn Cemetery and Old Side Cemetery for other Horn records.

William Darnell patented the E½ of SW¼ and W½ of SW¼ of this section. He sold some of his land to Joseph R. Dial in 1840, with no signature but his to the deed. There is a record of a William Darnell's marriage to Jeanette D. Gill 28 May 1840. She was the granddaughter of Joseph Dobbs. Some of the Darnells and Andersons were related. Winter Payne Darnell was a cousin of Melvira (Anderson) Jenkins. It is said he was called "Tump". His family went to Kemper County, Mississippi around Hopewell, west of DeKalb. Among those buried there are: Herbert Crofton Darnell born 1800 and died 1902. He was the son of R. W. and M. M. Darnell. John Darnell was born 1824 and died 1888. The above Darnells once lived in Sumter County. Thomas Darnell and wife Schaharrissa Darnell sold some of the land William Darnell patented, to Joseph R. Dial 26 January 1841. I believe it was this Thomas Darnell who married an Anderson, was probably closely related to both Classie Anderson Browning and to Vincent Anderson; Classie A. Browning had a daughter by the same name who married Peter Handley. This being true then Winter Payne "Tump" Darnell was the son of Thomas Darnell.

Section #10

Edmund R. Rhodes, John W. Kerr, David R. Wilson and Thomas Phillips patented land in this section. See John W. Kerr history under section #3.

David R. Wilson sold this land to Albert G. Dancy 10 January 1838. His wife was named Sara E.

Thomas Phillips and his wife Cyndrilla sold their land in this section.

Section #11

Those who patented land in this section were Charles Wall, Reuben Davidson, Hugh Wall and David J. Wilson.

Hugh Wall was the father of Charles Wall. Hugh died intestate; settlement in Orphans' Records Book 3 125, Book 4 page 206 and names heirs, Sara E. Wilson wife of David R. Wilson of Giles County, Tennessee; Mary wife of John W. Bodenhammer of Giles County, Tennessee; Charles L. Wall of Louisiana and minor heirs: Peter Bodenhammer heir of Franklin Bodenhammer and Franklin Wall 12 years, both beyond the limits of the State of Alabama.

Section #12

This section brings us to the one just north of Sumterville, and William Holland, Drury Jackson, Ephram Jackson and Lemmon Ward patented this entire section.

William Holland was the son of John Holland, Revolutionary Soldier who patented land in Section 6, Township 20, Range 2 West which was a little more than a mile from William's land. He is named in his father's will which is recorded in Sumter County. William Holland married Sary Davis in Marengo County, Alabama, 11 September 1821, Austin Lacy security. Sara (Sary) Davis born 16 October 1803, died 1866 in Texas was the daughter of Brooks H. Davis and wife Sara Davis. William Holland was born 19 November 1801 in Kentucky and died 28 June 1873. Both are buried in Centennial Cemetery, near Carthage, Texas. They had children as follows: Eli, Brooks, Thomas, William, Elizabeth, Amanda, Pinkney, Avarilla (married John B. Lacy), Pernecy (who married B. B. Lacy), and John who married Elizabeth Collier in Sumter County; there was also a daughter named Susan who married Henry J. Darnell. William Holland sold out to Samuel Speight 20 November 1843 Deed Book G - page 694.

Another son of John Holland was Anderson Holland who married Elizabeth Rainer in Marengo County, Alabama on 6 September 1821, Garrison Anderson, J.P. They had children: Bluford (who married Charlotte A. Davis 8 March 1845 - Marriage Book 1 page 319, Sumter County), F. M., William C. Vincent, Dulcina, Ann. This Anderson Holland was dead in 1842 when John Holland's will was probated as he named the above children as "the children of my son Anderson Holland." F. M. Holland married Tilitha Riggins.

Drury Jackson patented 160 acres (SW¼) in this section. He also bought land from Matthew A. and Leah Newton; and he sold some land to Lemmon Ward. Drury's wife was named Milly. Drury was in Marengo County, Alabama in the 1820's.

Lemmon Ward (Laman) patented land in SE¼ of this section.

Ephriam Jackson and wife Rhoda sold part of their land to Dempsey Cockrell. Ephriam died 1840. Rhoda, the widow, and Seaborn his brother, were administrators of the estate. See Orphans' Book 2 page 88. Ephram and Hiram held land jointly. Ephram, Hiram, Seaborn, Jacinth, and William were sons of Randall Jackson who died in 1839; however William had died prior to his father's death and left a son John R. Jackson. When Randall Jackson's estate was settled (page 249 - Book 2) the administrator stated all had been given their shares except the "estate of Ephriam Jackson." (See Sumterville Methodist Cemetery and Old Side Cemetery records for more Jackson history.)

Section #13

This is the section in which Sumterville is located. Joseph B. Jones, James L. Hutchins, Nicholas Keating, Zacheus Wilson patented this land. Joseph Jones owned the land where Sumterville lies. He sold some of it to William Patton. He married Margaret Patton 11 July 1834, supposedly the daughter of William Patton. She must have died before 1838 when William Patton died as he mentioned his wife, Eliza, a daughter Cynthia Meyers and son William S. Patton, a student, in his will.

See Methodist Cemetery for history of James L. Hutchins.

Nicholas Keating - no history to date.

Zacheus Wilson - no history to date.

Section #14

Terrance (Terry) Foy, Davis and Fiester Foy patented all the land in this section. Davis Foy was born in South Carolina about 1811 according to the 1850 Census. His wife was Eliza Amason and born in North Carolina about 1829; they married 28 March 1849 and had one child, Thomas T. who was 3 months old in 1850. Davis Foy's mother Nancy Foy was 67 at that time and was living in the home of her son. See Old Side Cemetery Records for Foy history.

Section #15

Davis Foy, Jeremiah Horne, Jabes Evans and Laman Ward patented the land in this section; the first two have been mentioned elsewhere, as has Laman Ward.

Jabes Evans - no history to date.

Section #16

Every 16th Section in the State of Alabama belonged to the schools, but under the terms of the Treaty of Dancing Rabbit Creek this 16th Section was received in trust by Anthony Winston for Daniel Green.

Section #17

Those who patented land in this section were Charity Pyle, Elizabeth Ann Pyle, Samuel B. Jackson, John E. Anderson, and Malachi Nettles.

Samuel Jackson sold his land to Zachariah Nettles 19 December 1835, no name on the deed but his. Zachariah Nettles married Mary A. Staggs 13 December 1841. Mary was the daughter of Zachariah Staggs according to marriage license in Book 1, Sumter County.

Malachi Nettles - no history to date.

John E. Anderson was the son of William and Elizabeth Anderson whose obituaries are in The Sumter County Whig. He was a brother of William G. Anderson, Sumter County's first Probate Judge. John Erwin Anderson was born circa 1796, in Greenville County, South Carolina, and died 1848, in Panola County, Texas. His wife was Cynthia D. Harper (sister of Sumter County's first Sheriff) born in Georgia 1798 and died after 1870. John E. Anderson appraised the property of Mason L. Anderson in 1838 - Alexander Anderson and Holland Jenkins were administrators of estate. John E. Anderson was security for Calvin Anderson in Marengo County, Alabama when Calvin married Bella Silman in 1824; in 1820 he was security in the marriage between William Mitchell and Sophia Lane in Marengo County; he and his wife Cynthia sold land to William Browning in 1828 and to John D. Collen in 1831, both of Marengo County. They sold land in Sumter County to John J. (or L.) Burton in 1838. John E. and Cynthia Anderson had a daughter Permilla who married Lewis L. Parham.

The Pyles patented land in other Townships in the county. More about them later.

Section #18

John Jackson, George W. Harper, David Jarrell, Alfred Yarbrough and James McCown patented the land in this section. It seems that those with money bought land anywhere in the county as an investment. After the land was cleared and a cabin built it could be sold for large profit. David Jarrell and his wife Mahala soon sold this land to Alfred Yarbrough. Ellender Jarrell, the daughter of David Jarrell married Stephen Grice 25 June 1843, John Grice security. John Jackson and wife Milly sold this land to Malichi Nettles and his land in Range 4 West of Township 20 to Alexander Birdsong.

Alfred Yarbrough was in Marengo County, Alabama before Sumter County was opened for settlement. In 1826 he sold land in Marengo County to Elish Yarbrough; and we find that Elish Yarbrough gave or deeded some land to

Lydia Yarbrough in 1825, "in consideration of natural affection and love I bear Lydia Yarbrough". It has not been determined just who were the parents of Alfred Yarbrough but to quote from a letter from G. W. Yarbrough, who has spent a life time tracing Yarbrough families says, to E. R. Hester of Arcadia, Louisiana: "Your Elizabeth Yarbrough Hester was a close relative of Alfred Yarbrough who settled in Sumter County; and they are of the group from whom Mrs. Nelle M. Jenkins is descended through Zachariah Yarbrough of Amelia County, Virginia and North Carolina". He went on to say that John Yarbrough Sr., was either an uncle or brother of Zachariah, and that John's wife was Mary and that John Jr. lived in Person County, N. C.

We believe that Randolph Hester, the husband of Elizabeth Yarbrough, knew the Yarbroughs of Troup County, Georgia, as there is an indenture in Sumter County between Randolph Hester and others of that Georgia County. (See Boney Cemetery records for other Hester history.)

There were two other sets of Yarbroughs in the early settling of Sumter County. One was William Yarbrough, brother of Manoah Yarbrough of St. Clair County, who came to Alabama through Tennessee, St. Clair County, Alabama, Greene County, Alabama and he had children George, Richard, Harvey, William C., Margaret Y. May, Mary Y. May (wives of John and Walter May, respectively), Temperance 6. Watkins -- see Orphans' Book 2 page 181, and Orphans' Book 3 page 265, Sumter County, Alabama. Harvey Yarbrough married a Miss Miller from Kemper County, Mississippi - a daughter of Dr. Miller who is said to have lived near old Moscow, in that county. These Yarbroughs all went to Smith County, Texas and lived as neighbors to George, Wiley, Burk and other Littleton Yarbrough (of St. Clair County, Alabama) children who called each other "cousin". Littleton Yarbrough was the son of Manoah and Mary (Cunningham) Yarbrough and the grandson of Zachariah Yarbrough.

Hon. Ralph Yarborough, Senator from Texas, is the grandson of Harvey Yarbrough who moved from Sumter County to Tyler, Texas. Mrs. Mary Yarbrough Herrin Adams, widow of W. T. Adams and daughter of Margaret Yarbrough who married W. H. Herrin (she was daughter of Littleton Yarbrough of St. Clair County, Alabama), told me in 1952 in Austin, Texas, that she knew the Hon. Ralph Yarborough's forebears in Tyler, Texas and "we were related even though we spelled the name Yarbrough differently." Mrs. Adams was 84 at the time. The name Yarbrough in Sumter County records is spelled Yarbrough, Yarborough, Yarbro, Yarber and Yarbre. Even brothers have been known to put an extra "o" in the name or to leave one out. Mrs. Svec of Houston, Texas is descended from Richard and Leanna (Brazile) Yarborough. George Yarborough married (1) a Miss Wyatt and (2) Ada Amason of Sumter County, Alabama. He also removed to Tyler, Texas and was neighbor to George Yarbrough, the 49er, a son of Littleton and Nancy (Ashcraft) Yarbrough of St. Clair County, Alabama. William H. Yarbrough, son of Charles, and grandson of Thomas (brother of Manoah formerly of Rowan County, N.C. and later of St. Clair County, Alabama) was also a neighbor of the other two sets of Yarbroughs and all claimed relationship. I have copies of letters written almost a century ago telling about members of these families - the above George Yarbrough, the 49er, was the great uncle of Nelle Morris Jenkins.

The other family of Yarbroughs in Sumter County in its early settling was the family of Ambrose Yarbrough born circa 1789/90 and his wife Phoebe. He was the grandson of Ambrose Yarbrough who is said to have come from Yorkshire, England ca 1710 - a member of the Yarbrough de Bateson branch of the family. He married into the Va. Yarbrough family which stemmed from Richard, the immigrant of 1643 and died 1702. The two branches of the family probably kept in touch with each other until after the death of Richard; that he came directly to this family in America attests this fact, and later, so G. W. Yarbrough informs me, they are found together in South Carolina. Mrs. Cleon Culpepper who lives south of Cuba in Sumter County is a descendant of Ambrose Yarbrough, Baptist Minister, who is buried near her home. These Yarbrough families will be dealt with in detail in a later volume. The members of this family settled in Mississippi and Louisiana.

George W. Harper was the first Sheriff of Sumter County (See Deed Book A page 8 Sumter County.) Security: Lodawick Moore, Samuel Grigsby, R. R. Moore and R. W. Lott. He married Malinda Moore, the daughter of Lodawick and Rachel Moore. George W. Harper was mentioned in the Lodawick Moore will as "my son-in-law" being a joint owner with him in a business. Will was proved 22 November 1841 - Will Book 1, Sumter County. Settlement of estate in Orphans' Minute Book #4 page 654. George W. Harper and his wife removed to Harpersville, Mississippi. Mary Ann Moore who married Albert G. Anderson, the first Tax Collector of Sumter County, was the niece of the above Malinda Moore Harper. Mary Ann was the daughter of Robert and Theodosia or Ladocia (Hamilton) Moore.

James McCown and his wife Elizabeth H. sold their land in this section to Eli Seales of Kemper County, Mississippi - See Deed Book A page 496.

Section #19

Glover and Lyons, Darling Seale, Pliny R. Fleming and Martin Simms patented the land in this section. No doubt but that Glover and Lyons bought this land to resell.

Section #20

Malachi Nettles, Elizabeth McLean, Joseph McLean, William H. Lacy and Henry J. Darnell patented the land in this section. However the McLeans never lived on their land. They sold their land to Alfred Yarbrough in 1836. The deeds show they were residents of Washington County at the time. Joseph McLean and H. A. McNiell were witnesses to Elizabeth McLean's signature.

William H. Lacy who settled E½ of SE¼ section 20 R 3 W married Elizabeth E. Anderson the daughter of John E. Anderson and granddaughter of William and Elizabeth (Easley) Anderson 12 December 1839. Removed to Panola County, Texas. They had children: Sara born 1842 in Texas, James K. Lacy born 1845, Louisa born 1846, Cynthia born 1847, and John born 1850.

Henry J. Darnell patented the 160 acres next to William H. Lacy. He married Susan Holland, the daughter of William and Sara (Davis) Holland.

Section #21

This section was patented by Sina Anderson and children Burbon Anderson, Amelia Anderson, and Mary Anderson "widow and heirs of Mason Lillard Anderson". He married Sina or Tina Donall (or Darnell) in Marengo County, Alabama, 19 September 1827. Mason L. Anderson died in Sumter County, Alabama the fall of 1834. The administrators of the estate were Alexander Anderson, and Holland Jenkins with A. G. Anderson and J. E. Anderson as securities. (The same ones who administered the estate of Vincent Anderson). Bailey Anderson and John E. Anderson appraised the estate. I believe that Vincent and Mason Lillard Anderson were brothers. Vincent's daughter Melvira who married Dominico Jenkins had a daughter named Clara Mason - Clara for Clara or Classie Anderson Browning and Mason for Mason L. Anderson. The widow of Mason L. Anderson sold her property to Pliny R. Fleming who patented land in same section.

Pliny R. Fleming records may be found in Bethel Cemetery records.

Section #22

Lemon Ward (Laman), Samuel Webb, Joseph Young, Edward McCord patented the land in this section.

Samuel Webb lived in Sumterville and kept the Inn where stage coaches stopped for refreshments for passengers and to change horses. Thomas Hodges really entered or patented this land in section 22 and assigned it to Samuel Webb (see Deed Book A - 225) just after he received his certificate of possession; but the deed signed in Washington in 1837 was made in Samuel Webb's name. There is an indenture in Deed Book D page 627 dated 12 November 1845, between Samuel Webb of Sumter County as 1st part and James D. Webb of Greene County, Alabama as 2nd part and James Webb of Orange County of North Carolina as 3rd part; certain slaves were were mortgaged to James Webb of the 3rd part for an indebtedness to him by Samuel Webb.

Section #23

Evan Bryant, Wiley Curry, Nathan Amason and Asa Amason patented all the land in section 23. Evan Bryant married the daughter of Bryant Richardson and his wife Uney (Ray) Richardson -- Cherry Lane Richardson. The Bryants, Richardsons along with five other families came to this county together in a wagon train. When they reached the Tombigbee River, on the west side in Greene County, it is said that they thought they had reached the Mississippi River. At that time they had no maps to guide them in their travels. They stopped and began to clear the forests and it was only when they went to apply for certificates did they realize their mistake. They stayed in Greene County until the Indians were sent to Oklahoma, under the Treaty Of Dancing Rabbit Creek, when the came to Sumter County, just across the Tombigbee River. Evan Bryant settled many estates, and was guardian to some of Bryant and Uney Richardson's children. (See Cherry Lane Bryant's obituary, and Old Side Cemetery records)

See Old Side Cemetery Records for Nathan Amason and Asa Amason records.

Wiley Curry - no history to date.

Section #24

Seaborn Jackson, Evan Bryant, John E. Brown, Ebenzer C. Pettigrew and Elisha T. Horne patented land in this section.

Seaborn Jackson was the son of Randall Jackson, as per will and settlement of estate of Randall Jackson as mentioned before. Seaborn was still in Sumter County in 1850 as the census shows him as family 204. He was 34 and was born in Georgia. His wife, Tobitha was 24 and was born in Alabama. His children were William B. aged 8, Mary J. age 6, Benj. F. age 4, and Charles F. was 1 year old. David P. Smith age 28 born in Virginia was living in their home.

Seaborn Jackson bought this land from William and Susannah Gilbert the parents of William Gilbert who married (1) Mrs. Samuel Speight, and (2) Catherine Poythress.

See John E. Brown Cemetery Records for this family.

Elisha T. Horne and his wife Marilda sold this land to Ebenezer C. Pettigrew 6 July 1835. He still lived in this area until after 1841 when he was listed in the voting list at Patton's Hill or Sumterville.

Ebenezer Pettigrew lived in Greene County along with the Horns and Richardsons before coming to Sumter. There was one, James Pettigrew, who married Nancy Richardson in Greene County on the 3rd of September 1825. Book 1 page 33. They lived in Township 19.

Section #25

This section was patented by Ebenezer Pettigrew, James Trible, Elisha Price and Wade R. Thomas.

The 1850 Census shows Wade R. Thomas as family 348. He gave his age as 46 and his birth place as North Carolina. His wife was Melissa, age was 43, born in North Carolina. The oldest child was Mary, 22 born in North Carolina, John H. was 19 and born in North Carolina, Martha J. was 10 and born in Alabama, Wade R. was 7 and born in Alabama, Morrison was 5 and born in Alabama, Sally was 2 and born in Alabama. Julia Horn was living with this family and she gave her age as 22, born in N.C. Julia Horn became the wife of Bennett B. Thomas (see Simms and Bennett Thomas records). Melissa was the wife of Wade R. Thomas was a Horne, whom he married in N.C., according to the tradition in the families concerned in Sumter County. The daughter of Wade R. Thomas, Martha J., married Dr. J. W. Epes, of Epes, Sumter County. (See Old Side Cemetery records.)

Elijah Price sold his land to Enoch Travis 20 March 1835. His was the only signature to the deed at this time.

James Trible - no history to date.

Section #26

Wilson G. Myers, William Patton, Morrison Thomas and William S. Patton were the first settlers in this section. Morrison Thomas, brother to Bennett B. and Wade R. Thomas married Patience Horn born 1805 - daughter of John and Aseneth (Simms) Horn. According to the Wade Thomas family records, Morrison Thomas and family removed to Grenada, Mississippi.

Wilson G. Myers came to Sumter County from Marengo County, Alabama. He was the son of James Myers and wife Martha Godfrey Myers, whose estate was settled 20 December 1842 - Orphans' Book 3 page 42. The estate was divided among the following: William G. Myers, George M. Myers, Wilson G. Myers, John M. Myers, John Phillips in right of his wife Martha G. Phillips, Asberry Myers, Joseph Read in right of his wife Ann D. Reed, Thomas M. Myers and Leonard D. Myers. (Asberry Myers died 1843 -- will probated 18 May 1843. He married Eliza McRae 19 January 1937.)

The above James Myers married Martha Godfrey, sister of William Godfrey of Sumter County. Their parents were William and Sara (Brittain) Godfrey. William Godfrey, Sr., was a Revolutionary Soldier.

Section #27

This section was settled by Samuel Webb, Henry Y. Webb, Lock Boyette and Edward Graves. See Old Side Cemetery Records for The Boyette history.

Edward Graves married Jane Taylor 27 March 1834 with William Bruton as security.

Leroy Boyette, son of Lock Boyette, married Mary L. Moore 14 May 1842. She was the daughter of Thomas Moore.

Section #28

Those who patented land in section 28 were Joseph Knight, Evant Anders, William Bruton, Stephen Andress and John McLean.

See Old Side Cemetery Records for Joseph Knight history.

The NE¼ was patented by Evant Andress of Monroe County. He and his wife Catherine probably bought it as an investment as they sold it to Samuel D. Murff in 1836. Evidently Stephen Andress and his wife Susan of Monroe County, also, bought their land in this section for the same reason as they sold to John Jackson the same year.

William Bruton married Jane Anderson in Marengo County 22 March 1822, Alexander Anderson, security. She evidently died as we find William C. Bruton married Matilda Lacy in Sumter County 24 April 1834. He sold his land to Morgan Smith in 1837. The two Williams might have been different people. William C. Bruton owned part of the same land that William Bruton patented and sold his part to James Bruton in 1835. There was no name but his on the deed. James Bruton gave his age as 48 and born in South Carolina when the 1850 Census was taken. His wife Lizzie gave her age as 40 and born in Kentucky. Elizabeth was 22, William H. was 19, Matilda was 16, Hellina A. was 12, Schell was 12, Leonocroles was 2 all the children born in Alabama. In this home Sara Anderson resided, and gave her age as 66 and born in S.C. (In some instances this name was written "Bruton" - in other instances it looked like "Burton".)

Stephen McLean

Joseph Knight was assignee of Samuel B. Lacy in 1834 before certificate of possession was issued. He married Rebecca Oneal 20 October 1847. Samuel B. Lacy was the only signature on the deed. (See Old Side Cemetery Records for Knight history.)

Evan and Catherine Evant of Monroe County sold their land to Samuel D. Murff in 1836. The Evant family did not live in Sumter County.

William Bruton married Matilda Lacy in Marengo County, Alabama. William Bruton sold this land to James H. Bruton 28 September 1836 - no name but his to the deed.

Stephen Andress and wife Susan, of Marengo County, Alabama sold their land to John Jackson in 1836.

Section #29

Section 29 was taken up by Elijah McCoy, Henry Darnell, John McLendon, and Gaines.

Section #30

Benj. Talliafarro, Whitfield and Wilson G. Myers patented the land in this section. Talliafarro (said to have been pronounced "Toliver") bought land all over the county, probably for investment. They finally went to Mobile where they made their home. Whitfield of Marengo County bought land in many parts of Marengo, Sumter and Greene Counties.

See another section for Wilson G. Myers.

Section #31

John J. Burton, Wilson Myers, Thomas Simpson and Austin H. Lacy patented this section. Austin H. Lacy died prior to 1843, for at that time, his widow Charlotte had remarried Isaac Spinks of Lauderdale County, Mississippi. She and her second husband asked at that time for a settlement of Austin H. Lacy estate.

Others in this section have been given elsewhere or will be given in another volume as they lived elsewhere in the county.

Section #32

Edward Graves, William Burton, Lewis Simmons, Anna Elliott, John Boyd and William C. Day patented land in this section.

William Burton who married Jane Anderson in Marengo County, Alabama, 22 March 1822, with Alexander Anderson as security sold this land in section to Morgan Smith. Others in this section have been mentioned elsewhere or will be mentioned later, except William C. Day and Anna Elliott.

Anna Knox Elliott was born 15 September 1792 and died 8 February 1851; she was the widow of Andrew Elliott born 11 July 1788, died 31 December 1833. Orphans Min. Book 1 page 549, Sumter County, Alabama shows final settlement of Andrew Elliott estate in 1838. But the vouchers are dated from 1834. John K. Elliott was administrator. Anna was to receive 1/5 of the estate; the remainder to be divided among the 6 heirs, viz: John Knox, Lucenda, Betty, Margaret, Martha, Mary Ann. (Rachel had died at the age of 12.)

David Elliott, the father of Andrew Elliott, was born in County Antrim, Belfast, Ireland 1747. He, at the age of 10 years, came to the Colonies with his father in 1757. The Knox family came over on the same boat; with them a daughter named Betsy or Elizabeth. also 10 years of age.

These two children grew up and married in 1773. David Elliott became chief hammerman for Byrd and Fullenwilder Iron Works in North Carolina, then removed to Pulaski, Tennessee where he died in 1804. His widow removed with her family to Greene County, Alabama near Moundville (now Hale County). David and Elizabeth or Betsy had the following children: John, David, Joe, Jenny, Rachel and Mary Elizabeth, (Elizabeth married William Cubley who died 2 February 1841, Elizabeth Cubley died 20 February 1841, John Knox Cubley died December 1839, another Cubley's name I could not make out. These faded names are on a fly leaf of Matthew Henry's Exposition of the Old and New Testament, published 1829 and belonged to Elizabeth Knox - Now owned by Mrs. Robert Knox Elliott of Emelle, Alabama. Jane married a Mr. Gibson) and three other girls.

Elizabeth or Betsey Knox Elliott died at the home of her son Joe in Moundville in 1852. The Re-issue of the Alabama Historical Quarterly, Winter Issue 1944, by Willo Publishing Company, Tuscaloosa, Alabama 1959 says "Elizabeth Knox Elliott was a Revolutionary Patriot in South Carolina during the Revolution. It stated that she molded bullets, provided clothing for the soldiers and carried messages for them. It stated she was born 1750 in Ireland and died 1852 at Moundville." David Elliott, husband of Elizabeth Knox Elliott, fought in the Revolutionary War for 7 years.

Andrew Elliott, their son, was with Jackson as body guard during the Indian Wars. Anna Knox, wife of Andrew Elliott, who patented land in this section was the daughter of Elizabeth Knox who founded Elizabeth Presbyterian Church in the southern part of Sumter County in 1834. Anna Knox had brothers John and Jimmy. John Knox died circa 1839/40. Orphans' Record Book 2 page 168, shows Elizabeth the relict. The Knox family is said to be descended from John Knox, the Presbyterian Reformer in Scotland.

Anna Elliott left a will recorded in Will Book 1 page 552, Sumter County. She mentioned daughters Mary A. Payne, Margaret Moore, Martha A. Elliott, granddaughter Mary A. E. Payne, daughter Lucinda Payne, son John Knox Elliott. The Exe'rs John Knox Elliott, David Elliott, Ambrose W. Jones. Signed Anna Elliott. Wit/ John Greenlees, John M. Boyd, J. C. Greenlees, 28 October 1850. Proved 17 February 1851.

We do not know where Anna and Andrew Elliott are buried but probably in a Payneville cemetery where there are many mounds but not a gravestone.

See Elliott family cemetery for more Elliotts; and Central Cemetery for some other members of this family.

William C. Day, who patented land in T. 32, married (1) Miss Pettus who had relatives at Gainesville. They had several children among whom were (a) Pettus died young, and (b) Carrie who married Mr. Die. Wm. C. Day married (2) to Mrs. Sara Ann Andrews, mother of Annie (Andrews) Jenkins. See Boney Cemetery records.

(Margaret J. Elliott married Roderick Ransom Moore - son of Robert and Ladocia, or Theodosia, Moore - 28 January 1847 Book 1 page 388. Margaret Cecile Moore Curlin (Mrs. L. C.) of Waxahachie, Texas is a granddaughter of Roderick and Margaret Moore.

Martha Amanda Elliott born 17 January 1830, died January 1862, married Andrew McNairy Moore born 19 August 1830. They were the parents of Margaret Ella Moore born 16 October 1852, Leodocia Ann Moore born 19 October 1854, and Fanny Moore who married Mr. Morgan and removed to Murpheysboro, Tennessee. Roderick Ransom Moore and Andrew McNairy Moore were the sons of Ladocia or Theodosia (Hamilton) Moore; and Margaret and Martha Elliott were the daughters of Andrew and Anna Elliott.

Even though the Loderick Moore family settled in Township 18 many of his children and grandchildren married into families in Township 19. I will give you the history of this family at this time. Loderick Moore's will is recorded in Will Book 1-208 in Sumter County. He lived in Marengo County before Sumter County was formed (see his wife's (Rachel Moore) obituary in Sumter County Whig for other places of residence. He mentioned his wife Rachel Moore, granddaughters Malindy Leatherman and Martha Fletcher, children of his deceased daughter Mary Washington Fletcher - the rest of the property to be divided into 11 equal parts, naming his children as follows: Alfred Moore, Anthony D. Kinard and Sara his wife, Marquis D. Moore, Eldridge Loftin and Elizabeth his wife, Rolly Morgan and Fanny his wife, Roderick Ransom Moore, George W. Harper and Malinda Franklin his wife, -- he especially stipulated that Nancy Ann Parker, his daughter, should have no part of his estate but 1 part should go to "the heirs of her body", 1 part to go to the heirs of Robert Moore deceased, and 1 part to go to the heirs of Arthur Moore deceased, (this makes 10 parts and the 11th to go to his widow, Rachel.) Signed Loderick Moore. 3 June 1849. Witnessed by Rufus Cotes, Ladocia Moore, George W. Harper.

The settlement of the estate of Loderick Moore shows the heirs of Robert Moore - 8 in number as follows: Hance H. Moore, Loderick Moore, John M. Boyd in right of his wife Louisa J., and minor heirs Roderick R. Moore, John W. Moore, Andrew M. Moore, Catherine E. Moore, Robert Moore.

The heirs of Nancy Ann Parker: Alfred Hudson, John Hudson, Lodowick Hudson, Henry Hudson, Eph Norman Hudson, Robert M. Hudson, Nancy Parker, Amanda Parker.

Heirs of Arthur Moore as named in settlement: William H. Moore, Mary and Martha Moore. Martha Fletcher granddaughter, had married Edward L. Jordan when she received her share of estate.

Deed Book A page 122 - 2 January 1835 Thomas Hamilton of Rutherford County, Tennessee, made the following Deed of Gift: "In consideration for the natural love and affection which I have for my sister

Theodoria Moore (the mother) and her children and those whom she may bear: Hance Moore, Lodowick Moore, Louisa Jane Moore, Roderick Ransom Moore, John Wesley Moore, Andrew McNairy Moore, and Catherine Elizzbeth Moore -... certain slaves conveyed unto Loderick Moore as trustee ... slaves for use of Theodosia (she called herself Ladocia) Moore and her children

Wit/ Alfred Moore and　　　　　　　　　　Signed, Thomas Hamilton.
Catherine Moore.　　　　　13 December 1834

Francis McNairy of Guilford County, North Carolina, whose home was used as a hospital after the Battle of Guilford Court House, is said to have been the father of Rachel (McNairy) Moore. It is also said that Francis McNairy's wife was named Mary Hamilton, perhaps the sister of Hance Hamilton of Revolutionary fame. It is farther said that the McNairys and Hamiltons came together from Lancaster County, Penna., to Guilford County, North Carolina, and intermarried many times. This being true, Robert Moore and his wife Theodosia or Ladocia (Hamilton) Moore were cousins.

The children of Francis born 1734 and Mary (Hamilton) McNairy were: John born 1762 and became a Judge, and his home was used by Cornwallis as Headquarters at one time, Nathaniel, James (whose descendants are said to have gone to Mississippi), Margaret born 1771, Andrew, Mary, Rachel, and Boyd born 1785. (Copied from Commercial Appeal of Memphis, 15 April 1931 - Dropped Stitches Column). Please note Rachel (McNairy) Moore's obituary in Sumter County Whig. The 1790 Census Records show Francis McNairy head of a household in Guilford County, North Carolina. He is mentioned in North Carolina Assembly as having been a Senator and and as having made a plea in behalf of Matthew Hamilton.

Andrew McNairy Moore, the son of Robert and Theodosia (Ladocia) Hamilton Moore, was Captain in the 40th Alabama Regiment, Company K and was in the Battles of Lookout Mountain, Missionary Ridge, Chickamauga, Vicksburg and some battles around Atlanta, Georgia. He was captured at Noon Day Creek, Georgia and put in prison at Johnson's Island on Lake Erie, 12 June 1864, released 12 June 1865. His brother Robert was in prison at Rock Island, Ill. (According to Mrs. Richard Prince, Shuqualak, Mississippi.)

According to Andrew McNairy Moore's family Bible record he was born 19 August 1830 near Linden, Alabama and died at Scooba, Mississippi 7 November 1897 (I have already given you the history of wife number 1 - Martha Amanda Elliott.) His 2nd wife was Mary McCaskell who was born 20 March 1837 and died at Binnsville, Mississippi 23 January 1891. They married 29 September 1865. She was the granddaughter ---- McCaskell, Revolutionary War Soldier. Andrew McNairy Moore and Mary McCaskell had children: Fannie Christiana Moore born 9 February 1868, Katie Hamilton Moore born 6 March 1873, Andrew McNairy Moore born and died 1874, and Carrie McNairy Moore born 25 June 1876. Katie Moore married Buck Clark 18 January 1899, Carrie Moore married Albert L. Morton 16 June 1897, Hance Hamilton Moore married Bertha Cloe Halsell 16 June 1897. Hance Hamilton Moore died at Shuqualak, Mississippi 28 April 1944 and his wife Bertha Cloe (Halsell) Moore whom he married 16 June 1897, was born 5 February 1879 and died at Scooba, Mississippi 14 October 1941.

Hance Hamilton Moore and his wife Bertha Cloe Moore had a daughter, Elizabeth, who married Richard Prince of Shuqualak, Mississippi.

There was a daughter of Robert and Theodosia (Hamilton) Moore named Kate (see settlement of estate of Loderick Moore) who married a Mr. Torry. They had a daughter, Dixie, who married a Speed at Coatopa and is buried at Brewersville. (See Brewersville Cemetery Records in a later volume.)

Another daughter Louisa J. Moore married John M. Boyd, son of John and Jennett (Dial) Boyd, of Payneville.

Other Moore Marriages

Hance H. Moore married Mariah Burney 30 October 1844.

Marcus D. Moore married Mary A. Bennett 7 January 1857.

Robert Moore married Mary Davis -failed to get the date- Book 2 page 370.

Even though the Flowers family settled in another part of the county, they are so tied in with those whose histories I am giving I will give their history here. Jacob D. Flowers was born 1792 in South Carolina and wife Mary Hendrick was born 1812 in South Carolina and settled in the Belmont District of Sumter County in the early 1830's. According to the 1850 Census their children were as follows: Thomas C(oleman) 16 born Alabama, (he married Molly Flanagan); Jacob D(orman) born in Alabama (married Tillie White); Jane born 1850, died 1914, married Mr. Vise; Temperance 12, (married Mr. McCormic); Anne (married Mr. Parker); Robert Baker born 11 January 1848, died 5 May 1913, married Sara Annie Caldwell born 10 January 1855, died 15 April 1921. Others named in the census were Mary A., James, Isabell, Bennett H., Sara J. 2 mo. (She was the above Jane who married Vise.)

The above Robert Baker Flowers who married Sara Annie Caldwell (she was born 10 January 1855 and died 15 April 1921. They were the parents of Thomas Coleman Flowers who married Jennie Tartt Brandon (see Elliott history), Murray Caldwell Flowers who married Florence Elliott (see Elliott history - Central Cemetery), Mary Florence Flowers who died young, Leslie Marshall Flowers who married Clara Melton. John Robert

Flowers born 10 June 1891, died 28 October 1948, married Kathleen Harper born 23 January 1899 (second husband H. C. Bert of Texas), Cedric Errol Flowers married Inez Frisbie.

The above Murray C. and Florence (Elliott) Flowers reared two sons to be grown: Murray C. Jr., killed in WWII, and Henry Hendricks who married Jean Elenor Mize and are parents of Henry Jr., and Richard Gean Flowers.

Robert Baker Flowers' wife, Sara Annie was the daughter of John and Sara (Horton) Caldwell (John Caldwell was married three times). The Caldwells are said to be related to John C. Calhoun. Sara Horton was the daughter of Col. Stephen Horton born 8 October 1811, died 25 August 1886, married 8 April 1831 in Greene County, Alabama Elizabeth Ann Coates.

John Robert Flowers who married Kathleen Harper (whose parents were Alice Enda (McMillan) and William Hudson Harper whose parents were Elizabeth Coates and Robert Harper, making Kathleen and John Robert Flowers distant cousins. The parents of Enda McMillan were Eliza Ann McPherson and Hugh McMillan.)

William Baker Flowers, son of Kathleen (Harper) and John Robert Flowers married Jennie Maude Shaw, the daughter of Eunice Carolyn (Morris) and James Spann Shaw. Eunice C. Shaw is the daughter of Jennie (Yarbrough) and Elbert Green Morris Jr., and niece of Nelle (Morris) Jenkins. J. S. Shaw is the son of Mary Helen (Straight) and Shelton Taylor Shaw. Jennie Maude (Shaw) and William Baker Flowers are parents of four children Camelia Kathleen, Aliceanne, Jeniker Erin, a son William Baker Flowers Jr.

William C. Day who also patented land in this, section 32, sold out and removed to Marion, Mississippi and married (2) Mrs. Sara Ann (Smith) Andrews, widow of Capt. William Penn Andrews - see Annie Andrews history in Boney Cemetery. William C. Andrews had at least one child, Cassie, by a previous marriage. She married a Die - last heard of she was living in Florida.

Section #33

William H. B. Lacy, Edwin Brownrigg, Anna Simmons, Guilford P. Daniel and Gaines-Whitfield settled in this section. W. H. B. Lacy married Helena Bruton 6 April 1836. In 1850 Census his wife was Wilphemia and he had a son Franklin B. 10 years old. Guilford P. Danniel married Elizabeth Johnson - license issued 4 November 1833.

Section #34

Thomas Moore, Nicholas Lacy, Thomas B. Tutt and Henry Bates patented this land in section 34. See Bethel Cemetery for Thomas Moore record.

Nicholas Lacy is buried in Lacy family cemetery. Nicholas' daughter Phoebe (Sheabee) married John Darden 9 May 1843 with Redden Darden, Security - notation: John Darden the son of Mrs. Margaret Stephens.

Evidently James B. Tutt had bought this land as an investment as it was sold to William Boulton October 1834. It was sold to "William Godfrey of Washington County, Alabama, George W. Myers agent. - Deed Book 1, page 90.

Section #35

Henry Smith, Sara Anderson, William Cooper and James B. Tutt bought land in this section from the Government. Henry Smith and James B. Tutt patented this land as an investment.

Sara Anderson was the widow of Vincent Anderson - see Section #6.

William Cooper and wife Frances sold their land to Henry Horn in 1836.

Section #36

Washington Drinkard, Elijah Price, Isaac N. Mitchell and John Kennedy patented land in this section; Washington Drinkard married Nancy Persons 9 January 1835 - they sold out to Nathan Johnson December 1836. See "McCainville" for Kennedy record.

Township 20N., Range 4 West

This is a fraction of a township, part of which lies in Mississippi. Most of the people who patented this land lived elsewhere in the county or out of the state. They are as follows: Christian Yarrell, William Bagley, Alfred Yarbrough, James Hamrick, John O. Marcy, Edward O. Marcy, Joel Lipscomb, James McCown, Moses Johnson, James Harper (he and his wife Tabitha sold to Wm. Earbee who sold to Wm. R. Sturdivant by 1837), Jeremiah Warsham, Daniel E. Harper (married Elizabeth Gorman 13 July 1836), Sharod H. Parker, Madison Taylor, William Wardlaw, William Ford, Warham Easley (his will is in Book 1, page 84 and mentioned son Creed T., daughter Martha Foreman - also spelled Foeman - wife Emily Easley, stated he held bill of sale for 3 slaves from Daniel Easley - recover and divide between children: Samuel W. Easley, Christopher B. Easley, and Martha Ann Foeman - minor heirs: Catherine, Maria, Elizabeth Jane, and Virginia Noble. Signature witnessed by Thomas Bartell, David Blackshear, P. B. May and J. A. Martiniere. We know by the witnesses, that Worham Easley lived near Belmont, so he was the one who helped to organize the county.) Others who patented this land: Mumford Lawson, Hugh McCann, Thomas Darnell, William Patton, John E. Anderson - many tracts - James J. Bruton and wife Patience sold to John McLendon January 1837. In Deed Book A in 1836 we find John J. Bruton (looks like Burton also) 1st part to Armistead Burwell and John Tayloe Lomack of Marengo County 2nd part and William M. Burwell of Franklin County, Virginia 3rd part - whereas James H. and John J. Burton (Bruton) owed William M. Burwell certain slaves etc.), Isaac Adair, Starling Gorman, James B. Pyle, John Stevens, John Jackson, (he and his wife Milly sold to Malichi Nettles who sold to Alexander Birdsong.)

Township 19N., Range 4 West

This is a fraction of a township, part of which lies in Mississippi. A great deal of this land was in woods, never cleared - so probably bought for speculation.

Section #1

George W. Harper, Joel Mallory and Starling Gorman settled this section. G. W. Harper was first sheriff in Sumter County, he later settled and founded Harpersville, Mississippi. His wife was Malinda Moore, daughter of Lodawick and Rachel Moore - in Mr. Moore's will he mentioned "my son-in-law George W. Harper."

Section #2

James P. Pyle and Starling Gorman patented this land.

Section #10

(Sections 4,5,6,7,8,9 lie in Mississippi.) John Greenlee, Alexander Walker patented this land. Tishobomattak, a Choctaw Indian, by the Treaty of Dancing Rabbit Creek was allowed 80 acres of land. The whites called this Indian "Tubby" which means "dead man". He finally sold his land to John Greenlee. A small creek flows through this land - it is known to this day as "Tubby's Creek". It was probably here that the first Baptist Church in confines of present Sumter County and 3rd in Alabama was located several years before the county was opened for settlement - see Owens History of Alabama. This site was near "outpost" for Fort Tombecbee.

Section #11

William Brewer, Hiram Payne, Alexander Breathit, Charles J. Puckett (See history of Payneville), and John Pyle who married Malinda Threadgill 18

June 1842 patented this section. William Brewer died before 1852, willed everything to wife Mary and daughter Martha E. Monett wife of James Monett. His son William executor - Book 2 page 20. He lived elsewhere in the county.

Section #12

William Payne and the men named in Section 11 patented this land. William Payne had no wife in 1836 when he sold some property.

Section #13

This section was taken up by Elisha Shelton, John P. Jones and Ransom T. Payne. (See history of Payneville for Payne.)

Section #14

This section was patented by those who have been mentioned before, and Austin Hitt who died ca 1853 - He named his wife Rebecca, and children: James A. Hitt, Sibell Hitt, Cornelia Hitt, Penelope Hitt, Clark Hitt, Nancy A. Hitt and Rebecca Hitt. Witnesses John A. McConnell and Jesse B. Thom. Another man in this section was James McCown who with wife Elizabeth sold land to Eli Seale, brother of Beaufort or Bufort Seale.

Section #15

This section was settled by those already named. (Sections 16, 17, 18, 19, 20 and 21 lie in Mississippi.)

Section #22

Beaufort (Bufort, Buford) Seale, Eli Seale and Harrison Evans patented this section. The father of Eli and Buford Seale was Jarvis Seale who removed to Greene County, Alabama from Wilkes County, Georgia. He married (1) Ann Yarbrough who died 26 December 1832. They were the parents of Anthony Seale who married Polly Bishop, Bufort Seale who married Mary Ann Evans, William Seale who married Jane Carr Elliott and Eli who married (1) Philida --- (2) Sara Alexander. Jarvis Seale married (2) Lucretia Oneal and had 4 children.

Section #23

This section was taken up by those already mentioned and by W. H. Smith.

Section #24

This section was patented by those already mentioned and by James Hodges, Jesse Ross, Stephen W. Clay, and Joseph Smith.

James Hodges was the son of Robert Hodges whose will is recorded in Book 1 Page 362, Sumter County, Alabama. He mentioned sons: James and Allen, grandsons: Amos, John P., James Allen; daughters (?) Melinda McDaniel, Karen or Caren Anderson, Celziam Hodges, Nancy Ann Hodges; granddaughter: Elizabeth Ross, grandson Thomas Hodges; daughter Cely Hellson, --witnessed Joseph Marlin and Jabel Faulkner. (The McDaniels lived at Sumterville and some of them are buried in Methodist Cemetery. J. W. Nixon, who married Alice Boyd, was also closely related to the McDaniels. Members of that family live in Demopolis and at Dancy, Alabama.

Section #25

Among those who took up this section were James Land - others already named.

Section #27

(Section #26 was taken up by those already mentioned.) Section #27 was patented by Geo. W. Freeland, John E. Shelton, Thadeus B. McGowan, Joe A. McGowan.

Sections #28, 29, 30, 31 and 32 lie in Mississippi.

Section #33 (a Fraction.)

This was patented by Francis Marlin. Section #34 was patented by those mentioned before.

Section #35

John Hand patented this land, and others with patents in this township.

Section #36

Besides those already mentioned Josiah Houston patented land in this section.

ERRATA

PAGE 55 - "His Mother" should be "her mother".

PAGE 59 - "Arch Richardson, Sr.," should be "Arch Richardson, Jr."

PAGE 60 - "Jacob Simms .. " should be "Jacob Horn married Millicent Thomas".

PAGE 62 - "Elisha Bell" should be "Elijah Bell".

PAGE 76 - Sallie Dial Hopper was "sister" of Jane Dial Boyd, not her "daughter".

PAGE 85 - "Site George S. Gaines" should be "site of Hamner".

PAGE 106 - "Austin Grover Boyd" (next to the last line) should be "Grover C. Boyd".

PAGE 191 - "John Horh" should be "John Horn".

PAGE 162 - "Spatt Cemetery" should be "Spratt Cemetery".

INDEX

A

ADAMS, Carol Ann.............112
   J. B....................... 19
   J. R.......................106
   Kate......................112
   Lloyd.....................112
   Mamie.....................106
   Mary Narze................106
   Mary J....................234
   Mr........................ 63
   Thomas....................134
   W. T......................234
ALBERTA, Bessie............... 73
ALBERTON, Frances............. 45
   Margaret.................. 45
ALCORN, Jeremiah..............115
   Margaret..................115
   Rebecca...................115
ALEXANDER, Della..............216
   Eli.......................115
   J. M......................216
   Margaret..................115
   Sara...................... 94
ALLEN, Ben....................219
   Joseph P..................184
ALLISON, Andy.................162
   Etta...................... 88
   John F....................209
   Lillis S..................159
   Mr........................173
   R. J......................195
   Ruby Nell.................111
ALLUMS, Prudence.............. 32
ALTMAN, John..................192
   William...................192
ALVIS, Ashley.................217
AMYL, Donalson................113
AMASON, Ada...................234
   Asa...................236, 237
   Elbert.................... 43
   Eli....................... 43
   Eliza.....................234
   Elizabeth................. 43
   Nannie.................... 43
   Nathan............143, 236, 237

ANDERSON, Albert G...13, 184, 189, 235
   Alexander.................227
   Alexander E...............233
   Amelia....................236
   Anna...................... 8
   Bailey W..............181, 184
   B.........................134
   Burbon....................236
   Calvin....................233
   Caroline..................184
   Cassa.................227, 229
   Catina.........127, 129, 181, 228
   Cynthia...................236
   Dorcas.............184, 223, 224
   Elizabeth........183, 184, 233, 236
   Family....................227
   Fred...................... 76
   Garrison..................231
   Helen.....................124
   Hulda.................184, 223
   James....................8, 12
   Jane..................239, 240
   Jean....................8, 184
   John.......8, 135, 184, 208, 227, 229
   John E........90, 184, 223, 233, 247
   John A................134, 228
   Karen..................... 92
   Letty.....................228
   Margaret..................134
   Mary..................184, 236
   Mason L...............223, 236
   Melvira...................227
   Mrs. Vincent..............127
   Narcissa...........129, 149, 228
   Pamilla................90, 233
   Rachel....................243
   Rebecca................... 76
   Robert....................184
   Sara.........246, 158, 226, 227, 239
   Scarlett..............184, 227
   Schaharissa...............181
   Sina......................236
   Vincent......140, 158, 184, 229, 246
   Willie Ann................223
   William......8, 9, 181, 184, 227, 233
   William G........8, 13, 144, 183, 233

William S. 51, 228
ANDREOLA, Howard N. 105
ANDRESS, Catherine. 239
    Evan. 239
    Stephen. 239
    Susan. 239
ANDREWS, Abraham. 138, 139
    Annie. 137, 139, 241
    Eli. 138
    Geo. W. 137
    Joel. 137, 139
    John. 138
    Henry. 139
    Mary. 138
    Robert. 138, 139
    Sarah Ann. 139, 241
    William P. 138, 139, 241
ANGLE, Allie Bell. 124
    Helen. 124
APPLEBY, Georgie. 96
ARMOUR, Mr. 125
ARMSTRONG, Agnes. 71
    Andrew a. 206
    Annie H. 154
    James. 71, 205
    Martha. 71
ARNOLD, John. 17
ARRINGTON, Anthony. 14
    A. J. 41
    Helen. 54
    J. J. 55
    Joseph. 203
    Mary J. 203
    Margaret. 54
    Patience A. 203
    R. H. 209
    Robert. 203
    Samuel. 214
    William. 87
    W. R. 41
ASHCRAFT, Nancy. 234
ASHFORD, Caroline E. 192
    James G. 192
    Martha. 174
    Samuel L. 174
    William. 174
ATTIKSON, Frank. 184
AUBREY, Margaret. 171
    Mary. 171
AULD, James. 11, 152

AUST, Betty. 108, 119
    Grover. 174
    James Leland. 108, 134
    Louise. 108
    Margie B. 119
    Monroe. 30
AXSON, Ellen. 47, 34
AYERS, Ann H. 216
    D. L. 216

B

BACHELOR, James L. 184
    Rebecca D. 184
BAGGETT, Catherine. 115
    Ed. 115
BAILEY, Cornelia A. 116
BAINE, Howard. 112
BAKER, Anthony. 31
    Billy. 27
    B. S. 211
    Edith. 68
    John. 31, 68
    Peggy. 68
BALDWIN, Helen. 215
BALLARD, James F. 152
    Jewel. 152
    Joseph F. 152
    Virginia 152
BARBOUR, Ruth. 76
BARD, Louise. 31
BARFIELD, Nannie K. 119
BARNES, A. G. 204
    Irvine. 166
    James. 38
    John R. 204
    Millicent. 166
    Sara. 32, 183
BARR, Julius. 209
    Susie. 209
BARROWS, George. 12
BARTELL, Thomas. 246
BASSETT, Frances. 24
BATTON, William. 185
BATY, Dorothy J. 108
    Eugene. 108
    J. B. 108
    Sara F. 108
    Terri Lnyy. 108
    Thomas H. 108

BAYLESS, Lucy................... 52
BEARD, Marguerite...............113
BEASLEY, Charles................ 12
BEAVERS, A. E...................208
BECK, Sallie McGill.............194
BEDELL, Albert A................211
BEIRNE, Andrew..................185
BELL, Alerena (Alice)........69, 156
    Cathy......................152
    David...................69, 152
    Elizabeth..................156
    Elijah.............49, 62, 80, 229
    Frank......................199
    James H..................... 69
    Irene......................174
    Laura...................62, 229
    Martha..................... 69
    Mary....................... 69
    Redman..................... 69
    William.................49, 69
BELTON, George.................. 12
BENEDICK, (family)..............139
BENNETT, Margaret............... 65
    Sarah E.................... 65
    W. H.......................214
BESTER, D. P....................193
    Eliza J....................193
BETHEL PRESBYTERIAN CEMETERY..68-84
BETHEL CEMETERY in alphabetical
order (Burwell, Daniel, Dozier,
Drummond, Fleming, Fulton, Hadden,
Hale, Hansel, Hodges, Holt, Jeter,
Kendall, Kerr, Lavender, McCorcle,
McDow, Mitchell, Moore, Ramsey,
Porter, Rix, Sanders, Silliman,
Smith, Templeton, Underwood, Wheelinf,
Woodard, Wreen,)...............68/84
BIBB, (family)..................123
BIGHAM, Martha J................ 73
    Mr......................... 86
    Samuel J................... 73
BILLINGS, (Carpetbagger).....129, 181
BIRDSONG, Alexander......184, 233, 247
BISHOP, Bobbie.................. 30
    John III................... 30
    Pamela..................... 30
    Polly...................94, 248
BLACK, Patricia Ann............. 39
BLACKBURN, Pamila...............193
BLACKSHEAR, David...............246

    Elizabeth.................. 83
    Nancy...................... 83
BLACKWELL, Harriett.............199
    Thomas.....................199
BLALOCK, John...................101
BOBBITT, R. P................... 52
BOBNETT, John M.................207
BODENHAMMER (family) 231
BOLDING, M. E...................208
BOLTON, Cora P.................. 83
BOND, Bob.......................167
    Margaret...............138, 167
    Madelyn F..................117
BONEY, Wimbeck..............126, 143
BONEY CEMETERY RECORDS -
    (Anderson, Boney, Cherry, Clark,
    Cobb, Davis, Bolsum, Fortner, Har-
    ry, Harper, Jenkins, Joyner, Kent,
    Kennon, Kirkland, Lacy, Lunceford,
    Massangale, McCrory, Murphy, Neely
    Newton, Parrish, Ramsey, Swain,
    Treadaway, Thomas, Willingham,
    White, Yarbrough.)......130-152
BOURDEAU, T. D..................209
BORDEN, Lillie.................. 69
BOSWELL, (family)...............109
BOWER, (family).................140
BOWLES, (family)................134
BOYD, A. F. J................... 96
    A. J....................... 72
    Alice..................249, 36
    Caddie..................... 72
    Conde......................146
    David...................12, 92
    Hugh.......................193
    Grover..................59, 94
    John..............63, 75, 225, 183
    J. W....................57, 193
    Lolita..................... 96
    Louise.....................242
    Margaret................... 76
    Matthew.................86, 91
    Mary....................... 72
    Olga....................... 94
    Philip..................... 76
    Ruby....................... 94
    Susan......................140
BOYD CEMETERY RECORDS.......100-125
    (Boyd, Dial, Danner, Davis, Daven-
    port, Hopper, Kelly, Moore, Powe,

Prestwood, Sutton, McCain, Plott, Thompson, Nixon.)
BOYETTE, Leroy................79, 239
    Lock.....................20, 238
    Mary L..................79, 239
    T. W........................192
BRADENBURG, (family)............68
BRADFORD, (family)..............193
BRAGG, (family).................185
BRAME, C. E......................12
BRANNON, Margaret B.............108
BRASHEARS, Jesse.................13
BREATHIT, Alexander..............94
BREWSTER, Mary..................151
BREWER, Amanda..................212
    Jane........................72
    Mary.......................248
    Matthew....................194
    Robert......................72
    William............94, 247, 93
BRIDGES, Jacob T................228
BRIDGMAN, Mary..................139
BRIGGS, (family).................74
    James M....................121
BRITTON, Mary....................26
BROCK, Lewis.....................13
BROCKWAY, D. S..................209
BROGAN, Ursula..................139
BROOLS, William M...............217
BROTHERS, (family)...............61
BROTHWAIT, Alexander............100
BROWN, (Bunyan family)..........134
    Charlie.....................46
    Ester......................214
    Frances L..................149
    Hiram.......................12
    Jeremaih.............16, 17, 186
    Jesse R....................120
    John E...............16, 17, 236
    Julia Kathleen..............25
    Maria......................227
    Mary........................12
    W. H........................26
    William....................226
BROWNING, John Bailey.......129, 142
    Classie....................230
    Laurel......................62
    Schaharissa.................31
BROWNING CEMETERY (Browning, Handley).....................181
BROWNRIGG, Edwin B...........63, 185

Wiley............................63
BROWNSON, John Milton............67
    Kate........................67
BRUNSON, (family)...............211
    Thomas M...................205
    W. A.......................206
BRUTON, (family)................239
    William...............130, 238
BRYANT, Cherry Lane......64, 200, 206
    E. N..............16, 36, 38, 200
    George W...................166
    Henrietta..................166
BUCHANNAN, (family).............143
    Clara Bell.................115
BUFFINGTON, Martha...............69
BUFORD, (family).................26
BULLOCK, B. F...................167
    Josephine...................62
BUNTIN (family)..................65
BURNES, Thomas...................97
BURT, Miss......................147
BURTON, (Cemetery)...............98
    (family)................96, 97
    Helena.....................143
    James......................247
    Lucenda....................227
    Patience...................247
    Susan F.....................62
    William C..................143
BURWELL, Armisted...............227
    Benj. P..............12, 21, 23
    Bessie......................23
    Jefferson...................87
    Sallie......................55
    William M..................247
BUSTIANT, Benj..................180
BUSTIN, William..................93
BOWLING, P. L....................47

C

Cade, Judith L..................174
Cahoon, Henry....................12
Caldwell, Carrie A..............220
    R. W.......................183
CALLICOAT, Queen Victoria.......115
CALLUMS, M.......................12
CALVERT, (family)...............100
    Mary........................96

CAMPBELL, (family)......76, 81, 89, 96
    Caroline.....................135
    David........................171
    John R.......................163
    Lillie........................68
    R. M.........................208
    Sandra.......................125
    Susannah.....................170
    William...................21, 135
CANNON, William.................101
CARDER, (family)...........17, 19, 20
CARLISLE, Martha................105
CAROTHERS, Rev.................17, 67
CARPENTER, Jubal.............43, 194
    Millicent.................44, 194
    Sarah.....................43, 194
CARR, (family)...................39
    A. J. (Mrs.).................207
    J. P.........................207
    Cecil.........................45
CARROLL, (family)...............124
    Ed...........................216
CARTER, (family)................227
CASSIDY, William P..............112
CATHY............................41
CENTRAL CEMETERY RECORDS....152-158
    (Boyd, Burton, Cobb, Crumm,
    Daniel, Dobbins, Elliott,
    Edmonds, Jenkins, Lang, Motes,
    Murray, Neville, Richardson,
    Stegall, Wooldridge.)
CHAFIN, (family)................177
CHAMBERS, Adams.................101
    James H......................91
    John........................222
CHANDLER, (family)..............118
CHAPMAN, Alexander..............185
    Bascom.......................28
    Charles E...................103
    Elizabeth...................103
    Florence.....................28
    Reuben..................185, 211
    Sarah H.................112, 125
    (Wm. P. family).............140
CHAPPELL, Hugh (family).........139
    George......................108
    Ruth........................108
CHERRY, Jarret (family).....31, 131
    Joshua..................31, 131
    A. E. (family)...............30
    Valera......................121

CHILD, W. H.....................221
CHISLOM, Lodie (family).........141
CHUTTEAU, Dr...............129, 181
CLARK, Ann.......................23
    Buck........................241
    Effie........................21
    Katie.......................241
    Jane........................186
    Virginia....................119
    William.....................186
CLAY, Stephens..........92, 94, 249
COATS, Mary.....................217
COBBS, Oscar (family)...........110
    Robert L. (family)...........61
    Rufus.......................137
    Virginia....................155
COBBS, Elizabeth Boon...........186
    James B.....................216
    Martha W.....................91
    Susie B.....................216
    Thomas......................216
COCKRELL, A. W..................162
    Catherine.................40, 64
    Dempsey.................194, 232
    Eva Nash....................201
    Mary S.......................40
    Millicent T.................194
    Nathan......................194
    W. A........................201
COFFIELD, Bessie................166
COIT, Miss......................109
COLEMAN, Wade (family)...........32
    Augustus....................195
    Ellis.......................118
    S. C........................118
    Shirley.....................118
    William H...................195
COLGIN, Clementine Georgians....185
    Edward B................8, 9, 185
    George J................12, 210
    William R....................12
COLLEN, John D..................233
COLLIER, Elizabeth..............131
COMMANDER, Irwin M. K(family)...109
COOK, J. M......................211
    Miss Dutch...................12
    Temperance A.................51
    Thomas L....................211
COON, C.........................194
COOPER, (family)................109
    Frances.....................246

Frankie......................163
John B......................13
William.....................246
COPELAND, Betty Ruth..........108
Preston.....................108
CORNICK, Sophia Mason......186, 194
Tully R..................186, 194
CORZINE, Isabel...............184
COX, Annie....................47
Dodson......................140
Meddie......................140
CRADDOCK, John (family).......124
CRACENS, Margaret J...........194
Mary........................210
Susan.......................12
CREIGHTON, (family)............61
CRENSHAW, Charles H...........186
Willis......................186
CROCKER, Clark.........16, 17, 38
J. W........................209
CROOM, Hardy B................185
James.......................185
Richard.....................185
Winifred....................185
CROSS, Austin.................113
Owen........................113
S. S. (Rev.)................12
Shirley.....................113
CRUMM, Vista K............74, 159
CRUMPTON, (family).............59
CUBLEY, John K................241
Elizabeth...................241
William.....................241
CULPEPPER, Cleon (Mrs.).......235
CUNNINGHAM, Eveline...........211
Mary Ann....................202
William.....................211
CURLIN, Margaret..............242
CURRY, Wiley..................236

D

DACY, Ruth Jo.................113
DANCY, Alaber G...............230
DANIEL, Alice Bell.............41
Betty J.....................106
Elizabeth...................245
Guilford....................245
James T............41, 156, 165
Kennith.....................106

Matilda.....................156
Rufus.......................165
W. S........................208
DANNEBURG, C. S................12
DANNER, Elizabeth.............100
Grace.......................120
Jacob G.....................101
DARDEN, John..................246
Phoebe L....................246
Redden......................246
DARLING, Carrie A.............145
Ida F.......................145
John........................119
DARNELL, (family).31, 56, 230, 231, 236
DAVENHAUER, David (family)....157
DAVENPORT, Queen V. (family)..116
Louise......................105
Nancy........................98
William B...................105
DAVID, M. V...................215
DAVIDSON, Frank...............215
Harry........................72
Mary.........................72
M. F.........................12
Mollie......................115
Reuben..................222, 224
Sadie L.....................115
Thomas J.................12, 20
W. Fayette...................15
DAVIS, Chesley (family)...195, 223
Stephen L. (family).........184
Eli.............14, 183, 193, 223
J. B........................157
John Le.................31, 222
Lee.........................119
Mary Amelia.................108
Mary E......................110
N. A.........................11
Rosa Knox...................157
Samuel......................195
Susan.......................108
William R..........108, 118, 172
DAVIS, CEMETERY(Danner, Davis)170-171
DAWKINS, Minnie...............135
DAY, Carrie...................241
Sara A......................245
William C...............241, 245
DEAN, Silas....................60
DEARMAN, Constance............118
Elisha......................212
John A......................118

J. M.	118
Mary F.	118
Mildred	118
Wilbur (Judge)	89
DeBERRY, Emily	60
James	60
DERBY, A. J.	208
C. A.	12
DeWITT, Joel L	105
Lulu	105
Mary Ann	105
DIAL, Clarence	97
David M.	26, 71, 74, 75, 78, 81, 82
Ed.	82, 130, 229
Emelle	229
Emma	229
Eliza	23
Florence K.	26, 74
Frances E.	24, 226
James	21, 24, 74
Jennett S.	17, 19, 26, 71, 81, 225
Jeremiah III	21, 22, 26, 102, 225
Jememiah Jr.	26, 102, 193
John	26, 102, 226
Joseph (family)	225
Summer	26
Telemachus	74
William	75, 81, 82, 102, 157, 224, 225
DICKINSON, Shadruck (family)	69
DICKSON, (family)	96
DILL, Adah Fulford	205
J. F.	205
DILLARD, Bob	125
Judge	8
Melvira	22
DILLARD CEMETERY RECORDS	179
DIXON, Martha	54
Mary	45
Nancy	45
DOLLAR, Ed	119
DORMAN, Elizabeth Grace	93
Henry M.	93
DOUGHTY, Gladys	55
Kay	55
Ormond	55
Preston	55
DOVE, Leodosia	104
Mick	104
DOWDLE, Elizabeth	100
Joseph P.	100
DOZIER, (family)	223
Elizabeth	27
DRAKE, Nathaniel B.	93
DRINKARD, Nancy	246
Washington	246
DuBOSE, Joel Campbell	13
DUKE, William	195
DRUMMOND, Amanda	70
David	70
Mary D.	184
Virginia A.	51
William	186
DUNN, Ed F.	141
DYSON, Angeline	152
DURANT, Bill (family)	125
DAUGHTERY, Mrs.	100

E

EAKINS, Ann	96
Elizabeth	167
Dorcas	143
George	101
Isabeea	96
Joseph	96
Maggie	114
Martha	143
Samuel	143
Sue	167
William	96, 114
EARBEE, William	196, 246
EARLE, Dr.	196
Samuel	30
EASLEY, Ann	183
Betsy	9
Christopher	246
Creed	246
Elizabeth	183
Daniel	246
Emily	246
John	183
Joyce	183
Martha	246
Robert	8, 183
Roderick	9
Sara	8
Samuel	246
Virginia Noble	246
Warham	8, 9, 183, 246
EASON, Carr	23

E. C. 46, 79, 208
E. K. 46
Elizabeth. 12
John T. 63, 196, 208
Joseph. 208
Henry. 46
Kessiah. 79, 92, 208
Winifred. 63
EATMAN, R. 93
EDMONDS, Alice. 214
Nellie. 214
Vivian M. 119
William. 214
EDWARDS, Elizabeth. 45
Rigdon. 90
Robert. 104
Washington. 20
William. 209
EGGAR, Mary. 9, 77
ELDRIDGE, Ann. 30
ELLIOTT, (family). 240-241
Anna. 17, 19, 91
Annie Bell. 59
Calvin. 59, 156
Clyde. 111
John Knox. 87, 241
Julia. 28
Julia k. 111
Robert Knox. 91
Rosa. 59
(Cemetery Records). 167-170
ELLIS, Colfield. 38
Patience. 166
Vivian. 55
W. R. 166
ELLISON, James. 12
ENGLAN, Ted. 156
ENGLISH, L. C. 117
Malcomb. 117
Stella. 117
ENNIS, Tempie Scruggs. 58
EPES, John Cross (family). 46
ERWIN, Ann. 8
ESSARY, Frances. 112
Ray. 112
Sidney R. 112
ESTES, Caldwell. 186
Jeremiah. 186
Margaret. 155
Maud. 155
R. T. 155

ETHRIDGE, Nathias. 12
EVANS, Harrison (family). 94
Ann. 140
Jabes. 231
Harrison. 248
Houston. 140
R. L. 161
EVANT, Catherine. 239
Evan. 239
EZELL, Sam. 211

F

FAIRES, Emma. 206
Rebecca. 206
FALKNER, Jabel. 216
FANT, Cordy. 91
Dottie L. 112
FARMER, (family). 152
Sarah. 124
FARRAR, John A. 105
Susan. 112
FARRES, J. W. 211
Mary L. 211
FAULKNER, Jabel. 12
James Davis. 48
FELLOWS, H. D. 219
FERRIS, Fergus P. 93
FIELD, David W. 164, 187
Louisa. 187
FIELDER, John. 20, 21
FINCH, John. 141
FISHER, Abraham. 20
FLEMING, Catherine. 20
James. 21
Mary B. 17, 19, 20
Mary Hannah. 23
P. R. 17, 19, 235
Robert. 20
FORTNER, Lucinda. 146
FLOWERS, Jacob (family). 244, 245
Ernest. 81
Murray. 155
Samuel. 214
William. 214
FLUKER, Minera. 217
William. 217
FOARD, Baldwin. 187
FOLSUM, Annie. 146
Ida F. 145

Squire.................127, 145
FORD, William....................246
FORT, Josephine................ 68
FOSTER, J. B....................209
   Margaret.....................132
   N. M......................... 12
   William C....................132
FOUST, J. E.....................212
FOY, Davis......................233
   Fiester......................232
   Martha....................... 45
   Nancy....................40, 232
   Terry.............16, 40, 45, 232
FRAZER, Micajah................. 12
FREELAND, William............... 95
FREEMAN, (family)...............177
FRENCH, Mary.................... 32
FRIERSON, Mary Ann.............. 68
   Susannah..................... 22
FULLER, Bessie (family)......... 43
   Ed........................... 43
   L. L.........................118
   Nathan....................... 12
   Ruby H.......................118
FULLINGHAM, P. M................ 12
FULSON, Jerry................... 91
FULTON, (family).............68-84
   Edwin........................110
   Elizabeth................20, 196
   James Hervey.............22, 196
   Mary.........................110
   Nancy J...................... 21
   William Frierson............. 20

G

GAGE, Betsy P................... 19
   David....................17, 19
   D........................20, 21
   Nancy........................ 17
GAROUTTE, Chellie...............113
   Amos.........................113
GARRISON, (family)..............207
GASTON, Martha L................ 72
GAY, Charlotte L................143
   Isaac Jesse..................143
   Jayle, Matthew............... 93
   Gee, Benj.................... 90
   John H....................... 90

Odell........................ 28
GEIGER.......................... 12
BIBBS, Edward...................211
   E. J. Jr..................... 76
   Louisa.......................211
   Rock A....................... 76
   Sarah E...................... 76
GIBSON, Jane....................241
   William A....................196
GILBERT, William (family)....30, 39
   Joseph F..................... 46
   Una.......................... 46
   William..................16, 210
GILES, Maria J..................227
GILLESPIE, (family).............205
   Robert.......................216
   Minnie.......................219
   Sarah........................219
GILLUM, Ina..................... 30
GILMER, John.................... 11
GILMORE, J. N..............209, 210
   Nancy........................187
   Willie Ann...................210
GODDARD, Ilsie..................106
   Raymond......................106
Godfrey, Annie.................. 61
   Dozier...................54, 197
   Earl......................... 61
   James M......................209
   Margaret..................... 54
   Martha...................54, 238
   Mary Julia................... 61
   Sara.........................238
   William......13, 54, 61, 104, 196, 238
GOGGANS, Louis Leon (family)107, 154
   Kim B........................106
   Mary Coefield................107
   Nellie Mae................... 26
GOODLOE, M. F...................221
GORDY, Glenn....................122
   J. D.........................122
   Mildred......................122
GORMAN, Starling........91, 94, 247
   Tyrell....................85, 94
GOULD, Daniel...................197
   Elizabeth A. L...............197
GOWDY, Allan....................218
   Elmer........................219
   George C.....................219
GRAHAM, Ernest (family).........117
   Sallie.......................218

T. R. 218
GRANT, F. M. 12
G. W. 12
GRANTHAM, (family) 81
GRAY, Oscar 60
Harriett 60
M. E. 189
GREENE, Charlotte 225
Daniel 93, 95, 226
Hollan A. 187
Matilda L. 196
T. S. 208
William H. 187, 191
GREENLEE, (family) 94, 96, 100
Hester 21
Isabella 17, 19
Robert 213
William 17, 19
GREER, Mr. 187
GREY, Lucinda 72
Washington 72
GRICE, Charity Woodward 82
Stephen 233
(family) 38-66
GREGORY, (family) 38-66
GRIFFIN, A. M. 85, 94
GRIGSBY, Lucinda 45
Luke 45
GRIMES, James 12
Missouri 124
GRISWOLD, Joel B. (family) 47
John 12
GRUBBS, Clifford (family) 61
GUNN, Louisa 187
Redford M. 164, 187
Robert Stacy 164, 187

H

Hadden, Isaac (family) 21
Robert W. 197
William H. 22
HAGGER, Thomas 38
HAGOOD, Ida (family) 38-66
HAILEY, (family) 96, 120
HAINSWORTH, James L. 194
HAIZE, dempsey S. 12
HALE, (family) 38-66
Joseph H. 219
Mary Isabella 219

R (H) 50, 209
Samuel 215
HALL, Col 210
John P. 91
William 90, 91
W. W. 12
HOLLIMAN, Cephas 109
Hattie Mary 109
Halsell, Nathan 12
Samuel 11, 198
HAMILTON, Hance 241
Mary 242
Thomas 242
HAMMELL, Virginia 61
HAMPTON, John P. 12
HAMRICK, John 225
HAND, John 95
S. P. 209
HANDCOCK, J. B. 188
Jane Green 188
HANDLEY, John L. 87, 98
Louise 22, 23, 31
Peter 31, 87, 98
HANNA, Andrew 91, 93
HANSEL, A. L. 73
T. D. 73
HARE, Willis V. 12
HARMAN, Winchester J. 13
HARPER, Bettie H. 212
Daniel E. 246
Edward 91
Elizabeth 72, 132, 246
Emma 132
George W. 13, 91, 235
James 246
James W. 212
Malinda M. 235
Margaret 72
Robert E. 212
Thomas 21, 91
Tibitha 246
Wyatt 72
HARRAN, James 12
HARRELL, (family) 198
HARRINGTON, Young J. 101
HARRIS, (family) 197
Delila 34
Edward 81
Eunice 148
H. H. 210
John E. 57

John..................34, 93, 149	HOLLINGWORTH, Jacob.............132
Mary S........................ 81	Simmons.....................132
Margaret...................... 34	Thomas......................132
Park..........................210	William R...................132
Reid..........................149	HOLLIS (family)................. 51
Richard.......................197	HOLLODAY, Isaphena.............. 66
Young W.......................218	HOLLOWAY, (family).............. 51
HARRY, Teenie....................119	HOLMES, Fred....................112
HART, Sarah L.................... 32	Louisa, L...................104
HARVEY, J. B....................209	HOLT, Bessie.................... 78
HARWELL, James D................. 23	Cadar.......................174
W. T........................ 23	James.......................174
HATCH, C. A...................... 12	Judy........................174
HATTON, John H..................101	LeRoy....................... 78
HEARD, Joel (family)............187	Thad........................ 78
HEDDLETON, Martha................ 22	HOOT, Buckie....................207
HELLSON, Cely.................... 92	Cornelia E..................207
HENAGAN, Darby..................209	R. D........................207
(family).......................219	HOPKINS, Devereux...............219
C. S........................202	Elizabeth W................. 22
HENDERSON, (family).............115	HOPPER (family)...........100, 125
HENDRICKS, J. H.................. 51	Elizabeth................... 96
Virginia A.................. 51	Hugh........................ 76
(family).................... 50	Mary Ann.................... 20
HERN, E. B......................218	William..................... 96
M. E........................218	HORN (family-see Old Side Cem.). 38
HENSON, J. M....................209	Elisha T....................237
HERBERT, Martha Ann.............. 27	Jere........................230
Richard. H.................. 27	Marilda.....................237
HESTER, Randolph (family)...151, 234	(Horn Cemetery).............166
HIGH, (family)................38-66	HORTON, Anna C..................245
HILL, Phoebe....................199	Louise......................158
HILMAN, (family)........197, 198, 207	Sarah.......................245
HINES, (family)................198	Stephen.....................245
HINSDALE, Charles................ 17	HOSTY, Carl G...................108
HITT, (family)............91, 94, 248	Jacqueline..................108
HODGES, (family)......91, 92, 125, 249	HOUSTON, Joe Clint..............218
Sarah Melissa............... 30	J. C........................209
HOGGER, Thomas................... 17	Josiah......................249
HOIT, Mr......................... 12	HOWARD, Bethel..................191
Z. M........................213	John.....................30, 124
HOLCOMBE, Alva................... 51	HOWELL, T. O. (family)..........110
HOLLAND, Anderson...............231	Mildred.....................105
Exum........................ 60	HUBBARD, Woodson................ 12
(family)....................228	HUDNALL, Jaunita................117
F. M........................231	Leon J......................117
John...............16, 30, 133, 222	HUDSON, (family)................242
Mary........................ 60	Sarah M.....................107
Tilitha.....................231	HUGHES, Dr...................... 81
William.....................133	Jennie...................... 81

HUNTER, Lebbens................ 91
   Marie........................200
   R. L.......................... 11
   T. A.......................... 12
HUTCHINS, (family)...........24-27
   James L......................232
   Jesse........................222
   Thomas H.................92, 222
HUTCHINSON (Hutcherson)
   Glennie......................109
   Washington P................. 38
HUTTON, C. M................... 67
HYNGUE, G. A...................119
   Ouida R......................119

I

INGE, Benjamin.................203
INGRAM, James.................. 12
   Margaret.....................102
IRBY, A........................202
IRWIN, Sarah................17, 38

J

JACKSON, Cornelius.............188
   Drury........................231
   Eleanor...................... 68
   Elizabeth................20, 188
   Erskine...................... 68
   (family).................232-237
   John R....................... 41
   Lane......................... 68
   Lucy......................... 41
   Mace.........................147
   Rebecca...................41, 64
   Sarah........................ 68
   Samuel.......................233
   Seaborn...................... 29
JAMISON, Nancy..............20, 22
   Thomas....................21, 22
JAMES, Ada.....................161
   Mary......................... 12
   Mrs.......................... 17
   W. H.........................209
JARMAN, W. T...................208
JARRELL, David.................233
   Ellenda......................233
   Mahala.......................233

JARRETT, Sallie................ 80
JEMISON, John S................188
JENKILES, A. N.................208
JENKINS, Anita.................111
   (family).....................228
   J. W.........................204
   Henry A..................51, 111
   T. L.....................131, 148
   Tom.......................... 49
JETER, Elelyn.................. 73
JOYNER (Joiner), Isophena...... 52
   Melvin....................... 52
   O. R.........................205
JOHNSON, Calvin................103
   Charles T....................217
   E............................105
   John.........................103
   John H....................... 79
   John S.......................188
   Malcom....................... 93
   Moses........................246
   Willie...............22, 79, 188
JOHNSTON, Willie Ann........... 23
JONES, Alice................... 49
   (family)..............61, 226-227
   Henry........................ 92
   Jabel........................198
   Jack......................... 49
   John C....................... 92
   Joseph.......................232
   Reuben.......................188
   Robert M..................... 55
   Wright....................17, 38
JONES, (Cemetery)..............178
JORDON, Prof................... 12
   Burwell P....................188
   Caroline.....................113
   Edward.......................242
   James........................113
   Martha.......................242
   Mary J.......................188
JOSEPH, J. M................... 23

K

KEATING, Nicholas..............232
KELLY, Isham H.................188
KELSEY, Nellie C...............221
KEMBLE, Aaron.................. 12

KENDALL, Amanda..........20, 21, 31
    Elizabeth................... 33
    J.......................... 93
    Jeremiah................... 92
    T. R....................20, 22
KENNARD, George................11
    James...................204, 205
    J. H....................... 11
KENNEDY, Benj. F..............198
    John....................... 53
    Harriett A................. 53
    N. B. (Dr.)...............210
    Renwick (Rev.)............. 10
    Sally Ann.................198
KENNON, Ester.................. 21
KERN, W. L...................161
KERR, Armstrong.............20, 73
    (family)................224-225
    Isaac F................... 23
    John...................... 16
    Joseph.................... 23
    J. W...................20, 22
    Logan..................... 23
    Margaret...........17, 19, 22, 23
    Sarah................17, 19, 22
    Susan..................... 22
    Virginia.................. 20
    William................16, 21
KEY, David M..................104
    George H..................104
    James T...................104
    Joel M....................104
    Hubbard...................104
    Martin....................104
    Nancy Ribb................104
KILLEN, Amarnath..............198
    Harris....................198
KILLINGSWORTH, B. G. (Mrs.).... 56
    (family)..................176
    Julia Praytor......17, 176, 201
KINDAL, Amanda................ 20
KING, Bonnie Jean.............106
    John L....................106
    Mrs. E.................48, 64
KINGLE, Blevens............... 46
    George P.................. 46
    Martha Mary............... 46
    Raymond................... 46
    Una E..................... 46
KINNARD, M. C.................204

KIRK, Betty M.................105
    James Drake...............105
    Laura Lee.................131
KIRKLAND, Elizabeth...........147
    D. L......................147
    Junius....................226
    (family)..................147
KNIGHT, Catherine............. 40
    Emaline................... 40
    Joseph....................239
    Martha.................... 40
KNIGHTEN, Annie............... 30
    Ellen..................... 30
    Ernest.................... 30
    Fannie.................... 30
    Herbert................... 30
    James..................... 30
    Leslie.................... 30
KNOX, Anna....................241
    Elizabeth.................241
    Jimmie....................241
    John......................241
KUHN, Jacob................... 11
    John...................... 11

L

LABUZAN, Charles (family).....199
LACY, Artemisa................ 40
    Austin....................240
    Elisha W..................132
    Franklin..................245
    Mary Ann.................. 53
    Nicholas..............245, 246
    Richard T.................132
    Samuel B..................239
    Thomas....................245
    William...................245
    Whilphema.................245
    (family)..............130-152
LACY CEMETERY.................180
LAKE, Joseph..................189
    Margaret G................189
LaLONDE, Lillian.............. 61
LAMPETER, P. G................201
LAND, Eliza...................109
    James..................94, 109
    Luther....................109
    Tilitha...................109
    William................... 14

LANDFAIR, H. L. 32
LANE, Tobias 56
LAUGHRIDGE, Andrew J. 20
LARKIN, J. 207
    Jo Ann 108
    Joyce 108
    Kenneth 108
    Malcolm 108
    Mary A. 199
    Michael 108
    R. 199
LANCASTER, L. 208
LAVENDER, Hugh (family) 121
    Bryan 91
    Jane 17, 19, 76
    Margaret 21
    Mary A. 20
    Rebecca S. 121
    Robert S. 17, 19, 121
    William 102, 121
    W. Urias 121
LAWRENCE, Betty 30
    Mary F. 188
    Tom, Jr. 30
    Tom, Dr. 30
    William H. 188
LAWSON, Mumford 247
LEE, Arthur 60
    Bettie J. 96
    James M. 218
LEMMON, Catherine 31
LEVERETT, Andrew J. 21
    Henry 21
LEWIS, Llewellyn (family) 39
    David 213
    Emma F. 106
    Llewellyn 53, 220
    W. C. 208
LIDIKAY, Erline 106
    Mack 106
    Tad 106
LIGHTSEY, Susan 103
LILLY, Mrs. 12
    T. A. 12
LINCH, James 20
LINDSAY, Mattie 213
LIPSCOM, Joel 246
LITTLE, Alice 49
    Blake 12, 41, 133
    Caroline 41
    Lethie 49

    Thomas W. 101
LOCKARD, Amanda T. 212
LOCKETT, Prof. 12
LOFTIN, Margaret 77
LOMACK, John Tayloe 247
LOOMIS, H. (Rev.) 195
LYNN, Agnes 199
    Meridith 199

Mc

McBRIDE, Fannie 52
McCAIN CEMETERY RECORDS 160-162
McCALL, Charles D. 132
    Susan C. 132
McCANN, Hugh 92-94
    Rachel 92-94
    William J. 207
McCaskell, Mary 243
McCLAIN, Elizabeth M. 104
McCLENDON, Bryant 12
    Burwell 12
McCONNELL, John A. 210, 217
    John 163
    Joseph 163, 217
    Mary E. 163
    Mary G. 210
    Marcus E. 163
McCONNICO, C. S. 200, 205
    Jacqueline 200
    Lena 123
    Maggie 200
McCORCLE, Amanda E. 20
    Andrew 20
    Joseph 20, 70
    Martha 20
    Violet 20, 70
McCORD, Edward 236
McCORMICK, John G. 12
    L. C. 218
    R. T. 12
McCOWN, Charlotte 164
    Elizabeth 164
    James 94, 246
    Jerome 164
McDANIEL, John M. 213
    Henry 208
    O. M. 12
    Mary Knox 213

Nancy............................ 76
McDONALD, Boyd.................212
 Maggie.......................212
 Mattie M.....................210
 M. B.........................210
 Marjorie Virginia............ 55
McDOW, Alexander................. 67
 Catherine. F................. 67
 Jane......................... 21
 John......................... 21
 (family) see Bether Cemetery
McELROY, I. R. (family).....200, 220
McENNIS, A. E.................... 12
 J. D........................202
McGOWEN, Thaddeus............95, 249
 Joe A.......................249
McKENLEY, David.................. 20
 Jane......................... 20
McKENSIE, H. S..................208
 Jane L....................... 32
McKERRALL, J....................204
McKINLEY, Eliza.................. 23
 Isabella..................... 23
 John......................... 23
 Mary Jane.................... 23
 Michael...................... 23
 Mitchell..................... 23
 Sara......................... 23
McKINSIE, Edgar J................ 36
 Jane......................... 36
 John......................... 36
McKNIGHT, W. T..................214
McLEAN, Bobbie..................119
 Bob.......................... 61
 Elizabeth...................235
 Joseph......................235
 Marjorie..................... 61
 Nancy Ellen.................. 61
 Turner......................119
McLENDON, John..................247
 Simon C...................... 12
McLEOD, Addie MacL............... 61
 Norman......................189
McLUNSEY, H. E. (Mrs.).......... 20
McMahon, Lizzie.................217
 R. G........................217
McMILLAN, Agnes.................218
 Archibald...................101
 Daniel....................91, 92
 Dora........................216

Drury............................ 19
Eliza...........................245
Enda............................245
Felix G.........................216
James...........................164
Jennie McR......................218
Hugh............................245
Nancy...........................164
McNAIRY, Andrew.................243
 Boyd........................243
 Francis.....................243
 John........................243
 Margaret....................243
 Mary........................243
 Nathaniel...................243
 Rachel......................243
McNIECE, John.................... 12
McNIELL, H. A...................235
McRae, Harriett Powe............. 27
 Marie.......................200
 Martha H....................200
 William P...................200

M

MACKEY, Kay.....................148
 George......................148
 Mike........................148
 Olive M.....................148
MAGGARD, David..................110
MALLORY, George M...............200
 Joel H...................... 91
MALONE, Mitchell..............11, 12
MANASCO, Jeremiah...............199
 Phoebe Hill.................199
MANNING, Sallie L................ 96
MARCY, Edward O.................246
 John O......................246
MARLIN, Francis.................249
MARR, Sarah P...................189
MARSH, Frank....................199
MARSHALL, J. B..................209
MARTIN, James...................189
 Francis..................... 95
MARTINIERE, Julius...........92, 94
MASON, Ann......................205
 George W................184, 215
 John........................211

R. S.	205
MASSEY, Emma A.	25
MATHRESS, Lermel	17, 36
MAURY, James W.	200
R. W.	200
MAY, Ansel	189
Ben	54
Bogan	202
Nannie F.	54
P. B.	246
MAYBERRY, G. E.	36
G. W.	31, 36
J. E.	36
MEADOW, Sara	39
MEEK, M. M.	20
Mrs.	71
Rosa Little	28
Susan	77
MELLARD, E. A.	199
Elisha	92
Elizabeth	199
MELLARD CEMETERY (Mellard, Willis)	173
MELLEN, C. H.	215
S. S.	215
MELTON, F.	209
Lorence H.	209
Mary	216
R. S.	209
MENDENHALL, Junius	47
Martha O.	47
Richard	47
MEREDITH, E. C.	20
Elisha	12
MERRITT, Fannie	218
George C.	218
METHODIST CEMETERY, Sumterville (Baker, Bancroft, Brown, Buford, Davis, Dial, Godfrey, Gilbert, Hodges, Holland, Hutchins, Jackson, Knight, McDaniel, McCain, Mitchell, McKinsie, Mayberry, Nance, Porter, Prince, Richardson, Somers, Webb.)	24-27
MILLER, Alice	109
C. B.	217
Joe R.	109
Kate	109
Martha E.	77
S. F.	14
T. K.	217
Robert D.	109

Velma	109
MIMMS, Seaborne	92
MIMMS CEMETERY.	172
MINNIECE, E. A.	79
J. A.	79
S. Evelyn	79
MITCHELL, Benj	23, 46, 224
David M.	79
Joseph Addison	46
Kessiah	22, 46
Nancy	23, 42
MOBLEY, Green B.	203
Henrietta	203
William A.	209
MONROE, E. W.	204, 220
John	220
MONTGOMERY, David	102
Laura	134
Willie Fayette	134
MOORE, A. E.	209
A. P.	109
Alfred	242, 243
Andrew	242, 243, 244
Arthur	243
Bertha	244
Bettie	209
Carrie	244
Catherine	244
David	92
Elizabeth	68
Fannie	244
Francis	100
Frank	92
Hance	242, 243
Harriett Cadmus	108
Ida	209
James	189
Jane	20
John	23, 209, 212
Katie	244
Loderick	104, 189, 235, 242, 243
Louisa	104, 107
Margaret	68, 242, 244
Martha	242
Mary	20, 42, 242, 243, 244
Marquis	243
Mark	96
Miaiah	244
Rachel	189, 242, 244
Robert	189, 242, 243
Roderick	242, 243

Theodosia..........189, 242, 243
Thomas...........17, 19, 20, 21, 68
William.........................14
MORRIS, Elbert G................245
   Jennie Yarbrough...............245
MORROW, Dorothy..................150
   Hugh...........................150
MORTON, Albert...................244
   Carrie.........................244
   Francis T.......................56
MOTES (family)...................154
MUFFITT, Jennett-----------------100
MURRAY, Sallie....................74
   Virginia...................74, 109
MULDREW, Elizabeth................12
MUNDY, Mary......................199
   Wesley A.......................199
MYERS, Asberry....................27
   Cynthia........................232
   Eliza..........................232
   (family).......................238
   James...........................27
   L. D............................12
   Martha G........................27

N

NANCE, Fannie Ella................37
   James Walker....................37
   Mary Ann........................37
   Nancy..........................221
   Thomas H........................37
   Sarah...........................37
   William.........................37
   W. T............................37
NASH, J. T.......................209
   Preston...................189, 215
NEELY, Henry F...................108
   Margaret.......................108
   Mary E.........................108
NEIL, Sara........................77
NEILSON, John (Mrs.).............161
NELSON, Thomas....................11
Nettles, Malichi............233, 247
   Mary Staggs....................233
NEWBERRY, Amelia..................30
   J. C............................30
   Larry...........................30
   Lucile..........................30

Michele...........................30
NEWELL, A. D.....................206
   Nancy..........................206
NEWTON, Anelia....................30
   J. C............................30
   Larry...........................30
   Leah...........................222
   Matthew........................222
NEVILL, Andrew....................20
   Lucy............................23
   Mary............................20
NIXON, Leslie....................157
NOBLE, Catherine.................246
   Elizabeth......................246
   Maria..........................246
   Virginia.......................246
NOONE, E. H.......................47
   Elizabeth W.....................47
NOYES, Eleanor C..................32
NUFFER, Prof......................12

O

O'CONNER, Burlyn.................151
   Louis T........................152
OLDE SIDE BAPTIST CEMETERY....38-66
OLIVER, Junie.....................46
   Marilyn.........................46
   Mary Ella (Lou).................46
   Melanie.........................47
   William E.......................46
O'NEAL, Cherry Lane..............200
   Harriett R......................65
   Lucretia........................94
   William....................65, 200
ORMOND, (family)..................55
   Cherry Ella.....................42
   Evan....................55, 71, 78
   John Fletcher...................42
   Thomas S........................36
   Tom........................16, 222
   William.........................71
ORR, Bob.........................148
   Elizabeth.......................77
   Louise.........................148

P

PAGE, Charles.....................12

PALMER, Luke	23	PEEL, (family)	30
PANKY, T. M. (family)	110	John	29
PARENT, Julia	189	Robert	29
Lewis	189	PEGUES	103
Mary L.	190	PERRY, John	93
PARHAM, Connie Jean	56	PETTIGREW, Ebenezer	237
J. C.	209	James	237
Lewis L.	90	Nanyc	237
Mary Ann	55	PETERS, E.	12
Matilda B.	56	PHARISS, Anthony	16
Matthew	55, 56	PHILLIPS, Cyndrilla	230
Nancy	56	Ellen	54
Permelia	90	Florence	54
PARK, James Vrrner	110	Jack	54
Mary E.	110	John	54, 201
Matthew B.	201	George M.	54
Robert	111	H. W. M.	201
PARKER, James L., Sr.	90, 94, 206, 196	Helen	54
K.	190	L. D.	201
Margaret	190	Margaret	27
Nancy	242	Martha G.	54, 201
Sharod	246	Sara J.	54
PARKER CEMETERY RECORDS	162-164	Thomas	230
PARRISH, Bruce R.	113	PHIPPS, Elizabeth	31
Chellie Caroline	113	Thomas H.	31
Elmira	113	PICKLES, George	91, 92
William E.	113	PICKENS, John C.	190
PATTON, Alice	213	PINSON, Annie Bell	30
Cynthia Myers	16	Geiger	30
D. U.	213	Hamet (Dr.)	30, 201
Eliza	16, 19	John H.	30
Joe	83	Chris (Mrs.)	72
Margaret	232	PIPEN, Loftin	91, 41
Nancy Elizabeth	83	Zelma	41
Thomas	93	Norflit	91
William	16, 232, 247	PIPKIN, Harriett	203
William S.	16	PITTARD, Irma	110
PAYNE, Bee	28	PLOTT, Catherine	62
Daniel	94	James	62, 121
Dillard	91, 92	S. E.	62, 121
James	91, 92	Walter	62
John K.	91	POINDEXTER, William R.	12
George	92	POPE, Leroy	190
Hiram	94, 294	PORTIS, Benj.	201
Laurana	91	Susan	202
Lucinda	241	PORTER, Thomas	12
Maty	91, 241	PORTOR, Eleanor	81
Ransom	85, 94	Margaret	31
Victoria	91	T. J.	31
William	91, 94	POSEY, M. B.	14

Sara H. 78
POST, Azubak. 200
POWE, Alice. 125
    Allen. 125
    Charles. 125
    Clara Jane. 104
    Josephine. 125
    Julia. 125
    Richard. 125
    W. H. Pegues. 103, 125
    William. 125
POWELL, Alama L. 218
    Ezekiel C. 218
    I. James. 218
POYTHRESS, Catherine. 29
    Catherine Preston. 79
    James Edward. 76
    Miss. 62
    Rebecca. 76
PRAYTOR, Hugh Boyd. 48
    Jabel. 204
    Middleton. 201, 216
PRICE, Elijah. 90
PRINCE, Barah E. 37
    Thomas. 30
    Elizabeth. 243
    Richard. 243
PUCKETT, Charles J. 13, 85, 92
PULLIUM, James. 208
PUSHMATAHA, Chief. 7
PYLE, Charity. 233
    Elizabeth. 233
    James. 247
    John. 247
    Matilda T. 247

R

RAINER, Lawrence. 72
    Stella. 72
RAMAGE, Laura. 209
    T. F. 209
RAMSEY, A. K. 204
    Mattie L. 210
    Susan. 204
RAMSAY, Alexander. 8
    Alice. 71
    Andrew H. 65, 71

George W. 9
Isabella. 19, 21
John. 56
Joseph R. 22, 68
Kate--. 56
Margaret. 21, 65, 68
Mary. 20, 21
Virginia. 56
Willie. 8, 78
RANDALL, Annie Laurie. 71
    Arthur. 71
RANDOLPH, Epes. 46
    Sarah. 46
RASSER, John. 90
REA, John. 146
    Lucy. 146
READ, Anna D. 54
    Joseph. 54
REEVES, Maurine. 158
    Woody. 158
REID, E. C. 209
    M. J. 220
    W. R. 220
RENFROE, Mary M. 56
    Molly E. 56
    Steve S. 56
RENWICK, Nathan. 101
RATCLIFF, Elizabeth. 209
REYNOLDS, Mrs. 161
RHEINSCHMIDT, Alice. 61
    Betty. 61
    Bill. 61
    Elizabeth ann. 61
RHODES, Edna M. 203
    James. 190, 203
    John P. 91
    Lucy. 27
RHYNE CEMETERY RECORDS. 169-170
RICHARDSON, Benj. J. 17
    Bryant. 16, 41, 42, 49, 203
    Cherry Lane. 200
    (family). 237
    Goin. 17
    Harriett. 200
    Rixie. 41, 64
    Oney. 41
    Washington. 17
RICHMOND, Rebecca J. 105
    William D. 105
RIED, Sara Hargrove. 9, 78

RIGDON, Arthur.................. 30
    Barney...................... 30
    Evelyn...................... 30
    Fannie...................... 30
    Roberta..................... 30
    Sara........................ 30
RILEY, B. J..................51,81
    L. V........................ 80
    Wiley....................... 80
    Willie...................... 81
RIX, Eleanor..............20,53,81
    Frederick................... 81
    George.................21,22,81
    Mary........................ 20
    Rebecca Dail.............22,81
ROBERTS, Joanna................. 12
    John.....................43,208
    Peter M.....................224
    Sallie 43,205
    Sara.....................43,221
    William H...................190
ROBERSON, James................. 22
ROBINSON, J. R..................141
    John.....................33, 93
    Jonah....................... 91
    Sarah.......................141
    Susan.......................141
ROGERS, Adeline.................117
    Edna........................150
    Ethel.......................117
    Eugene......................117
    Frederick M.................117
    George W....................203
    Henry H.....................202
    Jon.........................117
    Joseph...................90,202
    J. M........................ 12
    Mary....................117,202
    Rev.........................150
    Roselle.....................117
    Robert A....................117
    Sharrach.................... 90
    Thomas......................117
    Walter E....................117
    Walter T....................117
    William T...................117
ROOT, E......................... 12
ROSS, Elizabeth................. 92
    Jesse....................... 94
ROZELLE, Janice.................118

    H. B........................118
    Melainie....................118
RUMLEY, Martin..................202
RUSHING, Benjamin F.............105
    J. M........................190
    Mary....................105,190
    Shepard.....................190
    Stephen.....................190
RYON, Elizabeth S...............190
    Jason.......................190

S

SAMPLE, James................... 85
SANDERS, James L................134
    Keith....................... 75
    Larry....................... 75
    Lucile...................... 75
    Margaret....................134
    Moses M..................... 81
SAVAGE, Mary E..................113
    Owen........................113
    James....................... 13
    William.....................113
SCARBROUGH, A. R............210,214
    Sara A. Leitch.............. 76
    William H................... 76
SCOTT, Lillie Brame............. 39
SCRUGGS, Calvin.................134
    Josiah......................203
    J. O........................209
SEALE, Anthony................92,95
    B. B........................210
    Buford....................92,95
    Darling.....................235
    Eli.....................92,94,95
    Jane C...................... 84
    Jarvis....................92,94
    Lucretia.................... 94
    Mary Ann.................... 94
    Mary E......................212
    Philida..................... 94
    Polly....................... 94
    Sarah....................... 94
    Thomas F................110,212
SHAMBURGER, James A.............220
    Mary L......................220
    Sallie E....................220
SHAW (family)................... 81

SHELBY, Catherine............114
    Dorothy....................115
    E. B........................ 62
    J. L.......................207
    Helen R....................115
    Nina M.....................115
    Tamsy H....................114
SHELTON, Elisha............94, 95
    John E...................... 95
    Isreal...................... 92
    Robert R.................12, 95
SHEPPARD, Jackie Nell.......... 30
    Myrtle..................... 30
SHERER, Ellen..................191
    W. Waldo...................191
SHIELDS, J. J.................. 11
SHIPMAN, Eliza.............17, 20
    George J................... 20
    Jacob.....................17, 20
    Mrs........................ 21
SHOLL, E. H...................209
SHIRLEY, Catherine P.......... 30
    James...................... 30
SILBY, John H................. 93
SILLIMAN, Ann Pauline..........109
    Calvin.....................209
    John.......................109
    Mary.......................105
    Martha J...................105
    Susan......................105
    Thomas.................100, 105
SILMAN, Bella.................233
    Calvin.....................233
SIMMS, (family)...............229
    See Old Side Cemetery....38-66
    Keziah..................... 69
    Robert..................... 69
    William T................127, 202
    W. O.......................202
SIMMONS, Ann..................245
    Anna....................... 93
    Asberry.................... 93
    B. A....................... 93
    Barbara....................207
    E. W....................... 93
    J. H....................... 11
    Lewis S....................207
    Robert..................... 93
    William.................... 93
SIMPSON, Carra................ 55
    Gladys..................... 55
    Samuel..................... 55
SIMS, Flora................... 55
    Thomas H................... 31
SKINNER, Calvin............... 81
    Eleanor Portor............. 81
    Sallie..................... 81
SLEDGE, E. S................56, 57
    Mark.......................109
    Pauline....................109
    Susan......................109
    W. H.......................209
SMALL, Milton.................134
SMITH, Beulah Parker..........206
    Eviline....................191
    Henry...................17, 38
    James...................... 92
    Jane E.....................190
    John...................21, 72, 95
    John W..................... 91
    Joseph..................... 94
    Joshua..................... 40
    Louis (Pat)................ 72
    Lucy B..................21, 81
    Maggie..................... 78
    Mary Ann................... 72
    Murray F...................191
    N. O....................... 12
    Robert H...................191
    Roger...................... 78
    Samuel.....................206
    Sidney.....................188
    Sterling................... 81
    Thomas (Tip)............... 72
    T. B....................... 72
    William.................95, 93
    William H...............94, 95
    William R.................. 90
SNEDECOR, F. P................218
    Lucy.......................218
SMMERD, George................ 37
SOULE, John................... 21
SPEAR, C. A................... 12
SPEIGHT, Catherine............ 29
    Nancy Ann.................. 29
    Sammy Ann.................. 29
    Samuel..................... 29
SPIDLE, Carol Jane............ 76
    Francis Lynn............... 76
    Theodore M................. 76

SPINKS, Charlotte Lacy.........240
    Isaac....................240
SPRATT, James P.................217
    Helen E..................216
    Lewis....................78
    Maggie...................78, 217
SPRATT CEMETERY.................162
SPROTT, Mary....................214
    S. H.....................208
STAGGS, Mary....................233
    Zachariah................233
STANTON, James M................12
    Wiley....................14
STARK, Ellen....................31
    Emma.....................31
    Matthew..................31
    Thomas H.................31
STRAIGHT, Mary..................81
    Robert...................91
    William..................91
STEGALL, J. S...................158
    Matilda..................158
STEPHENS, John..................12, 247
STEWART, Amelia Ann.............27
    Fredrick.................27
    George...................109
    J. B. (Mrs.).............48
    Linda....................109
STINSON, Laurel.................62
    Lillibeck................62
    Sara Jackson.............52, 62
    W. R.....................62
STOKES, Eddie Mae...............119
    Jeff.....................119
STONE, Benj.....................12
STICKLER, George M..............152
    Mary A...................152
STROTHER, Edward H..............191
STRUMQUIST, Kenneth.............109
    Racheal..................109
STURDIVANT, William R...........246
SUMTER, General.................17
    SWANN, J. C..............216
        Matthew. P...........216
SYKES, (Mrs.)...................60

T

TALBERT, Mary...................76
TALLIAFARRO, Benj...............56
TALMAGE, J. C...................12
TARTT, Elizabeth................114
    Emily....................45
    Elnathan.................45, 114
    Enos.....................45, 114
    James B..................12
    Jonathan.................114
    Margaret.................114
    Mary C...................185
    Pernina..................114
    Sara.....................45
    Thomas M.................114
TAYLOR, Madison.................246
    Samuel...................12, 209
    William..................203
TEMPLETON, Mary Frances.........82
    T. J.....................23
THIGPEN, (family)...............133
THOMAS, (family)................238
    (See Old Side Cemetery)
    Elisha...................17
    Gray.....................125
    Morrison.................191
    Reuben...................127
    Richard..................96, 127
    Susannah B...............125
    William..................127
    Wiley....................33
THOMPSON, Alexander.............78
    Elizabeth................78
    Felix....................90
    Jacob E..................20
THREADGILL, Malinda.............94
TOBIN, Thomas M.................12
    TOMLINSON, Addie M.......61
        Em...................61
        Joe..................61
TOMPKINS, Bennett...............191
TRAVIS, Amos....................12
    Enoch....................91
TRAVIS CEMETERY.................165
PRESTWOOD, Austin68, 100, 104, 105, 113
    Chellie R................112
    Jonathan.................63
    John Thomas..............113
    Lucile...................113
    Mary.....................109
    Mary Boyd................63, 100
    Newton...................109

Thomas..................105
TREADWAY, Clara................112
    Dolly......................112
    Dolly Wise..................112
    Tracy......................112
    William....................112
TUREMAN, W. S..................60
TURK, Sam.....................88
TURNER, Bnejamin..............12
    Frances....................161
    James R....................114
    Matthew....................69
    Patience...................69
    Rebecca....................69
    Roselle....................117
    William D..................117
TURNIPSEED, John..............104
    Sarah O....................104
TUTT, Bettie..................206
    J. A.......................218
    James..................191, 245
    James F....................90
    Thomas.....................245
TWOMBY, R. D..................12
TYSON, Elizabeth Pate.........229
    Mason......................229

U

UNDERWOOD, Adelide Randolph....82
    E..........................82
    L. V.......................82
    Martha M...................82
    William....................27
UPCHURCH, Benjamin............91
USTICK, John Gano.............191

V

VANDYKE, George M.............184
    Hulda......................184
VERRELL, Mary.................191

W

WADDELL, Barbara..............111
    Edna.......................111
    Elsie......................111
    Frank......................111
    George.....................111
    Gillye.....................111
    Mary Ellen.................111
    Mattie.....................111
    Ruby...................96, 111
    Rufus......................111
    Sallie Bishop..............111
    Samson.....................111
    Wayne......................111
WADE, Emma....................75
WALKER, Alexander.............94
    Arch C.....................114
WALKINGS, Arnold..............56
WALL, Charles.................231
    Franklin...................231
    Hugh.......................231
WALTON, Sallie Ella...........55
    W. O.......................55
WAMMEL, Emaline...............72
WARD, Amanda..............184, 192
    A. S.......................216
    D. S.......................216
    Eleanor....................38
    Ellen......................47
    H. B.......................209
    Hulda......................192
    Jackson...............184, 194
    Jesse......................12
    John..................11, 20, 22
    H. B.......................209
    Mary...................20, 22
    M. C.......................14
    Sally A....................38
    W..........................11
WARF, Henry A.................134
    Lucinda....................134
WARDLAW, William..............246
WARHAM, Jeremiah..............246
WARREN, David.................130
WASHINGTON, W. B..............209
WATKINS, Annie P..............113
    W. L.......................113
WATSON, Inez..................30
    Jarred.....................202
    Martha.....................202
    Thomas F...................202
    Walter.....................30
WATSON CEMETERY............173-174

WATTS, C. H.............. 28
   J. R................... 217
   F. G................... 28
WAYNE, John.............. 11
WEAVER, James............ 76
   Ruby................... 76
   Ruth................... 76
WEBB, Henry Y............ 238
   James D................ 236
   Mr..................... 16,18
   R. D................... 209
   Sammie (Mrs.).......... 49
   Samuel................. 236,238
   Stephen................ 12
WEIGANT, Robert N........ 148
WHEAT, Bird.............. 11
   William................ 12
WHEELER, Eugene.......... 94
   James I................ 112
   Hodges................. 112
   H. N................... 217
   Ina Bell R............. 94
WHEELING, Ester.......... 82
   William................ 82
WHITE, Ben............... 213
   Dan Osborne............ 213
   George................. 1 55
   James.................. 93
   Jane................... 90
   Mr..................... 17
   Sallie Ella............ 55
   Sara................... 108
   Wiliam Goerge.......... 55
   W. O................... 109
WHITELY, Annie C......... 47
   Blair.................. 47
   Charles H.............. 47
   Elizabeth.............. 47
   Fitzhugh............... 47
   Florence J............. 47
   Goldie T............... 47
   Janie.................. 47
   John................... 47
   Lady................... 47
   Martha S............... 47
   Margaret............... 47
   Morrison............... 47
   Vernon................. 47
   Wade H................. 47
WHITFIELD, Annie......... 82
   Calvin................. 81

   Carrie................. 81
   Helen.................. 81,112
   LeGrands............... 112
   Walter................. 81
WHITSETT, John C......... 8,91,224
   Mary................... 22
WIDEMAN, R............... 208
WIGGINS, Margaret Hodges.. 76
WILKERSON, Cecil......... 76
   Elizabeth.............. 208
   H. T................... 208
   J. B................... 212
   John L................. 106
   Mary E................. 76
   Sallie................. 212
   Susan V................ 106
WILEY, William........... 80
WILLIAMS, David.......... 210
   J. B................... 207
   James.................. 17,238,176,188,192
   Jim.................... 176
   Lillie Marie........... 176
   Mike................... 176
   Price.................. 192
   Solomon................ 11
   Spottswood............. 220
   Z. R................... 207
WILLIS, Lona............. 41
   Will................... 41
WILSON, Allison.......... 218
   David R................ 230,231
   George................. 218
   C. B................... 11
   Jane................... 134
   J. R................... 64
   Martha................. 64
   Sarah E................ 230,231
   W...................... 101
   Sacheus................ 232
WINDHAM, James I......... 202
WIMBERLEY, Felix G....... 214
WINSTON, Amanda M........ 10
   Anthony................ 233
   William................ 213
   W. O................... 8,9,213
WOODARD, Charity......... 49,82
   Felix Hamilton......... 82
WOODRUFF, C. D........... 209
   Clair.................. 209
   John C................. 209

WOODSON, Warren............... 12
WRENN, Ella................... 48
 Elias..................... 12
 Eliza.................19, 22
 James..........19, 43, 48, 68
 Joe.....................43, 48
 Josiah......................68
 Margaret....................68
 Nannie......................68
 William (Mrs.)..............43
WRIGHT, Asa.................17, 38
 J. W.......................217
 Margaret T.................217
 Willie.....................217
WYATT, Ebenezer............... 29

Y

YARBROUGH, Alfred...17, 20, 55, 67, 233
 Ann........................ 94
 C. P....................... 12
 (family)...........233, 234, 235
 James Q.................55, 56
 J. P....................... 12
 Martha..................... 21
 Mary................17, 19, 55
 Mary Ann................... 55
 Parham..................55, 56
 Ralph.....................234
 Richard.................... 12
 Stephen.................... 12
YARBROUGH, Daniel............. 87
 Zachariah.................234
YOUNG, Joseph................236
 Thomas..................... 11
YORK, Helen................... 69

www.ingramcontent.com/pod-product-compliance
Lightning Source LLC
Chambersburg PA
CBHW020644300426
44112CB00007B/236